Java™ Structures

Data Structures in Java™ for the Principled Programmer

Second Edition

Duane A. Bailey

Mc Graw Hill

Boston   Burr Ridge, IL   Dubuque, IA   Madison, WI   New York   San Francisco   St. Louis
Bangkok   Bogotá   Caracas   Kuala Lumpur   Lisbon   London   Madrid   Mexico City
Milan   Montreal   New Delhi   Santiago   Seoul   Singapore   Sydney   Taipei   Toronto

McGraw-Hill Higher Education

A Division of The McGraw·Hill Companies

JAVA™ STRUCTURES: DATA STRUCTURES IN JAVA™ FOR THE PRINCIPLED PROGRAMMER, SECOND EDITION

Some ancillaries, including electronic and print components, may not be available to customers outside the United States.

This book is printed on acid-free paper.

International   1 2 3 4 5 6 7 8 9 0 QPF/QPF 0 9 8 7 6 5 4 3 2
Domestic   1 2 3 4 5 6 7 8 9 0 QPF/QPF 0 9 8 7 6 5 4 3 2

ISBN 0–07– 239909–0
ISBN 0–07–112163–3 (ISE)

Publisher: *Elizabeth A. Jones*
Sponsoring editor: *Kelly Lowery*
Developmental editor: *Melinda Dougharty*
Executive marketing manager: *John Wannemacher*
Senior project manager: *Joyce M. Berendes*
Senior production supervisor: *Laura Fuller*
Media project manager: *Jodi K. Banowetz*
Senior media technology producer: *Phillip Meek*
Designer: *David W. Hash*
Cover designer: *Rokusek Design*
Compositor: *Interactive Composition Corporation*
Typeface: *10/12 Computer Modern*
Printer: *Quebecor World Fairfield, PA*

Library of Congress Cataloging-in-Publication Data

Bailey, Duane A.
   Java™ structures : data structures in Java™ for the principled programmer / Duane A. Bailey. — 2nd ed.
      p.   cm.
   Includes bibliographical references and index.
   ISBN 0–07–239909–0 — ISBN 0–07–112163–3 (ISE)
   1. Java (Computer program language). 2. Data structures (Computer science). I. Title.

QA76.73.J38 B34   2003

                                                          2002070870
                                                          CIP

www.mhhe.com

Contents

for Mary,
my wife and best friend

without
the model of my mentors,
the comments of my colleagues,
the support of my students,
the friendship of my family
this book would never be

thank you!

Preface to the First Edition

"IT'S A WONDERFUL TIME TO BE ALIVE." At least that's what I've found myself saying over the past couple of decades. When I first started working with computers, they were resources used by a privileged (or in my case, persistent) few. They were physically large, and logically small. They were cast from iron. The challenge was to make these behemoths solve complex problems quickly.

Today, computers are everywhere. They are in the office and at home. They speak to us on telephones; they zap our food in the microwave. They make starting cars in New England a possibility. Everyone's using them. What has aided their introduction into society is their diminished size and cost, and increased capability. The challenge is to make these behemoths solve complex problems quickly.

Thus, while the computer and its applications have changed over time, the challenge remains the same: *How can we get the best performance out of the current technology?* The design and analysis of data structures lay the fundamental groundwork for a scientific understanding of what computers can do efficiently. The motivations for data structure design work accomplished three decades ago in assembly language at the keypunch are just as familiar to us today as we practice our craft in modern languages on computers on our laps. The focus of this material is the identification and development of relatively *abstract* principles for structuring data in ways that make programs efficient in terms of their consumption of resources, *as well as efficient in terms of "programmability."*

In the past, my students have encountered this material in Pascal, Modula-2, and, most recently, C++. None of these languages has been ideal, but each has been met with increasing expectation. This text uses The Java Programming Language[1]—"Java"—to structure data. Java is a new and exciting language that has received considerable public attention. At the time of this writing, for example, Java is one of the few tools that can effectively use the Internet as a computing resource. That particular aspect of Java is not touched on greatly in this text. Still, Internet-driven applications in Java will need supporting data structures. This book attempts to provide a fresh and focused approach to the design and implementation of classic structures in a manner that meshes well with existing Java packages. It is hoped that learning this material in Java will improve the way working programmers craft programs, and the way future designers craft languages.

Pedagogical Implications. This text was developed specifically for use with CS2 in a standard Computer Science curriculum. It is succinct in its approach, and requires, perhaps, a little more effort to read. I hope, though, that this text

---

[1] Java is a trademark of Sun Microsystems, Incorporated.

becomes not a brief encounter with object-oriented data structure design, but a touchstone for one's programming future.

The material presented in this text follows the syllabus I have used for several years at Williams. As students come to this course with experience using Java, the outline of the text may be followed directly. Where students are new to Java, a couple of weeks early in the semester will be necessary with a good companion text to introduce the student to new concepts, and an introductory Java language text or reference manual is recommended. For students that need a quick introduction to Java we provide a tutorial in Appendix B. While the text was designed as a whole, some may wish to eliminate less important topics and expand upon others. Students may wish to drop (or consider!) the section on induction (Section 4.2.2). The more nontraditional topics—including, for example, iteration and the notions of symmetry and friction—have been included because I believe they arm programmers with important mechanisms for implementing and analyzing problems. In many departments the subtleties of more advanced structures—maps (Chapter 14) and graphs (Chapter 15)—may be considered in an algorithms course. Chapter 5, a discussion of sorting, provides very important motivating examples and also begins an early investigation of algorithms. The chapter may be dropped when better examples are at hand, but students may find the refinements on implementing sorting interesting.

List

Associated with this text is a Java package of data structures that is freely available over the Internet for noncommercial purposes. I encourage students, educators, and budding software engineers to download it, tear it down, build it up, and generally enjoy it. In particular, students of this material are encouraged to follow along with the code online as they read. Also included is extensive documentation gleaned from the code by `javadoc`. All documentation—within the book and on the Web—includes pre- and postconditions. The motivation for this style of commenting is provided in Chapter 2. While it's hard to be militant about commenting, this style of documentation provides an obvious, structured approach to minimally documenting one's methods that students can appreciate and users will welcome. These resources, as well as many others, are available from McGraw-Hill at `http://www.mhhe.com/javastructures`.

nim

Three icons appear throughout the text, as they do in the margin. The top "compass" icon highlights the statement of a *principle*—a statement that encourages abstract discussion. The middle icon marks the first appearance of a particular class from the `structure` package. Students will find these files at McGraw-Hill, or locally, if they've been downloaded. The bottom icon similarly marks the appearance of example code.

Finally, I'd like to note an unfortunate movement away from studying the implementation of data structures, in favor of studying applications. In the extreme this is a disappointing and, perhaps, dangerous precedent. The design of a data structure is like the solution to a riddle: the process of developing the answer is as important as the answer itself. The text may, however, be used as a reference for using the `structure` package in other applications by selectively avoiding the discussions of implementation.

Preface to the Second Edition

Since the first edition of *Java Structures* support for writing programs in Java[2] has grown considerably. At that time the Java Development Toolkit consisted of 504 classes in 23 packages[3] In Java 1.2 (also called Java 2) Sun rolled out 1520 classes in 59 packages. This book is ready for Java 1.4, where the number of classes and packages continues to grow.

Most computer scientists are convinced of the utility of Java for programming in a well structured and platform independent manner. While there are still significant arguments about important aspects of the language (for example, support for generic types), the academic community is embracing Java, for example, as the subject of the Computer Science Advanced Placement Examination.

It might seem somewhat perplexing to think that many aspects of the original Java environment have been retracted (or *deprecated*) or reconsidered. The developers at Sun have one purpose in mind: to make Java the indispensable language of the current generation. As a result, documenting their progress on the development of data structures gives us valuable insight into the process of designing useful data structures for general purpose programming. Those students and faculty considering a move to this second edition of *Java Structures* will see first-hand some of the decisions that have been made in the intervening years. During that time, for example, the Collection-based classes were introduced, and are generally considered an improvement. Another force—one similar to calcification—has left a trail of backwards compatible features that are sometimes difficult to understand. For example, the Iterator class was introduced, but the Enumeration class was not deprecated. One subject of the first edition—the notion of Comparable classes—has been introduced into a number of important classes including String and Integer. This is a step forward and a reconsideration of what we have learned about that material has lead to important improvements in the text.

Since the main purpose of the text is to demonstrate the design and behavior of traditional data structures, we have not generally tracked the progress of Java where it blurs the view. For example, Java 2 introduces a List interface (we applaud) but the Vector class has been extended to include methods that are, essentially, motivated by linked lists (we wonder). As this text points out frequently, the purpose of an interface is often to provide *reduced* functionality. If the data structure does not *naturally* provide the functionality required by the application, it is probably not an effective tool for solving the problem: search elsewhere for an effective structure.

---

[2] The Java Programming Language is a trademark of Sun Microsystems, Incorporated.

[3] David Flanagan, et al., *Java in a Nutshell*, O'Reilly & Associates.

As of this writing, more than 100,000 individuals have searched for and downloaded the `structure` package. To facilitate using the comprehensive set of classes with the Java 2 environment, we have provided a number of features that support the use of the `structure` package in more concrete applications. Please see Appendix C.

Also new to this edition are more than 200 new problems, several dozen exercises, and over a dozen labs we regularly use at Williams.

Acknowledgments. Several students, instructors, and classes have helped to shape this edition of *Java Structures*. Parth Doshi and Alex Glenday—diligent Williams students—pointed out a large number of typos and stretches of logic. Kim Bruce, Andrea Danyluk, Jay Sachs, and Jim Teresco have taught this course at Williams over the past few years, and have provided useful feedback. I tip my hat to Bill Lenhart, a good friend and advisor, who has helped improve this text in subtle ways. To Sean Sandys I am indebted for showing me new ways to teach new minds.

The various reviewers have made, collectively, hundreds of pages of comments that have been incorporated (as much as possible) into this edition: Eleanor Hare and David Jacobs (Clemson University), Ram Athavale (North Carolina State University), Yannick Daoudi (McGill University), Walter Daugherty (Texas A&M University), Subodh Kumar (Johns Hopkins University), Toshimi Minoura (Oregon State University), Carolyn Schauble (Colorado State University), Val Tannen (University of Pennsylvania), Frank Tompa (University of Waterloo), Richard Wiener (University of Colorado at Colorado Springs), Cynthia Brown Zickos (University of Mississippi), and my good friend Robbie Moll (University of Massachusetts). Deborah Trytten (University of Oklahoma) has reviewed both editions! Still, until expert authoring systems are engineered, authors will remain human. Any mistakes left behind or introduced are purely those of the author.

The editors and staff at McGraw-Hill–Kelly Lowery, Melinda Dougharty, John Wannemacher, and Joyce Berendes–have attempted the impossible: to keep me within a deadline. David Hash, Phil Meek, and Jodi Banowetz are responsible for the look and feel of things. I am especially indebted to Lucy Mullins, Judy Gantenbein, and Patti Evers whose red pens have often shown me a better way.

Betsy Jones, publisher and advocate, has seen it all and yet kept the faith: thanks.

Be aware, though: long after these pages are found to be useless folly, my best work will be recognized in my children, Kate, Megan, and Ryan. None of these projects, of course, would be possible without the support of my best friend, my north star, and my partner, Mary.

Enjoy!

Duane A. Bailey
Williamstown, May 2002

Chapter 0

Introduction

Concepts:
▷ Approaches to this material
▷ Principles

This is an important notice.
Please have it translated.
—The Phone Company

YOUR MOTHER probably provided you with constructive toys, like blocks or Tinker Toys[1] or Legos. These toys are educational: they teach us to think spatially and to build increasingly complex structures. You develop modules that can be stuck together and rules that guide the building process.

If you are reading this book, you probably enjoyed playing with constructive toys. You consider writing programs an artistic process. You have grown from playing with blocks to writing programs. The same guidelines for building structures apply to writing programs, save one thing: there is, seemingly, no limit to the complexity of the programs you can write. *I lie.*

Well, almost. When writing large programs, the *data structures* that maintain the data in your program govern the space and time consumed by your running program. In addition, large programs take time to write. Using different structures can actually have an impact on how long it takes to *write* your program. Choosing the wrong structures can cause your program to run poorly or be difficult or impossible to implement effectively.

Thus, part of the program-writing process is choosing between different structures. Ideally you arrive at solutions by analyzing and comparing their various merits. This book focuses on the creation and analysis of traditional data structures in a modern programming environment, The Java Programming Language, or Java for short.

0.1 Read Me

As might be expected, each chapter is dedicated to a specific topic. Many of the topics are concerned with specific data structures. The structures we will investigate are abstracted from working implementations in Java that are available to you if you have access to the Internet.[2] Other topics concern the

---

[1] All trademarks are recognized.
[2] For more information, see http://www.cs.williams.edu/JavaStructures.

"tools of the trade." Some are mathematical and others are philosophical, but all consider the process of programming well.

The topics we cover are not all-inclusive. Some useful structures have been left out. Instead, we will opt to learn the *principles of programming data structures*, so that, down the road, you can design newer and better structures yourself.

Perhaps the most important aspect of this book is the set of problems at the end of each section. *All are important for you to consider.* For some problems I have attempted to place a reasonable hint or answer in the back of the book. Why should you do problems? Practice makes perfect. I could show you how to ride a unicycle, but if you never practiced, you would never learn. If you study and understand these problems, you will find your design and analytical skills are improved. As for your mother, she'll be proud of you.

Unicycles: the ultimate riding structure.

Sometimes we will introduce problems in the middle of the running text— these problems do not have answers (sometimes they are repeated as formal problems in the back of the chapter, where they *do* have answers)—they should be thought about carefully as you are reading along. You may find it useful to have a pencil and paper handy to help you "think" about these problems on the fly.

Exercise 0.1 *Call[3] your Mom and tell her you're completing your first exercise. If you don't have a phone handy, drop her a postcard. Ask her to verify that she's proud of you.*

Structure

This text is brief and to the point. Most of us are interested in experimenting. We will save as much time as possible for solving problems, perusing code, and practicing writing programs. As you read through each of the chapters, you might find it useful to read through the source code online. As we first consider the text of files online, the file name will appear in the margin, as you see here. The top icon refers to files in the `structure` package, while the bottom icon refers to files supporting examples.

Example

One more point—this book, like most projects, is an ongoing effort, and the latest thoughts are unlikely to have made it to the printed page. If you are in doubt, turn to the website for the latest comments. You will also find online documentation for each of the structures, generated from the code using `javadoc`. It is best to read the online version of the documentation for the most up-to-date details, as well as the documentation of several structures not formally presented within this text.

0.2   He Can't Say That, Can He?

Sure! Throughout this book are little political comments. These remarks may seem trivial at first blush. Skip them! If, however, you are interested in ways

---

[3] Don't e-mail her. Call her. Computers aren't everything, and they're a poor medium for a mother's pride.

to improve your skills as a programmer and a computer scientist, I invite you to read on. Sometimes these comments are so important that they appear as *principles*:

Principle 1 *The principled programmer understands a principle well enough to form an opinion about it.*

Self Check Problems

Solutions to these problems begin on page 427.

0.1   Where are the answers for "self check" problems found?

0.2   What are features of large programs?

0.3   Should you read the entire text?

0.4   Are *principles* statements of truth?

Problems

Solutions to the odd-numbered problems begin on page 437.

0.1   All odd problems have answers. Where do you find answers to problems? (Hint: See page 437.)

0.2   You are an experienced programmer. What five serious pieces of advice would you give a new programmer?

0.3   Surf to the website associated with this text and review the resources available to you.

0.4   Which of the following structures are described in this text (see Appendix D): BinarySearchTree, BinaryTree, BitSet, Map, Hashtable, List?

0.5   Surf to http://www.javasoft.com and review the Java resources available from Sun, the developers of Java.

0.6   Review documentation for Sun's java.util package. (See the Core API Documentation at http://www.javasoft.com.) Which of the following data structures are available in this package: BinarySearchTree, BinaryTree, BitSet, Dictionary, Hashtable, List?

0.7   Check your local library or bookstore for Java reference texts.

0.8   If you haven't done so already, learn how to use your local Java programming environment by writing a Java application to write a line of text. (Hint: Read Appendix B.)

0.9   Find the local documentation for the structure package. If none is to be found, remember that the same documentation is available over the Internet from http://www.cs.williams.edu/JavaStructures.

0.10   Find the examples electronically distributed with the structure package. Many of these examples are discussed later in this text.

Chapter 1

The Object-Oriented Method

Concepts:
▷ Data structures
▷ Abstract data types
▷ Objects
▷ Classes
▷ Interfaces

I will pick up the hook.
You will see something new.
Two things. And I call them
Thing One and Thing Two.
These Things will not bite you.
They want to have fun.
—Theodor Seuss Geisel

COMPUTER SCIENCE DOES NOT SUFFER the great history of many other disciplines. While other subjects have well-founded paradigms and methods, computer science still struggles with one important question: *What is the best method to write programs?* To date, we have no best answer. The focus of language designers is to develop programming languages that are simple to use but provide the power to accurately and efficiently describe the details of large programs and applications. The development of Java is one such effort.

Throughout this text we focus on developing data structures using *object-oriented programming*. Using this paradigm the programmer spends time developing templates for structures called *classes*. The templates are then used to construct *instances* or *objects*. A majority of the statements in object-oriented programs involve *sending messages* to objects to have them report or change their state. Running a program involves, then, the construction and coordination of objects. In this way languages like Java are *object-oriented*.

OOP:
Object-oriented
programming.

In all but the smallest programming projects, *abstraction* is a useful tool for writing working programs. In programming languages including Pascal, Scheme, and C, the details of a program's implementation are hidden away in its procedures or functions. This approach involves *procedural abstraction*. In object-oriented programming the details of the implementation of data structures are hidden away within its objects. This approach involves *data abstraction*. Many modern programming languages use object orientation to support basic abstractions of data. We review the details of data abstraction and the design of formal *interfaces* for objects in this chapter.

1.1   Data Abstraction and Encapsulation

If you purchase a donut from Neville's Bakery in North Adams, Massachusetts, you can identify it as a donut without knowing its ingredients. Donuts are circular, breadlike, and sweet. The particular ingredients in a donut are of little concern to you. Of course, Mrs. Neville is free to switch from one sweetener to another, as long as the taste is preserved.[1] The donut's ingredients list and its construction are details that probably do not interest you.

Mrs. Neville also programs robots.

Likewise, it is often unimportant to know how data structures are *implemented* in order to appreciate their *use*. For example, most of us are familiar with the workings or *semantics* of strings or arrays, but, if pressed, we might find it difficult to describe their *mechanics*: *Do all consecutive locations in the array appear close together in memory in your computer, or are they far apart?* The answer is: *it is unimportant.* As long as the array behaves like an array or the string behaves like a string we are happy. The less one knows about how arrays or strings are implemented, the less one becomes dependent on a particular implementation. Another way to think about this abstractly is that the data structure lives up to an implicit "contract": *a string is an ordered list of characters*, or *elements of an array may be accessed in any order*. The implementor of the data structure is free to construct it in any reasonable way, as long as all the terms of the contract are met. Since different implementors are in the habit of making very different implementation decisions, anything that helps to hide the implementation details—any means of using *abstraction*—serves to make the world a better place to program.

Macintosh and UNIX store strings differently.

When used correctly, object-oriented programming allows the programmer to separate the details that are important to the user from the details that are only important to the implementation. Later in this book we shall consider very general behavior of data structures; for example, in Section 9.1 we will study structures that allow the user only to remove the most recently added item. Such behavior is inherent to our most abstract understanding of how the data structure works. We can appreciate the unique behavior of this structure even though we haven't yet discussed how these structures might be implemented. Those abstract details that are important to the user of the structure—including abstract semantics of the methods—make up its *contract* or *interface*. The interface describes the abstract behavior of the structure. Most of us would agree that while strings and arrays are very similar structures, they behave differently: you can shrink or expand a string, while you cannot directly do the same with an array; you can print a string directly, while printing an array involves explicitly printing each of its elements. These distinctions suggest they have distinct abstract behaviors; there are distinctions in the design of their interfaces.

The unimportant details hidden from the user are part of what makes up

---

[1] Apple cider is often used to flavor donuts in New England, but that decision decidedly *changes* the flavor of the donut for the better. Some of the best apple cider donuts can be found at the Apple Barn in Vermont (http://www.theapplebarn.com).

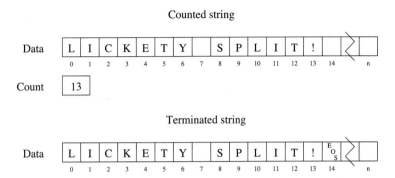

Figure 1.1 Two methods of implementing a string. A counted string explicitly records its length. The terminated string's length is determined by an end-of-string mark.

the *implementation*. We might decide (see Figure 1.1) that a string is to be constructed from a large array of characters with an attendant character count. Alternatively, we might specify the length implicitly by terminating the string with a special *end-of-string mark* that is not used for any other purpose. Both of these approaches are perfectly satisfactory, but there are trade-offs. The first implementation (called a *counted string*) has its length stored explicitly, while the length of the second implementation (called a *terminated string*) is implied. It takes longer to determine the length of a terminated string because we have to search for the end-of-string mark. On the other hand, the size of a terminated string is limited only by the amount of available memory, while the longest counted string is determined by the range of integers that can be stored in its length field (often this is only several hundred characters). If implementors can hide these details, users do not have to be distracted from their own important design work. As applications mature, a fixed interface to underlying objects allows alternative implementations of the object to be considered.

Data abstraction in languages like Java allows a structure to take responsibility for its own state. The structure knows how to maintain its own state without bothering the programmer. For example, if two strings have to be concatenated into a single string structure, a request might have to be made for a new allotment of memory. Thankfully, because strings know how to perform operations on themselves, the user doesn't have to worry about managing memory.

1.2 The Object Model

To facilitate the construction of well-designed objects, it is useful to have a design method in mind. As alluded to earlier, we will often visualize the data for our program as being managed by its objects. Each object manages its own data that determine its state. A point on a screen, for example, has two coordinates. A medical record maintains a name, a list of dependents, a medical history, and a reference to an insurance company. A strand of genetic material has a sequence of base pairs. To maintain a consistent state we imagine the program manipulates the data within its objects only through messages or *method calls* to the objects. A string might receive a message "tell me your length," while a medical record might receive a "change insurance" message. The string message simply accesses information, while the medical record method may involve changing several pieces of information in this and other objects in a consistent manner. If we directly modify the reference to the insurance company, we may forget to modify similar references in each of the dependents. For large applications with complex data structures, it can be extremely difficult to remember to coordinate all the operations that are necessary to move a single complex object from one consistent state to another. We opt, instead, to have the designer of the data structure provide us a method for carefully moving between states; this method is activated in response to a high-level message sent to the object.

This text, then, focuses on two important topics: (1) how we implement and evaluate objects with methods that are logically complex and (2) how we might use the objects we create. These objects typically represent *data structures*, our primary interest. Occasionally we will develop *control structures*—structures whose purpose is to control the manipulation of other objects. Control structures are an important concept and are described in detail in Chapter 7.

1.3   Object-Oriented Terminology

In Java, data abstraction is accomplished through *encapsulation* of data in an *object*—an instance of a *class*. Like a *record* in other languages, an object has *fields*. Unlike records, objects also contain *methods*. Fields and methods of an object may be declared `public`, which means that they are visible to entities outside the class, or `protected`, in which case they may only be accessed by code within methods of the class.[2] A typical class declaration is demonstrated by the following simple class that keeps track of the ratio of two integer values:

Ratio

```
public class Ratio
{
    protected int numerator;    // numerator of ratio
    protected int denominator;  // denominator of ratio

    public Ratio(int top, int bottom)
    // pre: bottom != 0
    // post: constructs a ratio equivalent to top::bottom
    {
        numerator = top;
```

---

[2] This is not quite the truth. For a discussion of the facts, see Appendix B.8.

```
        denominator = bottom;
        reduce();
    }

    public int getNumerator()
    // post: return the numerator of the fraction
    {
        return numerator;
    }

    public int getDenominator()
    // post: return the denominator of the fraction
    {
        return denominator;
    }

    public double getValue()
    // post: return the double equivalent of the ratio
    {
        return (double)numerator/(double)denominator;
    }

    public Ratio add(Ratio other)
    // pre: other is nonnull
    // post: return new fraction--the sum of this and other
    {
        return new Ratio(this.numerator*other.denominator+
                         this.denominator*other.numerator,
                         this.denominator*other.denominator);
    }

    protected void reduce()
    // post: numerator and denominator are set so that
    // the greatest common divisor of the numerator and denominator is 1
    {
        int divisor = gcd(numerator,denominator);
        numerator /= divisor;
        denominator /= divisor;
    }

    protected static int gcd(int a, int b)
    // pre: 0 <= a,b
    // post: computes the greatest integer value that divides a and b
    {
        if (a == 0) {
            if (b == 0) return 1;
            else return b;
        }
        if (b < a) return gcd(b,a);
        return gcd(b%a,a);
```

```
    }

    public String toString()
    // post: returns a string that represents this fraction
    {
        return getNumerator()+"/"+getDenominator();
    }
}
```

First, a `Ratio` object maintains the numerator and denominator as protected
`int`s that are not directly modifiable by the user. The `Ratio` method is a
constructor: a method whose name is the same as that of the class. (The
formal comments at the top of methods are pre- and postconditions; we discuss
these in detail in Chapter 2.) The constructor is called whenever a new `Ratio`
object is formed. Constructors initialize all the fields of the associated object,
placing the object into a predictable and consistent initial state. We declare the
constructors for a class `public`. To construct a new `Ratio` object, users will have
to call these methods. The `value` method returns a `double` that represents the
ratio, while the `getNumerator` and `getDenominator` methods fetch the current
values of the numerator and denominator of the fraction. The `add` method
is useful for adding one `Ratio` to another; the result is a newly constructed
`Ratio` object. Finally, the `toString` method generates the preferred printable
representation of the object; we have chosen to represent it in fractional form.

Two methods, `reduce` and `gcd`, are utility methods. The `gcd` method computes the greatest common divisor of two values using *Euclid's method*, one of
the oldest numerical algorithms used today. It is used by the `reduce` method to
reduce the numerator and denominator to lowest terms by removing any common factors. Both are declared `protected` because computing the reduction is
not a necessary (or obvious) operation to be performed on ratios of integers;
it's part of the implementation. The `gcd` method is declared `static` because
the algorithm can be used at any time—its utility is independent of the number
of `Ratio` objects that exist in our program. The `reduce` method, on the other
hand, works only with a `Ratio` object.

Exercise 1.1 *Nearly everything can be improved. Are there improvements that
might be made to the* `gcd` *method? Can you write the method iteratively? Is
iteration an improvement?*

As with the `Ratio` class, data fields are usually declared `protected`. To
manipulate protected fields the user must invoke `public` methods. The following
example demonstrates the manipulation of the `Ratio` class:

```
public static void main(String[] args)
{
    Ratio r = new Ratio(1,1);        // r == 1.0
    r = new Ratio(1,2);              // r == 0.5
    r.add(new Ratio(1,3));           // sum computed, but r still 0.5
    r = r.add(new Ratio(2,8));       // r == 0.75
```

```
        System.out.println(r.getValue()); // 0.75 printed
        System.out.println(r.toString());  // calls toString()
        System.out.println(r);  // calls toString()
    }
```

To understand the merit of this technique of class design, we might draw an analogy between a well-designed object and a lightbulb for your back porch. The protected fields and methods of an object are analogous to the internal design of the bulb. The observable features, including the voltage and the size of the socket, are provided without giving any details about the implementation of the object. If light socket manufacturers depended on a particular implementation of lightbulbs—for example the socket only supported bright xenon bulbs—it might ultimately restrict the variety of suppliers of lightbulbs in the future. Likewise, manufacturers of lightbulbs should be able to have a certain freedom in their implementation: as long as they only draw current in an agreed-upon way and as long as their bulb fits the socket, they should be free to use whatever design they want. Today, most lamps take either incandescent or fluorescent bulbs.

In the same way that fields are encapsulated by a class, classes may be encapsulated by a *package*. A package is a collection of related classes that implement some set of structures with a common theme. The classes of this text, for example, are members of the `structure` package. In the same way that there are users of classes, there are users of packages, and much of the analogy holds. In particular, classes may be declared `public`, in which case they may be used by anyone who *imports* the package into their program. If a class is not `public`, it is automatically considered `protected`. These `protected` classes may only be constructed and used by other classes within the same package.

1.4   A Special-Purpose Class: A Bank Account

We now look at the detailed construction of a simplistic class: a `BankAccount`. Many times, it is necessary to provide a tag associated with an instance of a data structure. You might imagine that your bank balance is kept in a database at your bank. When you get money for a trip through the Berkshires, you swipe your card through an automated teller bringing up your account. Your account number, presumably, is unique to your account. Nothing about you or your banking history is actually stored in your account number. Instead, that number is used to find the record linked to your account: the bank searches for a structure associated with the number you provide. Thus a `BankAccount` is a simple, but important, data structure. It has an `account` (an identifier that never changes) and a `balance` (that potentially *does* change). The public methods of such a structure are as follows:

Automated teller: a robotic palm reader.

```
public class BankAccount
{
    public BankAccount(String acc, double bal)
```

`BankAccount`

```
// pre: account is a string identifying the bank account
// balance is the starting balance
// post: constructs a bank account with desired balance

public boolean equals(Object other)
// pre: other is a valid bank account
// post: returns true if this bank account is the same as other

public String getAccount()
// post: returns the bank account number of this account

public double getBalance()
// post: returns the balance of this bank account

public void deposit(double amount)
// post: deposit money in the bank account

public void withdraw(double amount)
// pre: there are sufficient funds in the account
// post: withdraw money from the bank account
    }
```

The substance of these methods has purposefully been removed because, again, it is unimportant for us to know exactly how a BankAccount is implemented. We have ways to construct and compare BankAccounts, as well as ways to read the account number or balance, or update the balance.

Let's look at the implementation of these methods, individually. To build a new bank account, you must use the new operator to call the constructor with two parameters. The account number provided never changes over the life of the BankAccount—if it were necessary to change the value of the account number, a new BankAccount would have to be made, and the balance would have to be transferred from one to the other. The constructor plays the important role of performing the one-time initialization of the account number field. Here is the code for a BankAccount constructor:

```
protected String account;   // the account number
protected double balance;  // the balance associated with account

public BankAccount(String acc, double bal)
// pre: account is a string identifying the bank account
// balance is the starting balance
// post: constructs a bank account with desired balance
    {
        account = acc;
        balance = bal;
    }
```

Two fields—account and balance—of the BankAccount object are responsible for maintaining the object's state. The account keeps track of the account number, while the balance field maintains the balance.

Since account numbers are unique to `BankAccounts`, to check to see if two accounts are "the same," we need only compare the `account` fields. Here's the code:

```
public boolean equals(Object other)
// pre: other is a valid bank account
// post: returns true if this bank account is the same as other
{
    BankAccount that = (BankAccount)other;
    // two accounts are the same if account numbers are the same
    return this.account.equals(that.account);
}
```

Notice that the `BankAccount` equals method calls the `equals` method of the key, a `String`. Both `BankAccount` and `String` are nonprimitive types, or examples of `Objects`. Every object in Java has an `equals` method. If you don't explicitly provide one, the system will write one for you. Generally speaking, one should assume that the automatically written or *default* equals method is of little use. This notion of "equality" of objects is often based on the complexities of our abstraction; its design must be considered carefully.

One can ask the `BankAccount` about various aspects of its state by calling its `getAccount` or `getBalance` methods:

```
public String getAccount()
// post: returns the bank account number of this account
{
    return account;
}

public double getBalance()
// post: returns the balance of this bank account
{
    return balance;
}
```

These methods do little more than pass along the information found in the `account` and `balance` fields, respectively. We call such methods *accessors*. In a different implementation of the `BankAccount`, the balance would not have to be explicitly stored—the value might be, for example, the difference between two fields, `deposits` and `drafts`. Given the interface, it is not much of a concern to the user which implementation is used.

We provide two more methods, `deposit` and `withdraw`, that explicitly modify the current balance. These are *mutator* methods:

```
public void deposit(double amount)
// post: deposit money in the bank account
{
    balance = balance + amount;
}
```

```
public void withdraw(double amount)
// pre: there are sufficient funds in the account
// post: withdraw money from the bank account
{
    balance = balance - amount;
}
```

Because we would like to change the balance of the account, it is important to have a method that allows us to modify it. On the other hand, we purposefully don't have a setAccount method because we do not want the account number to be changed without a considerable amount of work (work that, by the way, models reality).

Here is a simple application that determines whether it is better to deposit $100 in an account that bears 5 percent interest for 10 years, or to deposit $100 in an account that bears $2\frac{1}{2}$ percent interest for 20 years. It makes use of the BankAccount object just outlined:

```
public static void main(String[] args)
{
    // Question: is it better to invest $100 over 10 years at 5%
    //           or to invest $100 over 20 years at 2.5% interest?
    BankAccount jd = new BankAccount("Jain Dough",100.00);
    BankAccount js = new BankAccount("Jon Smythe",100.00);

    for (int years = 0; years < 10; years++)
    {
        jd.deposit(jd.getBalance() * 0.05);
    }
    for (int years = 0; years < 20; years++)
    {
        js.deposit(js.getBalance() * 0.025);
    }
    System.out.println("Jain invests $100 over 10 years at 5%.");
    System.out.println("After 10 years " + jd.getAccount() +
                       " has $" + jd.getBalance());
    System.out.println("Jon invests $100 over 20 years at 2.5%.");
    System.out.println("After 20 years " + js.getAccount() +
                       " has $" + js.getBalance());
}
```

Exercise 1.2 *Which method of investment would you pick?*

1.5   A General-Purpose Class: An Association

At least Dr. Seuss started with 50 words! The following small application implements a Pig Latin translator based on a dictionary of nine words. The code makes use of an array of Associations, each of which establishes a relation between an English word and its Pig Latin translation. For each string passed as the argument to the `main` method, the dictionary is searched to determine the appropriate translation.

```java
public class atinLay {
    // a pig latin translator for nine words
    public static void main(String args[])
    {
        // build and fill out an array of nine translations
        Association dict[] = new Association[9];
        dict[0] = new Association("a","aay");
        dict[1] = new Association("bad","adbay");
        dict[2] = new Association("had","adhay");
        dict[3] = new Association("dad","adday");
        dict[4] = new Association("day","ayday");
        dict[5] = new Association("hop","ophay");
        dict[6] = new Association("on","onay");
        dict[7] = new Association("pop","oppay");
        dict[8] = new Association("sad","adsay");

        for (int argn = 0; argn < args.length; argn++)
        {   // for each argument
            for (int dictn = 0; dictn < dict.length; dictn++)
            {   // check each dictionary entry
                if (dict[dictn].getKey().equals(args[argn]))
                    System.out.println(dict[dictn].getValue());
            }
        }
    }
}
```

atinlay

When this application is run with the arguments `hop on pop`, the results are

```
ophay
onay
oppay
```

While this application may seem rather trivial, it is easy to imagine a large-scale application with similar needs.[3]

    We now consider the design of the `Association`. Notice that while the *type* of data maintained is different, the *purpose* of the `Association` is very similar to that of the `BankAccount` class we discussed in Section 1.4. An `Association` is a key-value pair such that the `key` cannot be modified. Here is the interface for the `Association` class:

```java
import java.util.Map;
```

Association

---

[3] Pig Latin has played an important role in undermining court-ordered restrictions placed on music piracy. When Napster—the rebel music trading firm—put in checks to recognize copyrighted music by title, traders used Pig Latin translators to foil the recognition software!

```
public class Association implements Map.Entry
{
    public Association(Object key, Object value)
    // pre: key is non-null
    // post: constructs a key-value pair

    public Association(Object key)
    // pre: key is non-null
    // post: constructs a key-value pair; value is null

    public boolean equals(Object other)
    // pre: other is non-null Association
    // post: returns true iff the keys are equal

    public Object getValue()
    // post: returns value from association

    public Object getKey()
    // post: returns key from association

    public Object setValue(Object value)
    // post: sets association's value to value
}
```

For the moment, we will ignore the references to Map and Map.entry; these will
be explained later, in Chapter 14. What distinguishes an Association from a
more specialized class, like BankAccount, is that the fields of an Association are
type Object. The use of the word Object in the definition of an Association
makes the definition very general: any value that is of type Object—any non-
primitive data type in Java—can be used for the key and value fields.

Unlike the BankAccount class, this class has two different constructors:

```
protected Object theKey; // the key of the key-value pair
protected Object theValue; // the value of the key-value pair

public Association(Object key, Object value)
// pre: key is non-null
// post: constructs a key-value pair
{
    Assert.pre(key != null, "Key must not be null.");
    theKey = key;
    theValue = value;
}

public Association(Object key)
// pre: key is non-null
// post: constructs a key-value pair; value is null
{
    this(key,null);
}
```

The first constructor—the constructor distinguished by having two parame-ters—allows the user to construct a new `Association` by initializing both fields. On occasion, however, we may wish to have an `Association` whose `key` field is set, but whose `value` field is left referencing nothing. (An example might be a medical record: initially the medical history is incomplete, perhaps waiting to be forwarded from a previous physician.) For this purpose, we provide a single parameter constructor that sets the `value` field to `null`. Note that we use `this(key,null)` as the body. The one-parameter constructor calls this object's two-parameter constructor with `null` as the second parameter. We write the constructors in this dependent manner so that if the underlying implementation of the `Association` had to be changed, only the two-parameter method would have to be updated. It also reduces the complexity of the code and saves your fingerprints!

Now, given a particular `Association`, it is useful to be able to retrieve the key or value. Since the implementation is hidden, no one outside the class is able to see it. Users must depend on the accessor methods to observe the data.

```
public Object getValue()
// post: returns value from association
{
    return theValue;
}

public Object getKey()
// post: returns key from association
{
    return theKey;
}
```

When necessary, the method `setValue` can be used to change the value associ-ated with the key. Thus, the `setValue` method simply takes its parameter and assigns it to the `value` field:

```
public Object setValue(Object value)
// post: sets association's value to value
{
    Object oldValue = theValue;
    theValue = value;
    return oldValue;
}
```

There are other methods that are made available to users of the `Association` class, but we will not discuss the details of that code until later. Some of the methods are required, some are useful, and some are just nice to have around. While the code may look complicated, we take the time to implement it correctly, so that *we will not have to reimplement it in the future.*

Principle 2 *Free the future: reuse code.*

It is difficult to fight the temptation to design data structures from scratch. We shall see, however, that many of the more complex structures would be very difficult to construct if we could not base our implementations on the results of previous work.

1.6 Sketching an Example: A Word List

Suppose we're interested in building a game of Hangman. The computer selects random words and we try to guess them. Over several games, the computer should pick a variety of words and, as each word is used, it should be removed from the word list. Using an object-oriented approach, we'll determine the essential features of a `WordList`, the Java object that maintains our list of words.

Our approach to designing the data structures has the following five informal steps:

1. Identify the types of operations you expect to perform on your object. What operations *access* your object only by reading its data? What operations might modify or *mutate* your objects?

2. Identify, given your operations, those data that support the *state* of your object. Information about an object's state is carried within the object between operations that modify the state. Since there may be many ways to encode the state of your object, your description of the state may be very general.

3. Identify any rules of consistency. In the `Ratio` class, for example, it would not be good to have a zero denominator. Also, the numerator and denominator should be in lowest terms.

4. Determine the number and form of the constructors. Constructors are synthetic: their sole responsibility is to get a new object into a good initial and consistent state. Don't forget to consider the best state for an object constructed using the parameterless *default constructor*.

5. Identify the types and kinds of information that, though declared `protected`, can *efficiently* provide the information needed by the `public` methods. Important choices about the internals of a data structure are usually made at this time. Sometimes, competing approaches are developed until a comparative evaluation can be made. That is the subject of much of this book.

The operations necessary to support a list of words can be sketched out easily, even if we don't know the intimate details of constructing the Hangman game itself. Once we see how the data structure is used, we have a handle on the design of the interface. Thinking about the overall design of Hangman, we can identify the following general use of the `WordList` object:

WordList

```
WordList list;                           // declaration
String targetWord;

list = new WordList(10);                 // construction
list.add("disambiguate");   // is this a word? how about ambiguate?
list.add("inputted");       // really? what verbification!
list.add("subbookkeeper");  // now that's coollooking!
while (!list.isEmpty())                  // game loop
{
    targetWord = list.selectAny();       // selection
    // ...play the game using target word...
    list.remove(targetWord);             // update
}
```

Let's consider these lines. One of the first lines (labeled `declaration`) declares a *reference* to a `WordList`. For a reference to refer to an object, the object must be constructed. We require, therefore, a constructor for a `WordList`. The `construction` line allocates an initially empty list of words ultimately containing as many as 10 words. We provide an upper limit on the number of words that are potentially stored in the list. (We'll see later that providing such information can be useful in designing efficient data structures.) On the next three lines, three (dubious) words are added to the list.

The `while` loop accomplishes the task of playing Hangman with the user. This is possible as long as the list of words is not empty. We use the `isEmpty` method to test this fact. At the beginning of each round of Hangman, a random word is selected (`selectAny`), setting the `targetWord` reference. To make things interesting, we presume that the `selectAny` method selects a random word each time. Once the round is finished, we use the `remove` method to remove the word from the word list, eliminating it as a choice in future rounds.

There are insights here. First, we have said very little about the Hangman game other than its interaction with our rather abstract list of words. The details of the screen's appearance, for example, do not play much of a role in understanding how the `WordList` structure works. We knew that a list was necessary for our program, and we considered the program *from the point of view of the object*. Second, we don't really know how the `WordList` is implemented. The words may be stored in an array, or in a file on disk, or they may use some technology that we don't currently understand. It is only important that we have *faith* that the structure can be implemented. We have sketched out the method headers, or *signatures*, of the `WordList` *interface*, and we have faith that an *implementation* supporting the interface can be built. Finally we note that what we have written is not a complete program. Still, from the viewpoint of the `WordList` structure, there are few details of the interface that are in question. A reasoned individual should be able to look at this design and say "this will work—provided it is implemented correctly." If a reviewer of the code were to ask a question about how the structure works, it would lead to a refinement of our understanding of the interface.

We have, then, the following required interface for the `WordList` class:

```
public class WordList
{
    public WordList(int size)
    // pre: size >= 0
    // post: construct a word list capable of holding "size" words

    public boolean isEmpty()
    // post: return true iff the word list contains no words

    public void add(String s)
    // post: add a word to the word list, if it is not already there

    public String selectAny()
    // pre: the word list is not empty
    // post: return a random word from the list

    public void remove(String word)
    // pre: word is not null
    // post: remove the word from the word list
}
```

We will leave the implementation details of this example until later. You might consider various ways that the WordList might be implemented. As long as the methods of the interface can be supported by your data structure, your implementation is valid.

Exercise 1.3 *Finish the sketch of the* WordList *class to include details about the state variables.*

1.7   Sketching an Example: A Rectangle Class

Suppose we are developing a graphics system that allows the programmer to draw on a DrawingWindow. This window has, associated with it, a Cartesian coordinate system that allows us to uniquely address each of the points within the window. Suppose, also, that we have methods for drawing line segments, say, using the Line object. How might we implement a rectangle—called a Rect—to be drawn in the drawing window?

One obvious goal would be to draw a Rect on the DrawingWindow. This might be accomplished by drawing four line segments. It would be useful to be able to draw a filled rectangle, or to erase a rectangle (think: draw a filled rectangle in the background color). We're not sure how to do this efficiently, but these latter methods seem plausible and consistent with the notion of drawing. (We should check to see if it is possible to draw in the background color.) This leads to the following methods:

Rect

```
public void fillOn(DrawingWindow d)
// pre: d is a valid drawing window
// post: the rectangle is filled on the drawing window d
```

```
public void clearOn(DrawingWindow d)
// pre: d is a valid drawing window
// post: the rectangle is erased from the drawing window

public void drawOn(DrawingWindow d)
// pre: d is a valid drawing window
// post: the rectangle is drawn on the drawing window
```

It might be useful to provide some methods to allow us to perform basic calculations—for example, we might want to find out if the mouse arrow is located within the `Rect`. These require accessors for all the obvious data. In the hope that we might use a `Rect` multiple times in multiple locations, we also provide methods for moving and reshaping the `Rect`.

```
public boolean contains(Pt p)
// pre: p is a valid point
// post: true iff p is within the rectangle

public int left()
// post: returns left coordinate of the rectangle

public void left(int x)
// post: sets left to x; dimensions remain unchanged

public int width()
// post: returns the width of the rectangle

public void width(int w)
// post: sets width of rectangle, center and height unchanged

public void center(Pt p)
// post: sets center of rect to p; dimensions remain unchanged

public void move(int dx, int dy)
// post: moves rectangle to left by dx and down by dy

public void moveTo(int left, int top)
// post: moves left top of rectangle to (left,top);
//         dimensions are unchanged

public void extend(int dx, int dy)
// post: moves sides of rectangle outward by dx and dy
```

Again, other approaches might be equally valid. No matter how we might represent a `Rect`, however, it seems that all rectangular regions with horizontal and vertical sides can be specified with four integers. We can, then, construct a `Rect` by specifying, say, the left and top coordinates and the width and height.

For consistency's sake, it seems appropriate to allow rectangles to be drawn anywhere (even off the screen), but the width and height should be non-negative values. We should make sure that these constraints appear in the documentation associated with the appropriate constructors and methods. (See Section 2.2 for more details on how to write these comments.)

Given our thinking, we have some obvious `Rect` constructors:

```
public Rect()
// post: constructs a trivial rectangle at origin

public Rect(Pt p1, Pt p2)
// post: constructs a rectangle between p1 and p2

public Rect(int x, int y, int w, int h)
// pre: w >= 0, h >= 0
// post: constructs a rectangle with upper left (x,y),
//        width w, height h
```

We should feel pleased with the progress we have made. We have developed the signatures for the rectangle interface, even though we have no immediate application. We also have some emerging answers on approaches to implementing the `Rect` internally. If we declare our `Rect` data protected, we can insulate ourselves from changes suggested by inefficiencies we may yet discover.

Exercise 1.4 *Given this sketch of the* `Rect` *interface, how would you declare the private data associated with the* `Rect` *object? Given your approach, describe how you might implement the* `center(int x, int y)` *method.*

1.8 Interfaces

Sometimes it is useful to describe the interface for a number of different classes, without committing to an implementation. For example, in later sections of this text we will implement a number of data structures that are able to be modified by adding or removing values. We can, for all of these classes, specify a few of their fundamental methods by using the Java `interface` declaration:

Structure

```
public interface Structure
{
    public int size();
    // post: computes number of elements contained in structure

    public boolean isEmpty();
    // post: return true iff the structure is empty

    public void clear();
    // post: the structure is empty

    public boolean contains(Object value);
    // pre: value is non-null
    // post: returns true iff value.equals some value in structure
```

```
    public void add(Object value);
    // pre: value is non-null
    // post: value has been added to the structure
    //       replacement policy is not specified

    public Object remove(Object value);
    // pre: value is non-null
    // post: value is removed from structure, if it was there

    public java.util.Enumeration elements();
    // post: returns an enumeration for traversing structure;
    //       all structure package implementations return
    //       an AbstractIterator

    public Iterator iterator();
    // post: returns an iterator for traversing structure;
    //       all structure package implementations return
    //       an AbstractIterator

    public Collection values();
    // post: returns a Collection that may be used with
    //       Java's Collection Framework
}
```

Notice that the body of each method has been replaced by a semicolon. It is, in fact, illegal to specify any code in a Java interface. Specifying just the method signatures in an interface is like writing boilerplate for a contract without committing to any implementation. When we decide that we are interested in constructing a new class, we can choose to have it *implement* the Structure interface. For example, our WordList structure of Section 1.6 might have made use of our Structure interface by beginning its declaration as follows:

```
    public class WordList implements Structure
```

WordList

When the WordList class is compiled by the Java compiler, it checks to see that each of the methods mentioned in the Structure interface—add, remove, size, and the others—is actually implemented. In this case, only isEmpty is part of the WordList specification, so we must either (1) not have WordList implement the Structure interface or (2) add the methods demanded by Structure.

Interfaces may be extended. Here, we have a possible definition of what it means to be a Set:

```
    public interface Set extends Structure
    {
        public void addAll(Structure other);
        // pre: other is non-null
        // post: values from other are added into this set
```

Set

```
public boolean containsAll(Structure other);
// pre: other is non-null
// post: returns true if every value in set is in other

public void removeAll(Structure other);
// pre: other is non-null
// post: values of this set contained in other are removed

public void retainAll(Structure other);
// pre: other is non-null
// post: values not appearing in the other structure are removed
}
```

A Set requires several set-manipulation methods—addAll (i.e., set union) retain-All (set intersection), and removeAll (set difference)—as well as the methods demanded by being a Structure. If we implement these methods for the WordList class and indicate that WordList implements Set, the WordList class could be used wherever either a Structure or Set is required. Currently, our WordList is close to, but not quite, a Structure. Applications that demand the functionality of a Structure will not be satisfied with a WordList. Having the class implement an interface increases the flexibility of its use. Still, it may require considerable work for us to upgrade the WordList class to the level of a Structure. It may even work against the design of the WordList to provide the missing methods. The choices we make are part of an ongoing design process that attempts to provide the best implementations of structures to meet the demands of the user.

1.9   Who Is the User?

When implementing data structures using classes and interfaces, it is sometimes hard to understand *why* we might be interested in hiding the implementation. After all, perhaps we know that ultimately we will be the only programmers making use of these structures. That might be a good point, except that if you are really a successful programmer, you will implement the data structure flawlessly this week, use it next week, and not return to look at the code for a long time. When you *do* return, your view is effectively that of a user of the code, with little or no memory of the implementation.

One side effect of this relationship is that we have all been reminded of the need to write comments. If you do not write comments, you will not be able to read the code. If, however, you design, document, and implement your interface carefully, you might not ever have to look at the implementation! That's good news because, for most of us, in a couple of months our code is as foreign to us as if someone else had implemented it. The end result: consider yourself a user and design and abide by your interface wherever possible. If you know of some public field that gives a hint of the implementation, do not make use of it. Instead, access the data through appropriate methods. You will be happy you did later, when you optimize your implementation.

Principle 3 *Design and abide by interfaces as though you were the user.*

A quick corollary to this statement is the following:

Principle 4 *Declare data fields* `protected`*.*

If the data are protected, you cannot access them from outside the class, and you are forced to abide by the restricted access of the interface.

1.10 Conclusions

The construction of substantial applications involves the development of complex and interacting structures. In object-oriented languages, we think of these structures as objects that communicate through the passing of messages or, more formally, the invocation of methods.

We use object orientation in Java to write the structures found in this book. It is possible, of course, to design data structures without object orientation, but any effective data structuring model ultimately depends on the use of some form of abstraction that allows the programmer to avoid considering the complexities of particular implementations.

In many languages, including Java, data abstraction is supported by separating the interface from the implementation of the data structure. To ensure that users cannot get past the interface to manipulate the structure in an uncontrolled fashion, the system controls access to fields, methods, and classes. The implementor plays an important role in making sure that the structure is usable, given the interface. This role is so important that we think of implementation as supporting the interface—sometimes usefully considered a *contract* between the implementor and the user. This analogy is useful because, as in the real world, if contracts are violated, someone gets upset!

Initial design of the interfaces for data structures arises from considering how they are used in simple applications. Those method calls that are required by the application determine the interface for the new structure and constrain, in various ways, the choices we make in implementing the object.

In our implementation of an `Association`, we can use the `Object` class—that class inherited by all other Java classes—to write very general data structures. The actual type of value that is stored in the `Association` is determined by the values passed to the constructors and mutators of the class. This ability to pass a subtype to any object that requires a super type is a strength of object-oriented languages—and helps to reduce the complexity of code.

Self Check Problems

Solutions to these problems begin on page 427.

1.1   What is meant by abstraction?

1.2   What is procedural abstraction?

1.3   What is data abstraction?

1.4   How does Java support the concept of a *message*?

1.5   What is the difference between an object and a class?

1.6   What makes up a method's signature?

1.7   What is the difference between an interface and an implementation?

1.8   What is the difference between an accessor and a mutator?

1.9   A general purpose class, such as an `Association`, often makes use of parameters of type `Object`. Why?

1.10   What is the difference between a reference and an object?

1.11   Who uses a class?

Problems

Solutions to the odd-numbered problems begin on page 437.

1.1   Which of the following are primitive Java types: `int`, `Integer`, `double`, `Double`, `String`, `char`, `Association`, `BankAccount`, `boolean`, `Boolean`?

1.2   Which of the following variables are associated with valid constructor calls?

```
BankAccount a,b,c,d,e,f;
Association g,h;
a = new BankAccount("Bob",300.0);
b = new BankAccount(300.0,"Bob");
c = new BankAccount(033414,300.0);
d = new BankAccount("Bob",300);
e = new BankAccount("Bob",new Double(300));
f = new BankAccount("Bob",(double)300);
g = new Association("Alice",300.0);
h = new Association("Alice",new Double(300));
```

1.3   For each pair of classes, indicate which class extends the other:

  a. `java.lang.Number`, `java.lang.Double`

  b. `java.lang.Number`, `java.lang.Integer`

  c. `java.lang.Number`, `java.lang.Object`

  d. `java.util.Stack`, `java.util.Vector`

    e. `java.util.Hashtable`, `java.util.Dictionary`

1.4   Rewrite the compound interest program (discussed when considering `BankAccounts` in Section 1.4) so that it uses `Associations`.

1.5   Write a program that attempts to modify one of the private fields of an `Association`. When does your environment detect the violation? What happens?

1.6   Finish the design of a `Ratio` class that implements a ratio between two integers. The class should support standard math operations: addition, subtraction, multiplication, and division. You should also be able to construct `Ratios` from either a numerator-denominator pair, or a single integer, or with no parameter at all (what is a reasonable default value?).

1.7   Amazing fact: If you construct a `Ratio` from two random integers, $0 < a, b$, the probability that $\frac{a}{b}$ is already in reduced terms is $\frac{6}{\pi^2}$. Use this fact to write a program to compute an approximation to π.

1.8   Design a class to represent a U.S. telephone number. It should support three types of constructors—one that accepts three numbers, representing area code, exchange, and extension; another that accepts two integers, representing a number within your local area code; and a third constructor that accepts a string of letters and numbers that represent the number (e.g., `"900-410-TIME"`). Provide a method that determines if the number is provided toll-free (such numbers have area codes of 800, 866, 877, 880, 881, 882, or 888).

1.9   Sometimes it is useful to measure the length of time it takes for a piece of code to run. (For example, it may help determine where optimizations of your code would be most effective.) Design a `Stopwatch` class to support timing of events. You should consider use of the millisecond clock in the Java environment, `System.currentTimeMillis()`. Like many stopwatches, it should support starting, temporary stopping, and a reset. The design of the protected section of the stopwatch should hide the implementation details.

1.10   Design a data structure in Java that represents a musical tone. A `tone` can be completely specified as a number of cycles per second (labeled Hz for hertz), or the number of half steps above a commonly agreed upon tone, such as A (in modern times, in the United States, considered to be 440 Hz). Higher tones have higher frequencies. Two tones are an octave (12 semitones) apart if one has a frequency twice the other. A half step or semitone increase in tone is $\sqrt[12]{2} \approx 1.06$ times higher. Your `tone` constructors should accept a frequency (a `double`) or a number of half steps (an `int`) above A. Imperfect frequencies should be tuned to the nearest half step. Once constructed, a tone should be able to provide its frequency in either cycles per second or half-steps above A.

1.11   Extend Problem 1.10 to allow a second parameter to each constructor to specify the definition of A upon which the `tone`'s definition is based. What modern tone most closely resembles that of modern middle C (9 semitones below A) if A is defined to be 415 Hz?

1.12   Design a data structure to represent a combination lock. When the lock is constructed, it is provided with an arbitrary length array of integers between

0 and 25 specifying a combination (if no combination is provided, $9 - 0 - 21 - 0$ is the default). Initially, it is locked. Two methods—**press** and `reset`—provide a means of entering a combination: **press** enters the next integer to be used toward matching the combination, while `reset` re-readies the lock for accepting the first integer of the combination. Only when **press** is used to match the last integer of the combination does the lock silently unlock. Mismatched integers require a call to the `reset` method before the combination can again be entered. The `isLocked` method returns true if and only if the lock is locked. The `lock` method locks and resets the lock. In the unlocked state only the `isLocked` and `lock` methods have effect. (Aside: Because of the physical construction of many combination locks, it is often the case that combinations have patterns. For example, a certain popular lock is constructed with a three-number combination. The first and last numbers result in the same remainder x when divided by 4. The middle number has remainder $(x + 2)\%4$ when divided by 4!)

1.13   Design a data structure to simulate the workings of a car radio. The state of the radio is on or off, and it may be used to listen to an AM or FM station. A dozen modifiable push buttons (identified by integers 1 through 12) allow the listener to store and recall AM or FM frequencies. AM frequencies can be represented by multiples of 10 in the range 530 to 1610. FM frequencies are found at multiples of 0.2 in the range 87.9 to 107.9.

1.14   Design a data structure to maintain the position of m coins of radius 1 through m on a board with $n \geq m$ squares numbered 0 through $n - 1$. You may provide whatever interface you find useful to allow your structure to represent any placement of coins, including stacks of coins in a single cell. A configuration is *valid* only if large coins are not stacked on small coins. Your structure should have an `isValid` method that returns true if the coins are in a valid position. (A problem related to this is discussed in Section 9.2.1.)

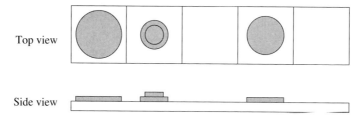

Top view

Side view

1.11 Laboratory: The Day of the Week Calculator

Objective. To (re)establish ties with Java: to write a program that reminds us of the particulars of numeric calculations and array manipulation in Java.

Discussion. In this lab we learn to compute the day of the week for any date between January 1, 1900, and December 31, 2099.[4] During this period of time, the only calendar adjustment is a leap-year correction every 4 years. (Years divisible by 100 are normally not leap years, but years divisible by 400 always are.) Knowing this, the method essentially computes the number of days since the beginning of the twentieth century in modulo 7 arithmetic. The computed remainder tells us the day of the week, where 0 is Saturday.

An essential feature of this algorithm involves remembering a short table of monthly adjustments. Each entry in the table corresponds to a month, where January is month 1 and December is month 12.

Month	1	2	3	4	5	6	7	8	9	10	11	12
Adjustment	1	4	4	0	2	5	0	3	6	1	4	6

If the year is divisible by 4 (it's a leap year) and the date is January or February, you must subtract 1 from the adjustment.

Remembering this table is equivalent to remembering how many days are in each month. Notice that 144 is 12^2, 025 is 5^2, 036 is 6^2, and 146 is a bit more than 12^2. Given this, the algorithm is fairly simple:

1. Write down the date numerically. The date consists of a month between 1 and 12, a day of the month between 1 and 31, and the number of years since 1900. Grace Hopper, computer language pioneer, was born December 9, 1906. That would be represented as year 6. Jana the Giraffe, of the National Zoo, was born on January 18, 2001. That year would be represented as year 101.

2. Compute the sum of the following quantities:

   - the month adjustment from the given table (e.g., 6 for Admiral Hopper)
   - the day of the month
   - the year
   - the whole number of times 4 divides the year (e.g., 25 for Jana the Giraffe)

---

[4] This particular technique is due to John Conway, of Princeton University. Professor Conway answers 10 day of the week problems before gaining access to his computer. His record is at the time of this writing well under 15 seconds for 10 correctly answered questions. See "Scientist at Work: John H. Conway; At Home in the Elusive World of Mathematics," *The New York Times*, October 12, 1993.

3. Compute the remainder of the sum of step 2, when divided by 7. The remainder gives the day of the week, where Saturday is 0, Sunday is 1, etc. Notice that we can compute the remainders *before* we compute the sum. You may also have to compute the remainder after the sum as well, but if you're doing this in your head, this considerably simplifies the arithmetic.

What day of the week was Tiger Woods born?

1. Tiger's birth date is 12-30-75.

2. Remembering that $18 \times 4 = 72$, we write the sum as follows:

$$6 + 30 + 75 + 18$$

which is equivalent to the following sum, modulo 7:

$$6 + 2 + 5 + 4 = 17 \equiv 3 \bmod 7$$

3. He was born on day 3, a Tuesday.

Now you practice: Which of Grace and Jana was born on a Thursday? (The other was born on a Sunday.)

Procedure. Write a Java program that performs Conway's day of the week challenge:

1. Develop an object that can hold a date.

2. Write a method to compute a random date between 1900 and 2099. How will you limit the range of days potentially generated for any particular month?

3. Write a method of your date class to compute the day of the week associated with a date. Be careful: the table given in the discussion has January as month 1, but Java would prefer it to be month 0! Don't forget to handle the birthday of Jimmy Dorsey (famous jazzman), February 29, 1904.

Jimmy was a Monday's child.

4. Your `main` method should repeatedly (1) print a random date, (2) read a predicted day of the week (as an integer/remainder), and (3) check the correctness of the guess. The program should stop when 10 dates have been guessed correctly and print the elapsed time. (You may wish to set this threshold lower while you're testing the program.)

Helpful Hints. You may find the following Java useful:

1. Random integers may be selected using the `java.util.Random` class:

```
Random r = new Random();
int month = (Math.abs(r.nextInt()) % 12) + 1;
```

You will need to `import java.util.Random;` at the top of your program to make use of this class. Be aware that you need to only construct one random number generator per program run. Also, the random number generator potentially returns negative numbers. If `Math.abs` is not used, these values generate negative remainders.

2. You can find out how many thousandths of seconds have elapsed since the 1960s, by calling the Java method, `System.currentTimeMillis()`. It returns a value of type `long`. We can use this to measure the duration of an experiment, with code similar to the following:

In 2001, 1 trillion millis since the '60s. Dig that!

```
long start = System.currentTimeMillis();
//
// place experiment to be timed here
//
long duration = System.currentTimeMillis()-start;
System.out.println("time: "+(duration/1000.0)+" seconds.");
```

The granularity of this timer isn't any better than a thousandth of a second. Still, we're probably not in Conway's league yet.

After you finish your program, you will find you can quickly learn to answer 10 of these day of the week challenges in less than a minute.

Thought Questions. Consider the following questions as you complete the lab:

1. True or not: In Java is it true that `(a % 7) == (a - a/7*7)` for a `>=` 0?

2. It's rough to start a week on Saturday. What adjustments would be necessary to have a remainder of 0 associated with Sunday? (This might allow a mnemonic of Nun-day, One-day, Twos-day, Wednesday, Fours-day, Fives-day, Saturday.)

3. Why do you *subtract* 1 in a leap year if the date falls before March?

4. It might be useful to compute the portion of any calculation associated with this year, modulo 7. Remembering that value will allow you to optimize your most frequent date calculations. What is the remainder associated with this year?

For years divisible by 28: think zero!

Notes:

Chapter 2

Comments, Conditions, and Assertions

Concepts:
▷ Preconditions
▷ Postconditions
▷ Assertions
▷ Copyrighting code

```
                              /* This is bogus code.
         Wizards are invited to improve it.   */
                                      —Anonymous
```

CONSIDER THIS: WE CALL OUR PROGRAMS "CODE"! The features of computer languages, including Java, are designed to help express algorithms in a manner that a machine can understand. Making a program run more efficiently often makes it less understandable. If language design was driven by the need to make the program readable by programmers, it would be hard to argue against programming in English.

Okay, perhaps French!

A *comment* is a carefully crafted piece of text that describes the state of the machine, the use of a variable, or the purpose of a control construct. Many of us, though, write comments for the same reason that we exercise: we feel guilty. You feel that, if you do not write comments in your code, you "just *know*" something bad is going to happen. Well, you are right. A comment you write today will help you out of a hole you dig tomorrow.

Ruth Krauss: "A hole is to dig."

All too often comments are hastily written after the fact, to help understand the code. The time spent thinking seriously about the code has long since passed, and the comment might not be right. If you write comments beforehand, while you are designing your code, it is more likely your comments will describe what you want to do as you carefully think it out. Then, when something goes wrong, the comment is there to help you figure out the code. In fairness, the code and the comment have a symbiotic relationship. Writing one or the other does not really feel complete, but writing both provides you with the redundancy of concept: one lucid and one as clear as Java.

The one disadvantage of comments is that, unlike code, they cannot be checked. Occasionally, programmers come across comments such as "If you think you understand this, you don't!" or "Are you reading this?" One could, of course, annotate programs with mathematical formulas. As the program is compiled, the mathematical comments are distilled into very concise descriptions

Semiformal convention: a meeting of tie haters.

of what should be going on. When the output from the program's code does not match the result of the formula, something is clearly wrong with your logic. But *which* logic? The writing of mathematical comments is a level of detail most programmers would prefer to avoid.

A compromise is a semiformal convention for comments that provide a reasonable documentation of *when* and *what* a program does. In the code associated with this book, we see one or two comments for each method or function that describe its purpose. These important comments are the *precondition* and *postcondition*.

2.1   Pre- and Postconditions

The *precondition* describes, as succinctly as possible in your native tongue, the conditions under which a method may be called and expected to produce correct results. Ideally the precondition expresses the *state* of the program. This state is usually cast in terms of the parameters passed to the routine. For example, the precondition on a square root function might be

sqrt

```
// pre: x is nonnegative
```

The authors of this square root function expect that the parameter is not a negative number. It is, of course, legal in Java to call a function or method if the precondition is not met, but it might not produce the desired result. When there is no precondition on a procedure, it may be called without failure.

The *postcondition* describes the state of the program once the routine has been completed, *provided the precondition was met*. Every routine should have some postcondition. If there were not a postcondition, then the routine would not change the state of the program, and the routine would have no effect! Always provide postconditions.

Pre- and postconditions do not force you to write code correctly. Nor do they help you find the problems that *do* occur. They can, however, provide you with a uniform method for documenting the programs you write, and they require more thought than the average comment. More thought put into programs lowers your average blood pressure and ultimately saves you time you might spend more usefully playing outside, visiting museums, or otherwise bettering your mind.

2.2   Assertions

In days gone by, homeowners would sew firecrackers in their curtains. If the house were to catch fire, the curtains would burn, setting off the firecrackers. It was an elementary but effective fire alarm.

And the batteries never needed replacing.

An *assertion* is an assumption you make about the state of your program. In Java, we will encode the assertion as a call to a function that verifies the state of the program. That function does nothing if the assertion is true, but it

halts your program with an error message if it is false. It is a firecracker to sew
in your program. If you sew enough assertions into your code, you will get an
early warning if you are about to be burned by your logic.

Principle 5 *Test assertions in your code.*

The `Assert` class provides several functions to help you test the state of your
program as it runs:

Assert

```
public class Assert
{
    static public void pre(boolean test, String message)
    // pre: result of precondition test
    // post: does nothing if test true, otherwise abort w/message

    static public void post(boolean test, String message)
    // pre: result of postcondition test
    // post: does nothing if test true, otherwise abort w/message

    static public void condition(boolean test, String message)
    // pre: result of general condition test
    // post: does nothing if test true, otherwise abort w/message

    static public void invariant(boolean test, String message)
    // pre: result of an invariant test
    // post: does nothing if test true, otherwise abort w/message

    static public void fail(String message)
    // post: throws error with message
}
```

Each of `pre`, `post`, `invariant`, and `condition` methods test to see if its first
argument—the assertion—is true. The `message` is used to indicate the condition
tested by the assertion. Here's an example of a check to make sure that the
precondition for the `sqrt` function was met:

```
public static double sqrt(double x)
// pre: x is nonnegative
// post: returns the square root of x
{
    Assert.pre(x >= 0,"the value is nonnegative.");
    double guess = 1.0;
    double guessSquared = guess * guess;

    while (Math.abs(x-guessSquared) >= 0.00000001) {
        // guess is off a bit, adjust
        guess += (x-guessSquared)/2.0/guess;
        guessSquared = guess*guess;
    }
    return guess;
}
```

Should we call `sqrt` with a negative value, the assertion fails, the message is printed out, and the program comes to a halt. Here's what appears at the display:

```
structure.FailedPrecondition:
Assertion that failed: A precondition: the value is nonnegative.
        at Assert.pre(Assert.java:17)
        at sqrt(examples.java:24)
        at main(examples.java:15)
```

The first two lines of this message indicate that a precondition (that `x` was non-negative) failed. This message was printed within `Assert.pre` on line 17 of the source, found in `Assert.java`. The next line of this *stack trace* indicates that the call to `Assert.pre` was made on line 24 of `examples.java` at the start of the `sqrt` function. This is the first line of the `sqrt` method. The problem is (probably) on line 15 of the main procedure of `examples.java`. Debugging our code should probably start in the `main` routine.

Beginning with Java 1.4, assertion testing is part of the formal Java language specification. The `assert` keyword can be used to perform many of the types of checks we have described. If, however, you are using an earlier version of Java, or you expect your users may wish to use a version of Java before version 1.4, you may find the `Assert` class to be a more portable approach to the testing of the conditions of one's code. A feature of language-based assertion testing is that the tests can be automatically removed at compile time when one feels secure about the way the code works. This may significantly improve performance of classes that heavily test conditions.

2.3   Craftsmanship

If you *really* desire to program well, a first step is to take pride in your work—pride enough to sign your name on everything you do. Through the centuries, fine furniture makers signed their work, painters finished their efforts by dabbing on their names, and authors inscribed their books. Programmers should stand behind their creations.

Computer software has the luxury of immediate copyright protection—it is a protection against piracy, and a modern statement that you stand behind the belief that what you do is worth fighting for. If you have crafted something as best you can, add a comment at the top of your code:

```
// Image compression barrel for downlink to robotic cow tipper.
// (c) 2001, 2002 duane r. bailey
```

If, of course, you *have* stolen work from another, avoid the comment and consider, heavily, the appropriate attribution.

2.4 Conclusions

Effective programmers consider their work a craft. Their constructions are well considered and documented. Comments are not necessary, but documentation makes working with a program much easier. One of the most important comments you can provide is your name—it suggests you are taking credit *and* responsibility for things you create. It makes our programming world less anonymous and more humane.

Special comments, including conditions and assertions, help the user and implementor of a method determine whether the method is used correctly. While it is difficult for compilers to determine the "spirit of the routine," the implementor is usually able to provide succinct checks of the sanity of the function. Five minutes of appropriate condition description and checking provided by the implementor can prevent hours of debugging by the user.

I've done my time!

Self Check Problems

Solutions to these problems begin on page 428.

2.1 Why is it necessary to provide pre- and postconditions?

2.2 What can be assumed if a method has no precondition?

2.3 Why is it not possible to have a method with no postcondition?

2.4 Object orientation allows us to hide unimportant details from the user. Why, then, must we put pre- and postconditions on hidden code?

Problems

Solutions to the odd-numbered problems begin on page 443.

2.1 What are the pre- and postconditions for the `length` method of the `java.lang.String` class?

2.2 What are the pre- and postconditions for `String`'s `charAt` method?

2.3 What are the pre- and postconditions for `String`'s `concat` method?

2.4 What are the pre- and postconditions for the `floor` function in the `java.lang.Math` class?

2.5 Improve the comments on an old program.

2.6 Each of the methods of `Assert` (`pre`, `post`, and `condition`) takes the same parameters. In what way do the methods function differently? (Write a test program to find out!)

2.7 What are the pre- and postconditions for `java.lang.Math.asin` class?

2.5 Laboratory: Using Javadoc Commenting

Objective. To learn how to generate formal documentation for your programs.

Discussion. The Javadoc program[1] allows the programmer to write comments in a manner that allows the generation web-based documentation. Programmers generating classes to be used by others are particularly encouraged to consider using Javadoc-based documentation. Such comments are portable, web-accessible, and they are directly extracted from the code.

In this lab, we will write documentation for an extended version of the Ratio class we first met in Chapter 1.

Comments used by Javadoc are delimited by a /** */ pair. Note that there are two asterisks in the start of the comment. Within the comment are a number of keywords, identified by a leading "at-sign" (@). These keywords identify the purpose of different comments you right. For example, the text following an @author comment identifies the programmer who originally authored the code. These comments, called Javadoc comments, appear *before* the objects they document. For example, the first few lines of the Assert class are:

```
package structure;
/**
 * A library of assertion testing and debugging procedures.
 * <p>
 * This class of static methods provides basic assertion testing
 * facilities.  An assertion is a condition that is expected to
 * be true at a certain point in the code.  Each of the
 * assertion-based routines in this class perform a verification
 * of the condition and do nothing (aside from testing side-effects)
 * if the condition holds.  If the condition fails, however, the
 * assertion throws an exception and prints the associated message,
 * that describes the condition that failed.  Basic support is
 * provided for testing general conditions, and pre- and
 * postconditions. There is also a facility for throwing a
 * failed condition for code that should not be executed.
 * <p>
 * Features similar to assertion testing are incorporated
 * in the Java 2 language beginning in SDK 1.4.
 * @author duane a. bailey
 */
public class Assert
{
    . . .
}
```

---

[1] Javadoc is a feature of command-line driven Java environments. Graphical environments likely provide Javadoc-like functionality, but pre- and postcondition support may not be available.

For each class you should provide any class-wide documentation, including id@author and `@version`-tagged comments.

Within the class definition, there should be a Javadoc comment for each instance variable and method. Typically, Javadoc comments for instance variables are short comments that describe the role of the variable in supporting the class state:

```
/**
 * Size of the structure.
 */
int size;
```

Comments for methods should include a description of the method's purpose. A comment should describe the purpose of each parameter (`@param`), as well as the form of the value returned (`@return`) for function-like methods. Programmers should also provide pre- and postconditions using the `@pre` and `@post` keywords.[2] Here is the documentation for a square root method.

```
/**
 *
 * This method computes the square root of a double value.
 * @param x The value whose root is to be computed.
 * @return The square root of x.
 * @pre x >= 0
 * @post computes the square root of x
 */
```

To complete this lab, you are to

1. Download a copy of the `Ratio.java` source from the *Java Structures* website. This version of the `Ratio` class does not include full comments.

2. Review the code and make sure that you understand the purpose of each of the methods.

3. At the top of the `Ratio.java` file, place a Javadoc comment that describes the class. The comment should describe the features of the class and an example of how the class might be used. Make sure that you include an `@author` comment (use your name).

4. Run the documentation generation facility for your particular environment. For Sun's Java environment, the Javadoc command takes a parameter that describes the location of the source code that is to be documented:

---

[2] In this book, where there are constraints on space, the pre- and postconditions are provided in non-Javadoc comments. Code available on the web, however, is uniformly commented using the Javadoc comments. Javadoc can be upgraded to recognize pre- and postconditions; details are available from the *Java Structures* website.

```
javadoc prog.java
```

The result is an `index.html` file in the current directory that contains links to all of the necessary documentation. View the documentation to make sure your description is formatted correctly.

5. Before each instance variable write a short Javadoc comment. The comment should begin with `/**` and end with `*/`. Generate and view the documentation and note the change in the documentation.

6. Directly before each method write a Javadoc comment that includes, at a minimum, one or two sentences that describe the method, a `@param` comment for each parameter in the method, a `@return` comment describing the value returned, and a `@pre` and `@post` comment describing the conditions.

   Generate and view the documentation and note the change in the documentation. If the documentation facility does not appear to recognize the `@pre` and `@post` keywords, the appropriate Javadoc doclet software has not been installed correctly. More information on installation of the Javadoc software can be found at the *Java Structures* website.

Notes:

Chapter 3

Vectors

Concepts:
▷ Vectors
▷ Extending arrays
▷ Matrices

Climb high, climb far,
your goal the sky, your aim the star.
—Inscription on a college staircase

THE BEHAVIOR OF A PROGRAM usually depends on its input. Suppose, for example, that we wish to write a program that reads in n String values. One approach would keep track of the n values with n String variables:

StringReader

```
public static void main(String args[])
{
    // read in n = 4 strings
    ReadStream r = new ReadStream();
    String v1, v2, v3, v4;
    v1 = r.readString();  // read a space-delimited word
    v2 = r.readString();
    v3 = r.readString();
    v4 = r.readString();
}
```

This approach is problematic for the programmer of a *scalable* application—an application that works with large sets of data as well as small. As soon as n changes from its current value of 4, it has to be rewritten. Scalable applications are not uncommon, and so we contemplate how they might be supported.

One approach is to use *arrays*. An array of n values acts, essentially, as a collection of similarly typed variables whose names can be computed at run time. A program reading n values is shown here:

```
public static void main(String args[])
{
    // read in n = 4 strings
    ReadStream r = new ReadStream();
    String data[];
    int n = 4;
    // allocate array of n String references:
    data = new String[n];
    for (int i = 0; i < n; i++)
```

```
        {
            data[i] = r.readString();
        }
    }
```

Here, n is a constant whose value is determined at compile time. As the program starts up, a new array of n integers is constructed and referenced through the variable named `data`.

All is fine, unless you want to read a different number of values. Then n has to be changed, and the program must be recompiled and rerun. Another solution is to pick an *upper bound* on the length of the array and only use the portion of the array that is necessary. Here's a modified procedure that uses up to one million array elements:

```
public static void main(String args[])
{
    // read in up to 1 million Strings
    ReadStream r = new ReadStream();
    String data[];
    int n = 0;
    data = new String[1000000];
    // read in strings until we hit end of file
    for (r.skipWhite(); !r.eof(); r.skipWhite())
    {
        data[n] = r.readString();
        n++;
    }
}
```

Unfortunately, if you are running your program on a small machine and have small amounts of data, you are in trouble (see Problem 3.9). Because the array is so large, it will not fit on your machine—even if you want to read small amounts of data. You have to recompile the program with a smaller upper bound and try again. All this seems rather silly, considering how simple the problem appears to be.

We might, of course, require the user to specify the maximum size of the array before the data are read, at *run time*. Once the size is specified, an appropriately sized array can be allocated. While this may appear easier to program, the burden has shifted to the *user* of the program: the user has to commit to a specific upper bound—beforehand:

```
public static void main(String args[])
{
    // read in as many Strings as demanded by input
    ReadStream r = new ReadStream();
    String data[];
    int n;
    // read in the number of strings to be read
    n = r.readInt();
```

```
    // allocate references for n strings
    data = new String[n];
    // read in the n strings
    for (int i = 0; i < n; i++)
    {
        data[i] = r.readString();
    }
}
```

A nice solution is to build a *vector*—an array whose size may easily be changed. Here is our `String` reading program retooled one last time, using `Vectors`:

```
public static void main(String args[])
{
    // read in an arbitrary number of strings
    ReadStream r = new ReadStream();
    Vector data;
    // allocate vector for storage
    data = new Vector();
    // read strings, adding them to end of vector, until eof
    for (r.skipWhite(); !r.eof(); r.skipWhite())
    {
        String s = r.readString();
        data.add(s);
    }
}
```

The `Vector` starts empty and expands (using the `add` method) with every `String` read from the input. Notice that the program doesn't explicitly keep track of the number of values stored in `data`, but that the number may be determined by a call to the `size` method.

3.1   The Interface

The semantics of a `Vector` are similar to the semantics of an array. Both can store multiple values that may be accessed in any order. We call this property *random access*. Unlike the array, however, the `Vector` starts empty and is extended to hold object references. In addition, values may be removed from the `Vector` causing it to shrink. To accomplish these same size-changing operations in an array, the array would have to be reallocated.

With these characteristics in mind, let us consider a portion of the interface for this structure:

```
public class Vector extends AbstractList implements Cloneable
{
    public Vector()
    // post: constructs a vector with capacity for 10 elements
```

Vector

```
      public Vector(int initialCapacity)
      // pre: initialCapacity >= 0
      // post: constructs an empty vector with initialCapacity capacity

      public void add(Object obj)
      // post: adds new element to end of possibly extended vector

      public Object remove(Object element)
      // post: element equal to parameter is removed and returned

      public Object get(int index)
      // pre: 0 <= index && index < size()
      // post: returns the element stored in location index

      public void add(int index, Object obj)
      // pre: 0 <= index <= size()
      // post: inserts new value in vector with desired index,
      //    moving elements from index to size()-1 to right

      public boolean isEmpty()
      // post: returns true iff there are no elements in the vector

      public Object remove(int where)
      // pre: 0 <= where && where < size()
      // post: indicated element is removed, size decreases by 1

      public Object set(int index, Object obj)
      // pre: 0 <= index && index < size()
      // post: element value is changed to obj; old value is returned

      public int size()
      // post: returns the size of the vector
}
```

First, the constructors allow construction of a Vector with an optional initial *capacity*. The capacity is the initial number of Vector locations that are reserved for expansion. The Vector starts empty and may be freely expanded to its capacity. At that point the Vector's memory is reallocated to handle further expansion. While the particulars of memory allocation and reallocation are hidden from the user, there is obvious benefit to specifying an appropriate initial capacity.

The one-parameter add method adds a value to the end of the Vector, expanding it. To insert a new value in the middle of the Vector, we use the two-parameter add method, which includes a location for insertion. To access an existing element, one calls get. If remove is called with an Object, it removes at most one element, selected by value. Another remove method shrinks the logical size of the Vector by removing an element from an indicated location. The set method is used to change a value in the Vector. Finally, two methods provide feedback about the current logical size of the `Vector`: `size` and `isEmpty`. The `size` method returns the number of values stored within the `Vector`. As elements are added to the `Vector`, the size increases from zero up to the capacity of the `Vector`. When the size is zero, then `isEmpty` returns `true`. The result is a data structure that provides constant-time access to data within the structure, without concern for determining explicit bounds on the structure's size.

There are several ways that a `Vector` is different than its array counterpart. First, while both the array and `Vector` maintain a number of references to objects, the `Vector` typically grows with use and stores a non-`null` reference in each entry. An array is a static structure whose entries may be initialized and used in any order and are often `null`. Second, the `Vector` has an *end* where elements can be appended, while the array does not directly support the concept of appending values. There are times, of course, when the append operation might not be a feature desired in the structure; either the `Vector` or array would be a suitable choice.

The interface for `Vector`s in the `structure` package was driven, almost exclusively, by the interface for Java's proprietary `java.util.Vector` class. Thus, while we do not have access to the code for that class, any program written to use Java's `Vector` class can be made to use the `Vector` class described here; their interfaces are consistent.

3.2 Example: The Word List Revisited

We now reconsider an implementation of the word list part of our Hangman program of Section 1.6 implemented directly using `Vector`s:

WordList

```
Vector list;
String targetWord;
java.util.Random generator = new java.util.Random();

list = new Vector(10);
list.add("clarify");
list.add("entered");
list.add("clerk");
while (list.size() != 0)
{
    {   // select a word from the list
        int index = Math.abs(generator.nextInt())%list.size();
        targetWord = (String)list.get(index);
    }
    // ... play the game using targetWord ...
    list.remove(targetWord);
}
```

Here, the operations of the `Vector` are seen to be very similar to the operations of the `WordList` program fragment shown on page 19. The `Vector` class, however, does not have a `selectAny` method. Instead, the bracketed code accomplishes that task. Since only `String`s are placed within the `Vector`, the assignment of `targetWord` involves a cast from `Object` (the type of value returned from the `get` method of `Vector`) to `String`. This cast is necessary for Java to be reassured that you're expecting an element of type `String` to be returned. If the cast were not provided, Java would complain that the types involved in the assignment were incompatible.

Now that we have an implementation of the Hangman code in terms of both the `WordList` and `Vector` structures, we can deduce an implementation of the `WordList` structure in terms of the `Vector` class. In this implementation, the `WordList` contains a `Vector` that is used to hold the various words, as well as the random number generator (the variable `generator` in the code shown above). To demonstrate the implementation, we look at the implementation of the `WordList`'s constructor and `selectAny` method:

```
protected Vector theList;
protected java.util.Random generator;

public WordList(int n)
{
    theList = new Vector(n);
    generator = new java.util.Random();
}

public String selectAny()
{
    int i = Math.abs(generator.nextInt())%theList.size();
    return (String)theList.get(i);
}
```

Clearly, the use of a `Vector` within the `WordList` is an improvement over the direct use of an array, just as the use of `WordList` is an improvement over the complications of directly using a `Vector` in the Hangman program.

3.3 Example: Word Frequency

Suppose one day you read a book, and within the first few pages you read "behemoth" twice. A mighty unusual writing style! Word frequencies within documents can yield interesting information.[1] Here is a little application for computing the frequency of words appearing on the input:

WordFreq

```
public static void main(String args[])
{
    Vector vocab = new Vector(1000);
    ReadStream r = new ReadStream();
    int i;
```

---

[1] Recently, using informal "literary forensics," Don Foster has identified the author of the anonymously penned book *Primary Colors* and is responsible for new attributions of poetry to Shakespeare. Foster also identified Major Henry Livingston Jr. as the true author of "The Night Before Christmas."

```
// for each word on input
for (r.skipWhite(); !r.eof(); r.skipWhite())
{
    Association wordInfo; // word-frequency association
    String vocabWord;     // word in the list

    // read in and tally instance of a word
    String word = r.readString();
    for (i = 0; i < vocab.size(); i++)
    {
        // get the association
        wordInfo = (Association)vocab.get(i);
        // get the word from the association
        vocabWord = (String)wordInfo.getKey();
        if (vocabWord.equals(word))
        {   // match: increment integer in association
            Integer f = (Integer)wordInfo.getValue();
            wordInfo.setValue(new Integer(f.intValue() + 1));
            break;
        }
    }
    // mismatch: add new word, frequency 1.
    if (i == vocab.size())
    {
        vocab.add(new Association(word,new Integer(1)));
    }
}
// print out the accumulated word frequencies
for (i = 0; i < vocab.size(); i++)
{
    Association wordInfo = (Association)vocab.get(i);
    System.out.println(
        wordInfo.getKey()+" occurs "+
        wordInfo.getValue()+" times.");
}
}
```

First, for each word found on the input, we maintain an `Association` between the word (a `String`) and its frequency (an `Integer`). Each element of the `Vector` is such an `Association`. Now, the outer loop at the top reads in each word. The inner loop scans through the `Vector` searching for matching words that might have been read in. Matching words have their values updated. New words cause the construction of a new `Association`. The second loop scans through the `Vector`, printing out each of the `Associations`.

Each of these applications demonstrates the most common use of `Vectors`—keeping track of data when the number of entries is not known far in advance. When considering the `List` data structure we will consider the efficiency of these algorithms and, if necessary, seek improvements.

3.4   The Implementation

Clearly, the `Vector` must be able to store a large number of similar items. We
choose, then, to have the implementation of the `Vector` maintain an array of
`Objects`, along with an integer that describes its current *size* or *extent*. When
the size is about to exceed the *capacity* (the length of the underlying array), the
`Vector`'s capacity is increased to hold the growing number of elements.

The constructor is responsible for allocation of the space and initializing the
local variables. The number of elements initially allocated for expansion can be
specified by the user:

Vector

```
protected Object elementData[];      // the data
protected int elementCount;          // number of elements in vector

public Vector()
// post: constructs a vector with capacity for 10 elements
{
    this(10); // call one-parameter constructor
}

public Vector(int initialCapacity)
// pre: initialCapacity >= 0
// post: constructs an empty vector with initialCapacity capacity
{
    Assert.pre(initialCapacity >= 0,"Nonnegative capacity.");
    elementData = new Object[initialCapacity];
    elementCount = 0;
}
```

Unlike other languages, all arrays within Java must be explicitly allocated. At
the time the array is allocated, the number of elements is specified. Thus, in the
constructor, the `new` operator allocates the number of elements desired by the
user. Since the size of an array can be gleaned from the array itself (by asking
for `elementData.length`), the value does not need to be explicitly stored within
the `Vector` object.[2]

To access and modify elements within a `Vector`, we use the following operations:

```
public Object get(int index)
// pre: 0 <= index && index < size()
// post: returns the element stored in location index
{
    return elementData[index];
}

public Object set(int index, Object obj)
```

---

[2] It could, of course, but explicitly storing it within the structure would mean that the
implementor would have to ensure that the stored value was always consistent with the value
accessible through the array's `length` variable.

```
// pre: 0 <= index && index < size()
// post: element value is changed to obj; old value is returned
{
    Object previous = elementData[index];
    elementData[index] = obj;
    return previous;
}
```

The arguments to both methods identify the location of the desired element. Because the index should be within the range of available values, the precondition states this fact.

For the accessor (get), the desired element is returned as the result. The set method allows the Object reference to be changed to a new value and returns the old value. These operations, effectively, translate operations on Vectors into operations on arrays.

Now consider the addition of an element to the Vector. One way this can be accomplished is through the use of the one-parameter add method. The task requires extending the size of the Vector and then storing the element at the location indexed by the current number of elements (this is the first free location within the Vector). Here is the Java method:

```
public void add(Object obj)
// post: adds new element to end of possibly extended vector
{
    ensureCapacity(elementCount+1);
    elementData[elementCount] = obj;
    elementCount++;
}
```

(We will discuss the method ensureCapacity later. Its purpose is simply to ensure that the data array actually has enough room to hold the indicated number of values.) Notice that, as with many modern languages, arrays are indexed starting at zero. There are many good reasons for doing this. There are probably just as many good reasons for not doing this, but the best defense is that this is what programmers are currently used to.

Principle 6 *Maintaining a consistent interface makes a structure useful.*

If one is interested in inserting an element in the middle of the Vector, it is necessary to use the two-parameter add method. The operation first creates an unused location at the desired point by shifting elements out of the way. Once the opening is created, the new element is inserted.

```
public void add(int index, Object obj)
// pre: 0 <= index <= size()
// post: inserts new value in vector with desired index,
//    moving elements from index to size()-1 to right
{
    int i;
    ensureCapacity(elementCount+1);
```

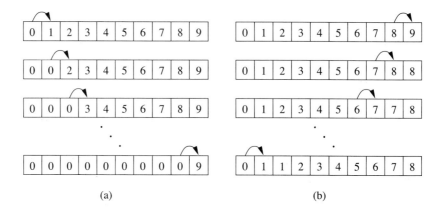

(a)   (b)

Figure 3.1 The incorrect (a) and correct (b) way of moving values in an array to make room for an inserted value.

```
// must copy from right to left to avoid destroying data
for (i = elementCount; i > index; i--) {
    elementData[i] = elementData[i-1];
}
// assertion: i == index and element[index] is available
elementData[index] = obj;
elementCount++;
}
```

Note that the loop that moves the elements higher in the array runs *backward*. To see why, it is only necessary to see what happens if the loop runs forward (see Figure 3.1a): the lowest element gets copied into higher and higher elements, ultimately copying over the entire **Vector** to the right of the insertion point. Figure 3.1b demonstrates the correct technique.

Removing an element from a specific location in the **Vector** is very similar, reversing the effect of add. Here, using an argument similar to the previous one, the loop moves in the forward direction:

```
public Object remove(int where)
// pre: 0 <= where && where < size()
// post: indicated element is removed, size decreases by 1
{
    Object result = get(where);
    elementCount--;
    while (where < elementCount) {
        elementData[where] = elementData[where+1];
        where++;
    }
    elementData[elementCount] = null; // free reference
```

```
        return result;
    }
```

We also allow the removal of a specific value from the `Vector`, by passing an example `Object` to `remove` (not shown). Within this code, the `equals` method of the value passed to the routine is used to compare it to values within the `Vector`. When (and if) a match is found, it is removed using the technique just described.

The methods having to do with size are relatively straightforward:

```
public boolean isEmpty()
// post: returns true iff there are no elements in the vector
{
    return size() == 0;
}

public int size()
// post: returns the size of the vector
{
    return elementCount;
}
```

The logical size of the `Vector` is the number of elements stored within the `Vector`, and it is empty when this size is zero.

3.5 Extensibility: A Feature

Sometimes, our initial estimate of the maximum number of values is too small. In this case, it is necessary to extend the capacity of the `Vector`, carefully maintaining the values already stored within the `Vector`. Fortunately, because we have packaged the implementation within an interface, it is only necessary to extend the functionality of the existing operations and provide some additional methods to describe the features.

A first approach might be to extend the `Vector` to include just as many elements as needed. Every time an element is added to the `Vector`, the number of elements is compared to the capacity of the array. If the capacity is used up, an array that is one element longer is allocated. This reallocation also requires copying of the existing data from one array to the other. Of course, for really long arrays, these copying operations would take a proportionally long time. Over time, as the array grows to n elements, the array data get copied many times. At the beginning, the array holds a single element, but it is expanded to hold two. The original element must be copied to the new space to complete the operation. When a third is added, the first two must be copied. The result is that

$$1 + 2 + 3 + \cdots + (n - 1) = \frac{n(n - 1)}{2}$$

elements are copied as the array grows to size n. (Proving this last formula is the core of Problem 3.8.) This is expensive since, if in the beginning we had just allocated the `Vector` with a capacity of n elements, none of the data items would have to be copied during extension!

It turns out there is a happy medium: every time you extend the array, just double its capacity. Now, if we reconsider the number of times that an item gets copied during the extension process, the result is dramatically different. Suppose, for neatness only, that n is a power of 2, and that the `Vector` started with a capacity of 1. What do we know? When the `Vector` was extended from capacity 1 to capacity 2, one element was copied. When the array was extended from capacity 2 to capacity 4, two elements were copied. When the array was extended from capacity 4 to capacity 8, four elements were copied. This continues until the last extension, when the `Vector` had its capacity extended from $\frac{n}{2}$ to n: then $\frac{n}{2}$ elements had to be preserved. The total number of times elements were copied is

$$1 + 2 + 4 + \cdots + \frac{n}{2} = n - 1$$

Thus, extension by doubling allows unlimited growth of the `Vector` with an overhead that is proportional to the ultimate length of the array. Another way to think about it is that there is a constant overhead in supporting each element of a `Vector` extended in this way.

The Java language specifies a `Vector` interface that allows the user to specify how the `Vector` is to be extended if its capacity is not sufficient for the current operation. When the `Vector` is constructed, a `capacityIncrement` is specified. This is simply the number of elements to be added to the underlying array when extension is required. A nonzero value for this increment leads to the n^2 behavior we saw before, but it may be useful if, for example, one does not have the luxury of being able to double the size of a large array. If the increment is zero, the doubling strategy is used.

Our design, then, demands another protected value to hold the increment; we call this `capacityIncrement`. This value is specified in a special constructor and is not changed during the life of the `Vector`:

```
protected int capacityIncrement;    // the rate of growth for vector

public Vector(int initialCapacity, int capacityIncr)
// pre: initialCapacity >= 0, capacityIncr >= 0
// post: constructs an empty vector with initialCapacity capacity
//    that extends capacity by capacityIncr, or doubles if 0
{
    Assert.pre(initialCapacity >= 0, "Nonnegative capacity.");
    elementData = new Object[initialCapacity];
    elementCount = 0;
    capacityIncrement = capacityIncr;
}
```

We are now prepared to investigate `ensureCapacity`, a method that, if necessary, resizes `Vector` to have a capacity of at least `minCapacity`:

```
    public void ensureCapacity(int minCapacity)
    // post: the capacity of this vector is at least minCapacity
    {
        if (elementData.length < minCapacity) {
            int newLength = elementData.length; // initial guess
            if (capacityIncrement == 0) {
                // increment of 0 suggests doubling (default)
                if (newLength == 0) newLength = 1;
                while (newLength < minCapacity) {
                    newLength *= 2;
                }
            } else {
                // increment != 0 suggests incremental increase
                while (newLength < minCapacity)
                {
                    newLength += capacityIncrement;
                }
            }
            // assertion: newLength > elementData.length.
            Object newElementData[] = new Object[newLength];
            int i;
            // copy old data to array
            for (i = 0; i < elementCount; i++) {
                newElementData[i] = elementData[i];
            }
            elementData = newElementData;
            // garbage collector will (eventually) pick up old elementData
        }
        // assertion: capacity is at least minCapacity
    }
```

This code deserves careful investigation. If the current length of the underlying array is already sufficient to provide minCapacity elements, then the method does nothing. On the other hand, if the Vector is too short, it must be extended. We use a loop here that determines the new capacity by doubling (if capacityIncrement is zero) or by directly incrementing if capacityIncrement is nonzero. In either case, by the time the loop is finished, the desired capacity is determined. At that point, an array of the appropriate size is allocated, the old values are copied over, and the old array is dereferenced in favor of the new.

3.6 Example: L-Systems

In the late 1960s biologists began to develop computational models for growth. One of the most successful models, *L-systems*, was developed by Aristid Lindenmayer. An L-system consists of a seed or *start string* of symbols derived from an alphabet, along with a number of rules for changing or *rewriting* the symbols, called *productions*. To simulate an interval of growth, strings are completely rewritten using the productions. When the rewriting begins with the start string, it is possible to iteratively simulate the growth of a simple organism. To demonstrate the complexity of this approach, we can use an alphabet of two characters—S (for stem) and L (for leaf). If the two productions

Before	After
S	L
L	SL

are used, we can generate the following strings over 6 time steps:

Time	String
0	S
1	L
2	SL
3	LSL
4	SLLSL
5	LSLSLLSL
6	SLLSLLSLSLLSL

Although there are some observations that might be made (there are never two consecutive Ss), any notion of a pattern in this string quickly breaks down. Still, many organisms display patterns that are motivated by the seemingly simple production system.

We can use Vectors to help us perform this rewriting process. By constructing two Character objects, L and S, we can store patterns in a Vector of references. The rewriting process involves constructing a new result Vector. Here is a program that would verify the growth pattern suggested in the table:

LSystem

```
public class LSystem
{   // constants that define the alphabet
    final static Character L = new Character('L');
    final static Character S = new Character('S');

    public static Vector rewrite(Vector s)
    // pre: s is a string of L and S values
    // post: returns a string rewritten by productions
    {
        Vector result = new Vector();
        for (int pos = 0; pos < s.size(); pos++)
        {
            // rewrite according to two different rules
            if (S == s.get(pos)) {
                result.add(L);
            } else if (L == s.get(pos)) {
                result.add(S); result.add(L);
            }
        }
        return result;
    }
}
```

```
public static void main(String[] args)
{
    Vector string = new Vector();
    string.add(S);

    // determine the number of strings
    ReadStream r = new ReadStream();
    int count = r.readInt();

    // write out the start string
    System.out.println(string);
    for (int i = 1; i <= count; i++)
    {
        string = rewrite(string);    // rewrite the string
        System.out.println(string); // print it out
    }
}
}
```

L-systems are an interesting example of a *grammar system*. The power of a grammar to generate complex structures—including languages and, biologically, plants—is of great interest to theoretical computer scientists.

3.7   Example: Vector-Based Sets

In Section 1.8 we discussed Java's interface for a Set. Mathematically, it is an unordered collection of unique values. The set abstraction is an important feature of many algorithms that appear in computer science, and so it is important that we actually consider a simple implementation before we go much further.

As we recall, the Set is an extension of the Structure interface. It demands that the programmer implement not only the basic Structure methods (add, contains, remove, etc.), but also the following methods of a Set. Here is the interface associated with a Vector-based implementation of a Set:

```
public class SetVector extends AbstractSet
{
    public SetVector()
    // post: constructs a new, empty set

    public SetVector(Structure other)
    // post: constructs a new set with elements from other

    public void clear()
    // post: elements of set are removed

    public boolean isEmpty()
    // post: returns true iff set is empty
```

SetVector

```
                    public void add(Object e)
                    // pre: e is non-null object
                    // post: adds element e to set

                    public Object remove(Object e)
                    // pre: e is non-null object
                    // post: e is removed from set, value returned

                    public boolean contains(Object e)
                    // pre: e is non-null
                    // post: returns true iff e is in set

                    public boolean containsAll(Structure other)
                    // pre: other is non-null reference to set
                    // post: returns true iff this set is subset of other

                    public Object clone()
                    // post: returns a copy of set

                    public void addAll(Structure other)
                    // pre: other is a non-null structure
                    // post: add all elements of other to set, if needed

                    public void retainAll(Structure other)
                    // pre: other is non-null reference to set
                    // post: returns set containing intersection of this and other

                    public void removeAll(Structure other)
                    // pre: other is non-null reference to set
                    // post: returns set containing difference of this and other

                    public Iterator iterator()
                    // post: returns traversal to traverse the elements of set

                    public int size()
                    // post: returns number of elements in set
                }
```

A SetVector might take the approach begun by the WordList implementation we have seen in Section 3.2: each element of the Set would be stored in a location in the Vector. Whenever a new value is to be added to the Set, it is only added if the Set does not already contain the value. When values are removed from the Set, the structure contracts. At all times, we are free to keep the order of the data in the Vector hidden from the user since the ordering of the values is not part of the abstraction.

We construct a SetVector using the following constructors, which initialize a protected Vector:

```
protected Vector data; // the underlying vector

public SetVector()
// post: constructs a new, empty set
{
    data = new Vector();
}

public SetVector(Structure other)
// post: constructs a new set with elements from other
{
    this();
    addAll(other);
}
```

The second constructor is a *copy constructor* that makes use of the union operator, `addAll`. Since the initial set is empty (the call to `this()` calls the first constructor), the `SetVector` essentially picks up all the values found in the other structure.

Most methods of the `Set` are adopted from the underlying `Vector` class. For example, the `remove` method simply calls the `remove` method of the `Vector`:

```
public Object remove(Object e)
// pre: e is non-null object
// post: e is removed from set, value returned
{
    return data.remove(e);
}
```

The `add` method, though, is responsible for ensuring that duplicate values are not added to the `Set`. It must first check to see if the value is already a member:

```
public void add(Object e)
// pre: e is non-null object
// post: adds element e to set
{
    if (!data.contains(e)) data.add(e);
}
```

To perform the more complex `Set`-specific operations (`addAll` and others), we must perform the specified operation for all the values of the other set. To accomplish this, we make use of an `Iterator`, a mechanism we will not study until Chapter 7, but which is nonetheless simple to understand. Here, for example, is the implementation of `addAll`, which attempts to `add` all the values found in the `other` structure:

```
public void addAll(Structure other)
// pre: other is a non-null structure
// post: add all elements of other to set, if needed
```

```
{
    Iterator yourElements = other.iterator();
    while (yourElements.hasNext())
    {
        add(yourElements.next());
    }
}
```

Other methods are defined in a straightforward manner.

3.8   Example: The Matrix Class

One application of the Vector class is to support a two-dimensional Vector-like
object: the *matrix*. Matrices are used in applications where two dimensions of
data are needed. Our Matrix class has the following methods:

Matrix

```
public class Matrix
{
    public Matrix(int h, int w)
    // pre: h >= 0, w >= 0;
    // post: constructs an h row by w column matrix

    public Object get(int row, int col)
    // pre: 0 <= row < height(), 0 <= col < width()
    // post: returns object at (row, col)

    public void set(int row, int col, Object value)
    // pre: 0 <= row < height(), 0 <= col < width()
    // post: changes location (row, col) to value

    public void addRow(int r)
    // pre: 0 <= r < height()
    // post: inserts row of null values to be row r

    public void addCol(int c)
    // pre: 0 <= c < width()
    // post: inserts column of null values to be column c

    public Vector removeRow(int r)
    // pre: 0 <= r < height()
    // post: removes row r and returns it as a Vector

    public Vector removeCol(int c)
    // pre: 0 <= c < width
    // post: removes column c and returns it as a vector

    public int width()
    // post: returns number of columns in matrix
```

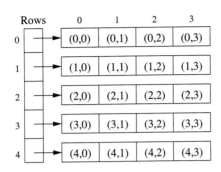

Figure 3.2 The `Matrix` class is represented as a `Vector` of rows, each of which is a `Vector` of references to `Objects`. Elements are labeled with their indices.

```
        public int height()
        // post: returns number of rows in matrix
    }
```

The two-parameter constructor specifies the width and height of the `Matrix`. Elements of the `Matrix` are initially `null`, but may be reset with the `set` method. This method, along with the `get` method, accepts two parameters that identify the row and the column of the value. To expand and shrink the `Matrix`, it is possible to insert and remove both rows and columns at any location. When a row or column is removed, a `Vector` of removed values is returned. The methods `height` and `width` return the number of rows and columns found within the `Matrix`, respectively.

To support this interface, we imagine that a `Matrix` is a `Vector` of rows, which are, themselves, `Vectors` of values (see Figure 3.2). While it is not strictly necessary, we explicitly keep track of the height and width of the `Matrix` (if we determine at some later date that keeping this information is unnecessary, the interface would hide the removal of these fields). Here, then, is the constructor for the `Matrix` class:

```
    protected int height, width; // size of matrix
    protected Vector rows;       // vector of row vectors

    public Matrix(int h, int w)
    // pre: h >= 0, w >= 0;
    // post: constructs an h row by w column matrix
    {
        height = h;  // initialize height and width
        width = w;
        // allocate a vector of rows
        rows = new Vector(height);
        for (int r = 0; r < height; r++)
```

```
{   // each row is allocated and filled with nulls
    Vector theRow = new Vector(width);
    rows.add(theRow);
    for (int c = 0; c < width; c++)
    {
        theRow.add(null);
    }
}
}
```

We allocate a Vector for holding the desired number of rows, and then, for each row, we construct a new Vector of the appropriate width. All the elements are initialized to null. It's not strictly necessary to do this initialization, but it's a good habit to get into.

The process of manipulating individual elements of the matrix is demonstrated by the get and set methods:

```
public Object get(int row, int col)
// pre: 0 <= row < height(), 0 <= col < width()
// post: returns object at (row, col)
{
    Assert.pre(0 <= row && row < height, "Row in bounds.");
    Assert.pre(0 <= col && col < width, "Col in bounds.");
    Vector theRow = (Vector)rows.get(row);
    return theRow.get(col);
}

public void set(int row, int col, Object value)
// pre: 0 <= row < height(), 0 <= col < width()
// post: changes location (row, col) to value
{
    Assert.pre(0 <= row && row < height, "Row in bounds.");
    Assert.pre(0 <= col && col < width, "Col in bounds.");
    Vector theRow = (Vector)rows.get(row);
    theRow.set(col,value);
}
```

The process of manipulating an element requires looking up a row within the rows table and finding the element within the row. It is also important to notice that in the set method, the row is found using the get method, while the element within the row is changed using the set method. Although the element within the row changes, the row itself is represented by the same vector.

Many of the same memory management issues discussed in reference to Vectors hold as well for the Matrix class. When a row or column needs to be expanded to make room for new elements (see Figure 3.3), it is vital that the management of the arrays within the Vector class be hidden. Still, with the addition of a row into the Matrix, it is necessary to allocate the new row object and to initialize each of the elements of the row to null:

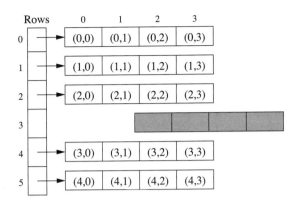

Figure 3.3   The insertion of a new row (gray) into an existing matrix. Indices are those associated with matrix *before* addRow. Compare with Figure 3.2.

```
public void addRow(int r)
// pre: 0 <= r < height()
// post: inserts row of null values to be row r
{
    Assert.pre(0 <= r && r < width, "Row in bounds.");
    height++;
    Vector theRow = new Vector(width);
    for (int c = 0; c < width; c++)
    {
        theRow.add(null);
    }
    rows.add(r,theRow);
}
```

We leave it to the reader to investigate the implementation of other **Matrix** methods. In addition, a number of problems consider common extensions to the **Matrix** class.

3.9   Conclusions

Most applications that accept data are made more versatile by not imposing constraints on the number of values processed by the application. Because the size of an array is fixed at the time it is allocated, programmers find it difficult to create size-independent code without the use of extensible data structures. The **Vector** and **Matrix** classes are examples of extensible structures.

Initially **Vectors** are empty, but can be easily expanded when necessary. When a programmer knows the upper bound on the **Vector** size, this information can be used to minimize the amount of copying necessary during the entire expansion process. When a bound is not known, we saw that doubling the allocated storage at expansion time can reduce the overall copying cost.

The implementation of `Vector` and `Matrix` classes is not trivial. Data abstraction hides many important housekeeping details. Fortunately, while these details are complex for the implementor, they can considerably reduce the complexity of applications that make use of the `Vector` and `Matrix` structures.

Self Check Problems

Solutions to these problems begin on page 428.

3.1   How are arrays and `Vectors` the same? How do they differ?

3.2   What is the difference between the `add(v)` and `add(i,v)` methods of `Vector`?

3.3   What is the difference between the `add(i,v)` method and the `set(i,v)` method?

3.4   What is the difference between the `remove(v)` method (`v` is an `Object` value), and the `remove(i)` (`i` is an `int`)?

3.5   What is the distinction between the *capacity* and *size* of a `Vector`?

3.6   Why is the use of a `Vector` an improvement over the use of an array in the implementation of Hangman in Section 3.2?

3.7   When inserting a value into a `Vector` why is it necessary to shift elements to the right starting at the high end of the `Vector`? (See Figure 3.1.)

3.8   By default, when the size first exceeds the capacity, the capacity of the `Vector` is doubled. Why?

3.9   What is the purpose of the following code?

```
elementData = new Object[initialCapacity];
```

What can be said about the values found in `elementData` after this code is executed?

3.10   When there is more than one constructor for a class, when and how do we indicate the appropriate method to use? Compare, for example,

```
Vector v = new Vector();
Vector w = new Vector(1000);
```

3.11   Is the row index of the `Matrix` bounded by the matrix height or width? When indexing a `Matrix` which is provided first, the row or the column?

Problems

Solutions to the odd-numbered problems begin on page 443.

3.1   Explain the difference between the *size* and *capacity* of a vector. Which is more important to the user?

3.2   The default capacity of a `Vector` in a `structure` package implementation is 10. It could have been one million. How would you determine a suitable value?

3.3   The implementation of `java.util.Vector` provides a method `trimTo-Size`. This method ensures that the capacity of the `Vector` is the same as its size. Why is this useful? Is it possible to trim the capacity of a `Vector` without using this method?

3.4   The implementation of `java.util.Vector` provides a method `setSize`. This method explicitly sets the size of the `Vector`. Why is this useful? Is it possible to set the size of the `Vector` without using this method?

3.5   Write a `Vector` method, `indexOf`, that returns the index of an object in the `Vector`. What should the method return if no object that is `equals` to this object can be found? What does `java.lang.Vector` do in this case? How long does this operation take to perform, on average?

3.6   Write a class called `BitVector` that has an interface similar to `Vector`, but the values stored within the `BitVector` are all known to be `boolean` (the primitive type). What is the primary advantage of having a special-purpose vector, like `BitVector`?

3.7   Suppose we desire to implement a method `reverse` for the `Vector` class. One approach would be to `remove` location 0 and to use `add` near the end or *tail* of the `Vector`. Defend or reject this suggested implementation. In either case, write the best method you can.

3.8   Suppose that a precisely sized array is used to hold data, and that each time the array size is to be increased, it is increased by exactly one and the data are copied over. Prove that, in the process of growing an array incrementally from size 0 to size n, approximately n^2 values must be copied.

3.9   What is the maximum length array of `Strings` you can allocate on your machine? (You needn't initialize the array.) What is the maximum length array of `boolean` you can allocate on your machine? What is to be learned from the ratio of these two values?

3.10   Implement the `Object`-based `remove` method for the `Vector` class.

3.11   In our discussion of L-systems, the resulting strings are always linear. Plants, however, often branch. Modify the `LSystem` program so that it includes the following three productions:

Before	After
S	T
T	U
U	V
V	W
W	[S]U

where [S] is represented by a new `Vector` that contains a single S. (To test to see if an `Object`, x, is a `Vector`, use the test x `instanceof Vector`.)

3.12 Finish the two-dimensional `Vector`-like structure `Matrix`. Each element of the `Matrix` is indexed by two integers that identify the row and column containing the value. Your class should support a constructor, methods `addRow` and `addCol` that append a row or column, the `get` and `set` methods, and `width` and `height` methods. In addition, you should be able to use the `removeRow` and `removeCol` methods.

3.13 Write `Matrix` methods for `add` and `multiply`. These methods should implement the standard matrix operations from linear algebra. What are the preconditions that are necessary for these methods?

3.14 A `Matrix` is useful for nonmathematical applications. Suppose, for example, that the owners of cars parked in a rectangular parking lot are stored in a `Matrix`. How would you design a new `Matrix` method to return the location of a particular value in the `Matrix`? (Such an extension implements an *associative memory*. We will discuss associative structures when we consider `Dictionary`s.)

3.15 An $m \times n$ `Matrix` could be implemented using a single `Vector` with mn locations. Assuming that this choice was made, implement the `get` method. What are the advantages and disadvantages of this implementation over the `Vector` of `Vectors` approach?

3.16 A *triangular matrix* is a two-dimensional structure with n rows. Row i has $i + 1$ columns (numbered 0 through i) in row i. Design a class that supports all the `Matrix` operations, except `addRow`, `removeRow`, `addCol`, and `removeCol`. You should also note that when a row and column must be specified, the row must be greater than or equal to the column.

3.17 A *symmetric matrix* is a two-dimensional `Matrix`-like structure such that the element at $[i][j]$ is the same element found at $[j][i]$. How would you implement each of the `Matrix` operations? The triangular matrix of Problem 3.16 may be useful here. Symmetric matrices are useful in implementing undirected graph structures.

3.18 Sometimes it is useful to keep an unordered list of characters (with ASCII codes 0 through 127), with no duplicates. Java, for example, has a `CharSet` class in the `java.util` package. Implement a class, `CharSet`, using a `Vector`. Your class should support (1) the creation of an empty set, (2) the addition of a single character to the set, (3) the check for a character in the set, (4) the union of two sets, and (5) a test for set equality.

3.10 Laboratory: The Silver Dollar Game

Objective. To implement a simple game using `Vectors` or arrays.

Discussion. The Silver Dollar Game is played between two players. An arbitrarily long strip of paper is marked off into squares:

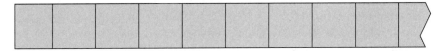

The game begins by placing silver dollars in a few of the squares. Each square holds at most one coin. Interesting games begin with some pairs of coins separated by one or more empty squares.

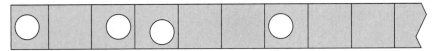

The goal is to move all the n coins to the leftmost n squares of the paper. This is accomplished by players alternately moving a single coin, constrained by the following rules:

1. Coins move only to the left.

2. No coin may pass another.

3. No square may hold more than one coin.

The last person to move is the winner.

Procedure. Write a program to facilitate playing the Silver Dollar Game. When the game starts, the computer has set up a random strip with 3 or more coins. Two players are then alternately presented with the current game state and are allowed to enter moves. If the coins are labeled 0 through $n-1$ from left to right, a move could be specified by a coin number and the number of squares to move the coin to the left. If the move is illegal, the player is repeatedly prompted to enter a revised move. Between turns the computer checks the board state to determine if the game has been won.

Here is one way to approach the problem:

1. Decide on an internal representation of the strip of coins. Does your representation store *all* the information necessary to play the game? Does your representation store *more* information than is necessary? Is it easy to test for a legal move? Is it easy to test for a win?

2. Develop a new class, `CoinStrip`, that keeps track of the state of the playing strip. There should be a constructor, which generates a random board. Another method, `toString`, returns a string representation of the coin strip. What other operations seem to be necessary? How are moves performed? How are rules enforced? How is a win detected?

3. Implement an application whose `main` method controls the play of a single game.

Thought Questions. Consider the following questions as you complete the lab:

Hint: When flipped, the Belgian Euro is heads 149 times out of 250.

1. How might one pick game sizes so that, say, one has a 50 percent chance of a game with three coins, a 25 percent chance of a game with four coins, a $12\frac{1}{2}$ percent chance of a game with five coins, and so on? Would your technique bias your choice of underlying data structure?

2. How might one generate games that are not immediate wins? Suppose you wanted to be guaranteed a game with the possibility of n moves?

3. Suppose the computer could occasionally provide good hints. What opportunities appear easy to recognize?

4. How might you write a method, `computerPlay`, where the computer plays to win?

5. A similar game, called Welter's Game (after C. P. Welter, who analyzed the game), allows the coins to pass each other. Would this modification of the rules change your implementation significantly?

Notes:

Chapter 4

Design Fundamentals

Concepts:

▷ Asymptotic analysis and big-O notation
▷ Time-space trade-off
▷ Back-of-the-envelope estimations
▷ Recursion and Induction

We shape clay into a pot,
but it is the emptiness inside
that holds whatever we want.
—Lao Tzu

PROGRAMMERS ARE CRAFTSMEN. Their medium—their programming language—often favors no particular design and pushes for an individual and artistic decision. Given the task of implementing a simple program, any two individuals are likely to make different decisions about their work. Because modern languages allow programmers a great deal of expression, implementations of data structures reflect considerable personal choice.

Some aspects of writing programs are, of course, taught and learned. For example, everyone agrees that commenting code is good. Programmers should write small and easily understood procedures. Other aspects of the design of programs, however, are only appreciated after considerable design experience. In fact, computer science as a whole has only recently developed tools for understanding what it means to say that an algorithm is "implemented nicely," or that a data structure "works efficiently." Since many data structures are quite subtle, it is important to develop a rich set of tools for developing and analyzing their performance.

In this chapter, we consider several important conceptual tools. *Big-O* complexity analysis provides a means of classifying the growth of functions and, therefore, the performance of the structures they describe. The concepts of *recursion* and *self-reference* make it possible to concisely code solutions to complex problems, and *mathematical induction* helps us demonstrate the important properties—including trends in performance—of traditional data structures. Finally, notions of symmetry and friction help us understand how to design data structures so that they have a reasonable look and feel.

4.1 Asymptotic Analysis Tools

We might be satisfied with evaluating the performance or *complexity* of data structures by precisely counting the number of statements executed or objects referenced. Yet, modern architectures may have execution speeds that vary as much as a factor of 10 or more. The accurate counting of any specific kind of operation alone does not give us much information about the actual running time of a specific implementation. Thus, while detailed accounting can be useful for understanding the fine distinctions between similar implementations, it is not generally necessary to make such detailed analyses of behavior. Distinctions between structures and algorithms, however, can often be identified by observing patterns of performance over a wide variety of problems.

4.1.1   Time and Space Complexity

What concerns the designer most are *trends* suggested by the various performance metrics as the problem size increases. Clearly, an algorithm that takes time proportional to the problem size degrades more slowly than algorithms that decay quadratically. Likewise, it is convenient to agree that any algorithm that takes time bounded by a polynomial in the problem size, is better than one that takes exponential time. Each of these rough characterizations—linear, quadratic, and so on—identifies a class of functions with similar growth behavior. To give us a better grasp on these classifications, we use *asymptotic* or *big-O* analysis to help us to describe and evaluate a function's growth.

Definition 4.1 *A function $f(n)$ is $O(g(n))$ (read "order g" or "big-O of g"), if and only if there exist two positive constants, c and n_0, such that*

$$|f(n)| \le c \cdot g(n)$$

for all $n \ge n_0$.

In this text, f will usually be a function of problem size that describes the utilization of some precious resource (e.g., time or space). This is a subtle definition (and one that is often stated incorrectly), so we carefully consider why each of the parts of the definition is necessary.

Most importantly, we would like to think of $g(n)$ as being proportional to an upper bound for $f(n)$ (see Figure 4.1). After some point, $f(n)$ does not exceed an "appropriately scaled" $g(n)$. The selection of an appropriate c allows us to enlarge $g(n)$ to the extent necessary to develop an upper bound. So, while $g(n)$ may not directly exceed $f(n)$, it might if it is multiplied by a constant larger than 1. If so, we would be happy to say that $f(n)$ has a trend that is no worse than that of $g(n)$. You will note that if $f(n)$ is $O(g(n))$, it is also $O(10 \cdot g(n))$ and $O(5 + g(n))$. Note, also, that c is positive. Generally we will attempt to bound $f(n)$ by positive functions.

Second, we are looking for long-term behavior. Since the most dramatic growth in functions is most evident for large values, we are happy to ignore "glitches" and anomalous behavior up to a certain point. That point is n_0. We *Nails = proofs.* do not care how big n_0 must be, as long as it can be nailed down to some fixed value when relating specific functions f and g.

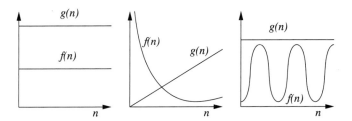

Figure 4.1 Examples of functions, $f(n)$, that are $O(g(n))$.

Third, we are not usually interested in whether the function $f(n)$ is negative or positive; we are just interested in the *magnitude* of its growth. In reality, most of the resources we consider (e.g., time and space) are measured as positive values and larger quantities of the resource are consumed as the problem grows in size; growth is usually positive.

Most functions we encounter fall into one of a few categories. A function that is bounded above by a constant is classified as $O(1)$.[1] The constant factor can be completely accounted for in the value of c in Definition 4.1. These functions measure size-independent characteristics of data structures. For example, the time it takes to assign a value to an arbitrary element of an array of size n is constant.

When a function grows proportionately to problem size, or *linearly*, we observe it is $O(n)$. Depending on what's being measured, this can be classified as "nice behavior." Summing the values in an n-element array, for example, can be accomplished in linear time. If we double the size of the array, we expect the time of the summation process to grow proportionately. Similarly, the `Vector` takes linear space. Most methods associated with the `Vector` class, if not constant, are linear in time and space. If we develop methods that manipulate the n elements of a `Vector` of numbers in *superlinear* time—faster than linear growth—we're not pleased, as we know it can be accomplished more efficiently.

Other functions grow *polynomially* and are $O(n^c)$, where c is some constant greater than 1. The function $n^2 + n$ is $O(n^2)$ (let $c = 2$ and $n_0 = 1$) and therefore grows as a quadratic. Many simple methods for sorting n elements of an array are quadratic. The space required to store a square matrix of size n takes quadratic space. Usually, we consider functions with polynomial growth to be fairly efficient, though we would like to see c remain small in practice. Because a function n^{c-1} is $O(n \cdot n^{c-1})$ (i.e., $O(n^c)$), we only need consider the growth of the most significant term of a polynomial function. (It is, after all, most significant!) The less significant terms are ultimately outstripped by the leading term.

What's your best guess for the time to assign a value?
$\frac{1}{1000}$ *second?*
$\frac{1}{1000000}$ *sec.?*
$\frac{1}{1000000000}$ *s.?*

Grass could be greener.

---

[1] It is also $O(13)$, but we try to avoid such distractions.

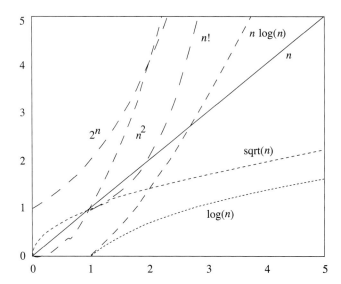

Figure 4.2   Near-origin details of common curves. Compare with Figure 4.3.

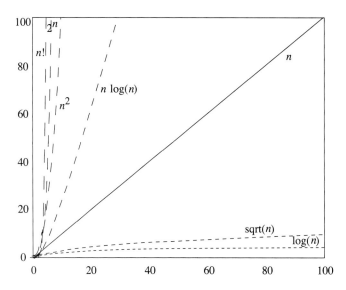

Figure 4.3   Long-range trends of common curves. Compare with Figure 4.2.

Some functions experience *exponential* growth (see Figures 4.2 and 4.3). The functions are $O(c^n)$, where c is a constant greater than 1. Enumerating all strings of length n or checking topological equivalence of circuits with n devices are classic examples of exponential algorithms. Constructing a list of the n-digit palindromes requires exponential time and space. The demands of an exponential process grow too quickly to make effective use of resources. As a result, we often think of functions with exponential behavior as being *intractable*. In the next section we will see that some recursive solutions to problems are exponential. While these solutions are not directly useful, simple insights can sometimes make these algorithms efficient.

"2002" is a palindrome.

4.1.2 Examples

A "Difference Table"

Suppose we're interested in printing a 10 by 10 table of differences between two integers (`row-col`) values. Each value in the table corresponds to the result of subtracting the row number from the column number:

```
0 -1 -2 -3 -4 -5 -6 -7 -8 -9
1 0 -1 -2 -3 -4 -5 -6 -7 -8
2 1 0 -1 -2 -3 -4 -5 -6 -7
3 2 1 0 -1 -2 -3 -4 -5 -6
4 3 2 1 0 -1 -2 -3 -4 -5
5 4 3 2 1 0 -1 -2 -3 -4
6 5 4 3 2 1 0 -1 -2 -3
7 6 5 4 3 2 1 0 -1 -2
8 7 6 5 4 3 2 1 0 -1
9 8 7 6 5 4 3 2 1 0
```

Analysis

As with most programs that generate two-dimensional output, we consider the use of a nested pair of loops:

```java
public static void diffTable(int n)
// pre: n >= 0
// post: print difference table of width n
{
    for (int row = 1; row <= n; row++)        // 1
    {
        for (int col = 1; col <= n; col++)    // 2
        {
            System.out.print(row-col+" ");    // 3
        }
        System.out.println();                 // 4
    }
}
```

Each of the loops executes n times. Since printing a value (line 3) takes constant time c_1, the inner loop at line 2 takes $c_1 n$ time. If line 4 takes constant time

c_2, then the outer loop at line 1 takes $n(c_1 n + c_2) = c_1 n^2 + c_2 n$ time. This polynomial is clearly $O(n^2)$ (take $c = c_1 + c_2$ and $n_0 = 1$). Doubling the problem size approximately quadruples the running time.

As a rule of thumb, each loop that performs n iterations multiplies the complexity of each iteration by a factor of n. Nested loops multiply the complexity of the most deeply nested code by another power of n. As we have seen, loops doubly nested around a simple statement often consume quadratic time.

Since there are only three variables in our difference method, it takes constant space—an amount of space that is independent of problem size.

A Multiplication Table

Unlike the difference operator, the multiplication operator is commutative, and the multiplication table is symmetric. Therefore, when printing a multiplication table of size n, only the "lower triangular" region is necessary:

```
1
2 4
3 6 9
4 8 12 16
5 10 15 20 25
6 12 18 24 30 36
7 14 21 28 35 42 49
8 16 24 32 40 48 56 64
9 18 27 36 45 54 63 72 81
10 20 30 40 50 60 70 80 90 100
```

Here is a Java method to print the above table:

```
public static void multTable(int n)
// pre: n >= 0
// post: print multiplication table
{
    for (int row = 1; row <= n; row++)        // 1
    {
        for (int col = 1; col <= row; col++)  // 2
        {
            System.out.print(row*col+" ");    // 3
        }
        System.out.println();                 // 4
    }
}
```

Clearly, this table can be printed at least as fast as our difference table—it has about half the entries—so it is, similarly, $O(n^2)$. Can this limit be improved? If lines 3 and 4 take constant times c_1 and c_2, respectively, then the overall time is approximately

$$(1c_1 + c_2) + (2c_1 + c_2) + \cdots + (nc_1 + c_2) = \frac{c_1 n(n+1)}{2} + nc_2 = \frac{c_1}{2}n^2 + (c_2 + \frac{c_1}{2})n$$

Clearly, no linear function will bound this function above, so the bound of $O(n^2)$ is a good estimate. Notice that we have, essentially, used the fastest growing term of the polynomial—n^2.

Notice that both of these programs print an "area" of values, each of which can be computed in constant time. Thus, the growth rate of the function is the growth rate of the area of the output—which is $O(n^2)$.

Building a Vector of Values

Often, it is useful to build a **Vector** containing specific values. For the purposes of this problem, we will assume the values are integers between 0 and $n - 1$, inclusive. Our first (and best) attempt expands the **Vector** in the natural manner:

```
public static Vector buildVector1(int n)
// pre: n >= 0
// post: construct a vector of size n of 1..n
{
    Vector v = new Vector(n);               // 1
    for (int i = 0; i < n; i++)             // 2
    {
        v.add(new Integer(i));              // 3
    }
    return v;                               // 4
}
```

We will assume (correctly) that lines 1 and 4 take constant time. The loop at line 2, however, takes n times the length of time it takes to add a single element. Review of that code will demonstrate that the addition of a new element to a **Vector** takes constant time, provided expansion is not necessary. Thus, the total running time is linear, $O(n)$. Notice that the process of building this **Vector** requires space that is linear as well. Clearly, if the method's purpose is to spend time initializing the elements of a **Vector**, it would be difficult for it to consume space at a faster rate than time.

A slightly different approach is demonstrated by the following code:

```
public static Vector buildVector2(int n)
// pre: n >= 0
// post: construct a vector of size n of 1..n
{
    Vector v = new Vector(n);               // 1
    for (int i = 0; i < n; i++)             // 2
    {
        v.add(0,new Integer(i));            // 3
    }
    return v;                               // 4
}
```

All the assumptions of `buildVector1` hold here, except that the cost of inserting a value at the *beginning* of a `Vector` is proportional to the `Vector`'s current length. On the first insertion, it takes about 1 unit of time, on the second, 2 units, and so on. The analysis of this method, then, is similar to that of the triangular multiplication table. Its running time is $O(n^2)$. Its space utilization, however, remains linear.

Printing a Table of Factors

Suppose we are interested in storing a table of factors of numbers between 1 and n. The beginning of such a table—the factors of values between 1 and 10—includes the following values:

```
1
1 2
1 3
1 2 4
1 5
1 2 3 6
1 7
1 2 4 8
1 3 9
1 2 5 10
```

How much space must be reserved for storing this table? This problem looks a little daunting because the number of factors associated with each line varies, but without any obvious pattern. Here's a program that generates the desired table:

```
public static Vector factTable(int n)
// pre: n > 0
// post: returns a table of factors of values 1 through n
{
    Vector table = new Vector();
    for (int i = 1; i <= n; i++)
    {
        Vector factors = new Vector();
        for (int f = 1; f <= i; f++)
        {
            if ((i % f) == 0) {
                factors.add(new Integer(f));
            }
        }
        table.add(factors);
    }
    return table;
}
```

To measure the table size we consider those lines that mention f as a factor. Clearly, f appears on every fth line. Thus, over n lines of the table there are

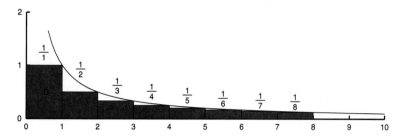

Figure 4.4 Estimating the sum of reciprocal values. Here, $\sum_{x=1}^{8} \frac{1}{x} \approx 2.72$ is no more than $1 + \int_{1}^{8} \frac{1}{x} dx = 1 + \ln 8 \approx 3.08$.

no more than $\frac{n}{f}$ lines that include f. Thus, we have as an upper bound on the table size:

$$\frac{n}{1} + \frac{n}{2} + \frac{n}{3} + \cdots + \frac{n}{n-1} + \frac{n}{n}$$

Factoring out n we have:

$$n \left(\frac{1}{1} + \frac{1}{2} + \frac{1}{3} + \cdots + \frac{1}{n-1} + \frac{1}{n} \right)$$

We note that these fractions fall on the curve $\frac{1}{x}$ (see Figure 4.4). We may compute the area of the curve—an upper bound on the sum—as:

$$n \sum_{x=1}^{n} \frac{1}{x} \leq n \left(1 + \int_{1}^{n} \frac{1}{x} dx \right)$$
$$\leq n(1 + \ln n - \ln 1)$$
$$\leq O(n \ln n)$$

The size of the table grows only a little faster than linearly. The time necessary to create the table, of course, is $O(n^2)$ since we check n factors for number n.

Exercise 4.1 *Slightly modify the method to construct the same table, but in $O(n\sqrt{n})$ time.*

Exercise 4.2 *Rewrite the method to construct the same table, but in $O(n \ln n)$ time.*

Finding a Space in a String

Some problems appear to have behavior that is more variable than the examples we have seen so far. Consider, for example, the code to locate the first space in a string:

```
static int findSpace(String s)
// pre: s is a string, possibly containing a space
// post: returns index of first space, or -1 if none found
{
    int i;
    for (i = 0; i < s.length(); i++)
    {
        if (' ' == s.charAt(i)) return i;
    }
    return -1;
}
```

This simple method checks each of the characters within a string. When one is found to be a space, the loop is terminated and the index is returned. If, of course, there is no space within the string, this must be verified by checking each character. Clearly, the time associated with this method is determined by the number of loops executed by the method. As a result, the time taken is linear in the length of the string.

We can, however, be more precise about its behavior using *best-*, *worst-*, and *average-case analyses*:

Best case. The best-case behavior is an upper bound on the shortest time that any problem of size n might take. Usually, best cases are associated with particularly nice arrangements of values—here, perhaps, a string with a space in the first position. In this case, our method takes at most constant time! It is important to note that the best case must be a problem of size n.

Worst case. The worst-case behavior is the longest time that any problem of size n might take. In our string-based procedure, our method will take the longest when there is no space in the string. In that case, the method consumes at most linear time. Unless we specify otherwise, we will use the worst-case consumption of resources to determine the complexity.

Average case. The average-case behavior is the complexity of solving an "average" problem of size n. Analysis involves computing a weighted sum of the cost (in time or space) of problems of size n. The weight of each problem is the probability that the problem would occur. If, in our example, we knew (somehow) that there was exactly one space in the string, and that it appears in any of the n positions with equal probability, we would deduce that, on average,

$$\sum_{i=1}^{n} \frac{1}{n}i = \frac{1}{n} \cdot 1 + \frac{1}{n} \cdot 2 + \cdots + \frac{1}{n} \cdot n = \frac{1}{n} \cdot \frac{n(n+1)}{2} = \frac{n+1}{2}$$

iterations would be necessary to locate the space. Our method has linear average-time complexity. If, however, we knew that the string was English prose of length n, the average complexity would be related to the average length of the first word, a value easily bounded above by a constant (say,

10). The weights of the first few terms would be large, while the weights associated with a large number of iterations or more would be zero. The average complexity would be constant. (In this case, the worst case would be constant as well.) Obviously determining the average-case complexity requires some understanding of the desired distributions of data.

German prose may require larger constants.

Best-, worst-, and average-case analyses will be important in helping us evaluate the theoretical complexities of the structures we develop. Some care, however, must be used when determining the growth rates of real Java. It is tempting, for example, to measure the space or time used by a data structure and fit a curve to it in hopes of getting a handle on its long-term growth. This approach should be avoided, if possible, as such statements can rarely be made with much security. Still, such techniques can be fruitfully used to verify that there is no *unexpected* behavior.

4.1.3   The Trading of Time and Space

Two resources coveted by programmers are time and space. When programs are run, the algorithms they incorporate and the data structures they utilize work together to consume time. This time is directly due to executing machine instructions. The fewer instructions executed, the faster the program goes.

Most of us have had an opportunity to return to old code and realize that useless instructions can be removed. For example, when we compute the table factors, we realized that we could speed up the process by checking fewer values for divisibility. Arguably, most programs are susceptible to some of this "instruction weeding," or *optimization*. On the other hand, it is clear that there must be a limit to the extent that an individual program can be improved. For some equivalent program, the removal of any statement causes the program to run incorrectly. This limit, in some sense, is an *information theoretic limit*: given the approach of the algorithm and the design of a data structure, no improvements can be made to the program to make it run faster. To be convinced that there is a firm limit, we would require a formal proof that no operation could be avoided. Such proofs can be difficult, especially without intimate knowledge of the language, its compiler, and the architecture that supports the running code. Nonetheless, the optimization of code is an important feature of making programs run quickly. Engineers put considerable effort into designing compilers to make automated optimization decisions. Most compilers, for example, will not generate instructions for *dead code*—statements that will never be executed. In the following Java code, for example, it is clear that the "then" portion of this code may be removed without fear:

```java
if (false)
{
    System.out.println("Man in the moon.");
} else {
    System.out.println("Pie in the sky.");
}
```

After compiler optimizations have been employed, though, there is a limit that can be placed on how fast the code can be made to run. We will assume—whenever we consider a time–space trade-off—that all reasonable efforts have been made to optimize the time and space utilization of a particular approach. Notice, however, that most optimizations performed by a compiler do not significantly affect the *asymptotic* running time of an algorithm. At most, they tend to speed up an algorithm by a constant factor, an amount that is easily absorbed in any theoretical analysis using big-O methods.

Appropriately implemented data structures can, however, yield significant performance improvements. Decisions about data structure design involve weighing—often using results of big-O analysis—the time and space requirements of a structure used to solve a problem. For example, in the `Vector` class, we opted to maintain a field, `elementCount`, that kept track of how many elements within the underlying array are actually being used. This variable became necessary when we realized that as the `Vector` expanded, the constant reallocation of the underlying memory could lead to quadratic time complexity over the life of the `Vector`. By storing a little more information (here, `elementCount`) we reduce the total complexity of expanding the `Vector`—our implementation, recall, requires $O(1)$ data-copying operations as the `Vector` expands. Since `Vector`s are very likely to expand in this way, we find it worthwhile to use this extra space. In other situations we will see that the trade-offs are less obvious and sometimes lead to the development of several implementations of a single data structure designed for various uses by the application designer.

The choice between implementations is sometimes difficult and may require analysis of the application: if `Vector`'s `add` method is to be called relatively infrequently, the time spent resizing the structure is relatively insignificant. On the other hand, if elements are to be added frequently, maintaining `elementCount` saves time. In any case, the careful analysis of trade-off between time and space is an important part of good data structure design.

4.1.4   Back-of-the-Envelope Estimations

A skill that is useful to the designer is the ability to develop good estimates of the time and space necessary to run an algorithm or program. It is one thing to develop a theoretical analysis of an algorithm, but it is quite another to develop a sense of the actual performance of a system. One useful technique is to apply any of a number of back-of-the-envelope approximations to estimating the performance of an algorithm.

The numbers that programmers work with on a day-to-day basis often vary in magnitude so much that it is difficult to develop much of a common sense for estimating things. It is useful, then, to keep a store of some simple figures that may help you to determine the performance—either in time or space—of a project. Here are some useful rules of thumb:

- Light travels one foot in a *nanosecond* (one billionth of a second).

- Approximately π ($\approx$ 3.15) hundredths of a second is a nanoyear (one billionth of a year).

- It takes between 1 and 10 nanoseconds (ns) to store a value in Java. Basic math operations take a similar length of time.

- An array assignment is approximately twice as slow as a regular assignment.

- A `Vector` assignment is approximately 50 times slower than a regular assignment.

- Modern computers execute 1 billion instructions per second.

- A character is represented by 8 bits (approximately 10).

- An Ethernet network can transmit at 100 million bits per second (expected throughput is nearer 10 million bits).

- Fewer than 100 words made up 50 percent of Shakespeare's writing; they have an average length of π. A core of 3000 words makes up 90 percent of his vocabulary; they have an average of 5.5 letters.

As an informal example of the process, we might attempt to answer the question: How many books can we store on a 10 gigabyte hard drive? First we will assume that 1 byte is used to store a character. Next, assuming that an average word has about 5 characters, and that a typewritten page has about 500 words per typewritten page, we have about 2500 characters per page. Another approximation might suggest 40 lines per page with 60 characters per line, or 2400 characters per page. For computational simplicity, we keep the 2500 character estimate. Next, we assume the average book has, say, 300 pages, so that the result is 0.75 million bytes required to store a text. Call it 1 million. A 10 gigabyte drive contains approximately 10 billion characters; this allows us to store approximately 10 thousand books.

A dictionary is a collection of approximately 250,000 words. How long might it take to compute the average length of words appearing in the dictionary? Assume that the dictionary is stored in memory and that the length of a word can be determined in constant time—perhaps 10 microseconds (μs). The length must be accumulated in a sum, taking an additional microsecond per word— let's ignore that time. The entire summation process takes, then, 2.5 seconds of time. (On the author's machine, it took 3.2 seconds.)

Exercise 4.3 *How many dots can be printed on a single sheet of paper? Assume, for example, your printer prints at 500 dots per inch. If a dot were used to represent a bit of information, how much text could be encoded on one page?*

As you gain experience designing data structures you will also develop a sense of the commitments necessary to support a structure that takes $O(n^2)$ space, or an algorithm that uses $O(n \log n)$ time.

4.2   Self-Reference

One of the most elegant techniques for constructing algorithms, data structures, and proofs is to utilize self-reference in the design. In this section we discuss applications of self-reference in programming—called *recursion*—and in proofs—called *proof by induction*. In both cases the difficulties of solving the problem outright are circumvented by developing a language that is rich enough to support the self-reference. The result is a compact technique for solving complex problems.

4.2.1   Recursion

When faced with a difficult problem of computation or structure, often the best solution can be specified in a *self-referential* or *recursive* manner. Usually, the difficulty of the problem is one of management of the resources that are to be used by the program. Recursion helps us tackle the problem by focusing on reducing the problem to one that is more manageable in size and then building up the answer. Through multiple, nested, progressive applications of the algorithm, a solution is constructed from the solutions of smaller problems.

Summing Integers

We first consider a simple, but classic, problem: suppose we are interested in computing the sum of the numbers from 0 through n.

$$\sum_{i=0}^{n} i = 0 + 1 + 2 + 3 + \cdots + n$$

One approach to the problem is to write a simple loop that over n iterations accumulates the result.

Recursion

```
public static int sum1(int n)
// pre: n >= 0
// post: compute the sum of 0..n
{
    int result = 0;
    for (int i = 1; i <= n; i++)
    {
        result = result + i;
    }
    return result;
}
```

The method starts by setting a partial sum to 0. If n is a value that is less than 1, then the loop will never execute. The result (0) is what we expect if $n = 0$. If n is greater than 0, then the loop executes and the initial portion of the partial sum is computed. After $n - 1$ loops, the sum of the first $n - 1$ terms is computed. The nth iteration simply adds in n. When the loop is finished,

result holds the sum of values 1 through n. We see, then, that this method works as advertised in the postcondition.

Suppose, now, that a second programmer is to solve the same problem. If the programmer is particularly lazy and has access to the **sum1** solution the following code also solves the problem:

```
public static int sum2(int n)
// pre: n >= 0
// post: compute the sum of 0..n
{
    if (n < 1) return 0;
    else return sum1(n-1) + n;
}
```

For the most trivial problem (any number less than 1), we return 0. For all other values of n, the programmer turns to **sum1** to solve the next simplest problem (the sum of integers 0 through $n-1$) and then adds n. Of course, this algorithm works as advertised in the postcondition, because it depends on **sum1** for all but the last step, and it then adds in the correct final addend, n.

Actually, if **sum2** calls *any* method that is able to compute the sum of numbers 0 through $n-1$, **sum2** works correctly. But, wait! The sum of integers is precisely what **sum2** is supposed to be computing! We use this observation to derive, then, the following *self-referential* method:

```
public static int sum3(int n)
// pre: n >= 0
// post: compute the sum of 0..n
{
    if (n < 1) return 0;         // base case
    else return sum3(n-1) + n;   // reduction, progress, solution
}
```

This code requires careful inspection (Figure 4.5). First, in the simplest or *base* cases (for $n < 1$), **sum3** returns 0. The second line is only executed when $n \geq 1$. It reduces the problem to a simpler problem—the sum of integers between 0 and $n-1$. As with all recursive programs, this requires a little work (a subtraction) to reduce the problem to one that is closer to the base case. Considering the problem $n + 1$ would have been fatal because it doesn't make suitable *progress* toward the base case. The subproblem is passed off to *another invocation* of **sum3**. Once that procedure computes its result (either immediately or, if necessary, through further recursion), a little more work is necessary to convert the solution of the problem of size $n - 1$ into a solution for a problem of size n. Here, we have simply added in n. Notice the operation involved in building the answer (addition) opposes the operation used to reduce the problem (subtraction). This is common in recursive procedures.

Principle 7 *Recursive structures must make "progress" toward a "base case."*

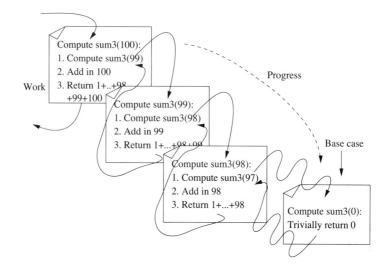

Figure 4.5 The "unrolling" of a procedure to recursively sum integers. Rightward arrows break the problem down; leftward arrows build up the solution.

We cast this principle in terms of "structures" because much of what we say about self-referential execution of code can be applied to self-referential structuring of data. Most difficulties with recursive structures (including recursive methods) stem from either incorrectly stating the base case or failing to make proper progress.

Inserting a Value into a Vector

Recursion is a natural method for accomplishing many complicated tasks on Vectors and arrays. For example, the `add(index,object)` method of the Vector class discussed on page 51 can be written as a recursive procedure. The essential concept is to insert the value into the Vector only after having moved the previous value out of the way. That value is inserted at the next larger location. This leads us to the following alternative to the standard Vector method:

Vector

```
public void add(int index, Object value)
// pre: 0 <= index <= size()
// post: inserts new value in vector with desired index
//    moving elements from index to size()-1 to right
{
    if (index >= size()) {
        add(value); // base case: add at end
    } else {
        Object previous = get(index); // work
```

```
            add(index+1,previous);   // progress through recursion
            set(index,value);   // work
    }
}
```

Note that the base case is identified through the need to apply a *trivial operation* rather than, say, the size of the index. Indeed, progress is determined by how close the index gets to the size of the `Vector`. Again, this is a linear or $O(n)$ process.

Printing a Vector of Values

In the previous example, the recursive routine was suitable for direct use by the user. Often, though, recursion demands additional parameters that encode, in some way, progress made toward the solution. These parameters can be confusing to users who, after all, are probably unaware of the details of the recursion. To avoid this confusion, we "wrap" the call to a protected recursive method in a public method. This hides the details of the initial recursive method call. Here, we investigate a printing extension to the `Vector` class:

```
public void print()
// post: print the elements of the vector
{
    printFrom(0);
}

protected void printFrom(int index)
// pre: index <= size()
// post: print elements indexed between index and size()
{
    if (index < size()) {
        System.out.println(get(index));
        printFrom(index+1);
    }
}
```

The `print` method wraps or hides the call to the recursive `printFrom` method. The recursive method accepts a single parameter that indicates the index of the first element that should be printed out. As progress is made, the initial index increases, leading to linear performance. To print the entire `Vector`, the recursive method is called with a value of zero.

It would appear that the base case is missing. In fact, it is indicated by the *failure* of the `if` statement. Even though the base case is to "do nothing," the `if` statement is absolutely necessary. Every terminating recursive method should have some conditional statement.

`PrintFrom` is an example of a *tail recursive* method. Any recursion happens just before exiting from the method. Tail recursive methods are particularly nice because good compilers can translate them into loops. Each iteration of the loop simulates the computation and return of another of the nested recursive procedure calls. Since there is one call for each of the n values, and the procedure performs a constant amount of work, the entire process takes $O(n)$ time.

Exercise 4.4 *Write a recursive method to print out the characters of a string with spaces between characters. Make sure your method does not print a leading or tailing space, unless it is a leading or trailing character of the original string.*

Computing Change in Postage Stamps

Suppose, when receiving change at the post office, you wished to be paid your change in various (useful) stamps. For example, at current rates, you might be interested in receiving either 37 cent stamps, 21 cent postcards, or penny stamps (just in case of a postage increase). For a particular amount, what is *the smallest number of stamps necessary* to make the change?

This problem is fairly complex because, after all, the minimum number of stamps needed to make 44 cents involves 4 stamps—two postcard stamps and two penny stamps—and *not* 8—a 37 cent stamp and 7 penny stamps. (The latter solution might be suggested by postal clerks used to dealing with U.S. coinage, which is fairly easily minimized.) We will initially approach this problem using recursion. Our solution will only report the minimum number of stamps returned. We leave it as an exercise to report the number of each type of stamp (consider Problem 4.22); that solution does not greatly change the approach of the problem.

If no change is required—a base case—the solution is simple: hand the customer zero stamps. If the change is anything more, we'll have to do some work. Consider the 44 cent problem. We know that some stamps will have to be given to the customer, but not the variety. We *do* know that the last stamp handed to the customer will either be a penny stamp, a 21 cent step, or a 37 cent stamp. If we could only solve three smaller minimization problems—the 43 cent problem, the 24 cent problem, and the 7 cent problem—then our answer would be one stamp more than the minimum of the answers to those three problems. (The answers to the three problems are 3, 4, and 7, respectively, so our answer should be 4.) Of course, we should ignore meaningless reduced problems: the −4 cent problem results from considering handing a 21 cent stamp over to solve the 17 cent problem.

Here is the `stampCount` method that computes the solution:

Recursive-
Postage

```
public final static int LETTER=37;
public final static int CARD=21;
public final static int PENNY=1;

public static int stampCount(int amount)
// pre: amount >= 0
// post: return *number* of stamps needed to make change
//       (only use letter, card, and penny stamps)
{
```

```
        int minStamps;
        Assert.pre(amount >= 0,"Reasonable amount of change.");
        if (amount == 0) return 0;
        // consider use of a penny stamp
        minStamps = 1+stampCount(amount-PENNY);
        // consider use of a post card stamp
        if (amount >= CARD) {
            int possible = 1+stampCount(amount-CARD);
            if (minStamps > possible) minStamps = possible;
        }
        // consider use of a letter stamp
        if (amount >= LETTER) {
            int possible = 1+stampCount(amount-LETTER);
            if (minStamps > possible) minStamps = possible;
        }
        return minStamps;
    }
```

For the nontrivial cases, the variable `minStamps` keeps track of the minimum number of stamps returned by any of these three subproblems. Since each method call potentially results in several recursive calls, the method is not tail recursive. While it is possible to solve this problem using iteration, recursion presents a very natural solution.

An Efficient Solution to the Postage Stamp Problem

If the same procedure were used to compute the minimum number of stamps to make 44 cents change, the `stampCount` procedure would be called 391 times. This number increases exponentially as the size of the problem increases (it is $O(3^n)$). Because 391 is greater than 44—the number of distinct subproblems—some subproblems are recomputed many times. For example, the 2 cent problem must be re-solved by every larger problem.

Making currency is illegal. Making change is not!

To reduce the number of calls, we can incorporate an array into the method. Each location **n** of the array stores either 0 or the answer to the problem of size **n**. If, when looking for an answer, the entry is 0, we invest time in computing the answer and *cache* it in the array for future use. This technique is called *dynamic programming* and yields an efficient linear algorithm. Here is our modified solution:

FullPostage

```
public static final int LETTER = 37; // letter rate
public static final int CARD = 21;   // post card rate
public static final int PENNY = 1;   // penny stamp

public static int stampCount(int amount)
// pre: amount >= 0
// post: return *number* of stamps needed to make change
//       (only use letter, post card, and penny stamps)
{
    return stampCount(amount, new int[amount+1]);
```

```
}

protected static int stampCount(int amount, int answer[])
// pre: amount >= 0; answer array has length >= amount
// post: return *number* of stamps needed to make change
//        (only use letter, post card, and penny stamps)
{
    int minStamps;
    Assert.pre(amount >= 0,"Reasonable amount of change.");
    if (amount == 0) return 0;
    if (answer[amount] != 0) return answer[amount];
    // consider use of a penny stamp
    minStamps = 1+stampCount(amount-1,answer);
    // consider use of a post card stamp
    if (amount >= CARD) {
        int possible = 1+stampCount(amount-CARD,answer);
        if (minStamps > possible) minStamps = possible;
    }
    // consider use of a letter stamp
    if (amount >= LETTER) {
        int possible = 1+stampCount(amount-LETTER,answer);
        if (minStamps > possible) minStamps = possible;
    }
    answer[amount] = minStamps;
    return minStamps;
}
```

When we call the method for the first time, we allocate an array of sufficient size (amount+1 because arrays are indexed beginning at zero) and pass it as answer in the protected two-parameter version of the method. If the answer is not found in the array, it is computed using up to three recursive calls that pass the array of previously computed answers. Just before returning, the newly computed answer is placed in the appropriate slot. In this way, when solutions are sought for this problem again, they can be retrieved without the overhead of redundant computation.

When we seek the solution to the 44 cent problem, 77 calls are made to the procedure. Only 44 of these get past the first few statements to potentially make recursive calls. The combination of the power recursion and the efficiency of dynamic programming yields elegant solutions to many seemingly difficult problems.

Exercise 4.5 *Explain why the dynamic programming approach to the problem runs in linear time.*

In the next section, we consider *induction*, a recursive proof technique. Induction is as elegant a means of proving theorems as recursion is for writing programs.

4.2.2   Mathematical Induction

The accurate analysis of data structures often requires mathematical proof. An effective proof technique that designers may apply to many computer science problems is *mathematical induction*. The technique is, essentially, the construction of a recursive proof. Just as we can solve some problems elegantly using recursion, some properties may be elegantly verified using induction.

A common template for proving statements by mathematical induction is as follows:

1. Begin your proof with "We will prove this using induction on the size of the problem." This informs the reader of your approach.

2. Directly prove whatever base cases are necessary. Strive, whenever possible to keep the number of cases small and the proofs as simple as possible.

3. State the assumption that the observation holds for all values from the base case, up to but not including the nth case. Sometimes this assumption can be relaxed in simple inductive proofs.

4. Prove, from simpler cases, that the nth case also holds.

5. Claim that, by mathematical induction on n, the observation is true for all cases more complex than the base case.

Individual proofs, of course, can deviate from this pattern, but most follow the given outline.

As an initial example, we construct a formula for computing the sum of integers between 0 and $n \geq 0$ inclusively. Recall that this result was used in Section 3.5 when we considered the cost of extending `Vectors`, and earlier, in Section 4.1.2, when we analyzed `buildVector2`. Proof of this statement also yields a constant-time method for implementing `sum3`.

Observation 4.1 $\sum_{i=0}^{n} i = \frac{n(n+1)}{2}$.

Proof: We prove this by induction. First, consider the simplest case, or *base case*. If $n = 0$, then the sum is 0. The formula gives us $\frac{0(0+1)}{2} = 0$. The observation appears to hold for the base case.

Now, suppose we know—for some reason—that our closed-form formula holds for all values between 0 (our base case) and $n - 1$. This knowledge may help us solve a more complex problem, namely, the sum of integers between 0 and n. The sum

$$0 + 1 + 2 + \cdots + (n - 1) + n$$

conveniently contains the sum of the first $n - 1$ integers, so we rewrite it as

$$[0 + 1 + 2 + \cdots + (n - 1)] + n$$

Because we have assumed that the sum of the natural numbers to $n - 1$ can be computed by the formula, we may rewrite the sum as

$$\left[\frac{(n-1)n}{2} \right] + n$$

The terms of this expression may be simplified and reorganized:

$$\frac{(n-1)n + 2n}{2} = \frac{n(n+1)}{2}$$

Thus given only the knowledge that the formula worked for $n - 1$, we have been able to extend it to n. It is not hard to convince yourself, then, that the observation holds for any nonnegative value of n. Our base case was for $n = 0$, so it must hold as well for $n = 1$. Since it holds for $n = 1$, it must hold for $n = 2$. In fact, it holds for any value of $n \geq 0$ by simply proving it holds for values $0, 1, 2, \ldots, n - 1$ and then observing it can be extended to n.◊

The induction can be viewed as a recursively constructed proof (consider Figure 4.6). Suppose we wish to see if our observation holds for $n = 100$. Our method requires us to show it holds for $n = 99$. Given that, it is a simple matter to extend the result to 100. Proving the result for $n = 99$, however, is *almost*[2] as difficult as it is for $n = 100$. We need to prove it for $n = 98$, and extend *that* result. This process of developing the proof for 100 eventually unravels into a recursive construction of a (very long) proof that demonstrates that the observation holds for values 0 through 99, and then 100.

99 cases left to prove! Take one down, pass it around, 98 cases left to prove! . . .

The whole process, like recursion, depends critically on the proof of appropriate base cases. In our proof of Observation 4.1, for example, we proved that the observation held for $n = 0$. If we do not prove this simple case, then our recursive construction of the proof for any value of $n \geq 0$ does not terminate: when we try to prove it holds for $n = 0$, we have no base case, and therefore must prove it holds for $n = -1$, and in proving that, we prove that it holds for $-2, -3, \ldots$, *ad infinitum*. The proof construction never terminates!

Our next example of proof by induction is a *correctness proof*. Our intent is to show that a piece of code runs as advertised. In this case, we reinvestigate sum3 from page 83:

```
public static int sum3(int n)
// pre: n >= 0
// post: compute the sum of 0..n
{
    if (n < 1) return 0;        // 1
    else return                 // 2
                sum3(           // 3
                  n-1           // 4
```

Recursion

---

[2] It is important, of course, to base your inductive step on simpler problems—problems that take you closer to your base case. If you avoid basing it on simpler cases, then the recursive proof will never be completely constructed, and the induction will fail.

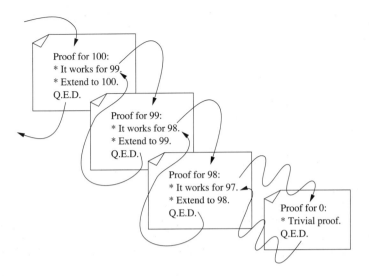

Figure 4.6 The process of proof by induction simulates the recursive construction of a proof. Compare with Figure 4.5.

```
         ) + n;  // 5
     }
```

(The code has been reformatted to allow discussion of portions of the computation.) As with our mathematical proofs, we state our result formally:

Observation 4.2 *Given that $n \geq 0$, the method* sum3 *computes the sum of the integers 0 through n, inclusive.*

Proof: Our proof is by induction, based on the parameter n. First, consider the action of sum3 when it is passed the parameter 0. The if statement of line 1 is true, and the program returns 0, the desired result.

We now consider n>0 and assume that the method computes the correct result for all values less that n. We extend our proof of correctness to the parameter value of n. Since n is greater than 0, the if of line 1 fails, and the else beginning on line 2 is considered. On line 4, the parameter is decremented, and on line 3, the recursion takes place. By our assumption, this recursive call returns the correct result—the sum of values between 0 and n-1, inclusive. Line 5 adds in the final value, and the entire result is returned. The program works correctly for a parameter n greater than 0. By induction on n, the method computes the correct result for all n>=0.⋄

Proofs of correctness are important steps in the process of verifying that code works as desired. Clearly, since induction and recursion have similar forms, the

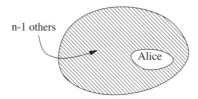

Figure 4.7   A group of n computer scientists composed of Alice and $n-1$ others.

application of inductive proof techniques to recursive methods often leads to straightforward proofs. Even when iteration is used, however, induction can be used to demonstrate assumptions made about loops, no matter the number of iterations.

We state here an important result that gives us a closed-form expression for computing the sum of powers of 2.

Observation 4.3 $\sum_{i=0}^{n} 2^i = 2^{n+1} - 1$.

Exercise 4.6 *Prove Observation 4.3.*

There are, of course, ways that the inductive proof can go awry. Not proving the appropriate base cases is the most common mistake and can lead to some interesting results. Here we prove what few have suspected all along:

Observation 4.4 *All computer scientists are good programmers.*

Warning: bad proof!   *Proof:*   We prove the observation is true, using mathematical induction. First, we use traditional techniques (examinations, etc.) to demonstrate that Alice is a good programmer.

Now, assume that our observation is true of any group of fewer than n computer scientists. Let's extend our result: select n computer scientists, including Alice (see Figure 4.7). Clearly, the subgroup consisting of all computer scientists that are "not Alice" is a group of $n-1$ computer scientists. Our assumption states that this group of $n-1$ computer scientists is made up of good programmers. So Alice and all the other computer scientists are good programmers. By induction on n, we have demonstrated that all computer scientists are good programmers.◊

This is a very interesting result, especially since it is not true. (Among other things, some computer scientists do not program computers!) How, then, were we successful in proving it? If you look carefully, our base case is Alice. The assumption, on the other hand, is based on *any* group of $n-1$ programmers. Unfortunately, since our only solid proof of quality programming is Alice, and non-Alice programmers cannot be reduced to cases involving Alice, our proof is fatally flawed.

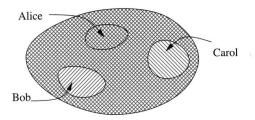

Figure 4.8   A group of n computer scientists, including Alice, Bob, and Carol.

Still, a slight reworking of the logic might make the proof of this observation possible. Since Alice is a computer scientist, we can attempt to prove the observation by induction on groups of computer scientists *that include Alice:*

Proof: We prove the observation by induction. First, as our base case, consider Alice. Alice is well known for being a good programmer. Now, assume that for any group of fewer than n computer scientists that includes Alice, the members are excellent programmers. Take n computer scientists, including Alice (see Figure 4.8). Select a non-Alice programmer. Call him Bob. If we consider all non-Bob computer scientists, we have a group of $n - 1$ computer scientists— including Alice. By our assumption, they must all be good. What about Bob? Select another non-Alice, non-Bob computer scientist from the group of n. Call her Carol. Carol must be a good programmer, because she was a member of the $n - 1$ non-Bob programmers. If we consider the $n - 1$ non-Carol programmers, the group includes both Alice and Bob. Because it includes Alice, the non-Carol programmers must all be good. Since Carol is a good programmer, then all n must program well. By induction on n, all groups of computer scientists that include Alice must be good programmers. Since the group of all computer scientists is finite, and it includes Alice, the entire population must program well. The observation holds!◇

Warning: bad proof, take 2!

This proof looks pretty solid—until you consider that in order for it to work, you must be able to distinguish between Alice, Bob, and Carol. There are three people. The proof of the three-person case depends directly on the observation holding for just two people. But we have not considered the two-person case! In fact, *that* is the hole in the argument. If we know of a bad programmer, Ted, we can say nothing about the group consisting of Alice and Ted (see Figure 4.9). As a result, we have a worrisome hole in the proof of the group consisting of Alice, Bob, and Ted. In the end, the attempt at a complete proof unravels.

What have we learned from this discussion? For an inductive proof, the base cases must be carefully enumerated and proved. When proving the inductive step, the step must be made upon a proved foundation. If not, the entire statement collapses. The subtlety of this difficulty should put us on alert: even the most thoughtful proofs can go awry if the base case is not well considered.

Lesson: it's hard to find good programmers.

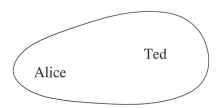

Figure 4.9   The proof does not hold for the simplest nontrivial case: Alice and any bad programmer.

We can now make a similar statement about recursion: it is important to identify and correctly code the base cases you need. If you don't, you run the risk that your method will fail to stop or will compute the wrong answer. One of the most difficult debugging situations occurs when multiple base cases are to be considered and only a few are actually programmed.

Our final investigation considers the implementation of a Java method to compute the following sequence of values:

$$0, 1, 1, 2, 3, 5, 8, 13, 21, \ldots$$

These values are the first of the sequence of *Fibonacci numbers*. Each value is the sum of the two values that fall before it. We should be careful—especially given our last discussion—that we have the base cases carefully considered. In this particular case, we must specify *two* initial values: 0 and 1.

This sequence may be familiar to you. If it is, you may have seen the definition of F_n, the nth value of the sequence as

$$F_n = \begin{cases} n & n = 0 \text{ or } n = 1 \\ F_{n-2} + F_{n-1} & n > 1 \end{cases}$$

The translation of this type of equation into Java is fairly straightforward. We make the following attempt:

Fibo

```
static public int fibo(int n)
// pre: n is a nonnegative integer
// post: result is the ith term from the sequence
//     0, 1, 1, 2, 3, 5, 8, 13, 21, 34, . . .
{
    Assert.pre(n >= 0, "Index is nonnegative.");
    // when n < 2, return n
    if (n == 0) return 0;                        // line 1
    else if (n == 1) return 1;                   // line 2
    // complex, self-referential case:
    else return fibo(n-2)+fibo(n-1);             // line 3
}
```

We now seek to prove that the recursive method computes and returns the nth member of the sequence.

Proof: First, suppose $n = 0$: the method returns 0, on line 1. Next, suppose that $n = 1$: the method returns 1, on line 2. So, for the two very simplest cases, the method computes the correct values. Now, suppose that $n > 1$, and furthermore, assume that `fibo` returns the correct value for all terms with index less than n. Since $n > 1$, lines 1 and 2 have no effect. Instead, the method resorts to using line 3 to compute the value. Since the method works for all values less than n, it specifically computes the two previous terms—F_{n-2} and F_{n-1}—correctly. The sum of these two values (F_n) is therefore computed and immediately returned on line 3. We have, then, by mathematical induction on n proved that $fibo(n)$ computes F_n for all $n \geq 0$.⋄

Another approach to computing Fibonacci numbers, of course, would be to use an iterative method:

```java
static public int fibo(int n)
// pre: n is a nonnegative integer
// post: result is the ith term from the sequence
//      0, 1, 1, 2, 3, 5, 8, 13, 21, 34, . . .
{
    Assert.pre(n >= 0, "Index is nonnegative.");
    int a = 0;
    int b = 1;
    if (n == 0) return a;        // line 1
    if (n == 1) return b;        // line 2
    // for large values of n, iteratively compute sequence
    int i=2,F;
    do
    {
        // Assertion: b is the i-1st member of the sequence
        //            a is the i-2nd member
        F = a + b;               // line 3
        // Assertion: F is the ith member
        // update previous two values:
        a = b;                   // line 4
        b = F;                   // line 5
        i++;                     // line 6
    } while (i <= n);            // line 7
    return F;                    // line 8
}
```

To demonstrate that such a program works, we perform a step-wise analysis of the method as it computes F_n.

Proof: Suppose $n = 0$. The condition in the `if` statement on line 1 is true and the value `a` (0) is returned. If $n = 1$, the condition on line 1 is false, but the `if` statement on line 2 is true and `b` (1) is returned. In both of these cases the correct value is returned.

We now investigate the loop. We notice that when the loop starts (it is a do loop, it must execute at least once if $n > 1$), a and b contain the values F_0 and F_1, and i is 2. Thus, the loop invariant before line 3 holds on the first iteration.

Now, assume that $i \geq 2$ and the loop invariant before line 3 holds. The effect of line 3 is to compute F_i from F_{i-1} and F_{i-2}. The result is placed in F, and the loop invariant after line 3 is met. The remaining statements, on lines 4 through 6 result in F_{i-2} in a and F_{i-1} in b. If the condition on line 7 should be true, we meet the loop invariant for the next iteration.

If the condition on line 7 should be false, then we note that this value of i is the first that is greater than n, so $F = F_{i-1} = F_n$, and the result returned is the correct result. ⬦

It is interesting to note that the initial values of the sequence are rather arbitrary, and that different natural phenomena related to Fibonacci numbers can be modeled by sequences that begin with different initial values.

4.3   Properties of Design

This section is dedicated to two informal properties of design that are referenced elsewhere within this text. The property of *symmetry* describes the predictability of a design, while *friction* describes the difficulty of moving a data structure from one state to another. Both terms extend the vocabulary of implementors when discussing design decisions.

4.3.1   Symmetry

For the most part, our instruction of computers occurs through programs. As a result, programs can be nonintuitive and hard to understand if they are not designed with human-readability in mind. On the other hand, a well-designed program can be used by a novice without a significant learning curve. Systems that are easy to use tend to survive longer.

The programmer, as a designer of a data structure, is responsible for delivering a usable implementation of an abstract data structure. For an implementation to be usable, it should provide access to the structure with methods that are predictable and easy to use. The notion of predictability is particularly difficult for designers of data structures to understand, and it is something often overlooked by novice programmers.

When designing a system (here, a program or data structure) a useful principle is to make its interface *symmetric*. What is symmetry? Symmetry allows one to view a system from different points of view and see similarities. Mathematicians would say that a system exhibits a symmetry if "it looks like itself under a nontrivial transformation." Given this, programmers consider asymmetries in transformed programs to be early warning signs of errors in logic.

Consider the following method (you will see this as part of the swap procedure of page 108). It exchanges two object references—data[i] and data[j].

```
int temp;
temp = data[i];
data[i] = data[j];
data[j] = temp;
```

Close inspection of this code demonstrates that it does what it claims to do. Even if we stand back, not thinking so much about the actual workings of the code, we can see that the code is pretty symmetric. For example, if we squint our eyes and look at the code from the standpoint of variable `data[i]`, we see it as:

```
int ...;
... = data[i];
data[i] = ...;
... = ...;
```

Here, `data[i]` is assigned to a variable, and a value is assigned to `data[i]`. We see a similar pattern with `data[j]`:

```
int ...;
... = ...;
... = data[j];
data[j] = ...;
```

While this is not direct proof that the code works, it is an indication that the code is, in some way, "symmetric," and that helps make the argument that it is well designed.

Not everything we do is symmetric. If we consider the `Association` class, for example, the key and value components of the `Association` are different. The value, of course, has two associated methods, `getValue` and `setValue`. The first of the methods reads and returns a value, while the second method consumes and sets a value. Everything is in balance, and so we are hopeful that the design of the structure is correct. On the other hand, the key can only be read: while there is a `getKey` method, there is no `setKey`. We have suggested good reasons for doing this. As long as you can make a good argument for asymmetry in design, the breaking of symmetry can be useful. Unreasoned asymmetry, however, is a sign of poor and unpredictable design.

Here are various ways that one can look at a system to evaluate it for symmetry:

1. Compare methods that extend the structure with methods that trim the structure. Do they have similar approaches? Are they similar in number?

2. Consider methods that read and write values. Can the input methods read what is written by the output methods? Can the writing methods write all values that can be read?

3. Are procedures that consume parameters matched by functions that deliver values?

4. Can points of potential garbage collection be equally balanced by `new` invocations?

5. In linked structures, does unlinking a value from the structure appear to be the reverse of linking a new value into the structure?

When asymmetries are found, it is important to consider why they occur. Arguments such as "I can't imagine that anyone would need an opposite method!" are usually unconvincing. Many methods are added to the structures, not because they are obviously necessary, but because there is no good argument against them. Sometimes, of course, the language or underlying system forces an asymmetry. In Java, for example, every `Object` has a `toString` method that converts an internal representation of an object to a human-readable form, but there's no `fromString` required method that reads the value of an `Object` from

Should ≠ will.   a `String`. There *should be*, but there isn't.

4.3.2   Friction

One of the obvious benefits of a data structure is that it provides a means of storing information. The ease with which the structure accepts and provides information about its contents can often be determined by its interface. Likewise, the difficulty of moving a data structure from one state to another determines, in some way, its "stiffness" or the amount of *friction* the structure provides when the state of the structure is to be modified.

One way that we might measure friction is to determine a sequence of logical states for the structure, and then determine the number of operations that are necessary to move the structure from each state to the next. If the number of operations is high, we imagine a certain degree of friction; if the operation count is low, the structure moves forward with relative ease.

Often we see that the less space provided to the structure, the more friction appears to be inherent in its structure. This friction can be good—it may make it less possible to get our structure into states that are inconsistent with the definition of the structure, or it may be bad—it may make it difficult to get something done.

4.4   Conclusions

Several formal concepts play an important role in modern data structure design—the use of big-O analysis to support claims of efficiency, the use of recursion to develop concise but powerful structures, and the use of induction to prove statements made about both data structures and algorithms. Mastery of these concepts improves one's approach to solving problems of data structure design.

The purpose of big-O analysis is to demonstrate upper bounds on the growth of functions that describe behavior of the structures we use. Since these are upper bounds, the tightest bounds provide the most information. Still, it is often not very difficult to identify the fastest-growing component of a function—analysis of that component is likely to lead to fairly tight bounds and useful results.

Self-reference is a powerful concept. When used to develop methods, we call this recursion. Recursion allows us to break down large problems into smaller problems whose solutions can be brought together to solve the original problem. Interestingly, recursion is often a suitable substitute for loops as a means of progressing through the problem solution, but compilers can often convert tail recursive code back into loops, for better performance. All terminating recursive methods involve at least one test that distinguishes the base case from the recursive, and every recursive program must eventually make progress toward a base case to construct a solution.

Mathematical induction provides a means of recursively generating proofs. Perhaps more than most other proof mechanisms, mathematical induction is a useful method for demonstrating a bound on a function, or the correct termination of a method. Since computers are not (yet) able to verify everyday inductive proofs, it is important that they be constructed with appropriate care. Knowing how to correctly base induction on special cases can be tricky and, as we have recently seen, difficult to verify.

In all these areas, practice makes perfect.

Self Check Problems

Solutions to these problems begin on page 430.

4.1   Suppose $f(x) = x$. What is its best growth rate, in big-O notation?

4.2   Suppose $f(x) = 3x$. What is its growth rate?

4.3   What is the growth rate of $f(x) = x + 900$?

4.4   How fast does $f(x)$ grow if $f(x) = x$ for odd integers and $f(x) = 900$ for even integers?

4.5   Evaluate and order the functions $\log_2 x$, $\sqrt{x}$, x, $30x$, x^2, 2^x, and $x!$ at $x = 2$, 4, 16, and 64. For each value of x, which is largest?

4.6   What are three features of recursive programs?

4.7   The latest Harry Potter book may be read by as much as 75 percent of the reading child population in the United States. Approximately how many child-years of reading time does this represent?

4.8   Given an infinite supply of 37 cent stamps, 21 cent stamps, and penny stamps a postmaster returns a minimum number of stamps composed of $c_{37}(x)$, $c_{21}(x)$, and $c_1(x)$ stamps for x dollars in change. What are the growth rates of these functions?

Problems

Solutions to the odd-numbered problems begin on page 448.

4.1   What is the time complexity associated with accessing a single value in an array? The `Vector` class is clearly more complex than the array. What is the time complexity of accessing an element with the `get` method?

4.2   What is the worst-case time complexity of the index-based `remove` code in the `Vector` class? What is the best-case time complexity? (You may assume the `Vector` does not get resized during this operation.)

4.3   What is the running time of the following method?

```
public static int reduce(int n)
{
    int result = 0;
    while (n > 1)
    {
        n = n/2;
        result = result+1;
    }
    return result;
}
```

4.4   What is the time complexity of determining the length of an n-character `null`-terminated string? What is the time complexity of determining the length of an n-character counted string?

4.5   What is the running time of the following matrix multiplication method?

```
// square matrix multiplication
// m1, m2, and result are n by n arrays
for (int row = 0; row < n; row++)
{
    for (int col = 0; col < n; col++)
    {
        int sum = 0;
        for (int entry = 0; entry < n; entry++)
        {
            sum = sum + m1[row][entry]*m2[entry][col];
        }
        result[row][col] = sum;
    }
}
```

4.6   In Definition 4.1 we see what it means for a function to be an upper bound. An alternative definition provides a *lower bound* for a function:

Definition 4.2 *A function $f(n)$ is $\Omega(g(n))$ (read "big-omega of g" or "at least order g"), if and only if there exist two positive constants, c and n_0, such that*

$$f(n) \geq c \cdot g(n)$$

for all $n \geq n_0$.

What is a lower bound on the time it takes to remove a value from a **Vector** by index?

4.7   What is a lower bound on adding a value to the end of a **Vector**? Does it matter that sometimes we may have to spend time doubling the size of the underlying array?

4.8   When discussing symmetry, we investigated a procedure that swapped two values within an array. Is it possible to write a routine that swaps two integer values? If so, provide the code; if not, indicate why.

4.9   For subtle reasons **String** objects cannot be modified. Instead, **Strings** are used as parameters to functions that build new **Strings**. Suppose that a is an n-character **String**. What is the time complexity of performing a=a+"!"?

4.10   Read Problem 4.9. Suppose that a and b are n-character **Strings**. What is the complexity of performing a=a+b?

4.11   What is the rate of growth (using big-O analysis) of the function $f(n) = n + \log n$? Justify your answer.

4.12   In this text, logarithms are assumed to be in base 2. Does it make a difference, from a complexity viewpoint?

4.13   What is the rate of growth of the function $\frac{1}{n} + 12$? Justify your answer.

4.14   What is the rate of growth of the function $\frac{\sin n}{n}$? Justify your answer.

4.15   Trick question: What is the rate of growth of $\tan n$?

4.16   Suppose n integers between 1 and 366 are presented as input, and you want to know if there are any duplicates. How would you solve this problem? What is the rate of growth of the function $T(n)$, describing the time it takes for you to determine if there are duplicates? (Hint: Pick an appropriate n_0.)

4.17   The first element of a *Syracuse sequence* is a positive integer s_0. The value s_i (for $i > 0$) is defined to be $s_{i-1}/2$ if s_{i-1} is even, or $3s_{i-1} + 1$ if s_{i-1} is odd. The sequence is finished when a 1 is encountered. Write a procedure to print the Syracuse sequence for any integer s_0. (It is not immediately obvious that this method should always terminate.)

4.18   Rewrite the **sqrt** function of Section 2.1 as a recursive procedure.

4.19   Write a recursive procedure to draw a line segment between (x_0, y_0) and (x_1, y_1) on a screen of pixels with integer coordinates. (Hint: The pixel closest to the midpoint is not far off the line segment.)

4.20   Rewrite the **reduce** method of Problem 4.3 as a recursive method.

4.21   One day you notice that integer multiplication no longer works. Write a recursive procedure to multiply two values a and b using only addition. What is the complexity of this function?

4.22   Modify the "stamp change" problem of Section 4.2.1 to report the number of each type of stamp to be found in the minimum stamp change.

4.23   Prove that $5^n - 4n - 1$ is divisible by 16 for all $n \geq 0$.

4.24   Prove Observation 4.3, that $\sum_{i=0}^{n} 2^i = 2^{n+1} - 1$ for $n \geq 0$.

4.25   Prove that a function n^c is $O(n^d)$ for any $d \geq c$.

4.26   Prove that $\sum_{i=1}^{n} 2i = n(n+1)$.

4.27   Prove that $\sum_{i=1}^{n} (2i-1) = n^2$.

4.28   Show that for $c \geq 2$ and $n \geq 0$, $\sum_{i=0}^{n} c^i = \frac{c^{n+1}+(c-2)}{c-1} - 1$.

4.29   Prove that $\sum_{i=1}^{n} \log i \leq n \log n$.

4.30   Some artists seek asymmetry. Physicists tell us the universe doesn't always appear symmetric. Why are we unfazed?

4.31   With a colleague, implement a fresh version of `Lists`. First, agree on the types and names of private fields. Then, going down the list of methods required by the `List` interface, split methods to be implemented between you by assigning every other method to your colleague. Bring the code together and compile it. What types of bugs occur? Did you depend on your colleague's code?

4.32   Consider the implementation of a `Ratio` data type. How does symmetry appear in this implementation?

4.33   In the `Vector` class, we extend by doubling, but we never discuss reducing by a similar technique. What is a good strategy?

4.34   Consider the following Java method:

```
static public int fido(int n)
// pre: n is a nonnegative integer
// post: result is the nth term from the sequence
//      1, 3, 7, 15, 31, 63, 127, ...
{
    int result = 1;
    if (n > 1) result = 1+fido(n-1)+fido(n-1);
    // assertion: the above if condition was tested
    //    fido(n) times while computing result
    return result;
}
```

a. What does it compute?

b. Prove or disprove the informal assertion following the `if` statement.

c. What is the time complexity of the method?

d. Why is `fido` an appropriate name for this method?

4.5 Laboratory: How Fast Is Java?

Objective. To develop an appreciation for the speed of basic Java operations including assignment of value to variables, arrays, and `Vectors`.

Discussion. How long does it take to add two integers in Java? How long does it take to assign a value to an entry in an array? The answers to these questions depend heavily on the type of environment a programmer is using and yet play an important role in evaluating the trade-offs in performance between different implementations of data structures.

If we are interested in estimating the time associated with an operation, it is difficult to measure it accurately with clocks available on most modern machines. If an operation takes 100 ns (*nanoseconds*, or billionths of a second), 10,000 of these operations can be performed within a single millisecond clock tick. It is unlikely that we would see a change in the millisecond clock while the operation is being performed.

One approach is to measure, say, the time it takes to perform a million of these operations, and divide that portion of the time associated with the operation by a million. The result *can* be a very accurate measurement of the time it takes to perform the operation. Several important things must be kept in mind:

- Different runs of the experiment can generate different times. This variation is unlikely to be due to significant differences in the speed of the operation, but instead to various interruptions that regularly occur when a program is running. Instead of computing the *average* of the running times, it is best to compute the *minimum* of the experiment's elapsed times. It's unlikely that this is much of an underestimate!

- Never perform input or output while you are timing an experiment. These operations are very expensive and variable. When reading or writing, make sure these operations appear before or after the experiment being timed.

- On modern systems there are many things happening concurrently with your program. Clocks tick forward, printer queues manage printers, network cards are accepting viruses. If you can keep your total experiment time below, say, a tenth of a second, it is likely that you will eliminate many of these distractions.

- The process of repeating an operation takes time. One of our tasks will be to measure the time it takes to execute an empty `for` loop. The loop, of course, is not really empty: it performs a test at the top of the loop and an increment at the bottom. Failing to account for the overhead of a `for` loop makes it impossible to measure any operation that is significantly faster.

- Good compilers can recognize certain operations that can be performed more efficiently in a different way. For example, traditional computers can assign a value of 0 much faster than the assignment of a value of 42. If an experiment yields an unexpectedly short operation time, change the Java to obscure any easy optimizations that may be performed. Don't forget to subtract the overhead of these obscuring operations!

Keeping a mindful eye on your experimental data will allow you to effectively measure very, very short events accurate to nanoseconds. In one nanosecond, light travels 11.80 inches!

Procedure. The ultimate goal of this experiment is a formally written lab report presenting your results. Carefully design your experiment, and be prepared to defend your approach. The data you collect here is experimental, and necessarily involves error. To reduce the errors described above, perform multiple runs of each experiment, and carefully document your findings. Your report should include results from the following experiments:

1. A description of the machine you are using. Make sure you use this machine for all of your experiments.

2. Write a short program to measure the time that elapses, say, when an empty `for` loop counts to one million. Print out the elapsed time, as well as the per-iteration elapsed time. Adjust the number of loops so that the total elapsed time falls between, say, one-hundredth and one-tenth of a second.

   Recall that we can measure times accurate to one-thousandth of a second using `System.currentTimeMillis()`:

   ```
   int i, loops;
   double speed;
   loops = 10000000;
   long start,stop,duration;

   start = System.currentTimeMillis();
   for (i = 0; i < loops; i++)
   {
       // code to be timed goes here
   }
   stop = System.currentTimeMillis();

   duration = stop-start;
   System.out.println("# Elapsed time: "+duration+"ms");
   System.out.println("# Mean time: "+
                   (((double)duration)/loops*NANOSPERMILLI)+
                   "nanoseconds");
   ```

3. Measure the time it takes to do a single integer assignment (e.g., `i=42;`). Do not forget to subtract the time associated with executing the `for` loop.

4. Measure the time it takes to assign an integer to an array entry. Make sure that the array has been allocated *before* starting the timing loop.

5. Measure the time it takes to assign a `String` reference to an array.

6. Measure the length of time it takes to assign a `String` to a `Vector`. (Note that it is not possible to directly assign an `int` to a `Vector` class.)

7. Copy one `Vector` to another, manually, using `set`. Carefully watch the elapsed time and do not include the time it takes to construct the two `Vectors`! Measure the time it takes to perform the copy for `Vectors` of different lengths. Does this appear to grow linearly?

Formally present your results in a write-up of your experiments.

Thought Questions. Consider the following questions as you complete the lab:

1. Your Java compiler and environment may have several switches that affect the performance of your program. For example, some environments allow the use of *just-in-time* (jit) compilers, that compile frequently used pieces of code (like your timing loop) into machine-specific instructions that are likely to execute faster. How does this affect your experiment?

2. How might you automatically guarantee that your total experiment time lasts between, say, 10 and 100 milliseconds?

3. It is, of course, possible for a timer to *underestimate* the running time of an instruction. For example, if you time a single assignment, it is certainly possible to get an elapsed time of 0—an impossibility. To what extent would a timing underestimate affect your results?

Notes:

Chapter 5

Sorting

"Come along, children. Follow me."
Before you could wink an eyelash
Jack, Knak, Lack, Mack,
Nack, Ouack, Pack, and Quack
fell into line, just as they had been taught.
—Robert McCloskey

COMPUTERS SPEND A CONSIDERABLE AMOUNT of their time keeping data in order. When we view a directory or folder, the items are sorted by name or type or modification date. When we search the Web, the results are returned sorted by "applicability." At the end of the month, our checks come back from the bank sorted by number, and our deposits are sorted by date. Clearly, in the grand scheme of things, sorting is an important function of computers. Not surprisingly, data structures can play a significant role in making sorts run quickly. This chapter begins an investigation of sorting methods.

5.1 Approaching the Problem

For the moment we assume that we will be sorting an unordered array of integers (see Figure 5.1a).[1] The problem is to arrange the integers so that every adjacent pair of values is in the correct order (see Figure 5.1b). A simple technique to sort the array is to pass through the array from left to right, swapping adjacent values that are out of order (see Figure 5.2). The exchange of values is accomplished with a utility method:

```
public static void swap(int data[], int i, int j)
// pre: 0 <= i,j < data.length
// post: data[i] and data[j] are exchanged
{
    int temp;
```

BubbleSort

---

[1] We focus on arrays of integers to maintain a simple approach. These techniques, of course, can be applied to vectors of objects, provided that some relative comparison can be made between two elements. This is discussed in Section 5.7.

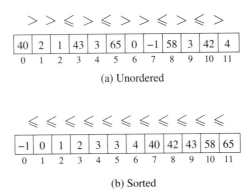

(a) Unordered

(b) Sorted

Figure 5.1   The relations between entries in unordered and sorted arrays of integers.

```
    temp = data[i];
    data[i] = data[j];
    data[j] = temp;
}
```

After a single pass the largest value will end up "bubbling" up to the high-indexed side of the array. The next pass will, at least, bubble up the next largest value, and so forth. The sort—called *bubble sort*—must be finished after $n - 1$ passes. Here is how we might write bubble sort in Java:

```
public static void bubbleSort(int data[], int n)
// pre: 0 <= n <= data.length
// post: values in data[0..n-1] in ascending order
{
    int numSorted = 0;      // number of values in order
    int index;              // general index
    while (numSorted < n)
    {
        // bubble a large element to higher array index
        for (index = 1; index < n-numSorted; index++)
        {
            if (data[index-1] > data[index])
                swap(data,index-1,index);
        }
        // at least one more value in place
        numSorted++;
    }
}
```

Observe that the only potentially time-consuming operations that occur in this sort are comparisons and exchanges. While the cost of comparing integers is

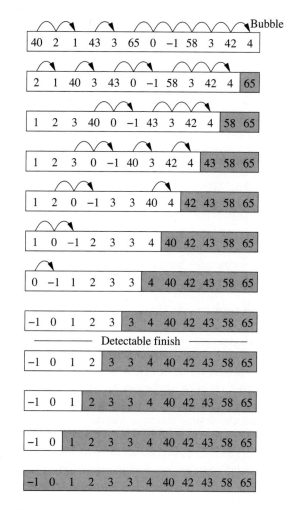

Figure 5.2 The passes of bubble sort: hops indicate "bubbling up" of large values. Shaded values are in sorted order. A pass with no exchanges indicates sorted data.

relatively small, if each element of the array were to contain a long string (for example, a DNA sequence) or a complex object (for example, a Library of Congress entry), then the comparison of two values might be a computationally intensive operation. Similarly, the cost of performing an exchange is to be avoided.[2] We can, therefore, restrict our attention to the number of comparison and exchange operations that occur in sorts in order to adequately evaluate their performance.

In bubble sort each pass of the bubbling phase performs $n-1$ comparisons and as many as $n-1$ exchanges. Thus the worst-case cost of performing bubble sort is $O((n-1)^2)$ or $O(n^2)$ operations. In the best case, none of the comparisons leads to an exchange. Even then, though, the algorithm has quadratic behavior.[3]

Most of us are inefficient sorters. Anyone having to sort a deck of cards or a stack of checks is familiar with the feeling that *there must be a better way to do this*. As we shall see, there probably is: most common sorting techniques used in day-to-day life run in $O(n^2)$ time, whereas the best single processor comparison-based sorting techniques are expected to run in only $O(n \log n)$ time. (If multiple processors are used, we can reduce this to $O(\log n)$ time, but that algorithm is beyond the scope of this text.) We shall investigate two sorting techniques that run in $O(n^2)$ time, on average, and two that run in $O(n \log n)$ time. In the end we will attempt to understand what makes the successful sorts successful.

Our first two sorting techniques are based on natural analogies.

5.2 Selection Sort

Children are perhaps the greatest advocates of *selection sort*. Every October, Halloween candies are consumed from best to worst. Whether daily sampling is limited or not, it is clear that choices of the next treat consumed are based on "the next biggest piece" or "the next-most favorite," and so on. Children consume treats in decreasing order of acceptability. Similarly, when we select plants from a greenhouse, check produce in the store, or pick strawberries from the farm we seek the best items first.

This selection process can be applied to an array of integers. Our goal is to identify the index of the largest element of the array. We begin by *assuming* that the first element is the largest, and then form a competition among all the remaining values. As we come across larger values, we update the index of the current maximum value. In the end, the index must point to the largest value. This code is idiomatic, so we isolate it here:

```
int index;   // general index
int max;     // index of largest value
```

SelectionSort

<hr>

[2] In languages like Java, where large objects are manipulated through references, the cost of an exchange is usually fairly trivial. In many languages, however, the cost of exchanging large values stored directly in the array is a real concern.

[3] If, as we noted in Figure 5.2, we detected the lack of exchanges, bubble sort would run in $O(n)$ time on data that were already sorted. Still, the average case would be quadratic.

```
// determine maximum value in array
max = 0;
for (index = 1; index < numUnsorted; index++)
{
    if (data[max] < data[index]) max = index;
}
```

(Notice that the maximum is not updated unless a *larger* value is found.) Now, consider where this maximum value would be found if the data were sorted: it should be clear to the right, in the highest indexed location. This is easily accomplished: we simply swap the last element of the unordered array with the maximum. Once this swap is completed, we know that at least that one value is in the correct location, and we logically reduce the size of the problem by one. If we remove the $n - 1$ largest values in successive passes (see Figure 5.3), we have selection sort. Here is how the entire method appears in Java:

```
public static void selectionSort(int data[], int n)
// pre: 0 <= n <= data.length
// post: values in data[0..n-1] are in ascending order
{
    int numUnsorted = n;
    int index;       // general index
    int max;         // index of largest value
    while (numUnsorted > 0)
    {
        // determine maximum value in array
        max = 0;
        for (index = 1; index < numUnsorted; index++)
        {
            if (data[max] < data[index]) max = index;
        }
        swap(data,max,numUnsorted-1);
        numUnsorted--;
    }
}
```

Selection sort potentially performs far fewer exchanges than bubble sort: selection sort performs exactly one per pass, while bubble sort performs as many as $n - 1$. Like bubble sort, however, selection sort demands $O(n^2)$ time for comparisons.

Interestingly, the performance of selection sort is independent of the order of the data: if the data are already sorted, it takes selection sort just as long to sort as if the data were unsorted. We can improve on this behavior through a slightly different analogy.

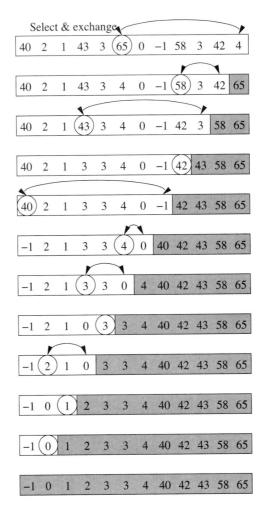

Figure 5.3   Profile of the passes of selection sort: shaded values are sorted. Circled values are maximum among unsorted values and are moved to the low end of sorted values on each pass.

5.3   Insertion Sort

Card players, when collecting a hand, often consider cards one at a time, inserting each into its sorted location. If we consider the "hand" to be the sorted portion of the array, and the "table" to be the unsorted portion, we develop a new sorting technique called *insertion sort*.

In the following Java implementation of insertion sort, the sorted values are kept in the low end of the array, and the unsorted values are found at the high end (see Figure 5.4). The algorithm consists of several "passes" of inserting the lowest-indexed unsorted value into the list of sorted values. Once this is done, of course, the list of sorted values increases by one. This process continues until each of the unsorted values has been incorporated into the sorted portion of the array. Here is the code:

InsertionSort

```java
public static void insertionSort(int data[], int n)
// pre: 0 <= n <= data.length
// post: values in data[0..n-1] are in ascending order
{
    int numSorted = 1;      // number of values in place
    int index;              // general index
    while (numSorted < n)
    {
        // take the first unsorted value
        int temp = data[numSorted];
        // ...and insert it among the sorted:
        for (index = numSorted; index > 0; index--)
        {
            if (temp < data[index-1])
            {
                data[index] = data[index-1];
            } else {
                break;
            }
        }
        // reinsert value
        data[index] = temp;
        numSorted++;
    }
}
```

A total of $n - 1$ passes are made over the array, with a new unsorted value inserted each time. The value inserted may not be a new minimum or maximum value. Indeed, if the array was initially unordered, the value will, on average, end up near the middle of the previously sorted values. On random data the running time of insertion sort is expected to be dominated by $O(n^2)$ compares and data movements (most of the compares will lead to the movement of a data value).

If the array is initially in order, one compare is needed at every pass to determine that the value is already in the correct location. Thus, the inner loop

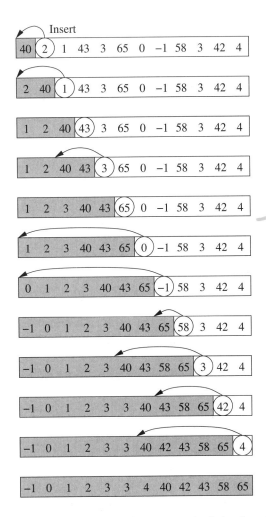

Figure 5.4   Profile of the passes of insertion sort: shaded values form a "hand" of sorted values. Circled values are successively inserted into the hand.

is executed exactly once for each of $n - 1$ passes. The best-case running time performance of the sort is therefore dominated by $O(n)$ comparisons (there are no movements of data within the array). Because of this characteristic, insertion sort is often used when data are very nearly ordered (imagine sorting a phone book after a month of new customers has been appended).

In contrast, if the array was previously in reverse order, the value must be compared with *every* sorted value to find the correct location. As the comparisons are made, the larger values are moved to the right to make room for the new value. The result is that each of $O(n^2)$ compares leads to a data movement, and the worst-case running time of the algorithm is $O(n^2)$.

Note that each of these sorts uses a linear number of data cells. Not every sorting technique is able to live within this constraint.

5.4   Mergesort

Suppose that two friends are to sort an array of values. One approach might be to divide the deck in half. Each person then sorts one of two half-decks. The sorted deck is then easily constructed by combining the two sorted half-decks. This careful interleaving of sorted values is called a *merge*.

It is straightforward to see that a merge takes at least $O(n)$ time, because every value has to be moved into the destination deck. Still, within $n - 1$ comparisons, the merge must be finished. Since each of the $n - 1$ comparisons (and potential movements of data) takes at most constant time, the merge is no worse than linear.

There are, of course, some tricky aspects to the merge operation—for example, it is possible that all the cards in one half-deck are smaller than all the cards in the other. Still, the performance of the following merge code is $O(n)$:

MergeSort

```
private static void merge(int data[], int temp[],
                          int low, int middle, int high)
// pre: data[middle..high] are ascending
//      temp[low..middle-1] are ascending
// post: data[low..high] contains all values in ascending order
{
    int ri = low; // result index
    int ti = low; // temp index
    int di = middle; // destination index
    // while two lists are not empty merge smaller value
    while (ti < middle && di <= high)
    {
        if (data[di] < temp[ti]) {
            data[ri++] = data[di++]; // smaller is in high data
        } else {
            data[ri++] = temp[ti++]; // smaller is in temp
        }
    }
    // possibly some values left in temp array
```

```
        while (ti < middle)
        {
            data[ri++] = temp[ti++];
        }
        // ...or some values left (in correct place) in data array
    }
```

This code is fairly general, but a little tricky to understand (see Figure 5.5). We assume that the data from the two lists are located in the two arrays—in the lower half of the range in `temp` and in the upper half of the range in `data` (see Figure 5.5a). The first loop compares the first remaining element of each list to determine which should be copied over to the result list first (Figure 5.5b). That loop continues until one list is emptied (Figure 5.5c). If `data` is the emptied list, the remainder of the `temp` list is transferred (Figure 5.5d). If the `temp` list was emptied, the remainder of the `data` list is already located in the correct place!

Returning to our two friends, we note that before the two lists are merged each of the two friends is faced with sorting half the cards. How should this be done? If a deck contains fewer than two cards, it's already sorted. Otherwise, each person could recursively hand off half of his or her respective deck (now one-fourth of the entire deck) to a new individual. Once these small sorts are finished, the quarter decks are merged, finishing the sort of the half decks, and the two half decks are merged to construct a completely sorted deck. Thus, we might consider a new sort, called *mergesort*, that recursively splits, sorts, and reconstructs, through merging, a deck of cards. The logical "phases" of mergesort are depicted in Figure 5.6.

```
    private static void mergeSortRecursive(int data[],
                                           int temp[],
                                           int low, int high)
    // pre: 0 <= low <= high < data.length
    // post: values in data[low..high] are in ascending order
    {
        int n = high-low+1;
        int middle = low + n/2;
        int i;

        if (n < 2) return;
        // move lower half of data into temporary storage
        for (i = low; i < middle; i++)
        {
            temp[i] = data[i];
        }
        // sort lower half of array
        mergeSortRecursive(temp,data,low,middle-1);
        // sort upper half of array
        mergeSortRecursive(data,temp,middle,high);
        // merge halves together
        merge(data,temp,low,middle,high);
    }
```

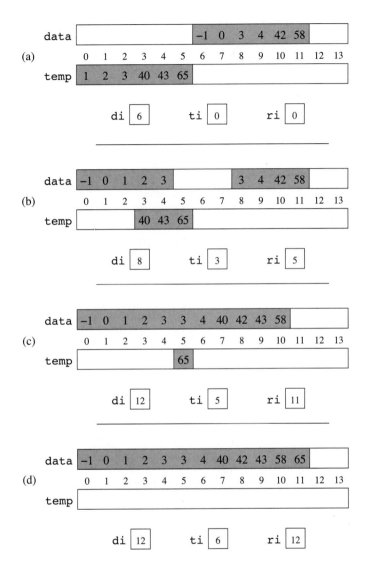

Figure 5.5 Four stages of a merge of two six element lists (shaded entries are participating values): (a) the initial location of data; (b) the merge of several values; (c) the point at which a list is emptied; and (d) the final result.

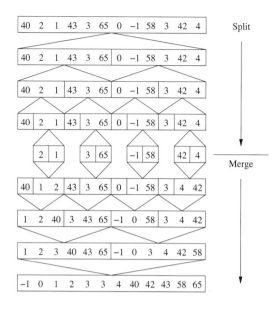

Figure 5.6 Profile of mergesort: values are recursively split into unsorted lists that are then recursively merged into ascending order.

Note that this sort requires a temporary array to perform the merging. This temporary array is only used by a single merge at a time, so it is allocated once and garbage collected after the sort. We hide this detail with a public wrapper procedure that allocates the array and calls the recursive sort:

```
public static void mergeSort(int data[], int n)
// pre: 0 <= n <= data.length
// post: values in data[0..n-1] are in ascending order
{
    mergeSortRecursive(data,new int[n],0,n-1);
}
```

Clearly, the depth of the splitting is determined by the number of times that n can be divided in two and still have a value of 1 or greater: $\log_2 n$. At each level of splitting, every value must be merged into its respective subarray. It follows that at each logical level, there are $O(n)$ compares over all the merges. Since there are $\log_2 n$ levels, we have $O(n \cdot \log n)$ units of work in performing a mergesort.

Mergesort is a common technique for sorting large sets of data that do not fit completely in fast memory. Instead, the data are saved in temporary files that are merged together. When the recursion splits the collection into subsets of a manageable size, they can be sorted using other techniques, if desired.

One of the unappealing aspects of mergesort is that it is difficult to merge two lists without significant extra memory. If we could avoid the use of this extra space without significant increases in the number of comparisons or data movements, then we would have an excellent sorting technique. Our next method demonstrates an $O(n \log n)$ method that requires significantly less space.

5.5   Quicksort

Since the process of sorting numbers consists of moving each value to its ultimate location in the sorted array, we might make some progress toward a solution if we could move *a single value* to its ultimate location. This idea forms the basis of a fast sorting technique called *quicksort*.

One way to find the correct location of, say, the leftmost value—called a *pivot*—in an unsorted array is to rearrange the values so that all the smaller values appear to the left of the pivot, and all the larger values appear to the right. One method of partitioning the data is shown here. It returns the final location for what was originally the leftmost value:

```
private static int partition(int data[], int left, int right)
// pre: left <= right
// post: data[left] placed in the correct (returned) location
{
    while (true)
    {
        // move right "pointer" toward left
        while (left < right && data[left] < data[right]) right--;
        if (left < right) swap(data,left++,right);
        else return left;
        // move left pointer toward right
        while (left < right && data[left] < data[right]) left++;
        if (left < right) swap(data,left,right--);
        else return right;
    }
}
```

QuickSort

The indices `left` and `right` start at the two ends of the array (see Figure 5.7) and move toward each other until they coincide. The pivot value, being leftmost in the array, is indexed by `left`. Everything to the left of `left` is smaller than the pivot, while everything to the right of `right` is larger. Each step of the main loop compares the left and right values and, if they're out of order, exchanges them. Every time an exchange occurs the index (`left` or `right`) that references the pivot value is alternated. In any case, the nonpivot variable is moved toward the other. Since, at each step, `left` and `right` move one step closer to each other, within n steps, `left` and `right` are equal, and they point to the current location of the pivot value. Since only smaller values are to the left of the pivot, and larger values are to the right, the pivot must be located in its final location. Values correctly located are shaded in Figure 5.8.

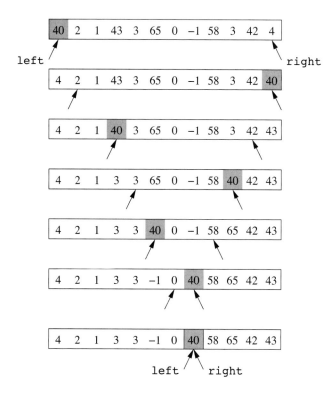

Figure 5.7   The partitioning of an array's values based on the (shaded) pivot value 40. Snapshots depict the state of the data after the **if** statements of the **partition** method.

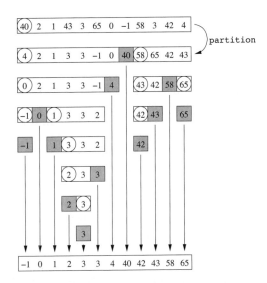

Figure 5.8   Profile of quicksort: leftmost value (the circled *pivot*) is used to position value in final location (indicated by shaded) and partition array into relatively smaller and larger values. Recursive application of partitioning leads to quicksort.

Because the pivot segregates the larger and smaller values, we know that none of these values will appear on the opposite side of the pivot in the final arrangement. This suggests that we can reduce the sorting of a problem of size n to two problems of size approximately $\frac{n}{2}$. To finish the sort, we need only recursively sort the values to the left and right of the pivot:

```
public static void quickSort(int data[], int n)
// post: the values in data[0..n-1] are in ascending order
{
    quickSortRecursive(data,0,n-1);
}

private static void quickSortRecursive(int data[],int left,int right)
// pre: left <= right
// post: data[left..right] in ascending order
{
    int pivot;    // the final location of the leftmost value
    if (left >= right) return;
    pivot = partition(data,left,right);      /* 1 - place pivot */
    quickSortRecursive(data,left,pivot-1); /* 2 - sort small */
    quickSortRecursive(data,pivot+1,right);/* 3 - sort large */
    /* done! */
}
```

In practice, of course, the splitting of the values is not always optimal (see the placement of the value 4 in Figure 5.8), but a careful analysis suggests that even with these "tough breaks" quicksort takes only $O(n \log n)$ time.

When either sorted or reverse-sorted data are to be sorted by quicksort, the results are disappointing. This is because the pivot value selected (here, the leftmost value) finds its ultimate location at one end of the array or the other. This reduces the sort of n values to $n - 1$ values (and *not* $n/2$), and the sort requires $O(n)$ passes of an $O(n)$ step partition. The result is an $O(n^2)$ sort. Since nearly sorted data are fairly common, this result is to be avoided.

Notice that picking the leftmost value is not special. If, instead, we attempt to find the correct location for the middle value, then other arrangements of data will cause the degenerate behavior. In short, for any specific or *deterministic* partitioning technique, a degenerate arrangement exists. The key to more consistent performance, then, is a *nondeterministic* partitioning that correctly places a value selected at random (see Problem 5.15). There is, of course, a very unlikely chance that the data are in order *and* the positions selected induce a degenerate behavior, but that chance is small and successive runs of the sorting algorithm on the same data are exceedingly unlikely to exhibit the same behavior. So, although the worst-case behavior is still $O(n^2)$, its expected behavior is $O(n \log n)$.

Quicksort is an excellent sort when data are to be sorted with little extra space. Because the speed of partitioning depends on the random access nature of arrays or `Vectors`, quicksort is not suitable when not used with random access structures. In these cases, however, other fast sorts are often possible.

5.6   Radix Sort

After investigating a number of algorithms that sort in $O(n^2)$ or $O(n \log n)$ time, one might wonder if it is possible to sort in linear time. If the right conditions hold, we can sort certain types of data in linear time. First, we must investigate a pseudogame, 52 pickup!

Suppose we drop a deck of 52 cards on the floor, and we want to not only pick them up, but we wish to sort them at the same time. It might be most natural to use an insertion sort: we keep a pile of sorted cards and, as we pick up new cards, we insert them in the deck in the appropriate position. A more efficient approach makes use of the fact that we know what the sorted deck looks like. We simply lay out the cards in a row, with each position in the row reserved for the particular card. As we pick up a card, we place it in its reserved location. In the end, all the cards are in their correct location and we collect them from left to right.

Exercise 5.1 *Explain why this sorting technique always takes $O(n)$ time for a deck of n cards.*

Such an approach is the basis for a general sorting technique called *bucket sort*. By quickly inspecting values (perhaps a word) we can approximately sort them into different buckets (perhaps based on the first letter). In a subsequent pass we can sort the values in each bucket with, perhaps a different sort. The buckets of sorted values are then accumulated, carefully maintaining the order of the buckets, and the result is completely sorted. Unfortunately, the worst-case behavior of this sorting technique is determined by the performance of the algorithm we use to sort each bucket of values.

Exercise 5.2 *Suppose we have n values and m buckets and we use insertion sort to perform the sort of each bucket. What is the worst-case time complexity of this sort?*

Such a technique can be used to sort integers, especially if we can partially sort the values based on a single digit. For example, we might develop a support function, `digit`, that, given a number n and a decimal place d, returns the value of the digit in the particular decimal place. If d was 0, it would return the units digit of n. Here is a recursive implementation:

```
public static int digit(int n, int d)
// pre: n >= 0 and d >= 0
// post: returns the value of the dth decimal place of n
//    where the units place has position 0
{
    if (d == 0) return n % 10;
    else return digit(n/10,d-1);
}
```

RadixSort

Here is the code for placing an array of integer values among 10 buckets, based on the value of digit d. For example, if we have numbers between 1 and 52 and we set d to 2, this code almost sorts the values based on their 10's digit.

```
public static void bucketPass(int data[], int d)
// pre: data is an array of data values, and d >= 0
// post: data is sorted by the digit found in location d;
// if two values have the same digit in location d, their
// relative positions do not change; i.e., they are not swapped
{
    int i,j;
    int value;
    // allocate some buckets
    Vector bucket[] = new Vector[10];
    // allocate Vectors to hold values in each bucket
    for (j = 0; j < 10; j++) bucket[j] = new Vector();
    // distribute the data among buckets
    int n = data.length;
    for (i = 0; i < n; i++)
    {
        value = data[i];
        // determine the d'th digit of value
        j = digit(value,d);
```

```
            // add data value to end of vector; keeps values in order
            bucket[j].add(new Integer(value));
        }
        // collect data from buckets back into array
        // collect in reverse order to unload Vectors
        // in linear time
        i = n;
        for (j = 9; j >= 0; j--)
        {
            // unload all values in bucket j
            while (!bucket[j].isEmpty())
            {
                i--;
                value = ((Integer)bucket[j].remove()).intValue();
                data[i] = value;
            }
        }
    }
```

We now have the tools to support a new sort, *radix sort*. The approach is to use the bucketPass code to sort all the values based on the units place. Next, all the values are sorted based on their 10's digit. The process continues until enough passes have been made to consider all the digits. If it is known that values are bounded above, then we can also bound the number of passes as well. Here is the code to perform a radix sort of values under 1 million (six passes):

```
public static void radixSort(int data[])
// pre: data is array of values; each is less than 10,000,000
// post: data in the array are sorted into increasing order
{
    for (int i = 0; i < 6; i++)
    {
        bucketPass(data,i);
    }
}
```

After the first bucketPass, the values are ordered, based on their units digit. All values that end in 0 are placed near the front of data (see Figure 5.9), all the values that end in 9 appear near the end. Among those values that end in 0, the values appear *in the order they originally appeared in the array*. In this regard, we can say that bucketPass is a *stable* sorting technique. All other things being equal, the values appear in their original order.

During the second pass, the values are sorted, based on their 10's digit. Again, if two values have the same 10's digit, the relative order of the values is maintained. That means, for example, that 140 will appear before 42, because after the first pass, the 140 appeared before the 42. The process continues, until all digits are considered. Here, six passes are performed, but only three are necessary (see Problem 5.9).

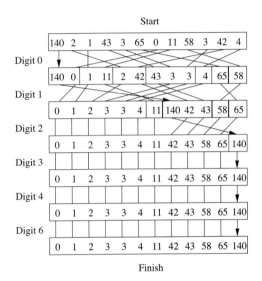

Figure 5.9 The state of the `data` array between the six passes of `radixSort`. The boundaries of the buckets are identified by vertical lines; bold lines indicate empty buckets. Since, on every pass, paths of incoming values to a bucket do not cross, the sort is stable. Notice that after three passes, the `radixSort` is finished. The same would be true, no matter the number of values, as long as they were all under 1000.

There are several important things to remember about the construction of this sort. First, `bucketPass` is stable. That condition is necessary if the work of previous passes is not to be undone. Secondly, the sort is unlikely to work if the passes are performed from the most significant digit toward the units digit. Finally, since the number of passes is independent of the size of the `data` array, the speed of the entire sort is proportional to the speed of a single pass. Careful design allows the `bucketPass` to be accomplished in $O(n)$ time. We see, then, that `radixSort` is a $O(n)$ sorting method.

While, theoretically, `radixSort` can be accomplished in linear time, practically, the constant of proportionality associated with the bound is large compared to the other sorts we have seen in this chapter. In practice, `radixSort` is inefficient compared to most other sorts.

5.7 Sorting Objects

Sorting arrays of integers is suitable for understanding the performance of various sorts, but it is hardly a real-world problem. Frequently, the object that needs to be sorted is an `Object` with many fields, only some of which are actually used in making a comparison.

Let's consider the problem of sorting the entries associated with an electronic phone book. The first step is to identify the structure of a single entry in the phone book. Perhaps it has the following form:

PhoneBook

```
class PhoneEntry
{
    String name;        // person's name
    String title;       // person's title
    int extension;      // telephone number
    int room;           // number of room
    String building;    // office building

    public PhoneEntry(String n, String t, int e,
                      String b, int r)
    // post: construct a new phone entry
    {
        ...
    }

    public int compareTo(PhoneEntry other)
    // pre: other is non-null
    // post: returns integer representing relation between values
    {
        return this.extension - other.extension;
    }
}
```

We have added the `compareTo` method to describe the relation between two entries in the phone book (the shaded fields of Figure 5.10). The `compareTo`

0	Blumenauer, Earl	Rep.	54881	1406	Longworth
1	DeFazio, Peter	Rep.	56416	2134	Rayburn
2	Hooley, Darlene	Rep.	55711	1130	Longworth
3	Smith, Gordon	Senator	43753	404	Russell
4	Walden, Greg	Rep.	56730	1404	Longworth
5	Wu, David	Rep.	50855	1023	Longworth
6	Wyden, Ron	Senator	45244	516	Hart

Data before sorting

0	Smith, Gordon	Senator	43753	404	Russell
1	Wyden, Ron	Senator	45244	516	Hart
2	Wu, David	Rep.	50855	1023	Longworth
3	Blumenauer, Earl	Rep.	54881	1406	Longworth
4	Hooley, Darlene	Rep.	55711	1130	Longworth
5	DeFazio, Peter	Rep.	56416	2134	Rayburn
6	Walden, Greg	Rep.	56730	1404	Longworth

Data after sorting by telephone

Figure 5.10   An array of phone entries for the 107th Congressional Delegation from Oregon State, before and after sorting by telephone (shaded).

method returns an integer that is less than, equal to, or greater than 0 when this is logically less than, equal to, or greater than other. We can now modify any of the sort techniques provided in the previous section to sort an array of phone entries:

```
public static void insertionSort(PhoneEntry data[], int n)
// pre: n <= data.length
// post: values in data[0..n-1] are in ascending order
{
    int numSorted = 1;     // number of values in place
    int index;             // general index
    while (numSorted < n)
    {
        // take the first unsorted value
        PhoneEntry temp = data[numSorted];
        // ...and insert it among the sorted:
        for (index = numSorted; index > 0; index--)
        {
```

```
                    if (temp.compareTo(data[index-1]) < 0)
                    {
                        data[index] = data[index-1];
                    } else {
                        break;
                    }
                }
                // reinsert value
                data[index] = temp;
                numSorted++;
            }
        }
```

Careful review of this insertion sort routine shows that all the < operators have been replaced by checks for negative `compareTo` values. The result is that the phone entries in the array are ordered by increasing phone number.

If two or more people use the same extension, then the order of the resulting entries depends on the stability of the sort. If the sort is stable, then the relative order of the phone entries with identical extensions in the sorted array is the same as their relative order in the unordered array. If the sort is not stable, no guarantee can be made. To ensure that entries are, say, sorted in increasing order by extension and, in case of shared phones, sorted by increasing name, the following `compareTo` method might be used:

```
public int compareTo(PhoneEntry other)
// pre: other is non-null
// post: returns integer representing relation between values
{
    if (this.extension != other.extension)
        return this.extension - other.extension;
    else return this.name.compareTo(other.name);
}
```

Correctly specifying the relation between two objects with the `compareTo` method can be difficult when the objects cannot be *totally ordered*. Is it always possible that one athletic team is strictly less than another? Is it always the case that one set contains another? No. These are examples of domains that are *partially ordered*. Usually, however, most types may be totally ordered, and imagining how one might *sort* a collection of objects forces a suitable relation between any pair.

5.8   Ordering Objects Using Comparators

The definition of the `compareTo` method for an object should define, in a sense, the natural ordering of the objects. So, for example, in the case of a phone book, the entries would ideally be ordered based on the name associated with the entry. Sometimes, however, the `compareTo` method does not provide the ordering desired, or worse, the `compareTo` method has not been defined for an object. In these cases, the programmer turns to a simple method for specifing an external comparison method called a *comparator*. A comparator is an object that contains a method that is capable of comparing two objects. Sorting methods, then, can be developed to apply a comparator to two objects when a comparison is to be performed. The beauty of this mechanism is that different comparators can be applied to the same data to sort in different orders or on different keys. In Java a comparator is any class that implements the `java.util.Comparator` interface. This interface provides the following method:

Comparator

```
package java.util;
public interface Comparator
{
    public abstract int compare(Object a, Object b);
    // pre: a and b are valid objects, likely of similar type
    // post: returns a value less than, equal to, or greater than 0
    //       if a is less than, equal to, or greater than b
}
```

Like the `compareTo` method we have seen earlier, the `compare` method returns an integer that identifies the relationship between two values. Unlike the `compareTo` method, however, the `compare` method is not associated with the compared objects. As a result, the comparator is not privy to the implementation of the objects; it must perform the comparison based on information that is gained from accessor methods.

As an example of the implementation of a `Comparator`, we consider the implementation of a case-insensitive comparison of `Strings`, called `Caseless-Comparator`. This comparison method converts both `String` objects to uppercase and then performs the standard `String` comparison:

Caseless-
Comparator

```
public class CaselessComparator implements java.util.Comparator
{
    public int compare(Object a, Object b)
    // pre: a and b are valid Strings
    // post: returns a value less than, equal to, or greater than 0
    //       if a is less than, equal to, or greater than b, without
    //       consideration of case
    {
        String upperA = ((String)a).toUpperCase();
        String upperB = ((String)b).toUpperCase();
        return upperA.compareTo(upperB);
    }
}
```

The result of the comparison is that strings that are spelled similarly in different cases appear together. For example, if an array contains the words of the children's tongue twister:

```
Fuzzy Wuzzy was a bear.
```

Fuzzy Wuzzy had no hair.
Fuzzy Wuzzy wasn't fuzzy, wuzzy?

we would expect the words to be sorted into the following order:

a bear. Fuzzy Fuzzy Fuzzy fuzzy, had hair.
no was wasn't Wuzzy Wuzzy Wuzzy wuzzy?

This should be compared with the standard ordering of String values, which
would generate the following output:

Fuzzy Fuzzy Fuzzy Wuzzy Wuzzy Wuzzy a bear.
fuzzy, had hair. no was wasn't wuzzy?

To use a Comparator in a sorting technique, we need only replace the use
of compareTo methods with compare methods from a Comparator. Here, for
example, is an insertion sort that makes use of a Comparator to order the values
in an array of Objects:

CompInsSort

```
public static void insertionSort(Object data[], Comparator c)
// pre: c compares objects found in data
// post: values in data[0..n-1] are in ascending order
{
    int numSorted = 1;      // number of values in place
    int index;              // general index
    int n = data.length;    // length of the array
    while (numSorted < n)
    {
        // take the first unsorted value
        Object temp = data[numSorted];
        // ...and insert it among the sorted:
        for (index = numSorted; index > 0; index--)
        {
            if (c.compare(temp,data[index-1]) < 0)
            {
                data[index] = data[index-1];
            } else {
                break;
            }
        }
        // reinsert value
        data[index] = temp;
        numSorted++;
    }
}
```

Note that in this description we don't see the particulars of the types involved.
Instead, all data are manipulated as Objects, which are specifically manipulated
by the compare method of the provided Comparator.

5.9 Vector-Based Sorting

We extend the phone book example one more time, by allowing the `PhoneEntrys` to be stored in a `Vector`. There are, of course, good reasons to use `Vector` over arrays, but there are some added complexities that should be considered. Here is an alternative Java implementation of `insertionSort` that is dedicated to the sorting of a `Vector` of `PhoneEntrys`:

PhoneBook

```java
protected void swap(int i, int j)
// pre: 0 <= i,j < this.size
// post: elements i and j are exchanged within the vector
{
    Object temp;
    temp = get(i);
    set(i,get(j));
    set(j,temp);
}


public void insertionSort()
// post: values of vector are in ascending order
{
    int numSorted = 0;      // number of values in place
    int index;              // general index
    while (numSorted < size())
    {
        // take the first unsorted value
        PhoneEntry temp = (PhoneEntry)get(numSorted);
        // ...and insert it among the sorted:
        for (index = numSorted; index > 0; index--)
        {
            if (temp.compareTo((PhoneEntry)get(index-1)) < 0)
            {
                set(index,get(index-1));
            } else {
                break;
            }
        }
        // reinsert value
        set(index,temp);
        numSorted++;
    }
}
```

Recall that, for `Vectors`, we use the `get` method to fetch a value and `set` to store. Since any type of object may be referenced by a vector entry, we verify the type expected when a value is retrieved from the vector. This is accomplished through a parenthesized *cast*. If the type of the fetched value doesn't match the type of the cast, the program throws a *class cast exception*. Here, we cast the result of `get` in the `compareTo` method to indicate that we are comparing `PhoneEntrys`.

It is unfortunate that the `insertionSort` has to be specially coded for use with the `PhoneEntry` objects.

Exercise 5.3 *Write an* `insertionSort` *that uses a* `Comparator` *to sort a* `Vector` *of objects.*

5.10   Conclusions

Sorting is an important and common process on computers. In this chapter we considered several sorting techniques with quadratic running times. Bubble sort approaches the problem by checking and rechecking the relationships between elements. Selection and insertion sorts are based on techniques that people commonly use. Of these, insertion sort is most frequently used; it is easily coded and provides excellent performance when data are nearly sorted.

Two recursive sorting techniques, mergesort and quicksort, use recursion to achieve $O(n \log n)$ running times, which are optimal for comparison-based techniques on single processors. Mergesort works well in a variety of situations, but often requires significant extra memory. Quicksort requires a random access structure, but runs with little space overhead. Quicksort is not a stable sort because it has the potential to swap two values with equivalent keys.

We have seen with radix sort, it is possible to have a linear sorting algorithm, but it cannot be based on compares. Instead, the technique involves carefully ordering values based on looking at portions of the key. The technique is, practically, not useful for general-purpose sorting, although for many years, punched cards were efficiently sorted using precisely the method described here.

Sorting is, arguably, the most frequently executed algorithm on computers today. When we consider the notion of an *ordered structure*, we will find that algorithms and structures work hand in hand to help keep data in the correct order.

Self Check Problems

Solutions to these problems begin on page 431.

5.1   Why does it facilitate the `swap` method to have a temporary reference?

5.2   Cover the numbers below with your hand. Now, moving your hand to the right, expose each number in turn. On a separate sheet of paper, keep the list of values you have encounted in order. At the end you have sorted all of the values. Which sorting technique are you using?

| 296 | 457 | -95 | 39 | 21 | 12 | 3.1 | 64 | 998 | 989 |

5.3   Copy the above table onto a piece of scrap paper. Start a column of numbers: write down the smallest table value you see into your column, crossing it out of the table. Continue until you have considered each of the values. What sorting technique are you using?

5.4   During spring cleaning, you decide to sort four months of checks returned with your bank statements. You decide to sort each month separately and go from there. Is this valid? If not, why. If it is, what happens next?

5.5   A postal employee approximately sorts mail into, say, 10 piles based on the magnitude of the street number of each address, pile 1 has 1-10, pile 2 has 11-20, etc. The letters are then collected together by increasing pile number. She then sorts them into a delivery crate with dividers labeled with street names. The order of streets corresponds to the order they appear on her mail route. What type of sort is she performing?

5.6   What is the purpose of the `compareTo` method?

Problems

Solutions to the odd-numbered problems begin on page 450.

5.1   Show that to exchange two integer values it is not strictly necessary to use a third, temporary integer variable. (Hint: Use addition and/or subtraction.)

5.2   We demonstrated that, in the worst case, bubble sort performs $O(n^2)$ operations. We assumed, however, that each pass performed approximately $O(n)$ operations. In fact, pass i performs as many as $O(n - i)$ operations, for $1 \leq i \leq n - 1$. Show that bubble sort still takes $O(n^2)$ time.

5.3   How does `bubbleSort` (as presented) perform in the best and average cases?

5.4   On any pass of bubble sort, if no exchanges are made, then the relations between all the values are those desired, and the sort is done. Using this information, how fast will bubble sort run in worst, best, and average cases?

5.5   How fast does selection sort run in the best, worst, and average cases?

5.6   How fast does insertion sort run in the best, worst, and average cases? Give examples of best- and worst-case input for insertion sort.

5.7   Running an actual program, count the number of compares needed to sort n values using insertion sort, where n varies (e.g., powers of 2). Plot your data. Do the same thing for quicksort. Do the curves appear as theoretically expected? Does insertion sort ever run faster than quicksort? If so, at what point does it run slower?

5.8   Comparing insertion sort to quicksort, it appears that quicksort sorts more quickly without any increase in space. Is that true?

5.9   At the end of the discussion on radix sort, we pointed out that the digit sorting passes must occur from right to left. Give an example of an array of 5 two-digit values that do not sort properly if you perform the passes left to right.

5.10   In radix sort, it might be useful to terminate the sorting process when numbers do not change position during a call to `bucketPass`. Should this modification be adopted or not?

5.11   Using the millisecond timer, determine the length of time it takes to perform an assignment of a nonzero value to an `int`. (Hint: It will take less than a millisecond, so you will have to design several experiments that measure thousands or millions of assignments; see the previous lab, on page 103, for details.)

5.12   Running an actual program, and using the millisecond timer, `System.-currentTimeMillis`, measure the length of time needed to sort arrays of data of various sizes using a sort of your choice. Repeat the experiment but use `Vector`s. Is there a difference? In either case, explain why. (Hint: You may have to develop code along the lines of Problem 5.11.)

5.13   A sort is said to be *stable* if the order of equal values is maintained throughout the sort. Bubble sort is stable, because whenever two equal values are compared, no exchange occurs. Which other sorts are stable (consider insertion sort, selection sort, mergesort, and quicksort)?

5.14   The `partition` function of quicksort could be changed as follows: To place the leftmost value in the correct location, count the number of values that are strictly less than the leftmost value. The resulting number is the correct index for the desired value. Exchange the leftmost value for the value at the indexed location. With all other code left as it is, does this support a correctly functioning quicksort? If not, explain why.

5.15   Modify the `partition` method used by quicksort so that the pivot is randomly selected. (Hint: Before partitioning, consider placing the randomly selected value at the left side of the array.)

5.16   Write a recursive `selectionSort` algorithm. (Hint: Each level of recursion positions a value in the correct location.)

5.17   Write a recursive `insertionSort` algorithm.

5.18   Some of the best-performing sorts depend on the best-performing shuffles. A good shuffling technique rearranges data into any arrangement with equal probability. Design the most efficient shuffling mechanism you can, and argue its quality. What is its performance?

5.19   Write a program called `shuffleSort`. It first checks to see if the data are in order. If they are, the sort is finished. If they aren't, the data are shuffled and the process repeats. What is the best-case running time? Is there a worst-case running time? Why or why not? If each time the data were shuffled they were arranged in a never-seen-before configuration, would this change your answer?

5.20   Write a program to sort a list of unique integers between 0 and 1 million, but only using 1000 32-bit integers of space. The integers are read from a file.

5.11 Laboratory: Sorting with Comparators

Objective. To gain experience with Java's `java.util.Comparator` interface.

Discussion. In Chapter 5 we have seen a number of different sorting techniques. Each of the techniques demonstrated was based on the fixed, natural ordering of values found in an array. In this lab we will modify the `Vector` class so that it provides a method, `sort`, that can be used—with the help of a `Comparator`—to order the elements of the `Vector` in any of a number of different ways.

Procedure. Develop an extension of `structure.Vector`, called `MyVector`, that includes a new method, `sort`.

Here are some steps toward implementing this new class:

1. Create a new class, `MyVector`, which is declared to be an extension of the `structure.Vector` class. You should write a default constructor for this class that simply calls `super();`. This will force the `structure.Vector` constructor to be called. This, in turn, will initialize the protected fields of the `Vector` class.

2. Construct a new `Vector` method called `sort`. It should have the following declaration:

   ```
   public void sort(Comparator c)
   // pre: c is a valid comparator
   // post: sorts this vector in order determined by c
   ```

   This method uses a `Comparator` type object to actually perform a sort of the values in `MyVector`. You may use any sort that you like.

3. Write an application that reads in a data file with several fields, and, depending on the `Comparator` used, sorts and prints the data in different orders.

Thought Questions. Consider the following questions as you complete the lab:

1. Suppose we write the following `Comparator`:

   ```java
   import structure.*;
   import java.util.Iterator;
   import java.util.Comparator;
   public class RevComparator implements Comparator
   {
       protected Comparator base;

       public RevComparator(Comparator baseCompare)
       {
           base = baseCompare;
   ```

```
        }

        public int compare(Object a, Object b)
        {
            return -base.compare(a,b);
        }
    }
```

What happens when we construct:

```
    MyVector v = new MyVector();
    ReadStream r = new ReadStream();

    for (r.skipWhite(); !r.eof(); r.skipWhite())
    {
        v.add(new Integer(r.readInt()));
    }

    Comparator c = new RevComparator(new IntegerComparator());
    v.sort(c);
```

2. In our examples, here, a new Comparator is necessary for each sorting order. How might it be possible to add state information (protected data) to the Comparator to allow it to sort in a variety of different ways? One might imagine, for example, a method called ascending that sets the Comparator to sort into increasing order. The descending method would set the Comparator to sort in reverse order.

Notes:

Chapter 6

A Design Method

Concepts:
▷ Signatures
▷ Interface design
▷ Abstract base classes

But, luckily, he kept his wits and his purple crayon.
—Crockett Johnson

THROUGHOUT THE REST of this book we consider a number of data structures–first from an abstract viewpoint and then as more detailed implementations. In the process of considering these implementations, we will use a simple design method that focuses on the staged development of interfaces and abstract base classes. Here, we outline the design method. In the first section we describe the process. The remaining sections are dedicated to developing several examples.

6.1 The Interface-Based Approach

As we have seen in our discussion of abstract data types, the public aspect of the data type—that part that users depend on—is almost entirely incorporated in the *interface*. In Java the interface is a formal feature of the language. Interfaces allow the programmer of an abstract data type to specify the *signatures* of each of the externally visible methods, as well as any constants that might be associated with implementations.

The development and adherence to the interface is the most important part of the development of an implementation. The process can be outlined as follows:

1. Design of the interface. The interface describes the common external features of all implementations.

2. An abstract implementation. The abstract implementation describes the common internal features of all implementations.

3. Extension of the abstract class. Each implementation suggests an independent approach to writing code that extends the abstract implementation and supports the required elements of the interface.

6.1.1   Design of the Interface

The designer first considers, in as much detail as possible, an abstract data structure's various internal *states*. For example, if we are to consider a `Vector` abstractly, we pull out a napkin, and draw an abstract `Vector` and we consider the various effects that `Vector` *operations* might have on its *structure*. In our napkin-as-design-tool strategy, we might find ourselves using ellipses to suggest that we expect the `Vector` to be unbounded in size; we might use outward arrows to suggest the effect of accessor methods or methods that remove values; and we might blot out old `Vector` values in favor of new values when mutators are used. The designer must develop, from these free-flowing abstract notions of a structure, a collection of precise notions of how structures are accessed and mutated. It is also important to understand which states of the abstract structure are valid, and how the various methods ensure that the structure moves from one valid state to the next.

Armed with this information, the designer develops the interface—the external description of how users of the structure can interact with it. This consists of

1. A list of constant (`final static`) values that help provide meaning to values associated with the abstract structure. For example, any models of an atom might provide constants for the masses of electrons, protons, and neutrons. Each of these constants is declared within the `atom` interface and becomes part of any implementation.

2. Implementation-independent publicly accessible methods that access or modify data. For example, if we described an interface for a time-of-day clock, methods for reading and setting the current time would be declared part of the public interface. A method that made the clock "tick," causing time to move forward, would not be declared as part of the interface because it would not be a feature visible to the user. From the user's standpoint, the clock ticks on its own. How the clock ticks is not an abstract feature of the clock.

3. If an interface appears to be a refinement of another interface, it is common practice to have the one `extend` the other. This is useful if the new objects should be usable wherever the previously declared values are used.

Once the interface has been defined, it can be put to immediate use. Potential users of the class can be asked to review it. In fact, application code can be written to make use of the new interface. Later, if particular implementations are developed, the application code can be put to use. It is important to remember, however, that the development of the application and the implementation of the data structure may both proceed at the same time.

6.1.2   Development of an Abstract Implementation

Once the interface has been outlined, it is useful for the designer to consider those functions of the structure that are implementation independent. These pieces are gathered together in a partial or *abstract* implementation of the interface called an *abstract base class*. Since some parts of the interface may not be implemented in the abstract base class—perhaps they require a commitment to a particular implementation approach—it is necessary for the class to be declared `abstract`. Once the abstract class is implemented, it may be used as a basis for developing extensions that describe particular implementations.

Some structures may have some built-in redundancy in their public methods. An interface supporting trigonometric calculations might, for example, have a method `tan` which computes its result from `sin` and `cos`. No matter how `sin` and `cos` are actually implemented, the `tan` method can be implemented in this manner. On the other hand, if a `tan` function can be computed in a more direct manner—one not dependent on `sin` and `cos`—a particular implementation might override the method outlined in the abstract base class.

A similar approach is taken in `Vector`-like classes that implement a backward-compatible `setElementAt` method based on the more recently added `set` method. Such a method might appear in an abstract base class as

Vector

```
public void setElementAt(Object obj, int index)
// pre: 0 <= index && index < size()
// post: element value is changed to obj
{
    set(index,obj);
}
```

Because such code cannot be included in any interface that might describe a `Vector`, we place the code in the abstract class.

Implementors of other abstract objects may find it useful to develop a common library of methods that support all implementations. These methods—often declared privately—are only made available to the implementor of the class. If they are utility methods (like `sin` and `sqrt`) that are not associated with a particular object, we also declare them `static`.

Thus the abstract base class provides the basis for all implementations of an interface. This includes implementation-independent code that need not be rewritten for each implementation. Even if an abstract base class is empty, it is useful to declare the class to facilitate the implementation of implementation-independent development later in the life of the data structure. It is frequently the case, for example, that code that appears in several implementations is removed from the specific implementations and shared from the abstract base class. When implementations are actually developed, they `extend` the associated abstract base class.

6.1.3   Implementation

When the abstract base class is finished, it is then possible for one or more implementations to be developed. Usually each of these implementations extends the work that was started in the abstract base class. For example, a `Fraction` interface might be implemented as the ratio of two values (as in the `Ratio` class we saw in Chapter 1), or it might be implemented as a `double`. In the latter case, the double is converted to an approximate ratio of two integers, the numerator and denominator. In both cases, it might be useful to declare an `AbstractFraction` class that includes a greatest common divisor (`gcd`) method. Such a method would be declared `protected` and `static`.

6.2   Example: Development of Generators

As an example, we develop several implementations of an object that generates a sequence of values—an object we will call a *generator*. Such an object might generate randomly selected values, or it might generate, incrementally, a sequence of primes.

We imagine the interface would include the following methods:

```
public interface Generator
{
    public void reset();
    // post: the generator is reset to the beginning of the sequence;
    //    the current value can be immediately retrieved with get.

    public int next();
    // post: returns true iff more elements are to be generated.

    public int get();
    // post: returns the current value of the generator.
}
```

Generator

The `Generator` is constructed and the `get` method can be used to get its initial value. When necessary, the `next` routine generates, one at a time, a sequence of integer values. Each call to `next` returns the next value in the sequence, a value that can be recalled using the `get` method. If necessary, the `reset` method can be used to restart the sequence of generated values.

The next step is to generate an abstract base class that implements the interface. For the `AbstractGenerator` we implement any of the methods that can be implemented in a general manner. We choose, here, for example, to provide a mechanism for the `next` method to save the current value:

```
abstract public class AbstractGenerator
    implements Generator
{
    protected int current;  // the last value saved
```

Abstract-
Generator

```
        public AbstractGenerator(int initial)
        // post: initialize the current value to initial
        {
            current = initial;
        }

        public AbstractGenerator()
        // post: initialize the current value to zero
        {
            this(0);
        }

        protected int set(int next)
        // post: sets the current value to next, and extends the sequence
        {
            int result = current;
            current = next;
            return result;
        }

        public int get()
        // post: returns the current value of the sequence
        {
            return current;
        }

        public void reset()
        // post: resets the Generator (by default, does nothing)
        {
        }
    }
```

The **current** variable keeps track of a single integer—ideally the last value generated. This value is the value returned by the **get** method. A hidden method—**set**—allows any implementation to set the value of **current**. It is expected that this is called by the **next** method of the particular implementation. By providing this code in the abstract base class, individual implementations needn't repeatedly reimplement this common code. By default, the **reset** method does nothing. If a particular generator does not require a **reset** method, the default method does nothing.

Here is a simple implementation of a **Generator** that generates a constant value. The value is provided in the constructor:

```
public class ConstantGenerator extends AbstractGenerator
{
    public ConstantGenerator(int c)
    // pre: c is the value to be generated.
    // post: constructs a generator that returns a constant value
    {
```

Constant-
Generator

```
            set(c);
        }

        public int next()
        // post: returns the constant value
        {
            return get();
        }
    }
```

The `set` method of the `AbstractGenerator` is called from the constructor, recording the constant value to be returned. This effectively implements the `get` method—that code was provided in the `AbstractGenerator` class. The `next` method simply returns the value available from the `get` method.

Another implementation of a `Generator` returns a sequence of prime numbers. In this case, the constructor sets the current value of the generator to 2—the first prime. The `next` method searches for the next prime and returns that value after it has been saved. Here, the private `set` and the public `get` methods from the `AbstractGenerator` class help to develop the state of the `Generator`:

PrimeGenerator

```
public class PrimeGenerator extends AbstractGenerator
{
    public PrimeGenerator()
    // post: construct a generator that delivers primes starting at 2.
    {
        reset();
    }

    public void reset()
    // post: reset the generator to return primes starting at 2
    {
        set(2);
    }

    public int next()
    // post: generate the next prime
    {
        int f,n = get();
        do
        {
            if (n == 2) n = 3;
            else n += 2;

            // check the next value
            for (f = 2; f*f <= n; f++)
            {
                if (0 ==(n % f)) break;
            }
```

```
        } while (f*f <= n);
        set(n);
        return n;
    }
}
```

Clearly, the `reset` method is responsible for restarting the sequence at 2. While it would be possible for each `Generator` to keep track of its current value in its own manner, placing that general code in the `AbstractGenerator` reduces the overall cost of keeping track of this information for each of the many implementations.

Exercise 6.1 *Implement a* `Generator` *that provides a stream of random integers. After a call to* `reset`*, the random sequence is "rewound" to return the same sequence again. Different generators should probably generate different sequences. (Hint: You may find it useful to use the* `setSeed` *method of* `java.util.Random`*.)*

6.3 Example: Playing Cards

Many games involve the use of playing cards. Not all decks of cards are the same. For example, a deck of bridge cards has four suits with thirteen cards in each suit. There are no jokers. Poker has a similar deck of cards, but various games include special joker or wild cards. A pinochle deck has 48 cards consisting of two copies of 9, jack, queen, king, 10, and ace in each of four suits. The ranking of cards places 10 between king and ace. A baccarat deck is as in bridge, except that face cards are worth nothing. Cribbage uses a standard deck of cards, with aces low.

While there are many differences among these card decks, there are some common features. In each, cards have a suit and a face (e.g., ace, king, 5). Most decks assign a value or rank to each of the cards. In many games it is desirable to be able to compare the relative values of two cards. With these features in mind, we can develop the following `Card` interface:

Card

```
public interface Card
{
    public static final int ACE = 1;
    public static final int JACK = 11;
    public static final int QUEEN = 12;
    public static final int KING = 13;
    public static final int JOKER = 14;
    public static final int CLUBS = 0;
    public static final int DIAMONDS = 1;
    public static final int HEARTS = 2;
    public static final int SPADES = 3;
    public int suit();
```

```
        // post: returns the suit of the card

        public int face();
        // post: returns the face of the card, e.g., ACE, 3, JACK

        public boolean isWild();
        // post: returns true iff this card is a wild card

        public int value();
        // post: return the point value of the card

        public int compareTo(Object other);
        // pre: other is valid Card
        // post: returns int <,==,> 0 if this card is <,==,> other

        public String toString();
        // post: returns a printable version of this card
    }
```

The card interface provides all the public methods that we need to have in our card games, but it does not provide any hints at how the cards are implemented. The interface also provides standard names for faces and suits that are passed to and returned from the various card methods.

In the expectation that most card implementations are similar to a standard deck of cards, we provide an AbstractCard class that keeps track of an integer—a card index—that may be changed with set or retrieved with get (both are protected methods):

AbstractCard

```
import java.util.Random;
public abstract class AbstractCard implements Card
{
    protected int cardIndex;
    protected static Random gen = new Random();

    public AbstractCard()
    // post: constructs a random card in a standard deck
    {
        set(randomIndex(52));
    }

    protected static int randomIndex(int max)
    // pre: max > 0
    // post: returns a random number n, 0 <= n < max
    {
        return Math.abs(gen.nextInt()) % max;
    }

    protected void set(int index)
    // post: this card has cardIndex index
    {
```

```
        cardIndex = index;
}

protected int get()
// post: returns this card's card index
{
        return cardIndex;
}

public int suit()
// post: returns the suit of the card
{
        return cardIndex / 13;
}

public int face()
// post: returns the face of the card, e.g. ACE, 3, JACK
{
        return (cardIndex % 13)+1;
}

public boolean isWild()
// post: returns true iff this card is a wild card
// (default is false)
{
        return false;
}

public int value()
// post: return the point value of the card, Ace..King
{
        return face();
}

public String toString()
// post: returns a printable version of this card
{
        String cardName = "";
        switch (face())
        {
          case ACE: cardName = "Ace"; break;
          case JACK: cardName = "Jack"; break;
          case QUEEN: cardName = "Queen"; break;
          case KING: cardName = "King"; break;
          default: cardName = cardName + face(); break;
        }
        switch (suit())
        {
          case HEARTS: cardName += " of Hearts"; break;
          case DIAMONDS: cardName += " of Diamonds"; break;
```

```
            case CLUBS: cardName += " of Clubs"; break;
            case SPADES: cardName += " of Spades"; break;
        }
        return cardName;
    }
}
```

Our abstract base class also provides a protected random number generator that returns values from 0 to max-1. We make use of this in the default constructor for a standard deck; it picks a random card from the usual 52. The cards are indexed from the ace of clubs through the king of spades. Thus, the `face` and `suit` methods must use division and modulo operators to split the card index into the two constituent parts. By default, the `value` method returns the face of the card as its value. This is likely to be different for different implementations of cards, as the face values of cards in different games vary considerably.

We also provide a standard `toString` method that allows us to easily print out a card. We do not provide a `compareTo` method because there are complexities with comparing cards that cannot be predicted at this stage. For example, in bridge, suits play a predominant role in comparing cards. In baccarat they do not.

Since a poker deck is very similar to our standard implementation, we find the `PokerCard` implementation is very short. All that is important is that we allow aces to have high values:

PokerCard

```
public class PokerCard extends AbstractCard
{
    public PokerCard(int face, int suit)
    // pre: face and suit have valid values
    // post: constructs a card with the particular face value
    {
        set(suit*13+face-1);
    }

    public PokerCard()
    // post: construct a random poker card.
    {
        // by default, calls the AbstractCard constructor
    }

    public int value()
    // post: returns rank of card - aces are high
    {
        if (face() == ACE) return KING+1;
        else return face();
    }

    public int compareTo(Object other)
    // pre: other is valid PokerCard
    // post: returns relationship between this card and other
```

```
    {
        PokerCard that = (PokerCard)other;
        return value()-that.value();
    }
}
```

Exercise 6.2 *Write the* `value` *and* `compareTo` *methods for a pair of cards where suits play an important role. Aces are high, and assume that suits are ranked clubs (low), diamonds, hearts, and spades (high). Assume that face values are only considered if the suits are the same; otherwise ranking of cards depends on their suits alone.*

The implementation of a pinochle card is particularly difficult. We are interested in providing the standard interface for a pinochle card, but we are faced with the fact that there are two copies each of the six cards 9, jack, queen, king, 10, and ace, in each of the four suits. Furthermore we assume that 10 has the unusual ranking between king and ace. Here's one approach:

PinochleCard

```
public class PinochleCard extends AbstractCard
{
    // cardIndex      face      suit
    // 0              9         clubs
    // 1              9         clubs (duplicate)
    // ...
    // 10             ACE       clubs
    // 11             ACE       clubs (duplicate)
    // 12             9         diamonds
    // 13             9         diamonds (duplicate)
    // ...
    // 47             ACE       spades (duplicate)

    public PinochleCard(int face, int suit, int copy)
    // pre: face and suit have valid values
    // post: constructs a card with the particular face value
    {
        if (face == ACE) face = KING+1;
        set((suit*2+copy)*6+face-9);
    }

    public PinochleCard()
    // post: construct a random Pinochle card.
    {
        set(randomIndex(48));
    }

    public int face()
    // post: returns the face value of the card (9 thru Ace)
    {
        int result = get()%6 + 9;
        if (result == 14) result = ACE;
```

```
        return result;
    }

    public int suit()
    // post: returns the suit of the card (there are duplicates!)
    {
        // this is tricky; we divide by 12 cards (including duplicates)
        // per suit, and again by 2 to remove the duplicate
        return cardIndex / 12 / 2;
    }

    public int value()
    // post: returns rank of card - aces are high
    {
        if (face() == ACE) return KING+2;
        else if (face() == 10) return KING+1;
        else return face();
    }

    public int compareTo(Object other)
    // pre: other is valid PinochleCard
    // post: returns relationship between this card and other
    {
        PinochleCard that = (PinochleCard)other;
        return value()-that.value();
    }
}
```

The difficulty is that there is more than one copy of a card. We choose to keep track of the extra copy, in case we need to distinguish between them at some point, but we treat duplicates the same in determining face value, suit, and relative rankings.

6.4 Conclusions

Throughout the remainder of this book we will find it useful to approach each type of data structure first in an abstract manner, and then provide the details of various implementations. While each implementation tends to have a distinct approach to supporting the abstract structure, many features are common to *all* implementations. The basic interface, for example, is a shared concept of the methods that are used to access the data structure. Other features—including common private methods and shared utility methods—are provided in a basic implementation called the *abstract base class*. This incomplete class serves as a single point of extension for many implementations; the public and private features of the abstract base class are shared (and possibly overridden) by the varied approaches to solving the problem.

Chapter 7

Iterators

Concepts:
▷ Iterators
▷ The **AbstractIterator** class
▷ **Vector** iterators
▷ Numeric iteration

One potato, two potato, three potato, four,
five potato, six potato, seven potato, more.
    —A child's iterator

PROGRAMS MOVE FROM ONE STATE TO ANOTHER. As we have seen, this "state" is composed of the current value of user variables as well as some notion of "where" the computer is executing the program. This chapter discusses *enumerations* and *iterators*—objects that hide the complexities of maintaining the state of a traversal of a data structure.

Ah! Interstate programs!

Consider a program that prints each of the values in a list. It is important to maintain enough information to know exactly "where we are" at all times. This might correspond to a reference to the current value. In other structures it may be less clear how the state of a traversal is maintained. Iterators help us hide these complexities. The careful design of these *control structures* involves, as always, the development of a useful interface that avoids compromising the iterator's implementation or harming the object it traverses.

7.1 Java's Enumeration Interface

Java defines an interface called an **Enumeration** that provides the user indirect, iterative access to each of the elements of an associated data structure, exactly once. The **Enumeration** is returned as the result of calling the **elements** method of various container classes. Every **Enumeration** provides two methods:

```
public interface java.util.Enumeration
{
    public abstract boolean hasMoreElements();
    // post: returns true iff enumeration has outstanding elements

    public abstract java.lang.Object nextElement();
    // pre: hasMoreElements
    // post: returns the next element to be visited in the traversal
}
```

Enumeration

The `hasMoreElements` method returns `true` if there are unvisited elements of the associated structure. When `hasMoreElements` returns `false`, the traversal is finished and the `Enumeration` expires. To access an element of the underlying structure, `nextElement` must be called. This method does two things: it returns a reference to the current element and then marks it visited. Typically `hasMoreElements` is the predicate of a `while` loop whose body processes a single element using `nextElement`. Clearly, `hasMoreElements` is an important method, as it provides a test to see if the precondition for the `nextElement` method is met.

The following code prints out a catchy phrase using a `Vector` enumeration:

HelloWorld

```java
public static void main(String args[])
{
    // construct a vector containing two strings:
    Vector v = new Vector();
    v.add("Hello");
    v.add("world!");

    // construct an enumeration to view values of v
    Enumeration i = (Enumeration)v.elements();
    while (i.hasMoreElements())
    {
        // SILLY: v.add(1,"silly");
        System.out.print(i.nextElement()+" ");
    }
    System.out.println();
}
```

When run, the following immortal words are printed:

```
Hello world!
```

There are some important caveats that come with the use of Java's `Enumeration` construct. First, it is important to avoid modifying the associated structure while the `Enumeration` is active or *live*. Uncommenting the line marked SILLY causes the following infinite output to begin:

```
Hello silly silly silly silly silly silly
```

A silly virus vector! Inserting the string `"silly"` as the new second element of the `Vector` causes it to expand each iteration of the loop, making it difficult for the `Enumeration` to detect the end of the `Vector`.

Principle 8 *Never modify a data structure while an associated* `Enumeration` *is live.*

Modifying the structure behind an `Enumeration` can lead to unpredictable results. Clearly, if the designer has done a good job, the implementations of both the `Enumeration` and its associated structure are hidden. Making assumptions about their interaction can be dangerous.

Another subtle aspect of `Enumerations` is that they do not guarantee a particular traversal order. All that is known is that each element will be visited exactly once before `hasMoreElements` becomes `false`. While we assume that our first example above will print out `Hello world!`, the opposite order may also be possible.

Presently, we develop the concept of an *iterator*.

7.2   The Iterator Interface

An `Iterator` is similar to an `Enumerator` except that the `Iterator` traverses an associated data structure in a predictable order. Since this is a *behavior* and not necessarily a characteristic of its *interface*, it cannot be controlled or verified by a Java compiler. Instead, we must assume that developers of `Iterators` will implement and document their structures in a manner consistent with the following interface:

```
public interface java.util.Iterator
{
    public abstract boolean hasNext();
    // post: returns true if there is at least one more value to visit

    public abstract java.lang.Object next();
    // pre: hasNext()
    // post: returns the next value to be visited
}
```

Iterator

While the `Iterator` is a feature built into the Java language, we will choose to implement our own `AbstractIterator` class.

```
public abstract class AbstractIterator
        implements Enumeration, Iterator
{
    public abstract void reset();
    // pre: iterator may be initialized or even amid-traversal
    // post: reset iterator to the beginning of the structure

    public abstract boolean hasNext();
    // post: true iff the iterator has more elements to visit

    public abstract Object get();
    // pre: there are more elements to be considered; hasNext()
    // post: returns current value; ie. value next() will return

    public abstract Object next();
    // pre: hasNext()
    // post: returns current value, and then increments iterator
```

Abstract-
Iterator

```
            public void remove()
            // pre: hasNext() is true and get() has not been called
            // post: the value has been removed from the structure
            {
                Assert.fail("Remove not implemented.");
            }

            final public boolean hasMoreElements()
            // post: returns true iff there are more elements
            {
                return hasNext();
            }

            final public Object nextElement()
            // pre: hasNext()
            // post: returns the current value and "increments" the iterator
            {
                return next();
            }
        }
    }
```

This abstract base class not only meets the `Iterator` interface, but also implements the `Enumeration` interface by recasting the `Enumeration` methods in terms of `Iterator` methods. We also provide some important methods that are not part of general `Iterator`s: reset and get. The reset method reinitializes the `AbstractIterator` for another traversal. The ability to traverse a structure multiple times can be useful when an algorithm makes multiple passes through a structure to perform a single logical operation. The same functionality can be achieved by constructing a new `AbstractIterator` between passes. The get method of the `AbstractIterator` retrieves a reference to the *current element* of the traversal. The same reference will be returned by the call to next. Unlike next, however, get does not push the traversal forward. This is useful when the current value of an `AbstractIterator` is needed at a point logically distant from the call to next.

The use of an `AbstractIterator` leads to the following idiomatic loop for traversing a structure:

HelloWorld

```
public static void main(String args[])
{
    // construct a vector containing two strings:
    Vector v = new Vector();
    AbstractIterator i;
    v.add("Hello");
    v.add("world!");

    // construct an iterator to view values of v
    for (i = (AbstractIterator)v.iterator(); i.hasNext(); i.next())
    {
```

```
            System.out.print(i.get()+" ");
        }
        System.out.println();
    }
```

The result is the expected `Hello world!`

7.3   Example: Vector Iterators

For our first example, we design an `Iterator` to traverse a `Vector` called,
not surprisingly, a `VectorIterator`. We do not expect the user to construct
`VectorIterators` directly—instead the `Vector` hides the construction and returns the new structure as a generic `Iterator`, as was seen in the `HelloWorld`
example. Here is the `iterator` method:

```
public Iterator iterator()
// post: returns an iterator allowing one to
//       view elements of vector
{
    return new VectorIterator(this);
}
```

Vector

When a `Vector` constructs an `Iterator`, it provides a reference to *itself* (`this`)
as a parameter. This reference is used by the `VectorIterator` to recall which
`Vector` it is traversing.

We now consider the interface for a `VectorIterator`:

```
class VectorIterator extends AbstractIterator
{
    public VectorIterator(Vector v)
    // post: constructs an initialized iterator associated with v

    public void reset()
    // post: the iterator is reset to the beginning of the traversal

    public boolean hasNext()
    // post: returns true if there is more structure to be traversed

    public Object get()
    // pre: traversal has more elements
    // post: returns the current value referenced by the iterator

    public Object next()
    // pre: traversal has more elements
    // post: increments the iterated traversal
}
```

Vector-
Iterator

As is usually the case, the nonconstructor methods of `VectorIterator` exactly
match those required by the `Iterator` interface. Here is how the `VectorIter-
ator` is constructed and initialized:

```
protected Vector theVector;
protected int current;

public VectorIterator(Vector v)
// post: constructs an initialized iterator associated with v
{
    theVector = v;
    reset();
}

public void reset()
// post: the iterator is reset to the beginning of the traversal
{
    current = 0;
}
```

The constructor saves a reference to the associated Vector and calls reset.
This logically attaches the Iterator to the Vector and makes the first element
(if one exists) current. Calling the reset method allows us to place all the
resetting code in one location.

To see if the traversal is finished, we invoke hasNext:

```
public boolean hasNext()
// post: returns true if there is more structure to be traversed
{
    return current < theVector.size();
}
```

This routine simply checks to see if the current index is valid. If the index is less
than the size of the Vector, then it can be used to retrieve a current element
from the Vector. The two value-returning methods are get and next:

```
public Object get()
// pre: traversal has more elements
// post: returns the current value referenced by the iterator
{
    return theVector.get(current);
}

public Object next()
// pre: traversal has more elements
// post: increments the iterated traversal
{
    return theVector.get(current++);
}
```

The get method simply returns the current element. It may be called arbitrarily
many times without pushing the traversal along. The next method, on the other
hand, returns the same reference, but only after having incremented current.
The next value in the Vector (again, if there is one) becomes the current value.

Since all the `Iterator` methods have been implemented, Java will allow a `VectorIterator` to be used anywhere an `Iterator` is required. In particular, it can now be returned from the `iterator` method of the `Vector` class.

Observe that while the user cannot directly construct a `VectorIterator` (it is a nonpublic class), the `Vector` can construct one on the user's behalf. This allows measured control over the agents that access data within the `Vector`. Also, an `Iterator` is a Java interface. It is not possible to directly construct an `Iterator`. We can, however, construct any class that implements the `Iterator` interface and use that as we would any instance of an `Iterator`.

Since an `AbstractIterator` implements the `Enumeration` interface, we may use the value returned by `Vector`'s iterator method as an `Enumeration` to access the data contained within the `Vector`. Of course, treating the `Vector-Iterator` as an `Enumeration` makes it difficult to call the `AbstractIterator` methods `reset` and `get`.

7.4   Example: Rethinking Generators

In Section 6.2 we discussed the construction of a class of objects that generated numeric values. These `Generator` objects are very similar to `Abstract-Iterators`—they have `next`, `get`, and `reset` methods. They lack, however, a `hasNext` method, mainly because of a lack of foresight, and because many sequences of integers are infinite—their `hasNext` would, essentially, always return true.

`Generators` are different from `Iterators` in another important way: `Generators` return the `int` type, while `Iterators` return `Objects`. Because of this, the `Iterator` interface is more general. Any `Object`, including `Integer` values, may be returned from an `Iterator`.

In this section we experiment with the construction of a numeric iterator—a `Generator`-like class that meets the `Iterator` interface. In particular, we are interested in constructing an `Iterator` that generates prime factors of a specific integer. The `PFIterator` accepts the integer to be factored as the sole parameter on the constructor:

```
import structure.AbstractIterator;
public class PFGenerator extends AbstractIterator
{
    // the original number to be factored
    protected int base;

    public PFGenerator(int value)
    // post: an iterator is constructed that factors numbers
    {
        base = value;
        reset();
    }
}
```

PFGenerator

The process of determining the prime factor involves reducing the number by a factor. Initially, the factor f starts at 2. It remains 2 as long as the reduced value is even. At that point, all the prime factors of 2 have been determined, and we next try 3. This process continues until the reduced value becomes 1.

Because we reduce the number at each step, we must keep a copy of the original value to support the reset method. When the iterator is reset, the original number is restored, and the current prime factor is set to 2.

```
// base, reduced by the prime factors discovered
protected int n;
// the current prime factor
protected int f;

public void reset()
// post: the iterator is reset to factoring the original value
{
    n = base;
    // initial guess at prime factor
    f = 2;
}
```

If, at any point, the number n has not been reduced to 1, prime factors remain undiscovered. When we need to find the current prime factor, we first check to see if f divides n—if it does, then f is a factor. If it does not, we simply increase f until it divides n. The next method is responsible for reducing n by a factor of f.

```
public boolean hasNext()
// post: returns true iff there are more prime factors to be considered
{
    return f <= n;          // there is a factor <= n
}

public Object next()
// post: returns the current prime factor and "increments" the iterator
{
    Object result = get();  // factor to return
    n /= f;                 // reduce n by factor
    return result;
}

public Object get()
// pre: hasNext()
// post: returns the current prime factor
{
    // make sure f is a factor of n
    while (f <= n && n%f != 0) f++;
    return new Integer(f);
}
```

We can now write a program that uses the iterator to print out the prime factors of the values presented on the command line of the Java program as it is run:

```
public static void main(String[]args)
{
    // for each of the command line arguments
    for (int i = 0; i < args.length; i++)
    {
        // determine the value
        int n = Integer.parseInt(args[i]);
        PFGenerator g = new PFGenerator(n);
        System.out.print(n+": ");
        // and print the prime factors of n
        while (g.hasNext()) System.out.print(g.next()+" ");
        System.out.println();
    }
}
```

For those programmers that prefer to use the `hasMoreElements` and `next-Element` methods of the `Enumeration` interface, those methods are automatically provided by the `AbstractIterator` base class, which `PFGenerator` extends.

Exercise 7.1 *The $3n+1$ sequence is computed in the following manner. Given a seed n, the next element of the sequence is $3n + 1$ if n is odd, or $n/2$ if n is even. This sequence of values stops whenever a 1 is encountered; this happens for all seeds ever tested. Write an `Iterator` that, given a seed, generates the sequence of values that ends with 1.*

7.5 Example: Filtering Iterators

We now consider the construction of a *filtering iterator*. Instead of traversing structures, a filtering iterator traverses another iterator! As an example, we construct an iterator that returns the unique values of a structure.

Before we consider the implementation, we demonstrate its use with a simple example. In the following code, suppose that `data` is a `Vector` of `Strings`, some of which may be duplicates. For example, the `Vector` could represent the text of the Gettysburg Address. The `iterator` method of `data` is used to construct a `VectorIterator`. This is, in turn, used as a parameter to the construction of a `UniqueFilter`. Once constructed, the filter can be used as a standard `Iterator`, but it only returns the first instance of each `String` appearing in the Vector:

```
Vector data = new Vector(1000);
    ...
AbstractIterator dataIterator = (AbstractIterator)data.iterator();
```

UniqueFilter

```
AbstractIterator ui = new UniqueFilter(dataIterator);
int count=0;

for (ui.reset(); ui.hasNext(); ui.next())
{
    System.out.print(ui.get()+" ");
    if (++count%7==0) System.out.println();
}
System.out.println();
```

The result of the program, when run on the Gettysburg Address, is the following output, which helps increase the vocabulary of this textbook by nearly 139 words:

```
four score and seven years ago our
fathers brought forth on this continent a
new nation conceived in liberty dedicated to
the proposition that all men are created
equal now we engaged great civil war
testing whether or any so can long
endure met battlefield of have come dedicate
portion field as final resting place for
those who here gave their lives might
live it is altogether fitting proper should
do but larger sense cannot consecrate hallow
ground brave living dead struggled consecrated far
above poor power add detract world will
little note nor remember what say itcan
never forget they did us rather be
unfinished work which fought thus nobly advanced
task remaining before from these honored take
increased devotion cause last full measure highly
resolve shall not died vain under God
birth freedom government people by perish earth
```

Fans of compact writing will find this unique.

The UniqueFilter provides the same interface as other iterators. Its constructor, however, takes a "base" Iterator as its parameter:

```
protected AbstractIterator base; // slave iterator
protected List observed;   // list of previous values

public UniqueFilter(AbstractIterator baseIterator)
// pre: baseIterator is a non-null iterator
// post: constructs unique-value filter
//       host iterator is reset
{
    base = baseIterator;
    reset();
}
```

```
public void reset()
// post: master and base iterators are reset
{
    base.reset();
    observed = new SinglyLinkedList();
}
```

When the filter is reset using the **reset** method, the base iterator is reset as
well. We then construct an empty **List** of words previously observed. As the
filter progresses, words encountered are incorporated into the **observed** list.

The current value is fetched by the **get** method. It just passes the request
along to the base iterator. A similar technique is used with the **hasNext** method:

```
public boolean hasNext()
// post: returns true if there are more values available
//       from base stream
{
    return base.hasNext();
}


public Object get()
// pre: traversal has more elements
// post: returns the current value referenced by the iterator
{
    return base.get();
}
```

Finally, the substance of the iterator is found in the remaining method, **next**:

```
public Object next()
// pre: traversal has more elements
// post: returns current value and increments the iterator
{
    Object current = base.next();
    // record observation of current value
    observed.add(current);
    // now seek next new value
    while (base.hasNext())
    {
        Object possible = base.get();
        if (!observed.contains(possible))
        {   // new value found! leave
            break;
        } else {
            // old value, continue
            base.next();
        }
    }
    return current;
}
```

Because this routine can only be called if there is a current value, we record the current value in the `observed` list. The method then increments the base iterator until a new, previously unobserved value is produced, or the base iterator runs dry.

Some subtle details are worth noting here. First, while we have used a `VectorIterator` on a `Vector` of `String`s, the `UniqueFilter` can be applied, as is, to any type of iterator and can deliver any type of value. All that is required is that the base type support the `equals` method. Secondly, as the filter iterator progresses, it forces the base iterator to progress, too. Because of this, two filters are usually not applied to the same base iterator, and the base iterator should never be modified while the filter is running.

7.6   Conclusions

We have seen that data structures can sometimes be used to control the way programs focus on and access data. This is made very explicit with Java's `Enumeration` construct that facilitates visiting all the elements of a structure.

When we wish to traverse the elements of a data structure in a predetermined order, we use an `Iterator`. The `Iterator` provides access to the elements of a structure using an interface that is similar to that of an `Enumeration`. The abstract base class `AbstractIterator` implements both the `Iterator` and `Enumeration` interfaces, and provides two new methods—`get` and `reset`—as well. We have also seen that there are weaknesses in the concept of both of these constructs, because they surrender some of the data hiding and access controls that are provided by the associated structure. Careful use of these controlling structures, however, can yield useful tools to make traversal of structures simpler.

Self Check Problems

Solutions to these problems begin on page 431.

7.1   Suppose `e` is an `Enumeration` over some data structure. Write a loop using `e` to print all the values of the data structure.

7.2   Suppose `i` is an `Iterator` over some data structure. Write a loop using `i` to print all the values of the data structure.

7.3   Suppose that `v` is a `Vector` of `Integer` values. Write a loop that will use an `Iterator` to print those `Integer` values that are even.

7.4   It is possible to write down the integers 1 through 15 in an order such that each adjacent pair of integers sums to a perfect square. Write a loop that prints `Perfect!` only if the adjacent `Integer` values generated by the `Iterator` `g` sum to perfect squares. (You needn't verify the number or range of values.)

Problems

Solutions to the odd-numbered problems begin on page 453.

7.1   Since the `get` method is available to the `AbstractIterator`, the `next` method does not appear to need to return a value. Why does our implementation return the value?

7.2   Write an `Iterator` that works on `Strings`. Each value returned should be an object of type `Character`.

7.3   Write an `Iterator` that returns a stream of `Integers` that are prime. How close is it to the `Generator` implementation of Section 6.2?

7.4   Write a filtering iterator, `ReverseIterator`, that reverses the stream of values produced by another `Iterator`. You may assume that the base `Iterator` will eventually have no more elements, but you may not bound the number.

7.5   Write a filtering iterator, `OrderedIterator`, that sorts the stream of values produced by another `Iterator`. You may assume that the base `Iterator` will eventually have no more elements, but you may not bound the number.

7.6   Write a filtering iterator, `ShuffleIterator`, that shuffles the stream of values produced by another `Iterator`. You may assume that the base `Iterator` will eventually have no more elements, but you may not bound the number.

7.7   Write a filtering iterator that takes a base iterator and an `Object` (called `predicate`) with a static `select` method defined. This iterator passes along only those values that generate `true` when passed to the `select` method of the `predicate` `Object`.

7.7   Laboratory: The Two-Towers Problem

Objective. To investigate a difficult problem using `Iterators`.

Discussion. Suppose that we are given n uniquely sized cubic blocks and that each block has a face area between 1 and n. Build two towers by stacking these blocks. How close can we get the heights of the two towers? The following two towers built by stacking 15 blocks, for example, differ in height by only 129 millions of an inch (each unit is one-tenth of an inch):

Still, this stacking is only the *second-best* solution! To find the best stacking, we could consider all the possible configurations.

We *do* know one thing: the total height of the two towers is computed by summing the heights of all the blocks:

$$h = \sum_{i=1}^{n} \sqrt{i}$$

If we consider all the *subsets* of the n blocks, we can think of the subset as the set of blocks that make up, say, the left tower. We need only keep track of that subset that comes closest to $h/2$ without exceeding it.

In this lab, we will represent a set of n distinct objects by a `Vector`, and we will construct an `Iterator` that returns each of the 2^n subsets.

Procedure. The trick to understanding how to generate a subset of n values from a `Vector` is to first consider how to generate a subset of indices of elements from 0 to $n - 1$. Once this simpler problem is solved, we can use the indices to help us build a `Vector` (or subset) of values identified by the indices.

There are exactly 2^n subsets of values 0 to $n-1$. We can see this by imagining that a coin is tossed n times—once for each value—and the value is added to the subset if the coin flip shows a head. Since there are $2 \times 2 \times \cdots \times 2 = 2^n$ different sequences of coin tosses, there are 2^n different sets.

We can also think of the coin tosses as determining the place values for n different digits in a binary number. The 2^n different sequences generate binary numbers in the range 0 through $2^n - 1$. Given this, we can see a line of attack: count from 0 to $2^n - 1$ and use the binary digits (*bits*) of the number to determine which of the original values of the `Vector` are to be included in a subset.

Computer scientists work with binary numbers frequently, so there are a number of useful things to remember:

- An `int` type is represented by 32 bits. A `long` is represented by 64 bits. For maximum flexibility, it would be useful to use `long` integers to represent sets of up to 64 elements.

- The *arithmetic shift* operator (`<<`) can be used to quickly compute powers of 2. The value 2^i can be computed by shifting a unit bit (1) i places to the left. In Java we write this `1<<i`. This works only for nonnegative, integral powers.

- The *bitwise and* of two integers can be used to determine the value of a single bit in a number's binary representation. To retrieve bit `i` of an integer `m` we need only compute `m & (1<<i)`.

Armed with this information, the process of generating subsets is fairly straightforward. One line of attack is the following:

1. Construct a new extension to the `AbstractIterator` class. (By extending the `AbstractIterator` we support both the `Iterator` and `Enumeration` interfaces.) This new class should have a constructor that takes a `Vector` as its sole argument. Subsets of this `Vector` will be returned as the `Iterator` progresses.

2. Internally, a `long` value is used to represent the current subset. This value increases from 0 (the empty set) to $2^n - 1$ (the entire set of values) as the `Iterator` progresses. Write a `reset` method that resets the subset counter to 0.

3. Write a `hasNext` method that returns `true` if the current value is a reasonable representation of a subset.

4. Write a `get` method that returns a new `Vector` of values that are part of the current subset. If bit `i` of the current counter is 1, element `i` of the `Vector` is included in the resulting subset `Vector`.

5. Write a `next` method. Remember it returns the current subset *before* incrementing the counter.

6. For an `Iterator` you would normally have to write a `remove` method. If you extend the `AbstractIterator` class, this method is provided and will do nothing (this is reasonable).

You can now test your new `SubsetIterator` by having it print all the subsets of a `Vector` of values. Remember to keep the `Vector` small. If the original values are all distinct, the subsets should all have different values.

To solve the two-towers problem, write a `main` method that inserts the values $\sqrt{1}$, $\sqrt{2}$,...,$\sqrt{n}$ as `Double` objects into a `Vector`. A `SubsetIterator` is then used to construct 2^n subsets of these values. The values of each subset are summed, and the sum that comes closest to, but does not exceed, the value $h/2$ is remembered. After all the subsets have been considered, print the best solution.

Thought Questions. Consider the following questions as you complete the lab:

1. What is the best solution to the 15-block problem?

2. This method of exhaustively checking the subsets of blocks will not work for very large problems. Consider, for example, the problem with 50 blocks: there are 2^{50} different subsets. One approach is to repeatedly pick and evaluate random subsets of blocks (stop the computation after 1 second of elapsed time, printing the best subset found). How would you implement `randomSubset`, a new `SubsetIterator` method that returns a random subset?

Notes:

Chapter 8

Lists

*He's makin' a list
and checkin' it twice!*
—Haven Gillespie

IMAGINE YOU ARE TO WRITE A ROBUST PROGRAM to handle varying amounts of data. An inventory program is a classic example. The same inventory program might be used to keep track of either tens of items, or millions. To support such applications, `Vectors` and arrays are not ideal. As they reach their capacity they must be expanded. Either this happens manually, as with arrays, or automatically, as with `Vectors`. In either case the penalty for growing the structure is the same over the growth of the structure. With a `Vector`, for example, when the structure must double in size, the cost of adding an element is proportional to the size of the `Vector`.

In this chapter, we develop the concept of a linked list. A *linked list* is a *dynamic structure* that grows and shrinks exactly when necessary and whose elements may be added in constant time. There is some cost for this dynamic behavior, however. As with `Vectors` and arrays, each of the elements of a linked-list has an associated index, but the elements of many linked list implementations cannot be efficiently accessed out of order or *accessed randomly*. Despite this one inefficiency, linked lists provide an important building block for the design of many effective data structures.

An analogy for linked lists is a child's string of snap-together beads. As we grow the string of beads, we attach and detach new beads on either the front (*head*) or rear (*tail*). Since there are two modifying operations that we can perform (*add* or *remove*) and two ends (at the location of the *first* or *last* element) there are four operations that change the length of the structure at the end.

If you have never seen these, visit your niece.

We may also wish to perform operations on the internal portion of the list. For example, we may test for inclusion (*Is* there a red bead?) or extract an element (*Remove* a red bead!). These operations require a traversal of the linked list from one of the two ends.

List

Now, let's see what the Java description of a list looks like:

```java
public interface List extends Structure
{
    public int size();
    // post: returns number of elements in list

    public boolean isEmpty();
    // post: returns true iff list has no elements

    public void clear();
    // post: empties list

    public void addFirst(Object value);
    // post: value is added to beginning of list

    public void addLast(Object value);
    // post: value is added to end of list

    public Object getFirst();
    // pre: list is not empty
    // post: returns first value in list

    public Object getLast();
    // pre: list is not empty
    // post: returns last value in list

    public Object removeFirst();
    // pre: list is not empty
    // post: removes first value from list

    public Object removeLast();
    // pre: list is not empty
    // post: removes last value from list

    public Object remove(Object value);
    // post: removes and returns element equal to value
    //       otherwise returns null

    public void add(Object value);
    // post: value is added to tail of list

    public Object remove();
    // pre: list has at least one element
    // post: removes last value found in list

    public Object get();
    // pre: list has at least one element
    // post: returns last value found in list
```

```
    public boolean contains(Object value);
    // pre: value is not null
    // post: returns true iff list contains an object equal to value

    public int indexOf(Object value);
    // pre: value is not null
    // post: returns (0-origin) index of value,
    //    or -1 if value is not found

    public int lastIndexOf(Object value);
    // pre: value is not null
    // post: returns (0-origin) index of value,
    //    or -1 if value is not found

    public Object get(int i);
    // pre: 0 <= i < size()
    // post: returns object found at that location

    public Object set(int i, Object o);
    // pre: 0 <= i < size()
    // post: sets ith entry of list to value o;
    //     returns old value

    public void add(int i, Object o);
    // pre: 0 <= i <= size()
    // post: adds ith entry of list to value o

    public Object remove(int i);
    // pre: 0 <= i < size()
    // post: removes and returns object found at that location

    public Iterator iterator();
    // post: returns an iterator allowing
    //     ordered traversal of elements in list
}
```

Again, because this structure is described as an `interface` (as opposed to a `class`) Java understands this to be a *contract* describing the methods that are required of lists. We might think of an interface as being a "structural precondition" describing the outward appearance of any "listlike" class. If we write our code in terms of this interface, we may only invoke methods specified within the contract.

Note that the `List` interface is an extension of the `Structure` interface that we have seen earlier, in Section 1.8. Thus, every `List` is also a `Structure`—a structure that supports operations like `add` and `remove` as well as other size-related methods. We will see, over the course of this text, several abstract types that may serve as `Structures`.

The interface, along with pre- and postconditions, makes many of the *implementation-independent* decisions about the semantics of associated structures.

When we develop specific implementations, we determine the *implementation-specific* features of the structure, including its performance. When we compare specific implementations, we compare their performance in terms of space and time. Often, performance can be used to help us select among different implementations for a specific use.

8.1   Example: A Unique Program

As an example of how we might use lists, we write a program that writes out the input with duplicate lines removed. The approach is to store each of the unique lines in a structure (`lines`) as they are printed out. When new lines are read in, they are compared against the existing list of unique, printed lines. If the current line (`current`) is not in the list, it is added. If the current line is in the list, it is ignored.

Unique

```
public static void main(String[] args)
{
    // input is read from System.in
    ReadStream s = new ReadStream(System.in);
    String current;                        // current line
    List lines = new SinglyLinkedList(); // list of unique lines

    // read a list of possibly duplicated lines
    while (!s.eof()) {
        current = s.readLine();
        // check to see if we need to add it
        if (!lines.contains(current)) {
            System.out.println(current);
            lines.add(current);
        }
    }
}
```

In this example we actually construct a particular type of list, a `SinglyLinked-List`. The details of that implementation, discussed in the next section, are not important to us because `lines` is declared to be a generic interface, a `List`. Accessing data through the `lines` variable, we are only allowed to invoke methods found in the `List` interface. On the other hand, if we are able to cast our algorithms in terms of `Lists`, any implementation of a `List` will support our program.

When given input

```
madam
I'm
Adam!
...
Adam!
I'm
```

```
Ada!
...
mad
am I...
madam
```

the program generates the following output:

```
madam
I'm
Adam!
...
Ada!
mad
am I...
```

Because there is no practical limit (other than the amount of memory available) on the length of a list, there is no practical limit on the size of the input that can be fed to the program. The list interface does not provide any hint of how the list is actually implemented, so it is difficult to estimate the performance of the program. It is likely, however, that the `contains` method—which is likely to have to consider every existing element of the list—and the `add` method—which might have to pass over every element to find its correct position—will govern the complexity of the management of this `List`. As we consider implementations of `Lists`, we should keep the performance of programs like `Unique` in mind.

8.2 Example: Free Lists

In situations where a pool of resources is to be managed, it is often convenient to allocate a large number and keep track of those that have not been allocated. This technique is often used to allocate chunks of physical memory that might eventually be allocated to individual applications or printers from a pool that might be used to service a particular type of printing request.

The following application maintains rental contracts for a small parking lot. We maintain each parking space using a simple class, `Space`:

ParkingLot

```
class Space
{   // structure describing parking space
    public final static int COMPACT = 0; // small space
    public final static int MINIVAN = 1; // medium space
    public final static int TRUCK = 2;   // large space
    protected int number;       // address in parking lot
    protected int size;         // size of space
    public Space(int n, int s)
    // post: construct parking space #n, size s
    {
        number = n;
        size = s;
```

```
        }
        public boolean equals(Object other)
        // pre: other is not null
        // post: true iff spaces are equivalent size
        {
            Space that = (Space)other;
            return this.size == that.size;
        }
    }
```

The lot consists of 10 spaces of various sizes: one large, six medium, and three small. Renters may rent a space if one of appropriate size can be found on the free list. The `equals` method of the `Space` class determines an appropriate match. The `rented` list maintains `Associations` between names and space descriptions. The following code initializes the free list so that it contains all the parking spaces, while the `rented` list is initially empty:

```
List free = new SinglyLinkedList();   // available
List rented = new SinglyLinkedList(); // rented spaces
for (int number = 0; number < 10; number++)
{
    if (number < 3) // three small spaces
        free.add(new Space(number,Space.COMPACT));
    else if (number < 9) // six medium spaces
        free.add(new Space(number,Space.MINIVAN));
    else // one large space
        free.add(new Space(number,Space.TRUCK));
}
```

The main loop of our program reads in commands from the keyboard—either `rent` or `return`:

```
ReadStream r = new ReadStream();
for (r.skipWhite(); !r.eof(); r.skipWhite())
{
    String command = r.readString(); // rent/return
        ...
}
System.out.println(free.size()+" slots remain available.");
```

Within the loop, when the `rent` command is entered, it is followed by the size of the space needed and the name of the renter. This information is used to construct a contract:

```
Space location;
if (command.equals("rent"))
{   // attempt to rent a parking space
    String size = r.readString();
    Space request;
    if (size.equals("small"))
```

```
            request = new Space(0,Space.COMPACT);
        else if (size.equals("medium"))
            request = new Space(0,Space.MINIVAN);
        else request = new Space(0,Space.TRUCK);
        // check free list for appropriate-sized space
        if (free.contains(request))
        {   // a space is available
            location = (Space)free.remove(request);
            String renter = r.readString(); // to whom?
            // link renter with space description
            rented.add(new Association(renter,location));
            System.out.println("Space "+location.number+" rented.");
        } else {
            System.out.println("No space available. Sorry.");
        }
    }
```

Notice that when the `contains` method is called on a `List`, a dummy element
is constructed to specify the type of object sought. When the dummy item is
used in the `remove` command, the actual item removed is returned. This allows
us to maintain a single copy of the object that describes a single parking space.

When the spaces are returned, they are returned by name. The contract is
looked up and the associated space is returned to the free list:

```
Space location;
if (command.equals("return")){
    String renter = r.readString(); // from whom?
    // template for finding "rental contract"
    Association query = new Association(renter);
    if (rented.contains(query))
    {   // contract found
        Association contract =
            (Association)rented.remove(query);
        location = (Space)contract.getValue(); // where?
        free.add(location); // put in free list
        System.out.println("Space "+location.number+" is now free.");
    } else {
        System.out.println("No space rented to "+renter);
    }
}
```

Here is a run of the program:

```
    rent small Alice
Space 0 rented.
    rent large Bob
Space 9 rented.
    rent small Carol
Space 1 rented.
    return Alice
```

```
Space 0 is now free.
   return David
No space rented to David
   rent small David
Space 2 rented.
   rent small Eva
Space 0 rented.
   quit
6 slots remain available.
```

Notice that when Alice's space is returned, it is not immediately reused because the free list contains other small, free spaces. The use of `addLast` instead of `addFirst` (or the equivalent method, `add`) would change the reallocation policy of the parking lot.

We now consider an abstract base class implementation of the `List` interface.

8.3   Partial Implementation: Abstract Lists

Although we don't have in mind any particular implementation, there are some pieces of code that may be written, given the little experience we already have with the use of `Lists`.

For example, we realize that it is useful to have a number of synonym methods for common operations that we perform on `Lists`. We have seen, for example, that the `add` method is another way of indicating we want to add a new value to one end of the `List`. Similarly, the parameterless `remove` method performs a `removeLast`. In turn `removeLast` is simply a shorthand for removing the value found at location `size()-1`.

AbstractList

```
public abstract class AbstractList
    extends AbstractStructure implements List
{
    public AbstractList()
    // post: does nothing
    {
    }

    public boolean isEmpty()
    // post: returns true iff list has no elements
    {
        return size() == 0;
    }

    public void addFirst(Object value)
    // post: value is added to beginning of list
    {
        add(0,value);
    }
```

```
public void addLast(Object value)
// post: value is added to end of list
{
    add(size(),value);
}

public Object getFirst()
// pre: list is not empty
// post: returns first value in list
{
    return get(0);
}

public Object getLast()
// pre: list is not empty
// post: returns last value in list
{
    return get(size()-1);
}

public Object removeFirst()
// pre: list is not empty
// post: removes first value from list
{
    return remove(0);
}

public Object removeLast()
// pre: list is not empty
// post: removes last value from list
{
    return remove(size()-1);
}

public void add(Object value)
// post: value is added to tail of list
{
    addLast(value);
}

public Object remove()
// pre: list has at least one element
// post: removes last value found in list
{
    return removeLast();
}

public Object get()
// pre: list has at least one element
// post: returns last value found in list
```

```
{
    return getLast();
}

public boolean contains(Object value)
// pre: value is not null
// post: returns true iff list contains an object equal to value
{
    return -1 != indexOf(value);
}
}
```

Position-independent operations, like `contains`, can be written in an implementation-independent manner. To see if a value is contained in a `List` we could simply determine its index with the `indexOf` method. If the value returned is −1, it was not in the list, otherwise the list contains the value. This approach to the implementation does not reduce the cost of performing the `contains` operation, but it *does* reduce the cost of *implementing* the `contains` operation: once the `indexOf` method is written, the `contains` method will be complete. When we expect that there will be multiple implementations of a class, supporting the implementations in the abstract base class can be cost effective. If improvements can be made on the generic code, each implementation has the option of providing an alternative version of the method.

Notice that we provide a parameterless constructor for `AbstractList` objects. Since the class is declared `abstract`, the constructor does not seem necessary. If, however, we write an implementation that extends the `AbstractList` class, the constructors for the implementation implicitly call the parameterless constructor for the `AbstractList` class. That constructor would be responsible for initializing any data associated with the `AbstractList` portion of the implementation. In the examples of the last chapter, we saw the `AbstractGenerator` initialized the `current` variable. Even if there is no class-specific data—as is true with the `AbstractList` class—it is good to get in the habit of writing these simple constructors.

We now consider a number of implementations of the `List` type. Each of these implementations is an extension of the `AbstractList` class. Some inherit the methods provided, while others override the selected method definitions to provide more efficient implementation.

8.4   Implementation: Singly Linked Lists

Dynamic memory is allocated using the **new** operator. Java programmers are accustomed to using the **new** operator whenever classes or arrays are to be allocated. The value returned from the **new** operator is a *reference* to the new object. Thus, whenever we declare an instance of a class, we are actually declaring a reference to one of those objects. Assignment of references provides multiple variables with access to a single, shared instance of an object.

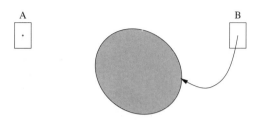

Figure 8.1 Pictures of a **null** reference (left) and a non-**null** reference to an instance of a class (right).

An instance of a class is like a helium-filled balloon. The balloon is the object being allocated. The string on the balloon is a convenient handle that we can use to hold onto with a hand. Anything that holds onto the string is a *reference*. Assignment of references is similar to asking another hand to "hold the balloon I'm holding." To not reference anything (to let go of the balloon) we can assign the reference the value **null**. If nothing references the balloon, then it floats away and we can no longer get access to the instance. When memory is not referenced in any way, it is recycled automatically by a *garbage collector*.

Principle 9 *When manipulating references, draw pictures.*

In this text, we will draw references as arrows pointing to their respective objects (Figure 8.1). When a reference is not referencing anything, we draw it as a dot. Since references can only be in one of two states—pointing to nothing or pointing to an object—these are the only pictures we will ever draw.

First garbage, now flies!

One approach to keeping track of arbitrarily large collections of objects is to use a *singly linked list* to dynamically allocate each chunk of memory "on the fly." As the chunks of memory are allocated, they are linked together to form the entire structure. This is accomplished by packaging with each user object a reference to the next object in the chain. Thus, a list of 10 items contains 10 elements, each of which contains a value as well as another element reference. Each element references the next, and the final element does not reference anything: it is assigned **null** (see Figure 8.2). Here, an implementation of a **SinglyLinkedListElement** contains an additional reference, **nextElement**:

```
public class SinglyLinkedListElement
{
    protected Object data; // value stored in this element
    protected SinglyLinkedListElement nextElement; // ref to next

    public SinglyLinkedListElement(Object v,
                         SinglyLinkedListElement next)
    // pre: v is a value, next is a reference to remainder of list
    // post: an element is constructed as the new head of list
```

**SinglyLinked-
ListElement**

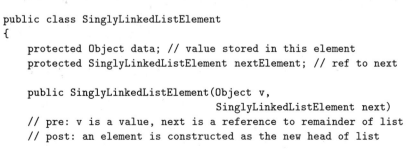

```
    {
        data = v;
        nextElement = next;
    }

    public SinglyLinkedListElement(Object v)
    // post: constructs a new tail of a list with value v
    {
        this(v,null);
    }

    public SinglyLinkedListElement next()
    // post: returns reference to next value in list
    {
        return nextElement;
    }

    public void setNext(SinglyLinkedListElement next)
    // post: sets reference to new next value
    {
        nextElement = next;
    }

    public Object value()
    // post: returns value associated with this element
    {
        return data;
    }

    public void setValue(Object value)
    // post: sets value associated with this element
    {
        data = value;
    }
}
```

When a list element is constructed, the value provided is stored away in the object. Here, `nextElement` is a reference to the next element in the list. We access the `nextElement` and `data` fields through `public` methods to avoid accessing protected fields. Notice that, for the first time, we see a self-referential data structure: the `SinglyLinkedListElement` object has a reference to a `SinglyLinkedListElement`. This is a feature common to structures whose size can increase dynamically. This class is declared `public` so that anyone can construct `SinglyLinkedListElement`s.

We now construct a new class that *implements* the `List` interface by extending the `AbstractList` base class. For that relation to be complete, it is necessary to provide a complete implementation of each of the methods promised by the interface. Failure to implement *any* of the methods leaves the implementation incomplete, leaving the class *abstract*.

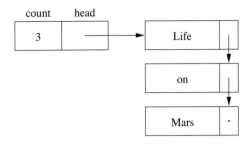

Figure 8.2 A nonempty singly linked list.

Figure 8.3 An empty singly linked list.

Our approach will be to maintain, in **head**, a reference to the first element of the list in a protected field (Figure 8.2). This initial element references the second element, and so on. The final element has a **null**-valued **next** reference. If there are no elements, **head** contains a **null** reference (Figure 8.3). We also maintain an integer that keeps track of the number of elements in the list. First, as with all classes, we need to specify protected data and a constructor:

```
protected int count;                       // list size
protected SinglyLinkedListElement head;    // ref. to first element

public SinglyLinkedList()
// post: generates an empty list
{
    head = null;
    count = 0;
}
```

SinglyLinked-
List

This code sets the **head** reference to **null** and the **count** field to 0. Notice that, by the end of the constructor, the list is in a consistent state.

Principle 10 *Every public method of an object should leave the object in a consistent state.*

What constitutes a "consistent state" depends on the particular structure, but in most cases the concept is reasonably clear. In the **SinglyLinkedList**, the constructor constructs a list that is empty.

The size-oriented methods are simply written in terms of the `count` identifier. The `size` method returns the number of elements in the list.

```
public int size()
// post: returns number of elements in list
{
    return count;
}
```

Recall that the `isEmpty` method described in the `AbstractList` class simply returns whether or not the `size` method would return 0. There's a great advantage to calling the `size` method to implement `isEmpty`: if we ever change the implementation, we need only change the implementation of `size`.

Both of these methods could avoid referencing the `count` field, by traversing each of the `next` references. In this alternative code we use the analogy of a *finger* referencing each of the elements in the list. Every time the finger references a new element, we increment a counter. The result is the number of elements. This time-consuming process is equivalent to constructing the information stored explicitly in the `count` field.

```
public int size()
// post: returns number of elements in list
{
    // number of elements we've seen in list
    int elementCount = 0;
    // reference to potential first element
    SinglyLinkedListElement finger = head;

    while (finger != null) {
        // finger references a new element, count it
        elementCount++;
        // reference possible next element
        finger = finger.next();
    }
    return elementCount;
}
```

Note that `isEmpty` does not need to change.[1] It is early verification that the interface for `size` helps to hide the implementation.

The decision between the two implementations has little impact on the user of the class, as long as both implementations meet the postconditions. Since the user is insulated from the details of the implementation, the decision can be made *even after applications have been written*. If, for example, an environment is memory-poor, it might be wise to avoid the use of the `count` field and instead traverse the list to determine the number of elements by counting them. If, however, a machine is slow but memory-rich, then the first implementation would be preferred. Both implementations could be made available, with the

---

[1] In either case, the method `isEmpty` could be written more efficiently, checking a `null head` reference.

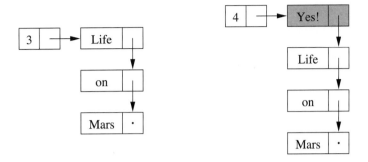

Figure 8.4 A singly linked list before and after the call to `addFirst`. Shaded value is added to the list. The `removeFirst` method reverses this process and returns value.

user selecting the appropriate design, based on broad guidelines (e.g., memory versus speed). If this trade-off does not appear dramatic, you might consider Problem 8.10. We also discuss space–time trade-offs in more detail in Chapter 9.

Let us now consider the implementation of the methods that manipulate items at the head of the list (see Figure 8.4). First, to add an element at the head of the list, we simply need to create a new `SinglyLinkedListElement` that has the appropriate value and references the very first element of the list (currently, `head`). The head of the new list is simply a reference to the new element. Finally, we modify the `count` variable to reflect an increase in the number of elements.

```java
public void addFirst(Object value)
// post: value is added to beginning of list
{
    // note order that things happen:
    // head is parameter, then assigned
    head = new SinglyLinkedListElement(value, head);
    count++;
}
```

Removing a value should simply perform the reverse process. We copy the reference[2] to a temporary variable where it can be held for return, and then we simply move the head reference down the list. Once completed, the value is returned.

```java
public Object removeFirst()
// pre: list is not empty
// post: removes and returns value from beginning of list
```

---

[2] Remember: The assignment operator *does not* copy the value, just the reference. If you want a reference to a *new* element, you should use the **new** operator and explicitly create a new object to be referenced.

```
{
    SinglyLinkedListElement temp = head;
    head = head.next(); // move head down list
    count--;
    return temp.value();
}
```

Notice that `removeFirst` returns a value. Why not? Since `addFirst` "absorbs" a value, `removeFirst` should do the reverse and "emit" one. Typically, the caller will not dispose of the value, but re-insert it into another data structure. Of course, if the value is not desired, the user can avoid assigning it a variable, and it will be garbage-collected at some later time. Since we think of these two operations as being inverses of each other, it is only natural to have them balance the consumption of objects in this way.

Principle 11 *Symmetry is good.*

One interesting exception to Principle 11 only occurs in languages like Java, where a garbage collector manages the recycling of dynamic memory. Clearly, `addFirst` must construct a new element to hold the value for the list. On the other hand, `removeFirst` does not explicitly *get rid* of the element. This is because after `removeFirst` is finished, there are no references to the element that was just removed. Since there are no references to the object, the garbage collector can be assured that the object can be recycled. All of this makes the programmer a little more lax about thinking about when memory has been logically freed. In languages without garbage collection, a "dispose" operation must be called for any object allocated by a **new** command. Forgetting to dispose of your garbage properly can be a rude shock, causing your program to run out of precious memory. We call this a *memory leak*. Java avoids all of this by collecting your garbage for you.

There's one more method that we provide for the sake of completeness: `getFirst`. It is a *nondestructive* method that returns a reference to the first value in the list; the list is not modified by this method; we just get access to the data:

```
public Object getFirst()
// pre: list is not empty
// post: returns first value in list
{
    return head.value();
}
```

Next, we must write the methods that manipulate the tail of the list (see Figure 8.5). While the interface makes these methods appear similar to those that manipulate the head of the list, our implementation has a natural bias against tail-oriented methods. Access through a single reference to the head of the list makes it difficult to get to the end of a long singly linked list. More "energy" will have to be put into manipulating items at the tail of the list. Let's see how these methods are implemented:

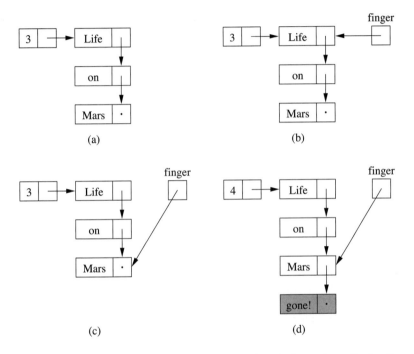

Figure 8.5 The process of adding a new value (shaded) to the tail of a list. The `finger` reference keeps track of progress while searching for the element whose reference must be modified.

```
public void addLast(Object value)
// post: adds value to end of list
{
    // location for new value
    SinglyLinkedListElement temp =
        new SinglyLinkedListElement(value,null);
    if (head != null)
    {
        // pointer to possible tail
        SinglyLinkedListElement finger = head;
        while (finger.next() != null)
        {
            finger = finger.next();
        }
        finger.setNext(temp);
    } else head = temp;
    count++;
}

public Object removeLast()
// pre: list is not empty
// post: removes last value from list
{
    SinglyLinkedListElement finger = head;
    SinglyLinkedListElement previous = null;
    Assert.pre(head != null,"List is not empty.");
    while (finger.next() != null) // find end of list
    {
        previous = finger;
        finger = finger.next();
    }
    // finger is null, or points to end of list
    if (previous == null)
    {
        // has exactly one element
        head = null;
    }
    else
    {
        // pointer to last element is reset
        previous.setNext(null);
    }
    count--;
    return finger.value();
}
```

Each of these (complex) methods uses the finger-based list traversal technique. We reference each element of the list, starting at the top and moving downward, until we finally reach the tail. At that point we have constructed the desired reference to the end of the list, and we continue as we would have in the head-manipulating methods. We have to be aware of one slight problem that concerns the very simplest case—when the list is empty. If there are no elements, then `finger` never becomes non-`null`, and we have to write special code to manipulate the `head` reference.

To support the `add` and `remove` methods of the `Structure` (and thus `List`) interface, we had them call the `addLast` and `removeLast` methods, respectively. Given their expense, there might be a good argument to have them manipulate values at the head of the list, but that leads to an inconsistency with other potential implementations. The correct choice in design is not always obvious.

Several methods potentially work in the context of the middle of lists—including `contains` and `remove`. Here, the code becomes particularly tricky because we cannot depend on lists having any values, and, for `remove`, we must carefully handle the boundary cases—when the elements are the first or last elements of the list. Errors in code usually occur at these difficult points, so it is important to make sure they are tested.

Principle 12 *Test the boundaries of your structures and methods.*

Here is the code for these methods:

```
public boolean contains(Object value)
// pre: value is not null
// post: returns true iff value is found in list
{
    SinglyLinkedListElement finger = head;
    while (finger != null &&
           !finger.value().equals(value))
    {
        finger = finger.next();
    }
    return finger != null;
}

public Object remove(Object value)
// pre: value is not null
// post: removes first element with matching value, if any
{
    SinglyLinkedListElement finger = head;
    SinglyLinkedListElement previous = null;
    while (finger != null &&
           !finger.value().equals(value))
    {
        previous = finger;
        finger = finger.next();
    }
    // finger points to target value
    if (finger != null) {
        // we found element to remove
        if (previous == null) // it is first
```

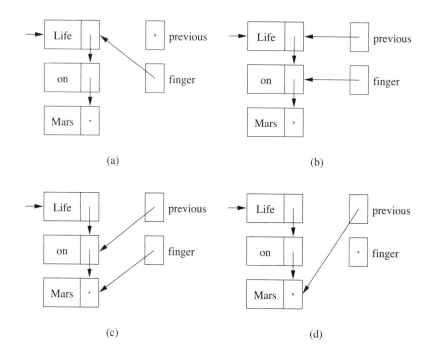

Figure 8.6 The relation between `finger` and `previous`. The target element is (a) the head of the list, (b) in the middle, (c) at the tail, or (d) not present.

```
    {
        head = finger.next();
    } else {                    // it's not first
        previous.setNext(finger.next());
    }
    count--;
    return finger.value();
}
// didn't find it, return null
return null;
}
```

In the `contains` method we call the value's `equals` method to test to see if the values are logically equal. Comparing the values with the `==` operator checks to see if the references are the same (i.e., that they are, in fact, the same object). We are interested in finding a logically equal object, so we invoke the object's `equals` method.

Some fancy reference manipulation is needed in any routine that removes an element from the list. When we find the target value, the `finger` variable has moved too far down to help with removing the element. By the time `finger` references the element holding the target value, we lose the reference to the previous element—precisely the element that needs to have its `next` reference reset when the value is removed. To avoid this difficulty, we keep another reference, local to the particular method, that is either `null` or references the element just before `finger`. When (and if) we find a value to be removed, the element to be fixed is referenced by `previous` (Figure 8.6). Of course, if `previous` is `null`, we must be removing the first element, and we update the `head` reference. All of this can be very difficult to write correctly, which is another good reason to write it carefully once and reuse the code whenever possible (see Principle 2, *Free the future: Reuse code*).

One final method with subtle behavior is the `clear` method. This removes all the elements from the list. In Java, this is accomplished by clearing the reference to the head and adjusting the list size:

```
public void clear()
// post: removes all elements from list
{
    head = null;
    count = 0;
}
```

All that happens is that `head` stops referencing the list. Instead, it is explicitly made to reference nothing. What happens to the elements of the list? When the garbage collector comes along, it notices that the first element of the former list is not referenced by anything—after all it was only referenced by `head` before. So, the garbage collector collects that first element as garbage. It is pretty easy to see that if anything is referenced *only by* garbage, it *is* garbage. Thus, the second element (as well as the value referenced by the first element) will be marked as garbage, and so forth. This cascading identification of garbage elements is responsible for recycling all the elements of the list and, potentially, the `Object`s they reference. (If the list-referenced objects are referenced outside of the list, they *may* not be garbage after all!)

You are what references you.

We have left to this point the implementation of general methods for supporting indexed versions of `add` and `remove`. These routines insert and remove values found at particular offsets from the beginning of this list. Careful inspection of the `AbstractList` class shows that we have chosen to implement `addFirst` and similar procedures in terms of the generic `add` and `remove` routines. We have, however, already seen quite efficient implementations of these routines. Instead, we choose to make use of the end-based routines to handle special cases of the generic problem.

Here, we approach the adding of a value to the middle of a list. An index is passed with a value and indicates the desired index of the value in the augmented list. A finger keeps track of our progress in finding the correct location.

```
public void add(int i, Object o)
// pre: 0 <= i <= size()
// post: adds ith entry of list to value o
{
    Assert.pre((0 <= i)  && (i <= size())),
                "Index in range.");
    if (i == size()) {
        addLast(o);
    } else if (i == 0) {
        addFirst(o);
    } else {
        SinglyLinkedListElement previous = null;
        SinglyLinkedListElement finger = head;
        // search for ith position, or end of list
        while (i > 0)
        {
            previous = finger;
            finger = finger.next();
            i--;
        }
        // create new value to insert in correct position
        SinglyLinkedListElement current =
            new SinglyLinkedListElement(o,finger);
        count++;
        // make previous value point to new value
        previous.setNext(current);
    }
}
```

Some thought demonstrates that the general code can be considerably simplified if the boundary cases (adding near the ends) can be handled directly. By handling the head and tail cases we can be sure that the new value will be inserted in a location that has a non-null previous value, as well as a non-null next value. The loop is simpler, then, and the routine runs considerably faster.

A similar approach is used in the indexed remove routine:

```
public Object remove(int i)
// pre: 0 <= i < size()
// post: removes and returns object found at that location
{
    Assert.pre((0 <= i) && (i < size())),
                "Index in range.");
    if (i == 0) return removeFirst();
    else if (i == size()-1) return removeLast();
    SinglyLinkedListElement previous = null;
    SinglyLinkedListElement finger = head;
    // search for value indexed, keep track of previous
    while (i > 0)
    {
        previous = finger;
```

```
            finger = finger.next();
            i--;
    }
    // in list, somewhere in middle
    previous.setNext(finger.next());
    count--;
    // finger's value is old value, return it
    return finger.value();
}
```

Exercise 8.1 *Implement the indexed* set *and* get *routines. You may assume the existence of* setFirst, setLast, getFirst, *and* getLast.

We now consider another implementation of the list interface that makes use of two references per element.   *Swoon!*

8.5 Implementation: Doubly Linked Lists

In Section 8.4, we saw indications that some operations can take more "energy" to perform than others, and expending energy takes time. Operations such as modifying the tail of a singly linked list can take significantly longer than those that modify the head. If we, as users of lists, expect to modify the tail of the list frequently, we might be willing to make our code more complex, or use more space to store our data structure if we could be assured of significant reductions in time spent manipulating the list.

We now consider an implementation of a *doubly linked list*. In a doubly linked list, each element points not only to the next element in the list, but also to the previous element (see Figure 8.7). The first and last elements, of course, have null previousElement and nextElement references, respectively.

In addition to maintaining a second reference within each element, we will also consider the addition of a reference to the tail of the list (see Figure 8.8). This one reference provides us direct access to the end of the list and has the potential to improve the addLast and removeLast methods.

A cursory glance at the resulting data structure identifies that it is more *symmetric* with respect to the head and tail of the list. Writing the tail-related methods can be accomplished by a simple rewriting of the head-related methods. Symmetry is a powerful concept in the design of complex structures; if something is asymmetric, you should step back and ask yourself why.

Principle 13 *Question asymmetry.*

We begin by constructing a DoublyLinkedListElement structure that parallels the SinglyLinkedListElement. The major difference is the addition of the previous reference that refers to the element that occurs immediately before this element in the doubly linked list. One side effect of doubling the number of references is that we duplicate some of the information.

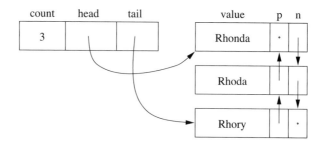

Figure 8.7   A nonempty doubly linked list.

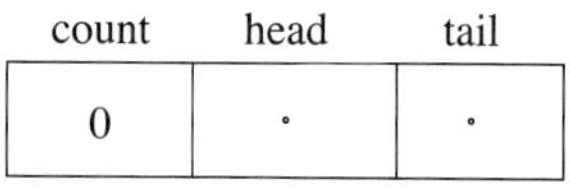

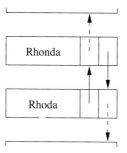

Figure 8.8   An empty doubly linked list.

Figure 8.9   Rhonda's next reference duplicates Rhoda's previous reference.

If we look at two adjacent elements Rhonda and Rhoda in a doubly linked list, their mutual adjacency is recorded in two references (Figure 8.9): Rhonda's *Say* that *twice!* nextElement reference refers to Rhoda, while Rhoda's previousElement reference refers to Rhonda. Whenever one of the references is modified, the other must be modified also. When we construct a new DoublyLinkedListElement, we set both the nextElement and previousElement references. If either is non-null, a reference in the newly adjacent structure must be updated. *If we fail to do this, the data structure is left in an inconsistent state.*

Here's the code:

```
protected Object data;
protected DoublyLinkedListElement nextElement;
protected DoublyLinkedListElement previousElement;

public DoublyLinkedListElement(Object v,
                   DoublyLinkedListElement next,
                   DoublyLinkedListElement previous)
{
    data = v;
    nextElement = next;
    if (nextElement != null)
        nextElement.previousElement = this;
    previousElement = previous;
    if (previousElement != null)
        previousElement.nextElement = this;
}

public DoublyLinkedListElement(Object v)
// post: constructs a single element
{
    this(v,null,null);
}
```

DoublyLinked-
ListElement

Now we construct the class describing the doubly linked list, proper. As with any implementation of the list interface, it is necessary for our new Doubly-LinkedList to provide code for each method not addressed in the AbstractList class. The constructor simply sets the head and tail references to null and the count to 0—the state identifying an empty list:

```
protected int count;
protected DoublyLinkedListElement head;
protected DoublyLinkedListElement tail;

public DoublyLinkedList()
// post: constructs an empty list
{
    head = null;
    tail = null;
    count = 0;
}
```

DoublyLinked-
List

Many of the fast methods of `SinglyLinkedLists`, like `addFirst`, require only minor modifications to maintain the extra references.

```
public void addFirst(Object value)
// pre: value is not null
// post: adds element to head of list
{
    // construct a new element, making it head
    head = new DoublyLinkedListElement(value, head, null);
    // fix tail, if necessary
    if (tail == null) tail = head;
    count++;
}
```

The payoff for all our extra references comes when we implement methods like those modifying the tail of the list:

```
public void addLast(Object value)
// pre: value is not null
// post: adds new value to tail of list
{
    // construct new element
    tail = new DoublyLinkedListElement(value, null, tail);
    // fix up head
    if (head == null) head = tail;
    count++;
}
```

```
public Object removeLast()
// pre: list is not empty
// post: removes value from tail of list
{
    Assert.pre(!isEmpty(),"List is not empty.");
    DoublyLinkedListElement temp = tail;
    tail = tail.previous();
    if (tail == null) {
        head = null;
    } else {
        tail.setNext(null);
    }
    count--;
    return temp.value();
}
```

Here, it is easy to see that head- and tail-based methods are textually similar, making it easier to verify that they are written correctly. Special care needs to be taken when these procedures handle a list that newly becomes either empty or not empty. In these cases, *both* the `head` and `tail` references must be modified to maintain a consistent view of the list. Some people consider the careful manipulation of these references so time-consuming and error-prone that they dedicate an unused element that permanently resides at the head of the list. It is never seen or modified by the user, and it can simplify the code. Here, for example, are the addLast and removeLast methods for this type of list:

```
public void addLast(Object value)
{
    // construct new element
    tail = new DoublyLinkedListElement(value, null, tail);
    count++;
}

public Object removeLast()
{
    Assert.pre(!isEmpty(),"List is not empty.");
    DoublyLinkedListElement temp = tail;
    tail = tail.previous();
    tail.setNext(null);
    count--;
    return temp.value();
}
```

The reserved-element technique increases the amount of space necessary to store a DoublyLinkedList by the size of a single element. The choice is left to the implementor and is another example of a time–space trade-off.

Returning to our original implementation, we note that remove is simplified by the addition of the previous reference:

```
public Object remove(Object value)
// pre: value is not null.  List can be empty
// post: first element matching value is removed from list
{
    DoublyLinkedListElement finger = head;
    while (finger != null &&
            !finger.value().equals(value))
    {
        finger = finger.next();
    }
    if (finger != null)
    {
        // fix next field of element above
        if (finger.previous() != null)
        {
            finger.previous().setNext(finger.next());
        } else {
            head = finger.next();
        }
        // fix previous field of element below
        if (finger.next() != null)
        {
            finger.next().setPrevious(finger.previous());
        } else {
```

```
            tail = finger.previous();
        }
        count--;                    // fewer elements
        return finger.value();
    }
    return null;
}
```

Because every element keeps track of its previous element, there is no difficulty in finding it from the element that is to be removed. Of course, once the removal is to be done, several references need to be updated, and they must be assigned carefully to avoid problems when removing the first or last value of a list.

The List interface requires the implementation of two index-based methods called indexOf and lastIndexOf. These routines return the index associated with the first (or last) element that is equivalent to a particular value. The indexOf method is similar to the implementation of contains, but it returns the index of the element, instead of the element itself. For DoublyLinkedLists, the lastIndexOf method performs the same search, *but starts at the tail of the list.* It is, essentially, the mirror image of an indexOf method.

```
public int lastIndexOf(Object value)
// pre: value is not null
// post: returns the (0-origin) index of value,
//    or -1 if value is not found
{
    int i = size()-1;
    DoublyLinkedListElement finger = tail;
    // search for last matching value, result is desired index
    while (finger != null && !finger.value().equals(value))
    {
        finger = finger.previous();
        i--;
    }
    if (finger == null)
    {   // value not found, return indicator
        return -1;
    } else {
        // value found, return index
        return i;
    }
}
```

8.6   Implementation: Circularly Linked Lists

Careful inspection of the singly linked list implementation identifies one seemingly unnecessary piece of data: the final reference of the list. This reference is always null, but takes up as much space as any varying reference. At the same time, we were motivated to add a tail reference in the doubly linked list to help

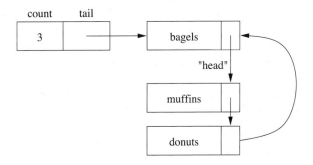

Figure 8.10   A nonempty circularly linked list.

us access either end of the list with equal ease. Perhaps we could use the last reference as the extra reference we need to keep track of one of the ends!

The tail wags the dog.

Here's the technique: Instead of keeping track of both a head and a tail reference, we explicitly keep only the reference to the tail. Since this element would normally have a `null` reference, we use that reference to refer, implicitly, to the head (see Figure 8.10). This implementation marries the speed of the `DoublyLinkedList` with the space needed by the `SinglyLinkedList`. In fact, we are able to make use of the `SinglyLinkedListElement` class as the basis for our implementation. To build an empty list we initialize the tail to `null` and the `count` to 0:

CircularList

```
protected SinglyLinkedListElement tail;
protected int count;

public CircularList()
// pre: constructs a new circular list
{
    tail = null;
    count = 0;
}
```

Whenever access to the head of the list is necessary, we use `tail.next()`, instead.[3] Thus, methods that manipulate the head of the list are only slight modifications of the implementations we have seen before for singly and doubly linked lists. Here is how we add a value to the head of the list:

```
public void addFirst(Object value)
// pre: value non-null
// post: adds element to head of list
```

---

[3] This longhand even works in the case when there is exactly one element, since its next reference points to itself.

```
{
    SinglyLinkedListElement temp =
        new SinglyLinkedListElement(value);
    if (tail == null) { // first value added
        tail = temp;
        tail.setNext(tail);
    } else { // element exists in list
        temp.setNext(tail.next());
        tail.setNext(temp);
    }
    count++;
}
```

Now, to add an element to the end of the list, we first add it to the head, and then "rotate" the list by moving the `tail` down the list. The overall effect is to have added the element to the tail!

```
public void addLast(Object value)
// pre: value non-null
// post: adds element to tail of list
{
    // new entry:
    addFirst(value);
    tail = tail.next();
}
```

The "recycling" of the tail reference as a new head reference does not solve all our problems. Careful thought will demonstrate that the removal of a value from the tail of the list remains a difficult problem. Because we only have access to the tail of the list, and not the value that precedes it, it is difficult to remove the final value. To accomplish this, we must iterate through the structure, looking for an element that refers to the same element as the tail reference.

```
public Object removeLast()
// pre: !isEmpty()
// post: returns and removes value from tail of list
{
    Assert.pre(!isEmpty(),"list is not empty.");
    SinglyLinkedListElement finger = tail;
    while (finger.next() != tail) {
        finger = finger.next();
    }
    // finger now points to second-to-last value
    SinglyLinkedListElement temp = tail;
    if (finger == tail)
    {
        tail = null;
    } else {
        finger.setNext(tail.next());
        tail = finger;
```

```
        }
        count--;
        return temp.value();
    }
```

There are two approaches to improving the performance of this operation. First, we could reconsider the **previous** links of the doubly linked list. There's not much advantage to doing this, and if we did, we could then keep the head reference instead of the tail reference. The second technique is to point instead to the element before the tail; that is the subject of Problem 8.11.

8.7 Implementation: Vectors

Careful inspection of the **List** interface makes it clear that the **Vector** class actually implements the **List** interface. Thus, we can augment the **Vector** definition with the phrase **implements List**.

With such varied implementations, it is important to identify the situations where each of the particular implementations is most efficient. As we had noted before, the **Vector** is a good random access data structure. Elements in the middle of the **Vector** can be accessed with little overhead. On the other hand, the operations of adding or removing a value from the front of the **Vector** are potentially inefficient, since a large number of values must be moved in each case.

In contrast, the dynamically allocated lists manipulate the head of the list quite efficiently, but do not allow the random access of the structure without a significant cost. When the tail of a dynamically allocated list must be accessed quickly, the **DoublyLinkedList** or **CircularList** classes should be used.

Exercise 8.2 *In Exercise 5.3 (see page 132) we wrote a version of* **insertionSort** *that sorts* **Vector***s. Follow up on that work by making whatever modification would be necessary to have the* **insertionSort** *work on any type of* **List***.*

8.8 List Iterators

The observant reader will note that all classes that implement the **Structure** class (see page 24) are required to provide an **iterator** method. Since the **List** interface extends the **Structure** interface, all **List**s are required to implement an **iterator** method. We sketch the details of an **Iterator** over **SinglyLinkedList**s here. Implementations of other **List**-based iterators are similar.

When implementing the **VectorIterator** it may be desirable to use only methods available through the **Vector**'s public interface to access the **Vector**'s data. Considering the **List** interface—an interface biased toward manipulating the ends of the structure—it is not clear how a traversal might be accomplished without disturbing the underlying **List**. Since several **Iterator**s may be active on a single List at a time, it is important not to disturb the host structure. As a result, efficient implementations of ListIterators must make use of the protected fields of the List object.

The SinglyLinkedListIterator implements all the standard Iterator methods. To maintain its positioning within the List, the iterator maintains two references: the head of the associated list and a reference to the current node. The constructor and initialization methods appear as follows:

SinglyLinked-
ListIterator

```
protected SinglyLinkedListElement current;
protected SinglyLinkedListElement head;

public SinglyLinkedListIterator(SinglyLinkedListElement t)
// post: returns an iterator that traverses a linked list
{
    head = t;
    reset();
}

public void reset()
// post: iterator is reset to beginning of traversal
{
    current = head;
}
```

When called by the SinglyLinkedList's iterator method, the protected head reference is passed along. The constructor caches away this value for use in reset. The reset routine is then responsible for initializing current to the value of head. The Iterator is able to refer to the SinglyLinkedListElements because both structures are in the same package.

The value-returning routines visit each element and "increment" the current reference by following the next reference:

```
protected SinglyLinkedListElement current;
protected SinglyLinkedListElement head;

public boolean hasNext()
// post: returns true if there is more structure to be viewed:
//       i.e., if value (next) can return a useful value.
{
    return current != null;
}

public Object next()
// pre: traversal has more elements
// post: returns current value and increments iterator
{
    Object temp = current.value();
    current = current.next();
    return temp;
}
```

The traversal is finished when the `current` reference "falls off" the end of the `List` and becomes `null`.

Observe that the `Iterator` is able to develop references to values that are not accessible through the public interface of the underlying `List` structure. While it is of obvious utility to access the middle elements of the `List`, these references could be used to modify the associated `List` structure. If the objects referred to through the `Iterator` are modified, this underlying structure could become corrupted. One solution to the problem is to return copies or *clones* of the current object, but then the references returned are not really part of the `List`. The best advice is to think of the values returned by the `Iterator` as *read-only*.

Principle 14 *Assume that values returned by iterators are read-only.*

8.9 Conclusions

In this chapter we have developed the notion of a list and three different implementations. One of the features of the list is that as each of the elements is added to the list, the structure is expanded dynamically, using dynamic memory. To aid in keeping track of an arbitrarily large number of chunks of dynamic memory, we allocate, with each chunk, at least one reference for keeping track of logically nearby memory.

Although the description of the interface for lists is quite detailed, none of the details of any particular implementation show through the interface. This approach to designing data structures makes it less possible for applications to depend on the peculiarities of any particular implementation, making it more likely that implementations can be improved without having to reconsider individual applications.

Finally, as we investigated each of the three implementations, it became clear that there were certain basic trade-offs in good data structure design. Increased speed is often matched by an increased need for space, and an increase in complexity makes the code less maintainable. We discuss these trade-offs in more detail in upcoming chapters.

Self Check Problems

Solutions to these problems begin on page 432.

8.1   What are the essential distinctions between the List types and the Vector implementation?

8.2   Why do most List implementations make use of one or more references for each stored value?

8.3   How do we know if a structure qualifies as a List?

8.4   If class C extends the SinglyLinkedList class, is it a SinglyLinkedList? Is it a List? Is it an AbstractList? Is it a DoublyLinkedList?

8.5   The DoublyLinkedList class has elements with two pointers, while the SinglyLinkedList class has elements with one pointer. Is DoublyLinkedList a SinglyLinkedList with additional information?

8.6   Why do we have a tail reference in the DoublyLinkedList?

8.7   Why don't we have a tail reference in the SinglyLinkedList?

8.8   The ListVector implementation of a List is potentially slow? Why might we use it, in any case?

8.9   The AbstractList class does not make use of any element types or references. Why?

8.10   If you use the add method to add an element to a List, to which end does it get added?

8.11   The get and set methods take an integer index. Which element of the list is referred to by index 1?

Problems

Solutions to the odd-numbered problems begin on page 457.

8.1   When considering a data structure it is important to see how it works in the *boundary cases*. Given an empty List, which methods may be called without violating preconditions?

8.2   Compare the implementation of getLast for each of the three List types we have seen in this chapter.

8.3   From within Java programs, you may access information on the Web using URL's (uniform resource locators). Programmers at MindSlave software (working on their new NetPotato browser) would like to keep track of a potentially large bookmark list of frequently visited URL's. It would be most useful if they had arbitrary access to the values saved within the list. Is a List an appropriate data structure? (Hint: If not, why?)

8.4   Write a List method, equals, that returns true exactly when the elements of two lists are pair-wise equal. Ideally, your implementation should work for any List implementation, without change.

8.5   Write a method of `SinglyLinkedList`, called `reverse`, that reverses the order of the elements in the list. This method should be *destructive*—it should modify the list upon which it acts.

8.6   Write a method of `DoublyLinkedList`, called `reverse`, that reverses the order of the elements in the list. This method should be destructive.

8.7   Write a method of `CircularList`, called `reverse`, that reverses the order of the element in the list. This method should be destructive.

8.8   Each of the n references in a singly linked list are needed if we wish to remove the final element. In a doubly linked list, are each of the additional n `previous` references necessary if we want to remove the tail of the list in constant time? (Hint: What would happen if we mixed `SinglyLinkedListElements` and `DoublyLinkedListElements`?)

8.9   Design a method that inserts an object into the middle of a `CircularList`.

8.10   Which implementation of the `size` and `isEmpty` methods would you use if you had the potential for a million-element list. (Consider the problem of keeping track of the alumni for the University of Michigan.) How would you choose if you had the potential for a million small lists. (Consider the problem of keeping track of the dependents for each of a million income-tax returns.)

8.11   One way to make all the circular list operations run quickly is to keep track of the element that points to the last element in the list. If we call this `penultimate`, then the tail is referenced by `penultimate.next`, and the head by `penultimate.next.next`. What are the disadvantages of this?

8.12   Suppose we read n integers $1, 2, \ldots, n$ from the input, in order. Flipping a coin, we add each new value to either the head or tail of the list. Does this shuffle the data? (Hint: See Problem 5.18.)

8.13   Measure the performance of `addFirst`, `remove(Object)`, and `removeLast` for each of the three implementations (you may include `Vectors`, if you wish). Which implementations perform best for small lists? Which implementations perform best for large lists?

8.14   Consider the implementation of an `insertionSort` that works on `Lists`. (See Exercises 5.3 and 8.2.) What is the worst-case performance of this sort? Be careful.

8.15   Implement a recursive version of the `size` method for `SinglyLinkedLists`. (Hint: A wrapper may be useful.)

8.16   Implement a recursive version of the `contains` method for `SinglyLinkedLists`.

8.17   Suppose the `add` of the `Unique` program is replaced by `addFirst` and the program is run on (for example) the first chapter of Mark Twain's *Tom Sawyer*. Why does the modified program run as much as 25 percent *slower* than the program using the `add` (i.e., `addLast`) method? (Hint: Mark Twain didn't write randomly.)

8.18   Describe an implementation for an iterator associated with `CircularLists`.

8.10   Laboratory: Lists with Dummy Nodes

Objective. To gain experience implementing List-like objects.

Discussion. Anyone attempting to understand the workings of a doubly linked list understands that it is potentially difficult to keep track of the references. One of the problems with writing code associated with linked structures is that there are frequently *boundary cases*. These are special cases that must be handled carefully because the "common" path through the code makes an assumption that does not hold in the special case.

Take, for example, the addFirst method for DoublyLinkedLists:

```
public void addFirst(Object value)
// pre: value is not null
// post: adds element to head of list
{
    // construct a new element, making it head
    head = new DoublyLinkedListElement(value, head, null);
    // fix tail, if necessary
    if (tail == null) tail = head;
    count++;
}
```

The presence of the if statement suggests that sometimes the code must reassign the value of the tail reference. Indeed, if the list is empty, the first element must give an initial non-null value to tail. Keeping track of the various special cases associated with a structure can be very time consuming and error-prone.

One way that the complexity of the code can be reduced is to introduce *dummy nodes*. Usually, there is one dummy node associated with each external reference associated with the structure. In the DoublyLinkedList, for example, we have two references (head and tail); both will refer to a dedicated dummy node:

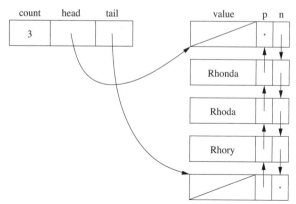

These nodes appear to the code to be normal elements of the list. In fact, they do not hold any useful data. They are completely hidden by the abstraction of the data structure. They are *transparent*.

Because most of the boundary cases are associated with maintaining the correct values of external references and because these external references are now "hidden" behind their respective dummy nodes, most of the method code is simplified. This comes at some cost: the dummy nodes take a small amount of space, and they must be explicitly stepped over if we work at either end of the list. On the other hand, the total amount of code to be written is likely to be reduced, and the running time of many methods decreases if the special condition testing would have been expensive.

Procedure. In this lab we will extend the DoublyLinkedList, building a new class, LinkedList, that makes use of two dummy nodes: one at the head of the list, and one at the end.

LinkedList

You should begin taking a copy of the LinkedList.java starter file. This file simply declares LinkedList to be an extension of the structure package's DoublyLinkedList class. The code associated with each of the existing methods is similar to the code from DoublyLinkedList. You should replace that code with working code that makes use of two dummy nodes:

1. First, recall that the three-parameter constructor for DoublyLinkedList-Elements takes a value and two references—the nodes that are to be **next** and **previous** to this new node. That constructor will also update the **next** and **previous** nodes to point to the newly constructed node. You may find it useful to use the one-parameter constructor, which builds a node with **null next** and **previous** references.

2. Replace the constructor for the LinkedList. Instead of constructing **head** and **tail** references that are **null**, you should construct two dummy nodes; one node is referred to by **head** and the other by **tail**. These dummy nodes should point to each other in the natural way. Because these dummy nodes replace the **null** references of the DoublyLinkedList class, we will not see any need for **null** values in the rest of the code. Amen.

3. Check and make necessary modifications to **size**, **isEmpty**, and **clear**.

4. Now, construct two important **protected** methods. The method **insert-After** takes a **value** and a reference to a node, **previous**. It inserts a new node with the value **value** that directly follows **previous**. It should be declared **protected** because we are not interested in making it a formal feature of the class. The other method, **remove**, is given a reference to a node. It should unlink the node from the linked list and return the value stored in the node. You should, of course, assume that the node removed is not one of the dummy nodes. These methods should be simple with no **if** statements.

5. Using **insertAfter** and **remove**, replace the code for **addFirst**, **addLast**, **getFirst**, **getLast**, **removeFirst**, and **removeLast**. These methods should be very simple (perhaps one line each), with no **if** statements.

6. Next, replace the code for the indexed versions of methods `add`, `remove`, `get`, and `set`. Each of these should make use of methods you have already written. They should work without any special `if` statements.

7. Finally, replace the versions of methods `indexOf`, `lastIndexOf`, and `contains` (which can be written using `indexOf`), and the `remove` method that takes an object. Each of these searches for the location of a value in the list and then performs an action. You will find that each of these methods is simplified, making no reference to the `null` reference.

Thought Questions. Consider the following questions as you complete the lab:

1. The three-parameter constructor for `DoublyLinkedListElement`s makes use of two `if` statements. Suppose that you replace the calls to this constructor with the one-parameter constructor and manually use `setNext` and `setPrevious` to set the appropriate references. The `if` statements disappear. Why?

2. The `contains` method can be written making use of the `indexOf` method, but not the other way around. Why?

3. Notice that we could have replaced the method `insertAfter` with a similar method, `insertBefore`. This method inserts a new value *before* the indicated node. Some changes would have to be made to your code. There does not appear, however, to be a choice between versions of `remove`. Why is this the case? (Hint: Do you ever pass a dummy node to `remove`?)

4. Even though we don't need to have the special cases in, for example, the indexed version of `add`, it is desirable to handle one or more cases in a special way. What are the cases, and why is it desirable?

5. Which file is bigger: your final result source or the original?

Notes:

Chapter 9

Linear Structures

> *"Rule Forty-two.*
> *All persons more than a mile high to leave the court."...*
> *"Well, I shan't go," said Alice; "Besides*
> *that's not a regular rule: you just invented it now."*
> *"It's the oldest rule in the book," said the King.*
> *"Then it ought to be Number One," said Alice.*
> —Charles Lutwidge Dodgson

THE STATE OF SOME STRUCTURES REFLECTS THEIR HISTORY. Many systems—for example, a line at a ticket booth or, as Alice presumes, the King's book of rules—modify their state using two pivotal operations: *add* and *remove*. As with most data structures, when values are added and removed the structure grows and shrinks. *Linear structures*, however, shrink in a predetermined manner: values are removed in an order based only on the order they were added. All linear structures abide by a very simple interface:

```
public interface Linear extends Structure
{
    public void add(Object value);
    // pre: value is non-null
    // post: the value is added to the collection,
    //       the consistent replacement policy is not specified

    public Object get();
    // pre: structure is not empty
    // post: returns reference to next object to be removed

    public Object remove();
    // pre: structure is not empty
    // post: removes an object from store

    public int size();
    // post: returns the number of elements in the structure

    public boolean empty();
    // post: returns true if and only if the linear structure is empty
}
```

Linear

For each structure the **add** and **remove** methods are used to insert new values into the linear structure and remove those values later. A few utility routines are also provided: `get` retrieves a copy of the value that would be removed next, while `size` returns the size of the structure and `empty` returns whether or not the linear structure is empty.

One thing that is important to note is that the `empty` method seems to provide the same features as the `isEmpty` method we have seen in previous structures. This is a common feature of ongoing data structure design—as structures evolve, aliases for methods arise. In this case, many native classes of Java actually have an `empty` method. We provide that for compatibility; we implement it in our abstract implementation of the `Linear` interface. The `empty` method simply calls the `isEmpty` method required by the `Structure` interface and ultimately coded by the particular `Linear` implementation.

Abstract-
Linear

```
abstract public class AbstractLinear extends AbstractStructure
    implements Linear
{
    public boolean empty()
    // post: return true iff the linear structure is empty
    {
        return isEmpty();
    }

    public Object remove(Object o)
    // pre: value is non-null
    // post: value is removed from linear structure, if it was there
    {
        Assert.fail("Method not implemented.");
        // never reaches this statement:
        return null;
    }
}
```

Since our `Linear` interface extends our notion of `Structure`, so we will also be required to implement the methods of that interface. In particular, the `remove(Object)` method is required. We use the `AbstractLinear` implementation to provide a default version of the `remove` method that indicates it is not yet implemented. The benefits of making `Linear` classes instances of `Structure` outweigh the perfect fit of the `Structure` interface.

Since `AbstractLinear` extends `AbstractStructure`, any features of the `AbstractStructure` implementation are enjoyed by the `AbstractLinear` interface as well.

We are now ready to implement several implementations of the `Linear` interface. The two that we will look at carefully in this chapter, *stacks* and *queues*, are the most common—and most widely useful—examples of linear data structures we will encounter.

9.1 Stacks

Our first linear structure is a *stack*. A stack is a collection of items that exhibit the behavior that *the last item in is the first item out*. It is a *LIFO* ("lie-foe") structure. The `add` method pushes an item onto the stack, while `remove` pops off the item that was pushed on most recently. We will provide the traditionally named methods `push` and `pop` as alternatives for `add` and `remove`, respectively. We will use these stack-specific terms when we wish to emphasize the LIFO quality. A nondestructive operation, `get`, returns the top element of the `Stack`— the element that would be returned next. Since it is meaningless to `remove` or `get` a `Stack` that is empty, it is important to have access to the size methods (`empty` and `size`). Here is the interface that defines what it means to be a `Stack`:

Stack

```
public interface Stack extends Linear
{
    public void add(Object item);
    // post: item is added to stack
    //       will be popped next if no intervening add

    public void push(Object item);
    // post: item is added to stack
    //       will be popped next if no intervening push

    public Object remove();
    // pre: stack is not empty
    // post: most recently added item is removed and returned

    public Object pop();
    // pre: stack is not empty
    // post: most recently pushed item is removed and returned

    public Object get();
    // pre: stack is not empty
    // post: top value (next to be popped) is returned

    public Object getFirst();
    // pre: stack is not empty
    // post: top value (next to be popped) is returned

    public Object peek();
    // pre: stack is not empty
    // post: top value (next to be popped) is returned

    public boolean empty();
    // post: returns true if and only if the stack is empty

    public int size();
    // post: returns the number of elements in the stack
```

}

To maintain applications that are consistent with Java's `java.util.Stack` the alternative operations of `push` and `pop` may be preferred in some of our discussions.

9.1.1 Example: Simulating Recursion

Earlier we mentioned that tail recursive methods could be transformed to use loops. More complex recursive methods—especially those that perform multiple recursive calls—can be more complex to implement. In this section, we focus on the implementation of an iterative version of the quicksort sorting algorithm. Before we turn to the implementation, we will investigate the calling mechanisms of languages like Java.

Data available to well-designed methods come mainly from two locations: the method's parameters and its local variables. These values help to define the method's current *state*. In addition to the explicit values, implicit parameters also play a role. Let us consider the recursive version of quicksort we saw earlier:

QuickSort

```
private static void quickSortRecursive(int data[],int left,int right)
// pre: left <= right
// post: data[left..right] in ascending order
{
    int pivot;   // the final location of the leftmost value
    if (left >= right) return;
    pivot = partition(data,left,right);     /* 1 - place pivot */
    quickSortRecursive(data,left,pivot-1);  /* 2 - sort small */
    quickSortRecursive(data,pivot+1,right); /* 3 - sort large */
    /* done! */
}
```

The *flow of control* in most methods is from top to bottom. If the machine stops execution, it is found to be executing one of the statements. In our recursive quicksort, there are three main points of execution: (1) before the first recursive call, (2) before the second recursive call, and (3) just before the return. To focus on what needs to be accomplished, the computer keeps a special reference to the code, called a *program counter*. For the purposes of our exercise, we will assume the program counter takes on the value 1, 2, or 3, depending on its location within the routine.

These values—the parameters, the local variables, and the program counter—reside in a structure called a *call frame*. Whenever a method is called, a new call frame is constructed and filled out with appropriate values. Because many methods may be active at the same time (methods can call each other), there are usually several active call frames. These frames are maintained in a *call stack*. Since the first method to return is the last method called, a stack seems appropriate. Figure 9.1 describes the relationship between the call frames of the call stack and a partial run of quicksort.

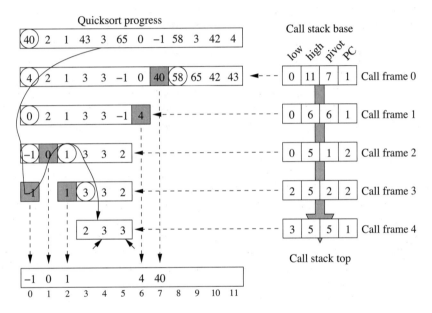

Figure 9.1   A partially complete quicksort and its call stack. The quicksort routine is currently partitioning the three-element subarray containing 2, 3, and 3. The curve indicates the progress of recursion in quicksort to this point.

Our approach is to construct a stack of frames that describes the progress of the various "virtually recursive" calls to quicksort. Each frame must maintain enough information to simulate the actual call frame of the recursive routine:

```
class callFrame
{
    int pivot;// location of pivot
    int low;  // left index
    int high; // right index
    int PC; // next statement (see numbering in recursive code)

    public callFrame(int l, int h)
    // post: generate new call frame with low and high as passed
    {
        low = l; high = h; PC = 1;
    }
}
```

Just as with real call frames, it's possible for variables to be uninitialized (e.g., pivot)! We can consider an iterative version of quicksort:

```
public static void quickSortIterative(int data[], int n)
// pre: n <= data.length
// post: data[0..n-1] in ascending order
{
    Stack callStack = new StackList();
    callStack.push(new callFrame(0,n-1));
    while (!callStack.isEmpty())
    {   // some "virtual" method outstanding
        callFrame curr = (callFrame)callStack.get();
        if (curr.PC == 1) { // partition and sort lower
            // return if trivial
            if (curr.low >= curr.high) { callStack.pop(); continue; }
            // place the pivot at the correct location
            curr.pivot = partition(data,curr.low,curr.high);
            curr.PC++;
            // sort the smaller values...
            callStack.push(new callFrame(curr.low,curr.pivot-1));
        } else if (curr.PC == 2) { // sort upper
            curr.PC++;
            // sort the larger values....
            callStack.push(new callFrame(curr.pivot+1,curr.high));
        } else { callStack.pop(); continue; } // return
    }
}
```

We begin by creating a new stack initialized with a callFrame that simulates first call to the recursive routine. The low and high variables of the frame are initialized to 0 and $n-1$ respectively, and we are about to execute statement 1. As long as there is a call frame on the stack, some invocation of quicksort is still executing. Looking at the top frame, we conditionally execute the code associated with each statement number. For example, statement 1 returns (by popping off the top call frame) if `low` and `high` suggest a trivial sort. Each variable is prefixed by `curr` because the local variables reside within the call frame, `curr`. When we would execute a recursive call, we instead increment the "program counter" and push a new frame on the stack with appropriate initialization of local variables. Because each local variable appears in several places on the call stack, recursive procedures appear to have fewer local variables. The conversion of recursion to iteration, then, requires more explicit handling of local storage during execution.

The sort continues until all the call frames are popped off. This happens when each method reaches statement 3, that is, when the recursive quicksort would have returned.

We now discuss two implementations of `Stacks`: one based on a `Vector` and one based on a `List`.

9.1.2 Vector-Based Stacks

Let us consider a traditional stack-based analogy: the storage of trays in a fast-food restaurant. At the beginning of a meal, you are given a tray from a stack. The process of removing a tray is the popping of a tray off the stack. When trays are returned, they are pushed back on the stack.

Now, assume that the side of the tray holder is marked in a rulerlike fashion, perhaps to measure the number of trays stacked. Squinting one's eyes, this looks like a sideways vector:

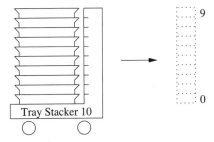

Following our analogy, the implementation of a `Stack` using a `Vector` can be accomplished by aligning the "top" of the `Stack` with the "end" of the `Vector` (see Figure 9.2). We provide two constructors, including one that provides the `Vector` with the initial capacity:

```
protected Vector data;

public StackVector()
// post: an empty stack is created
{
    data = new Vector();
}
```

StackVector

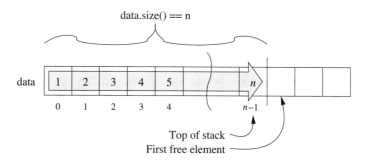

Figure 9.2 A `Vector`-based stack containing n elements. The top of the stack is implied by the length of the underlying vector. The arrow demonstrates the direction of growth.

```
public StackVector(int size)
// post: an empty stack with initial capacity of size is created
{
    data = new Vector(size);
}
```

To add elements on the `Stack`, we simply use the `add` method of the `Vector`. When an element is to be removed from the `Stack`, we carefully remove the last element, returning its value.

```
public void add(Object item)
// post: item is added to stack
//       will be popped next if no intervening add
{
    data.add(item);
}

public Object remove()
// pre: stack is not empty
// post: most recently added item is removed and returned
{
    return data.remove(size()-1);
}
```

The `add` method appends the element to the end of the `Vector`, extending it if necessary. Notice that if the vector has n elements, this element is written to slot n, increasing the number of elements to $n+1$. Removing an element reverses this process: it removes and returns the last element. (Note the invocation of our principle of symmetry, here. We will depend on this notion in our design of a number of `add` and `remove` method pairs.) The `get` method is like `remove`, except that the stack is not modified. The size of the stack is easily determined by requesting the same information from the underlying `Vector`. Of course when the `Vector` is empty, so is the `Stack` it supports.[1]

```
public boolean isEmpty()
// post: returns true if and only if the stack is empty
{
    return size() == 0;
}

public int size()
// post: returns the number of elements in stack
{
    return data.size();
}

public void clear()
// post: removes all elements from stack
{
    data.clear();
}
```

The `clear` method is required because the `Stack` indirectly extends the `Structure` interface.

9.1.3 List-Based Stacks

Only the top "end" of the stack ever gets modified. It is reasonable, then, to seek an efficient implementation of a `Stack` using a `SinglyLinkedList`. Because our `SinglyLinkedList` manipulates its head more efficiently than its tail, we align the `Stack` top with the head of the `SinglyLinkedList` (see Figure 9.3).

The `add` method simply performs an `addFirst`, and the `remove` operation performs `removeFirst`. Since we have implemented the list's `remove` operation so that it returns the value removed, the value can be passed along through the stack's `remove` method.

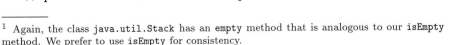

StackList

```
public void add(Object value)
// post: adds an element to stack;
//       will be next element popped if no intervening push
{
    data.addFirst(value);
}

public Object remove()
// pre: stack is not empty
// post: removes and returns the top element from stack
```

---

[1] Again, the class `java.util.Stack` has an `empty` method that is analogous to our `isEmpty` method. We prefer to use `isEmpty` for consistency.

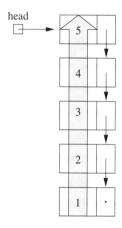

Figure 9.3   A stack implemented using a singly-linked list. The arrow demonstrates the direction of stack growth.

```
    {
        return data.removeFirst();
    }
```

The remaining methods are simply the obvious wrappers for similar methods from the `SinglyLinkedList`. Because the stack operations are trivial representations of the linked-list operations, their complexities are all the same as the corresponding operations found in linked lists—each takes constant time.

It should be noted that any structure implementing the `List` interface would be sufficient for implementing a `Stack`. The distinction, however, between the various lists we have seen presented here has focused on providing quick access to the tail of the list. Since stacks do not require access to the tail, the alternative implementations of list structure do not provide any benefit. Thus we use the `SinglyLinkedList` implementation.

9.1.4   Comparisons

Clearly, stacks are easily implemented using the structures we have seen so far. In fact, the complexities of those operations make it difficult to decide which of the classes is better. How can we make the decision?

Let's consider each a little more carefully. First, in terms of time, both underlying structures provide efficient implementations. In addition, both structures provide (virtually) unlimited extension of the structure. Their difference stems from a difference in approach for expanding the structure. In the case of the vector, the structure is responsible for deciding when the structure is extended. Because the structure grows by doubling, the reallocation of memory occurs increasingly less often, but *when* that reallocation occurs, it takes an increasingly long time. So, while the *amortized* cost of dynamically extending vectors is constant time per element, the incremental cost of extending the vector either is zero (if no extension actually occurs) or is occasionally proportional to the size of the vector. Some applications may not be tolerant of this great variation in the cost of extending the structure. In those cases the `StackList` implementation should be considered.

The constant incremental overhead of expanding the `StackList` structure, however, comes at a price. Since each element of the list structure requires a reference to the list that follows, there is a potentially significant overhead in terms of space. If the items stored in the stack are roughly the size of a reference, the overhead is significant. If, however, the size of a reference is insignificant when compared to the size of the elements stored, the increase in space used may be reasonable.

9.2 Queues

Most of us have participated in queues—at movie theaters, toll booths, or ice cream shops, or while waiting for a communal bathroom in a large family! A *queue*, like a stack, is an ordered collection of elements with tightly controlled access to the structure. Unlike a stack, however, *the first item in is the first item out*. We call it a *FIFO* ("fie-foe") structure. FIFO's are useful because they maintain the order of the data that run through them.

The primary operations of queues are to *enqueue* and *dequeue* elements. Again, to support the `Linear` interface, we supply the **add** and **remove** methods as alternatives. Elements are added at the *tail* of the structure, where they then pass through the structure, eventually reaching the *head* where they are removed. The interface provides a number of other features we have seen already:

Queue

```
public interface Queue
    extends Linear
{
    public void add(Object value);
    // post: the value is added to the tail of the structure

    public void enqueue(Object value);
    // post: the value is added to the tail of the structure

    public Object remove();
    // pre: the queue is not empty
    // post: the head of the queue is removed and returned

    public Object dequeue();
    // pre: the queue is not empty
    // post: the head of the queue is removed and returned
```

```
                    public Object getFirst();
                    // pre: the queue is not empty
                    // post: the element at the head of the queue is returned

                    public Object get();
                    // pre: the queue is not empty
                    // post: the element at the head of the queue is returned

                    public Object peek();
                    // pre: the queue is not empty
                    // post: the element at the head of the queue is returned

                    public boolean empty();
                    // post: returns true if and only if the queue is empty

                    public int size();
                    // post: returns the number of elements in the queue
                }
```

As with the Stack definition, the Queue interface describes necessary characteristics of a class, but not the code to implement it. We use, instead, the AbstractQueue class to provide any code that might be of general use in implementing queues. Here, for example, we provide the various traditional aliases for the standard operations add and remove required by the Linear interface:

AbstractQueue

```
public abstract class AbstractQueue
    extends AbstractLinear implements Queue
{
    public void enqueue(Object item)
    // post: the value is added to the tail of the structure
    {
        add(item);
    }

    public Object dequeue()
    // pre: the queue is not empty
    // post: the head of the queue is removed and returned
    {
        return remove();
    }

    public Object getFirst()
    // pre: the queue is not empty
    // post: the element at the head of the queue is returned
    {
        return get();
    }

    public Object peek()
    // pre: the queue is not empty
```

```
    // post: the element at the head of the queue is returned
    {
        return get();
    }
}
```

We will use this abstraction implementation as the basis for the various implementations of queues that we see in this chapter.

9.2.1   Example: Solving a Coin Puzzle

As an example of an application of queues, we consider an interesting coin puzzle (see Figure 9.4). A dime, penny, nickel, and quarter are arranged in decreasing size in each of the leftmost four squares of a five-square board. The object is to reverse the order of the coins and to leave them in the rightmost four slots, in the least number of moves. In each move a single coin moves to the left or right. Coins may be stacked, but only the top coin is allowed to move. When a coin moves, it may not land off the board or on a smaller coin. A typical intermediate legal position is shown in the middle of Figure 9.4. From this point, the nickel may move right and the dime may move in either direction.

We begin by defining a "board state." This object keeps track of the positions of each of the four coins, as well as the series of board states that lead to this state from the start. Its implementation is an interesting problem (see Problem 1.14). We outline its interface here:

CoinPuzzle

```
    class State
    {
        public static final int DIME=0;     // coins
        public static final int PENNY=1;
        public static final int NICKEL=2;
        public static final int QUARTER=3;
        public static final int LEFT = -1; // directions
        public static final int RIGHT = 1;

        public State()
        // post: construct initial layout of coins

        public State(State prior)
        // pre: prior is a non-null state
        // post: constructs a copy of that state to be successor state

        public boolean done()
        // post: returns true if state is the finish state

        public boolean validMove(int coin, int direction)
        // pre: State.DIME <= coin <= State.QUARTER
        //      direction = State.left or State.right
        // post: returns true if coin can be moved in desired direction
```

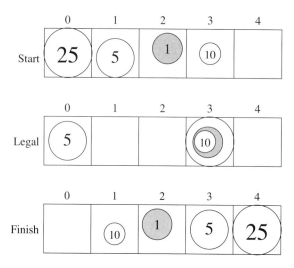

Figure 9.4 A four-coin puzzle. Top and bottom orientations depict the start and finish positions. A typical legal position is shown in the middle.

```
public State move(int coin, int direction)
// pre: coin and direction describe valid move
// post: coin is moved in that direction

public int printMoves()
// post: print moves up to and including this point

public int id()
// post: construct an integer representing state
//       states of coins are equal iff id's are equal
}
```

The parameterless constructor builds a board in the initial state, while the one-parameter constructor generates a new state to follow `prior`. The `done` method checks for a state that is in the final position. Coins (identified by constants such as `State.PENNY`) are moved in different directions (e.g., `State.LEFT`), but only if the move is valid. Once the final state is found, the intermediate states leading to a particular board position are printed with `printMoves`.

Once the `State` class has been defined, it is a fairly simple matter to solve the puzzle:

```
public static void main(String args[])
{
    Queue pool = new QueueList();
    State board = new State();
```

```
          BitSet seen = new BitSet(5*5*5*5);
          pool.add(board);
          while (!pool.isEmpty())
          {
              board = (State)pool.remove();
              if (board.done()) break;
              int moveCode = board.id();
              if (seen.contains(moveCode)) continue;
              seen.add(moveCode);
              for (int coin = State.DIME; coin <= State.QUARTER; coin++)
              {
                  if (board.validMove(coin,State.LEFT))
                      pool.add(board.move(coin,State.LEFT));
                  if (board.validMove(coin,State.RIGHT))
                      pool.add(board.move(coin,State.RIGHT));
              }
          }
          board.printMoves();
      }
```

We begin by keeping a pool of potentially unvisited board states. This queue
initially includes the single starting board position. At each stage of the loop an
unvisited board position is checked. If it is not the finish position, the boards
generated by the legal moves from the current position are added to the state
pool. Processing continues until the final position is encountered. At that point,
the intermediate positions are printed out.

Because the pool is a FIFO, each unvisited position near the head of the
queue must be at least as close to the initial position as those found near the
end. Thus, when the final position is found, the distance from the start position
(in moves) is a minimum!

A subtle point in this code is the use of the id function and the BitSet.[2]
The id function returns a small integer (between 0 and $5^5 - 1$) that uniquely
identifies the state of the board. These integers are kept in the set. If, in the
future, a board position with a previously encountered state number is found,
the state can safely be ignored. Without this optimization, it becomes difficult
to avoid processing previously visited positions hundreds or thousands of times
before a solution is found. We will leave it to the reader to find the solution
either manually or automatically. (The fastest solution involves 22 moves.)

We now investigate three different implementations of queues, based on
Lists, Vectors, and arrays. Each has its merits and drawbacks, so we consider them carefully.

---

[2] BitSets are part of the java.util package, and we provide public implementations of these
and other sets in the structure package. They are not discussed formally within this text.

9.2.2 List-Based Queues

Drawing upon our various analogies with real life, it is clear that there are *two* points of interest in a queue: the head and the tail. This two-ended view of queues makes the list a natural structure to support the queue. In this implementation, the head and tail of the queue correspond to the head and tail of the list. The major difference is that a queue is restricted to peeking at and removing values from the head and appending elements to the tail. Lists, on the other hand, allow adding and removing values from both ends.

This discussion leads us to the following protected field within the `QueueList` structure:

```
protected List data;
```

QueueList

When we consider the constructor, however, we are forced to consider more carefully which implementation of a list is actually most suitable. While for the stack the `SinglyLinkedList` was ideal, that implementation only provides efficient manipulation of the head of the list. To get fast access to both ends of the list, we are forced to consider either the `DoublyLinkedList` or the `CircularList`. Either would be time-efficient here, but we choose the more compact `CircularList` (see Figure 9.5). We now consider our constructor:

```
public QueueList()
// post: constructs a new, empty queue
{
    data = new CircularList();
}
```

Notice that, because the `List` structure has unbounded size, the `Queue` structure built atop it is also unbounded. This is a nice feature, since many applications of queues have no easily estimated upper bound.

To add a value to the queue, we simply add an element to the tail of the list. Removing a value from the list provides what we need for the `remove` operation. (Note, once again, that the decision to have `remove` operations symmetric with the `add` operations was the right decision.)

```
public void add(Object value)
// post: the value is added to the tail of the structure
{
    data.addLast(value);
}

public Object remove()
// pre: the queue is not empty
// post: the head of the queue is removed and returned
{
    return data.removeFirst();
}
```

The needs of the `remove` operation are satisfied by the `removeFirst` operation on a `List`, so very little code needs to be written. The simplicity of these methods demonstrates how *code reuse* can make the implementation of structures less difficult. This is particularly dramatic when we consider the implementation of the size-related methods of the `QueueList` structure:

```
public Object get()
// pre: the queue is not empty
// post: the element at the head of the queue is returned
{
    return data.getFirst();
}

public int size()
// post: returns the number of elements in the queue
{
    return data.size();
}

public void clear()
// post: removes all elements from the queue
{
    data.clear();
}

public boolean isEmpty()
// post: returns true iff the queue is empty
{
    return data.isEmpty();
}
```

Because the `QueueList` is a rewrapping of the `List` structure, the complexity of each of the methods corresponds to the complexity of the underlying `List` implementation. For `CircularLists`, most of the operations can be performed in constant time.

We now consider two implementations that do not use dynamically linked structures for their underpinnings. While these structures have drawbacks, they are useful when space is a concern or when the size of the queue can be bounded above.

9.2.3 Vector-Based Queues

The lure of implementing structures through code reuse can lead to performance problems if the underlying structure is not well considered. Thus, while we have advocated hiding the unnecessary details of the implementation within the object, it is important to have a sense of the *complexity* of the object's methods, if the object is the basis for supporting larger structures.

Principle 15 *Understand the complexity of the structures you use.*

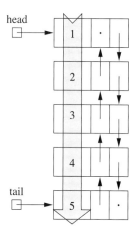

Figure 9.5 A `Queue` implemented using a `List`. The head of the `List` corresponds to the head of the `Queue`.

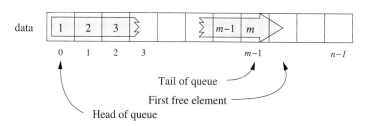

Figure 9.6 A `Queue` implemented atop a `Vector`. As elements are added (enqueued), the `Queue` expands the `Vector`. As elements are removed, the leftmost element is removed, shrinking the `Vector`.

We will return to this issue a number of times. Careful design of data structures sometimes involves careful reconsideration of the performance of structures.

Now, let's consider an implementation of `Queues` using `Vectors`. Recall that a `Vector` is a linear structure whose values can be randomly accessed and modified. We will, again, reconsider the `Vector` as a two-ended structure in our attempt to implement a queue (see Figure 9.6). The head of the queue will be found in the first location of the `Vector`, and the tail of the queue will be found in the last. (The index associated with each element will, essentially, enumerate the order in which they would be removed in the future.)

The constructor creates an empty `QueueVector` by creating an empty `Vector`. When an upper bound is provided, the second `QueueVector` constructor passes that information along to the `Vector`:

```
protected Vector data;

public QueueVector()
// post: constructs an empty queue
{
    data = new Vector();
}

public QueueVector(int size)
// post: constructs an empty queue of appropriate size
{
    data = new Vector(size);
}
```

QueueVector

Adding an element to the end of the queue is as simple as adding an element to the end of the `Vector`. This is accomplished through the `Vector` method `addElement`.

```
public void add(Object value)
// post: the value is added to the tail of the structure
{
    data.add(value);
}
```

As with the `remove` method of the `StackVector` class, remove the first element of the `Vector`, and return the returned value.

```
public Object remove()
// pre: the queue is not empty
// post: the head of the queue is removed and returned
{
    return data.remove(0);
}
```

As usual, the remaining methods rewrap similar `Vector` methods in the expected way. Because of the restricted nature of this linear structure, we take care not to publicize any features of the `Vector` class that violate the basic restrictions of a `Linear` interface.

When considering the complexity of these methods, it is important to keep in mind the underlying complexities of the `Vector`. For example, adding a value to the "end" of the `Vector` can be accomplished, on average, in constant time.[3] That method, `add`, is so special in its simplicity that it was distinguished from the general `add(int)` method: the latter operation has time complexity that is expected to be $O(n)$, where n is the length of the `Vector`. The worst-case

---

[3] It can vary considerably if the `Vector` requires reallocation of memory, but the average time (as we saw in Section 3.5) is still constant time.

behavior, when a value is added at the front of the `Vector`, is $O(n)$. All the existing elements must be moved to the right to make room for the new value.

A similar situation occurs when we consider the removal of values from a `Vector`. Unfortunately, the case we need to use—removing an element from the beginning of a `Vector`—is precisely the worst case. It requires removing the value and then shifting $n-1$ elements to the left, one slot. That $O(n)$ behavior slows down our `remove` operation, probably by an unacceptable amount. For example, the process of adding n elements to a queue and then dequeuing them takes about $O(n^2)$ time, which may not be acceptable.

Even though the implementation seemed straightforward, we pay a significant price for this code reuse. If we could remove a value from the `Vector` without having to move the other elements, the complexity of these operations could be simplified. We consider that approach in our implementation of the `Queue` interface using arrays of objects.

9.2.4 Array-Based Queues

If we can determine an upper bound for the size of the queue we need, we can gain some efficiency because we need not worry so much about managing the memory we use. Keyboard hardware, for example, often implements a queue of keystrokes that are to be shipped off to the attached processor. The size of that queue can be easily bounded above by, say, several hundred keystrokes. Notice, by the way, that this does not limit the number of elements that can run through the queue, only the number of values that can be resident within the queue *simultaneously*.

Fast typists, take note!

Once the array has been allocated, we simply place enqueued values in successive locations within the array, starting at location 0. The head of the queue—the location containing the oldest element—is initially found at location 0. As elements are removed, we return the value stored at the head of the queue, and move the head toward the right in the array. All the operations must explicitly store and maintain the size of the queue in a counter. This counter should be a nonnegative number less than the length of the array.

One potential problem occurs when a value is removed from the very end of the array. Under normal circumstances, the head of the queue would move to the right, but we now need to have it wrap around. One common solution is to use modular arithmetic. When the head moves too far to the right, its value, `head`, is no longer less than the length of the array, `data.length`. After moving the head to the right (by adding 1 to `head`), we simply compute the remainder when dividing by `data.length`. This always returns a valid index for the array, `data`, and it indexes the value just to the right, in wrap-around fashion (see Figure 9.7). It should be noted, at this point, that remainder computation is reasonable for positive values; if `head` were ever to become negative, one must take care to check to see if a negative remainder might occur. If that appears to be a possibility, simply adding `data.length` to the value before remainder computation fixes the problem in a portable way.

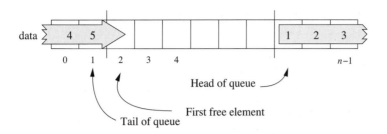

Figure 9.7 A `Queue` implemented atop an array. As elements are added (enqueued), the queue wraps from the back to the front of the array.

Our `QueueArray` implementation, then, requires three values: an array of objects that we allocate once and never expand, the index of the head of the queue, and the number of elements currently stored within the queue.

QueueArray

```
protected Object data[]; // an array of the data
protected int head; // next dequeue-able value
protected int count; // current size of queue
```

Given an upper bound, the constructor allocates the array and sets the `head` and `count` variables to 0. The initial value of `head` could, actually, be any value between 0 and `size-1`, but we use 0, for neatness.

42 isn't the ultimate answer, then?

```
public QueueArray(int size)
// post: create a queue capable of holding at most size values
{
    data = new Object[size];
    head = 0;
    count = 0;
}
```

The `add` and `remove` methods appear more complex than their `QueueVector` counterparts, but review of the implementation of the `Vector` class proves their similarity. The `add` method adds a value at the logical end of the queue—the first free slot in the array—in wrap-around fashion. That location is `count` slots to the right of the head of the queue and is computed using modular arithmetic; `remove` is similar, but carefully moves the `head` to the right. The reader should verify that, in a valid `QueueArray`, the value of `head` will never pass the value of `tail`.

```
public void add(Object value)
// pre: the queue is not full
// post: the value is added to the tail of the structure
{
    Assert.pre(!isFull(),"Queue is not full.");
```

```
    int tail = (head + count) % data.length;
    data[tail] = value;
    count++;
}

public Object remove()
// pre: the queue is not empty
// post: the head of the queue is removed and returned
{
    Assert.pre(!isEmpty(),"The queue is not empty.");
    Object value = data[head];
    head = (head + 1) % data.length;
    count--;
    return value;
}
```

The **get** method just provides quick access to the **head** entry of the array.

```
public Object get()
// pre: the queue is not empty
// post: the element at the head of the queue is returned
{
    Assert.pre(!isEmpty(),"The queue is not empty.");
    return data[head];
}
```

Because we are directly using arrays, we do not have the luxury of previously constructed size-oriented methods, so we are forced to implement these directly. Again, the cost of an efficient implementation can mean less code reuse—or increased original code and the potential for error.

```
public int size()
// post: returns the number of elements in the queue
{
    return count;
}

public void clear()
// post: removes all elements from the queue
{
    // we could remove all the elements from the queue
    count = 0;
    head = 0;
}

public boolean isFull()
// post: returns true if the queue is at its capacity
{
    return count == data.length;
}
```

```
public boolean isEmpty()
// post: returns true iff the queue is empty
{
    return count == 0;
}
```

Alternative Array Implementations

One aesthetic drawback of the implementation of queues described is that symmetric operations—add and remove—do not lead to symmetric code. There are several reasons for this, but we might uncover some of the details by reconsidering the implementations.

Two variables, head and count, are responsible for *encoding* (in an asymmetric way) the information that might be more symmetrically encoded using two variables, say head and tail. For the sake of argument, suppose that head points to the oldest value in the queue, while tail points to the oldest value *not* in the queue—the value to the right of the last value in the queue. A simple test to see if the queue is empty is to check to see if head == tail. Strangely enough this also appears to be a test to see if the queue is full! Since a queue should never be simultaneously empty and full, this problem must be addressed.

Suppose the array has length l. Then both head and tail have a range of 0 to $l - 1$. They take on l values apiece. Now consider all queues with head values stored beginning at location 0. The head is fixed at 0, but tail may take on any of the l values between 0 and $l - 1$, inclusive. The queues represented, however, have $l + 1$ potential states: an empty queue, a queue with one value, a queue with two values, up to a queue with l values. Because there are $l + 1$ queues, they cannot be adequately represented by a pair of variables that can support only l different states. There are several solutions to this conflict that we outline momentarily and discuss in problems at the end of the chapter.

1. A boolean variable, queueEmpty, could be added to distinguish between the two states where head and tail are identical. Code written using this technique is clean and symmetric. The disadvantage of this technique is that more code must be written to maintain the extra variable.

2. An array element logically to the left of the head of the queue can be reserved. The queue is full if there are $l - 1$ values within the queue. Since it would not be possible to add a value when the queue is full, the tail and head variables would never "become equal" through expansion. The only significant difference is the allocation of an extra reserved cell, and a change in the isFull method to see if the tail is just to the logical left of the head. The disadvantage of this technique is that it requires the allocation of another array element. When objects are large, this cost may be prohibitively expensive. (Again, in Java, an Object is a small reference to the actual memory used, so the cost is fairly insignificant. In

other languages, where instances are stored directly, and not as references, this cost may be prohibitively expensive.)

Our actual implementation, of course, provides a third solution to the problem. While we like our solution, data abstraction allows us to hide any changes we might make if we change our minds.

9.3 Example: Solving Mazes

To demonstrate the utility of stacks and queues, we consider the automated solution of a maze. A *maze* is simply a matrix of cells that are adjacent to one another. The user begins in a special *start cell* and seeks a path of adjacent cells that lead to the *finish cell*.

One general approach to solving a maze (or any other search problem) is to consider unvisited cells as potential tasks. Each unvisited cell represents the task of *finding a path from that cell to the finish*. Some cells, of course, may not be reachable from the start position, so they are tasks we seek to avoid. Other cells lead us on trails from the start to finish. Viewed in this manner, we can use the linear structure to help us solve the problem by keeping track of outstanding tasks—unvisited cells adjacent to visited cells.

In the following program, we make use of two abstract classes, `Position` and `Maze`. A `Position` is used to identify a unique location within a maze. Any `Position` can be transformed into another `Position` by asking it for an adjacent position to the north, south, east, or west. Here is the class:

MazeRunner

```
class Position
{
    public Position north()
    // post: returns position above

    public Position south()
    // post: returns position below

    public Position east()
    // post: returns position to right

    public Position west()
    // post: returns position to left

    public boolean equals(Object other)
    // post: returns true iff objects represent same position
}
```

The interface for the `Maze` class reads a maze description from a file and generates the appropriate adjacency of cells. We ignore the implementation that is not important to us at this point (it is available online):

```
class Maze
{
    public Maze(String filename)
    // pre: filename is the name of a maze file. # is a wall.
    //      's' marks the start, 'f' marks the finish.
    // post: reads and constructs maze from file <filename>

    public void visit(Position p)
    // pre: p is a position within the maze
    // post: cell at position p is set to visited

    public boolean isVisited(Position p)
    // pre: p is a position within the maze
    // pos: returns true if the position has been visited

    public Position start()
    // post: returns start position

    public Position finish()
    // post: returns finish position

    public boolean isClear(Position p)
    // post: returns true iff p is a clear location within the maze
}
```

Now, once we have the structures supporting the construction of mazes, we can use a Linear structure to organize the search for a solution in a Maze:

```
public static void main(String[] arguments)
{
    Maze m = new Maze(arguments[0]); // the maze
    Position goal = m.finish(); // where the finish is
    Position square = null; // the current position
    // a linear structure to manage search
    Linear todo = new StackList();

    // begin by priming the queue(stack) w/starting position
    todo.add(m.start());
    while (!todo.isEmpty()) // while we haven't finished exploring
    {
        // take the top position from the stack and check for finish
        square = (Position)todo.remove();
        if (m.isVisited(square)) continue; // been here before
        if (square.equals(goal)) {
            System.out.println(m); // print solution
            break;
        }
        // not finished.
        // visit this location, and add neighbors to pool
        m.visit(square);
```

```
####################        ####################
#s#        #f   #    #       #s#         #f...#...#
# ####### #### # # #         #.####### ####.#.#.#
#         #  # ### #         #........#..#.###.#
##### ### #         #        ##### ###.#........#
#   # #   ####### ##         #   # #...#######.##
#   # # ### #   # #          #   # #.### #...#..#
#   # # #   # # ## #         #   # #.#...#.#.##.#
#     #   #   #    #         #     #...#...#....#
####################        ####################
```

Figure 9.8 A classic maze and its solution found using a stack. Dots indicate locations in the maze visited during the solution process.

```
            if (m.isClear(square.north())) todo.add(square.north());
            if (m.isClear(square.west()))  todo.add(square.west());
            if (m.isClear(square.south())) todo.add(square.south());
            if (m.isClear(square.east()))  todo.add(square.east());
        }
    }
```

We begin by placing the start position on the stack. If, ultimately, the stack is emptied, a solution is impossible. If the stack is not empty, the top position is removed and considered, if not visited. If an unvisited cell is not the finish, the cell is marked visited, and open neighboring cells are added to the stack.

Notice that since the underlying data structure is a `Stack`, the order in which the neighboring positions are pushed on the stack is the reverse of the order in which they will be considered. The result is that the program prefers to head east before any other direction. This can be seen as it gets distracted by going
No: east at the right border of the maze of Figure 9.8. Because stacks are LIFO
Go west structures, the search for a solution prefers to deepen the search rather than
young Maze! investigate alternatives. If a queue was used as the linear structure, the search would expand along a frontier of cells that are equidistant from the start. The solution found, then, would be the most direct route from start to finish, just as in the coin puzzle.

9.4 Conclusions

In this chapter we have investigated two important linear structures: the `Stack` and the `Queue`. Each implements `add` and `remove` operations. Traditional implementations of `Stack`s refer to these operations as `push` and `pop`, while traditional `Queue` methods are called `enqueue` and `dequeue`. Since these structures are often used to solve similar problems (e.g., search problems), they share a common `Linear` interface.

There are many different ways to implement each of these linear structures, and we have investigated a number—including implementations using arrays. Because of the trade-offs between speed and versatility, each implementation has its own particular strengths. Still, for many applications where performance is less important, we can select an implementation and use it without great concern because a common interface allows us to freely swap implementations.

We have seen a number of examples that use `Linear` structures to solve complex problems. Since stacks are used to maintain the state of executing methods, we have seen that recursive programs can be converted to iterative programs that maintain an explicit stack. Two explicit search problems—the coin puzzle and the maze—have an obvious relation. Because the coin puzzle searches for a short solution, we use a queue to maintain the pool of goal candidates. For the maze, we chose a stack, but a queue is often just as effective. The coin puzzle can be thought of as a maze whose rules determine the location of the barriers between board positions.

Self Check Problems

Solutions to these problems begin on page 433.

9.1 Is a `Stack` a `Linear`? Is it a `List`? An `AbstractLinear`? A `Queue`?

9.2 Is a `Stack` a `List`? Is a `StackList` a `List`? Is a `StackList` a `Stack`?

9.3 Why might we use generic `Queues` in our code, instead of `QueueLists`?

9.4 Is it possible to construct a new `Queue` directly?

9.5 If you are in a line to wash your car, are you in a queue or a stack?

9.6 Suppose you surf to a page on the Web about gardening. From there, you surf to a page about flowers. From there, you surf to a flower seed distributor. When you push the "go back" button, you return to the flower page. What structure is your history stored in?

9.7 In a breadth-first search, what is special about the first solution found?

9.8 You are in a garden maze and you are optimistically racing to the center. Are you more likely to use a stack-based depth-first search, or a queue-based breadth-first search?

9.9 Why do we use modular arithmetic in the `QueueArray` implementation?

Problems

Solutions to the odd-numbered problems begin on page 460.

9.1 Suppose we push each of the integers $1, 2, \ldots, n$, in order, on a stack, and then perform $m \le n$ `pop` operations. What is the final state of the stack?

9.2 Suppose we enqueue each of the integers $1, 2, \ldots, n$, in order, into a queue, and then perform $m \le n$ `dequeue` operations. What is the final state of the queue?

9.3   Suppose you wish to fill a stack with a copy of another, maintaining the order of elements. Using only `Stack` operations, describe how this would be done. How many additional stacks are necessary?

9.4   Suppose you wish to reverse the order of elements of a stack. Using only `Stack` operations, describe how this would be done. How many additional stacks are necessary?

9.5   Suppose you wish to copy a queue into another, preserving the order of elements. Using only `Queue` operations, describe how this would be done.

9.6   In the discussion of radix sort (see Section 5.6) we discussed an implementation of a procedure `bucketPass` that sorted integer values based on a digit of the number. It was important that the sort was stable—that values with similar digits remained in their original relative order. Unfortunately, our implementation used `Vector`s, and to have `bucketPass` work in $O(n)$ time, it was important to add and remove values from the end of the `Vector`. It was also necessary to unload the buckets in reverse order, a process that was rather obscure. Is it possible to clean this code up using a `Stack` or a `Queue`? One of these two will allow us to unload the buckets into the data array in increasing order. Does this improved version run as quickly (in terms of big-O)?

9.7   Suppose you wish to reverse the order of elements of a queue. Using only `Queue` operations, describe how this would be done. (Hint: While you can't use a stack, you can use something similar.)

9.8   Over time, the elements 1, 2, and 3 are pushed onto the stack in that order. What sequence(s) of popping the elements off the stack is impossible?

9.9   Generalize the solution to Problem 9.8. If elements $1, 2, 3, \ldots, n$ are pushed onto a stack in that order, what sequences of popping the elements off the stack are not permissible?

9.10   Over time, the elements 1, 2, and 3 are added to a queue, in that order. What sequence(s) of removing the elements from the queue is impossible, if any?

9.11   Generalize the solution to Problem 9.10. If elements $1, 2, 3, \ldots, n$ are added to a queue in that order, what sequences of removing the elements are not permissible?

9.12   It is conceivable that one linear structure is more general than another. (a) Is it possible to implement a `Queue` using a `Stack`? What is the complexity of each of the `Queue` operations? (b) Is it possible to implement a `Stack` using a `Queue`? What are the complexities of the various `Stack` methods?

9.13   Describe how we might efficiently implement a `Queue` as a pair of `Stacks`, called a "stack pair." (Hint: Think of one of the stacks as the head of the queue and the other as the tail.)

9.14   The implementation of `QueueLists` makes use of a `CircularList`. Implement `QueueLists` in a manner that is efficient in time and space using `SinglyLinkedListElement` with a head and tail reference.

9.15   Burger Death needs to keep track of orders placed at the drive-up window. Design a data structure to support their ordering system.

9.5 Laboratory: A Stack-Based Language

Objective. To implement a PostScript-based calculator.

Discussion. In this lab we will investigate a small portion of a stack-based language called PostScript. You will probably recognize that PostScript is a file format often used with printers. In fact, the file you send to your printer is a program that instructs your printer to draw the appropriate output. PostScript is stack-based: integral to the language is an operand stack. Each operation that is executed pops its operands from the stack and pushes on a result. There are other notable examples of stack-based languages, including `forth`, a language commonly used by astronomers to program telescopes. If you have an older Hewlett-Packard calculator, it likely uses a stack-based input mechanism to perform calculations.

We will implement a few of the math operators available in PostScript.

To see how PostScript works, you can run a PostScript simulator. (A good simulator for PostScript is the freely available `ghostscript` utility. It is available from `www.gnu.org`.) If you have a simulator handy, you might try the following example inputs. (To exit a PostScript simulator, type `quit`.)

1. The following program computes $1 + 1$:

   ```
   1 1 add pstack
   ```

   Every item you type in is a *token*. Tokens include numbers, booleans, or symbols. Here, we've typed in two numeric tokens, followed by two symbolic tokens. Each number is pushed on the internal stack of operands. When the `add` token is encountered, it causes PostScript to pop off two values and add them together. The result is pushed back on the stack. (Other mathematical operations include `sub`, `mul`, and `div`.) The `pstack` command causes the entire stack to be printed to the console.

2. Provided the stack contains at least one value, the `pop` operator can be used to remove it. Thus, the following computes 2 and prints nothing:

   ```
   1 1 add pop pstack
   ```

3. The following "program" computes $1 + 3 * 4$:

   ```
   1 3 4 mul add pstack
   ```

   The result computed here, 13, is different than what is computed by the following program:

   ```
   1 3 add 4 mul pstack
   ```

   In the latter case the addition is performed first, computing 16.

4. Some operations simply move values about. You can duplicate values—the following squares the number 10.1:

```
10.1 dup mul pstack pop
```

The `exch` operator to exchange two values, computing $1 - 3$:

```
3 1 exch sub pstack pop
```

5. Comparison operations compute logical values:

```
1 2 eq pstack pop
```

tests for equality of 1 and 2, and leaves `false` on the stack. The program

```
1 1 eq pstack pop
```

yields a value of `true`.

6. Symbols are defined using the `def` operation. To define a symbolic value we specify a "quoted" symbol (preceded by a slash) and the value, all followed by the operator `def`:

```
/pi 3.141592653 def
```

Once we define a symbol, we can use it in computations:

```
/radius 1.6 def
pi radius dup mul mul pstack pop
```

computes and prints the area of a circle with radius 1.6. After the pop, the stack is empty.

Procedure. Write a program that simulates the behavior of this small subset of PostScript. To help you accomplish this, we've created three classes that you will find useful:

Token

- **Token.** An immutable (constant) object that contains a double, boolean, or symbol. Different constructors allow you to construct different `Token` values. The class also provides methods to determine the type and value of a token.

Reader

- **Reader.** A class that allows you to read `Tokens` from an input stream. The typical use of a reader is as follows:

```
Reader r = new Reader();
Token t;
while (r.hasNext())
{
    t = (Token)r.next();
    if (t.isSymbol() && // only if symbol:
        t.getSymbol().equals("quit")) break;
    // process token
}
```

This is actually our first use of an `Iterator`. It always returns an `Object` of type `Token`.

- `SymbolTable`. An object that allows you to keep track of `String`–`Token` associations. Here is an example of how to save and recall the value of π:

```
SymbolTable table = new SymbolTable();
// sometime later:
table.add("pi",new Token(3.141592653));
// sometime even later:
if (table.contains("pi"))
{
    Token token = table.get("pi");
    System.out.println(token.getNumber());
}
```

SymbolTable

You should familiarize yourself with these classes before you launch into writing your interpreter.

To complete your project, you should implement the PostScript commands pstack, add, sub, mul, div, dup, exch, eq, ne, def, pop, quit. Also implement the nonstandard PostScript command ptable that prints the symbol table.

Thought Questions. Consider the following questions as you complete the lab:

1. If we are performing an eq operation, is it necessary to assume that the values on the top of the stack are, say, numbers?

2. The pstack operation should print the contents of the operand stack without destroying it. What is the most elegant way of doing this? (There are many choices.)

3. PostScript also has a notion of a *procedure*. A procedure is a series of Tokens surrounded by braces (e.g., { 2 add }). The Token class reads procedures and stores the procedure's Tokens in a List. The Reader class has a constructor that takes a List as a parameter and returns a Reader that iteratively returns Tokens from its list. Can you augment your PostScript interpreter to handle the definition of functions like area, below?

```
/pi 3.141592653 def
/area { dup mul pi mul } def
1.6 area
9 area pstack
quit
```

Such a PostScript program defines a new procedure called **area** that computes πr^2 where r is the value found on the top of the stack when the procedure is called. The result of running this code would be

```
254.469004893
8.042477191680002
```

4. How might you implement the `if` operator? The `if` operator takes a
   boolean and a token (usually a procedure) and executes the token if the
   boolean is true. This would allow the definition of the absolute value
   function (given a less than operator, `lt`):

   ```
   /abs { 0 lt { -1 mul } if } def
   3 abs
   -3 abs
   eq pstack
   ```

   The result is `true`.

5. What does the following do?

   ```
   /count { dup 1 ne { dup 1 sub count } if } def
   10 count pstack
   ```

Notes:

9.6 Laboratory: The Web Crawler

Objective. To crawl over web pages in a breadth-first manner.

Discussion. Web crawling devices are a fact of life. These programs automatically venture out on the Web and internalize documents. Their actions are based on the links between pages. The data structures involved in keeping track of the progress of an avid web crawler are quite complex: imagine, for example, how difficult it must be for such a device to keep from chasing loops of references between pages.

In this lab we will build a web crawler that determines the distance from one page to another. If page A references page B, the distance from A to B is 1. Notice that page B may not have any links on it, so the distance from B to A may not be defined.

Here is an approach to determining the distance from page A to arbitrary page B:

- Start a list of pages to consider. This list has two columns: the page, and its distance from A. We can, for example, put page A on this list, and assign it a distance of zero. If we ever see page B on this list, the problem is solved: just print out the distance associated with B.

- Remove the first page on our list: call it page X with distance d from page A. If X has the same URL as B, B must be distance d from A. Otherwise, consider any link off of page X: either it points to a page we've already seen on our list (it has a distance d or less), or it is a new page. If it's a new page we haven't encountered, add it to the end of our list and associate with it a distance $d + 1$—it's a link farther from A than page X. We consider all the links off of page X before considering a new page from our list.

If the list is a FIFO, this process is a *breadth-first* traversal, and the distance associated with B is the shortest distance possible. We can essentially think of the Web as a large maze that we're exploring.

Procedure. Necessary for this lab is a class `HTML`. It defines a reference to a textual (HTML) web page. The constructor takes a URL that identifies which page you're interested in:

```
HTML page = new HTML("http://www.yahoo.com");
```

HTML

Only pages that appear to have valid HTML code can actually be inspected (other types of pages will appear empty). Once the reference is made to the page, you can get its content with the method `content`:

```
System.out.println(page.content());
```

Two methods allow you to get the URL's associated with each link on a page: `hasNext` and `nextURL`. The `hasNext` method returns `true` if there are more links you have not yet considered. The `nextURL` method returns a URL (a `String`) that is pointed to by this page. Here's a typical loop that prints all the links associated with a page:

```
int i = 0;
while (page.hasNext())
{
    System.out.println(i+": "+page.nextURL());
    i++;
}
```

For the sake of speed, the HTML method downloads 10K of information. For simple pages, this covers at least the first visible page on the screen, and it might be argued that the most important links to other pages probably appear within this short start (many crawlers, for example, limit their investigations to the first part of a document). You can change the size of the document considered in the constructor:

```
HTML page = new HTML("http://www.yahoo.com",20*1024);
```

You should probably keep this within a reasonable range, to limit the total impact on memory.

Write a program that will tell us the maximum number of links (found on the first page of a document) that are necessary to get from your home page to any other page within your personal web. You can identify these pages because they all begin with the same prefix. We might think of this as a crude estimate of the "depth" or "diameter" of a site.

Thought Questions. Consider the following questions as you complete the lab:

1. How do your results change when you change the buffer size for the page to 2K? 50K? Under what conditions would a large buffer change cause the diameter of a Web to decrease? Under what conditions would this change cause the diameter of a Web to increase?

Notes:

Chapter 10

Ordered Structures

Concepts:
▷ The Comparable interface
▷ The Comparator
▷ The OrderedStructure interface
▷ The OrderedVector
▷ The OrderedList

"Make no mistake about it.
A miracle has happened...
we have no ordinary pig."
"Well," said Mrs. Zuckerman,
"it seems to me you're a little off.
It seems to me we have
no ordinary spider."
—Elwyn Brooks White

WE HAVE MADE NO ASSUMPTIONS about the type of data we store within our structures—so far. Instead, we have assumed only that the data referenced are a subclass of the type Object. Recall that *all* classes are subtypes of Object in Java, so this is hardly a constraint. Data structures serve a purpose, often helping us perform tasks more complex than "just holding data." For example, we used the Stack and Queue classes to *guide* a search through search space in the previous chapter.

One important use of data structures is to help keep data in order—the smallest value in the structure might be stored close to the front, while the largest value would be stored close to the rear. Once a structure is ordered it becomes potentially useful as a mechanism for sorting: we simply insert our possibly unordered data into the structure and then extract the values in order. To do this, however, it is necessary to *compare* data values to see if they are in the correct order. In this chapter we will discuss approaches to the various problems associated with maintaining ordered structures. First we review material we first encountered when we considered sorting.

10.1 Comparable Objects Revisited

In languages like C++ it is possible to *override* the comparison operators (<, >, ==, etc.). When two objects are compared using these operators, a user-written method is called. Java does not support overriding of built-in operators. Thus, it is useful to come up with a convention for supporting *comparable* data.

First, let's look closely at the interface for Java's Object. Since every class inherits and extends the interface of the Object class, each of its methods may be applied to any class. For example, the equals method allows us to check if an `Object` is logically equal to another `Object`. In contrast, the `==` operator compares two *references* to see if they refer to the same *instance* of an object.

By default, the `equals` function returns `true` whenever two references point to exactly the same object. This is often not the correct comparison—often we wish to have different instances of the same type be equal—so the class designer should consider rewriting it as a class-specific method.

For our purposes, we wish to require of comparable classes a method that determines the relative order of objects. How do we *require* this? Through an interface! Since an interface is a contract, we simply wrap the `compareTo` method in a language-wide interface, `Comparable`:

Comparable

```
public interface java.lang.Comparable
{
    public int compareTo(Object that);
}
```

This is pretty simple: When we want to compare two objects, we simply call the `compareTo` method of one on another. Now, if we require that an object be a `Comparable` object, then we know that it may be compared to similarly typed data using the `compareTo` method.

10.1.1   Example: Comparable Ratios

Common types, such as `Integers` and `Strings`, include a `compareTo` method. In this section we add methods to make the `Ratio` class comparable. Recall that a `Ratio` has the following interface:

Ratio

```
public class Ratio
        implements Comparable
{
    public Ratio(int top, int bottom)
    // pre: bottom != 0
    // post: constructs a ratio equivalent to top::bottom

    public int getNumerator()
    // post: return the numerator of the fraction

    public int getDenominator()
    // post: return the denominator of the fraction

    public double getValue()
    // post: return the double equivalent of the ratio

    public Ratio add(Ratio other)
    // pre: other is nonnull
    // post: return new fraction--the sum of this and other

    public String toString()
    // post: returns a string that represents this fraction
```

```
    public int compareTo(Object other)
    // pre: other is non-null and type Ratio
    // post: returns value <, ==, > 0 if this value is <, ==, > that

    public boolean equals(Object that)
    // pre: that is type Ratio
    // post: returns true iff this ratio is the same as that ratio
}
```

A `Ratio` is constructed by passing it a pair of integers. These integers are cached away—we cannot tell how—where they can later be used to compare their ratio with another `Ratio`. The protected data and the constructor that initializes them appear as follows:

```
protected int numerator;    // numerator of ratio
protected int denominator;  // denominator of ratio

public Ratio(int top, int bottom)
// pre: bottom != 0
// post: constructs a ratio equivalent to top::bottom
{
    numerator = top;
    denominator = bottom;
    reduce();
}
```

We can see, now, that this class has a pair of protected `int`s to hold the values. Let us turn to the `compareTo` method. Since the `Comparable` interface declares the `compareTo` method to take an `Object` parameter, it is necessary to declare the parameter as an `Object`, even though we expect the parameter to be a `Ratio`. We could have declared the `compareTo` method to take a `Ratio`, but then the method would not have matched the `Comparable` `compareTo` method. Here is what we do:

```
public int compareTo(Object other)
// pre: other is non-null and type Ratio
// post: returns value <, ==, > 0 if this value is <, ==, > that
{
    Assert.pre(other instanceof Ratio,"other is a Ratio type");
    Ratio that = (Ratio)other;
    return this.getNumerator()*that.getDenominator()-
            that.getNumerator()*this.getDenominator();
}
```

Before we do anything with the object passed in, we invoke Java's built-in `instanceof` operator. This operator returns `true` when the object on the left can be considered an object of the type on the right. To convey to Java that we require the parameter to be a `Ratio`, we *cast*, on the right side of the second line, the value of the parameter. This cast simply tells Java to consider `other` to be a `Ratio` (an implementation of `Comparable`) for use in the assignment. The third and fourth lines, then, check the order of two ratios: the values stored within `this` object are compared to the values stored in `that` object.

We now consider the `equals` method:

```
public boolean equals(Object that)
// pre: that is type Ratio
// post: returns true iff this ratio is the same as that ratio
{
    return compareTo(that) == 0;
}
```

Conveniently, the `equals` method can be cast in terms of the `compareTo` method. For the `Ratio` class, the `compareTo` method is not much more expensive to compute than the `equals`, so this "handing off" of the work does not cost much. For more complex classes, the `compareTo` method may be so expensive that a consistent `equals` method can be constructed using independently considered code. In either case, it is important that `equals` return `true` exactly when the `compareTo` method returns 0.

Note also that the parameter to the `equals` method is declared as an `Object`. If it is not, then the programmer is writing a *new* method, rather than overriding the default method inherited from the `Object` class. Since equivalent `Ratios` may refer to different object instances, comparing references is not appropriate. Failure to implement the `equals` (or `compareTo`) method can lead to very subtle logical errors.

Principle 16 *Declare parameters of overriding methods with the most general types possible.*

To reiterate, failure to correctly declare these methods as generally as possible makes it unlikely that Java will call the correct method.

10.1.2   Example: Comparable Associations

Let us return now to the idea of an `Association`. An `Association` is a key-value pair, bound together in a single class. For the same reasons that it is sometimes nice to be able to compare integers, it is often useful to compare `Associations`. Recall that when we constructed an `Association` we took great care in defining the `equals` operator to work on just the key field of the `Association`. Similarly, when we extend the concept of an `Association` to its `Comparable` equivalent, we will have to be just as careful in constructing the `compareTo` method.

Comparable-
Association

Unlike the `Ratio` class, the `ComparableAssociation` can be declared an extension of the `Association` class. The outline of this extension appears as follows:

```
public class ComparableAssociation extends Association
    implements Comparable
```

```
{

    public ComparableAssociation(Comparable key)
    // pre: key is non-null
    // post: constructs comparable association with null value

    public ComparableAssociation(Comparable key, Object value)
    // pre: key is non-null
    // post: constructs association between a comparable key and a value

    public int compareTo(Object other)
    // pre: other is non-null ComparableAssociation
    // post: returns integer representing relation between values
}
```

Notice that there are very few methods. Since ComparableAssociation is an *extension* of the Association class, all the methods written for Association are available for use with ComparableAssociations. The only additions are those shown here. Because one of the additional methods is the compareTo method, it meets the specification of what it means to be Comparable; thus we claim it implements the Comparable interface.

Let's look carefully at the implementation. As with the Association class, there are two constructors for ComparableAssociations. The first constructor initializes the key and sets the value reference to null, while the second initializes both key and value:

```
public ComparableAssociation(Comparable key)
// pre: key is non-null
// post: constructs comparable association with null value
{
    this(key,null);
}

public ComparableAssociation(Comparable key, Object value)
// pre: key is non-null
// post: constructs association between a comparable key and a value
{
    super(key,value);
}
```

Remember that there are two special methods available to constructors: this and super. The this method calls another constructor with a different set of parameters (if the parameters are not different, the constructor could be recursive!). We write one very general purpose constructor, and any special-purpose constructors call the general constructor with reconsidered parameter values. The super method is a means of calling the constructor for the superclass—the class we are extending—Association. The second constructor simply calls the constructor for the superclass. The first constructor calls the second constructor (which, in turn, calls the superclass's constructor) with a null value field. All

of this is necessary to be able to construct `ComparableAssociations` using the
`Association`'s constructors.

Now, the `compareTo` method is a little tricky:

```
public int compareTo(Object other)
// pre: other is non-null ComparableAssociation
// post: returns integer representing relation between values
{
    Assert.pre(other instanceof ComparableAssociation,
               "compareTo expects a ComparableAssociation");
    ComparableAssociation that = (ComparableAssociation)other;
    Comparable thisKey = (Comparable)this.getKey();
    Comparable thatKey = (Comparable)that.getKey();

    return thisKey.compareTo(thatKey);
}
```

Because the `compareTo` method must implement the `Comparable` interface, its
parameter is an `Object`. In fact, the precondition requires the parameter to be
a `ComparableAssociation`. We access the parameter through an intermediate,
temporary variable, `that`, that has type `ComparableAssociation`.

Principle 17 *Avoid multiple casts of the same object by assigning the value to
a temporary variable.*

Since `ComparableAssociations` are associations with comparable keys, we
know that the `key` within the association has a `compareTo` method. Java is
not able to figure this out, so we must give it hints, by casting the appropriate
`key` references. Casting, here, is essentially a catalyst to get Java to verify
that a referenced object has certain type characteristics. In any case, we get
access to both `keys` through independent variables. These allow us to make
the comparison by calling the `compareTo` method on the comparable objects.
Very little logic is directly encoded in these routines; we mostly make use of the
prewritten code to accomplish what we need.

In the next few sections we consider features that we can provide to existing
data structures, provided that the underlying data are known to be comparable.

10.2 Keeping Structures Ordered

We can make use of the natural ordering of classes suggested by the `compareTo`
method to organize our structure. Keeping data in order, however, places significant constraints on the type of operations that should be allowed. If a comparable value is added to a structure that orders its elements, the relative position
of the new value is determined by the data, not the structure. Since this placement decision is predetermined, ordered structures have little flexibility in their
interface. It is not possible, for example, to insert data at random locations.
While simpler to use, these operations also tend to be more costly than their

unordered counterparts. Typically, the increased *energy* required is the result of an increase in the friction associated with decisions needed to accomplish add and remove.

The implementation of the various structures we see in the remainder of this chapter leads to simpler algorithms for sorting, as we will see in Section 10.2.3.

10.2.1 The OrderedStructure Interface

Recall that a Structure is any traversable structure that allows us to add and remove elements and perform membership checks (see Section 1.8). Since the Structure interface also requires the usual size-related methods (e.g., size, isEmpty, clear), none of these methods actually requires that the data within the structure be kept in order. To ensure that the structures we create order their data, we make them abide by an extended interface—an OrderedStructure:

```
public interface OrderedStructure extends Structure
{
}
```

Ordered-
Structure

Amazingly enough we have accomplished something for nothing! Actually, what is happening is that we are using the *type* to store the fact that the data are kept in sorted order. Implied in this, of course, is that we are working with Comparable values.

The emperor wears no clothes!

10.2.2 The Ordered Vector and Binary Search

We can now consider the implementation of an ordered Vector of values. Since it implements an OrderedStructure, we know that the order in which elements are added does not directly determine the order in which they are ultimately removed. Instead, when elements are added to an OrderedVector, they are kept ascending in their natural order.

Constructing an ordered Vector requires little more than allocating the underlying vector:

```
public OrderedVector()
// post: constructs an empty, ordered vector
{
    data = new Vector();
}
```

OrderedVector

Rather obviously, if there are no elements in the underlying Vector, then all of the elements are in order. Initially, at least, the structure is in a consistent state. We must always be mindful of consistency.

Because finding the correct location for a value is important to both adding and removing values, we focus on the development of an appropriate search technique for OrderedVectors. This process is much like looking up a word in a dictionary, or a name in a phone book (see Figure 10.1). First we look at the value halfway through the Vector and determine if the value for which we are looking is bigger or smaller than this *median*. If it is smaller, we restart our search with the left half of the structure. If it is bigger, we restart our search with the right half of the `Vector`. Whenever we consider a section of the `Vector` consisting of a single element, the search can be terminated, with the success of the search dependent on whether or not the indicated element contains the desired value. This approach is called *binary search*.

We present here the code for determining the index of a value in an `Ordered-Vector`. Be aware that if the value is not in the `Vector`, the routine returns the ideal location to insert the value. This may be a location that is outside the `Vector`.

```
protected int indexOf(Comparable target)
{
    Comparable midValue;
    int low = 0;   // lowest possible location
    int high = data.size(); // highest possible location
    int mid = (low + high)/2; // low <= mid <= high
    // mid == high iff low == high
    while (low < high) {
        // get median value
        midValue = (Comparable)data.get(mid);
        // determine on which side median resides:
        if (midValue.compareTo(target) < 0) {
            low = mid+1;
        } else {
            high = mid;
        }
        // low <= high
        // recompute median index
        mid = (low+high)/2;
    }
    return low;
}
```

For each iteration through the loop, `low` and `high` determine the bounds of the `Vector` currently being searched. `mid` is computed to be the middle element (if there are an even number of elements being considered, it is the leftmost of the two middle elements). This middle element is compared with the parameter, and the bounds are adjusted to further constrain the search. Since the portion of the `Vector` participating in the search is roughly halved each time, the total number of times around the loop is approximately $O(\log n)$. This is a considerable improvement over the implementation of the `indexOf` method for `Vector`s of arbitrary elements—that routine is *linear* in the size of the structure.

Notice that `indexOf` is declared as a **protected** member of the class. This makes it impossible for a user to call directly, and makes it more difficult for a user to write code that depends on the underlying implementation. To convince yourself of the utility of this, both `OrderedStructures` of this chapter have exactly the same interface (so these two data types can be interchanged), but they

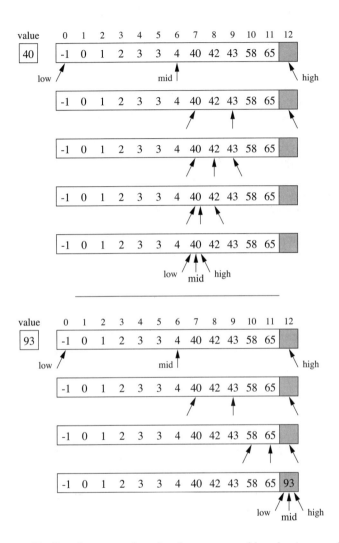

Figure 10.1   Finding the correct location for a comparable value in an ordered array. The top search finds a value in the array; the bottom search fails to find the value, but finds the correct point of insertion. The shaded area is not part of the `Vector` during search.

are completely different structures. If the `indexOf` method were made public, then code could be written that makes use of this `Vector`-specific method, and it would be impossible to switch implementations.

Implementation of the `indexOf` method makes most of the nontrivial `OrderedVector` methods more straightforward. The `add` operator simply adds an element to the `Vector` in the location indicated by the `indexOf` operator:

```
public void add(Object value)
// pre: value is non-null
// post: inserts value, leaves vector in order
{
    int position = indexOf((Comparable)value);
    data.add(position,value);
}
```

It is interesting to note that the cost of looking up the value is $O(\log n)$, but the `insertElementAt` for relatively "small" values *can* take $O(n)$ time to insert. Thus, the worst-case (and expected—see Problem 10.6) time complexity of the `add` operation is $O(n)$, linear in the size of the structure. In reality, for large `Vectors`, the time required to find the index of a value using the `OrderedVector` method is significantly reduced over the time required using the underlying `Vector` method. If the cost of comparing two objects exceeds the cost of assigning one object to another, the use of binary search can be expected to reduce the cost of the `add` operation by as much as a factor of 2.

Both `contains` and `remove` can also make use of the `indexOf` operator. First, we consider testing to see if an element is contained by the `OrderedVector`:

```
public boolean contains(Object value)
// pre: value is non-null
// post: returns true if the value is in the vector
{
    int position = indexOf((Comparable)value);
    return (position < size()) &&
            data.get(position).equals(value);
}
```

We simply attempt to find the item in the `Vector`, and if the location returned contains the value we desire, we return `true`; otherwise we return `false`. Since `indexOf` takes $O(\log n)$ time and the check for element equality is constant, the total complexity of the operation is $O(\log n)$. The `Vector` version of the same operation is $O(n)$ time. This is a considerable improvement.

The `return` statement, you will note, returns the result of a *logical and* (`&&`) operator. This is a *short-circuiting* operator: if, after evaluating the left half of the expression, the ultimate value of the expression is known to be false, then the second expression is not evaluated. That behavior is used here to avoid calling the `get` operator with a `position` that might exceed the size of the structure, that is, the length of the `Vector`. This is a feature of many languages, but a potential trap if you ever consider reordering your boolean expressions.

Removing a value from an `OrderedVector` involves finding it within the `Vector` and then explicitly extracting it from the structure:

```
public Object remove(Object value)
// pre: value is non-null
// post: removes one instance of value, if found in vector
{
    if (contains(value)) {
        // we know value is pointed to by indexOf
        int position = indexOf((Comparable)value);
        // since vector contains value, position < size()
        // keep track of the value for return
        Object target = data.get(position);
        // remove the value from the underlying vector
        data.remove(position);
        return target;
    }
    return null;
}
```

Like `add`, the operation has complexity $O(n)$. But it executes faster than its `Vector` equivalent, `removeElement`.

Note that by keeping the elements sorted, we have made adding and removing an element from the `OrderedVector` relatively symmetric: the expected complexity of each method is $O(n)$. Yet, in the underlying `Vector`, an `addElement` operation takes constant time, while the `removeElement` operation takes $O(n)$ time.

Extracting values in order from an `OrderedStructure` is accomplished by an iterator returned from the `elements` method. Because the elements are stored in the correct order in the `Vector`, the method need only return the value of the `Vector`'s `iterator` method:

```
public Iterator iterator()
// post: returns an iterator for traversing vector
{
    return data.iterator();
}
```

The ease of implementing this particular method reassures us that our layout of values within the vector (in ascending order) is appropriate. The rest of the `OrderedVector` operators repackage similar operators from the `Vector` class:

```
public boolean isEmpty()
// post: returns true if the OrderedVector is empty
{
    return data.size() == 0;
}
```

```
public void clear()
// post: vector is emptied
{
    data.setSize(0);
}

public int size()
// post: returns the number of elements in vector
{
    return data.size();
}
```

This "repackaging" brings up a point: *Why is it necessary?* If one were to, instead, consider the `OrderedVector` to be an *extension* of the `Vector` class, much of this repackaging would be unnecessary, because each of the repackaged methods could be inherited, and those—like `add`, `contains`, and `remove`—that required substantial reconsideration could be rewritten overriding the methods provided in the underlying `Vector` class.

That's all true! There's one substantial drawback, however, that is uncovered by asking a simple question: *Is an* `OrderedVector` *suitably used wherever a* `Vector` *is used?* The answer is: *No!* Consider the following hypothetical code that allocates an `OrderedVector` for use as a `Vector`:

```
static void main(String args[])
{
    OrderedVector v = new OrderedVector();

    v.add("Michael's Pizza");
    v.add(1,"Cozy Pizza");
    v.add(0,"Hot Tomatoes Pizza");;
}
```

First, the `add` methods are not methods for `OrderedVectors`. Assuming this could be done, the semantics become problematic. We are inserting elements at specific locations within a `Vector`, but it is really an `OrderedVector`. The values inserted violate the ordering of elements and the postconditions of the `add` method of the `OrderedVector`.

We now consider a simple application of `OrderedStructures`—sorting.

10.2.3   Example: Sorting Revisited

Now that we have seen the implementation of an `OrderedStructure`, we can use these structures to sort comparable values. (If values are not comparable, it is hard to see how they might be sorted, but we will see an approach in Section 10.2.4.) Here is a program to sort integers appearing on the input:

```
public static void main(String[] args)
{
    ReadStream r = new ReadStream(System.in);
    OrderedStructure o = new OrderedVector();
    // read in integers
    for (r.skipWhite(); !r.eof(); r.skipWhite())
    {
        o.add(new Integer(r.readInt()));
    }
    // and print them out, in order
    Iterator i = o.iterator();
    while (i.hasNext())
    {
        System.out.println(i.next());
    }
}
```

Sort

In this simple program a sequence of numbers is read from the input stream. Each number is placed within an `Integer` that is then inserted into the `Ordered-Structure`, in this case an `OrderedVector`. The insertion of this value into the `Vector` may involve moving, on average, $\frac{n}{2}$ elements out of the way. As the n values are added to the `Vector`, a total of $O(n^2)$ values have to be moved. The overall effect of this loop is to perform insertion sort! Once the values have been inserted in the ordered structure, we can use an iterator to traverse the `Vector` in order and print out the values in order. If the `OrderedVector` is substituted with any structure that meets the `OrderedStructure` interface, similar results are generated, but the performance of the sorting algorithm is determined by the complexity of insertion.

Now, what should happen if we don't have a `Comparable` data type?

10.2.4 A Comparator-based Approach

Sometimes it is not immediately obvious how we should generally order a specific data type, or we are hard-pressed to commit to one particular ordering for our data. In these cases we find it useful to allow ordered structures to be ordered in alternative ways. One approach is to have the ordered structure keep track of a `Comparator` that can be used when the `compareTo` method does not seem appropriate. For example, when constructing a list of `Integer` values, it may be useful to have them sorted in descending order.

The approach seems workable, but somewhat difficult when a comparison needs to actually be made. We must, at that time, check to see if a `Comparator` has somehow been associated with the structure and make either a `Comparator`-based `compare` or a class-based `compareTo` method call. We can greatly simplify the code if we assume that a `Comparator` method can always be used: we construct a `Comparator`, the `structure` package's `NaturalComparator`, that calls the `compareTo` method of the particular elements and returns that value for `compare`:

Natural-
Comparator

```
import java.util.Comparator;
public class NaturalComparator implements Comparator
{
    public int compare(Object a, Object b)
    // pre: a, b non-null, and b is same type as a
    // post: returns value <, ==, > 0 if a <, ==, > b
    {
        return ((Comparable)a).compareTo(b);
    }

    public boolean equals(Object b)
    // post: returns true if b is a NaturalComparator
    {
        return (b != null) && (b instanceof NaturalComparator);
    }
}
```

The NaturalComparator, can then serve as a default comparison method in classes that wish to make exclusive use of the Comparator-based approach.

To demonstrate the power of the Comparator-based approach we can develop a notion of Comparator composition: one Comparator can be used to modify the effects of a *base* Comparator. Besides the NaturalComparator, the structure package also provides a ReverseComparator class. This class keeps track of its base Comparator in a protected variable, base. When a ReverseComparator is constructed, another Comparator can be passed to it to reverse. Frequently we expect to use this class to reverse the natural order of values, so we provide a parameterless constructor that forces the base Comparator to be NaturalComparator:

Reverse-
Comparator

```
protected Comparator base; // comparator whose ordering is reversed

public ReverseComparator()
// post: constructs a comparator that orders in reverse order
{
    base = new NaturalComparator();
}

public ReverseComparator(Comparator base)
// post: constructs a Comparator that orders in reverse order of base
{
    this.base = base;
}
```

We are now ready to implement the comparison method. We simply call the compare method of the base Comparator and reverse its sign. This effectively reverses the relation between values.

```
public int compare(Object a, Object b)
// pre: a, b non-null, and b is of type of a
```

```
// post: returns value <, ==, > 0 if a <, ==, > b
{
    return -base.compare(a,b);
}
```

Note that formerly equal values are still equal under the `ReverseComparator` transformation.

We now turn to an implementaton of an `OrderedStructure` that makes exclusive use of `Comparators` to keep its elements in order.

10.2.5 The Ordered List

Arbitrarily inserting an element into a list is difficult, since it requires moving to the middle of the list to perform the addition. The lists we have developed are biased toward addition and removal of values from their ends. Thus, we choose to use the underlying structure of a `SinglyLinkedList` to provide the basis for our `OrderedList` class. As promised, we will also support orderings through the use of `Comparators`. First, we declare the class as an implementation of the `OrderedStructure` interface:

OrderedList

```
public class OrderedList
        extends AbstractStructure implements OrderedStructure
```

The instance variables describe a singly linked list as well as a `Comparator` to determine the ordering. The constructors set up the structure by initializing the protected variables using the `clear` method:

```
protected SinglyLinkedListElement data; // smallest value
protected int count;        // number of values in list
protected Comparator ordering;     // the comparison function

public OrderedList()
// post: constructs an empty ordered list
{
    this(new NaturalComparator());
}

public OrderedList(Comparator ordering)
// post: constructs an empty ordered list ordered by ordering
{
    this.ordering = ordering;
    clear();
}

public void clear()
// post: the ordered list is empty
{
    data = null;
    count = 0;
}
```

Again, the advantage of this technique is that changes to the initialization of the underlying data structure can be made in one place within the code.

By default, the `OrderedList` keeps its elements in the order determined by the `compareTo` method. The `NaturalOrder` comparator does precisely that. If an alternative ordering is desired, the constructor for the `OrderedList` can be given a `Comparator` that can be used to guide the ordering of the elements in the list.

To warm up to the methods that we will soon have to write, let's consider implementation of the `contains` method. It uses the finger technique from our work with `SinglyLinkedLists`:

```
public boolean contains(Object value)
// pre: value is a non-null comparable object
// post: returns true iff contains value
{
    SinglyLinkedListElement finger = data; // target
    Comparable cValue = (Comparable)value; // value sought
    // search down list until we fall off or find bigger value
    while ((finger != null) &&
            ordering.compare(finger.value(),cValue) < 0)
    {
        finger = finger.next();
    }
    return finger != null && cValue.equals(finger.value());
}
```

This code is very similar to the *linear search* `contains` method of the `Singly-LinkedList` class. However, because the list is always kept in order, it can stop searching if it finds an element that is larger than the desired element. This leads to a behavior that is linear in the size of the list, but in the case when a value is not in the list, it terminates—on average—halfway down the list. For programs that make heavy use of looking up values in the structure, this can yield dramatic improvements in speed.

Note the use of the `compare` method in the `ordering` Comparator. No matter what order the elements have been inserted, the `ordering` is responsible for keeping them in the order specified.

Exercise 10.1 *What would be necessary to allow the user of an* `OrderedStructure` *to provide an alternative ordering* during *the lifetime of a class? This method might be called* `sortBy` *and would take a* `Comparator` *as its sole parameter.*

Now, let us consider the addition of an element to the `OrderedList`. Since the elements of the `OrderedList` are kept in order constantly, we must be careful to preserve that ordering after we have inserted the value. Here is the code:

```
public void add(Object value)
// pre: value is non-null
// post: value is added to the list, leaving it in order
{
    SinglyLinkedListElement previous = null; // element to adjust
    SinglyLinkedListElement finger = data;   // target element
    Comparable cValue = (Comparable)value;   // inserted value
    // search for the correct location
    while ((finger != null) &&
            ordering.compare(finger.value(),cValue) < 0)
    {
        previous = finger;
        finger = finger.next();
    }
    // spot is found, insert
    if (previous == null) // check for insert at top
    {
        data = new SinglyLinkedListElement(cValue,data);
    } else {
        previous.setNext(
            new SinglyLinkedListElement(cValue,previous.next()));
    }
    count++;
}
```

Here we use the finger technique with an additional **previous** reference to help
the insertion of the new element. The first loop takes, on average, linear time
to find a position where the value can be inserted. After the loop, the **previous**
reference refers to the element that will refer to the new element, or is **null**, if
the element should be inserted at the head of the list. Notice that we use the
SinglyLinkedListElement methods to ensure that we reuse code that works
and to make sure that the elements are constructed with reasonable values in
their fields.

One of the most common mistakes made is to forget to do important bookkeeping. Remember to increment **count** when inserting a value and to decrement
count when removing a value. When designing and implementing structures,
it is sometimes useful to look at each method from the point of view of each of
the bookkeeping variables that you maintain.

Principle 18 *Consider your code from different points of view.*

Removing a value from the **OrderedList** first performs a check to see if the
value is included, and then, if it is, removes it. When removing the value, we
return a reference to the value found in the list.

```
public Object remove(Object value)
// pre: value is non-null
// post: an instance of value is removed, if in list
{
```

```
            SinglyLinkedListElement previous = null; // element to adjust
            SinglyLinkedListElement finger = data;    // target element
            Comparable cValue = (Comparable)value;    // value to remove
            // search for value or fall off list
            while ((finger != null) &&
                    ordering.compare(finger.value(),cValue) < 0)
            {
                previous = finger;
                finger = finger.next();
            }
            // did we find it?
            if ((finger != null) && cValue.equals(finger.value())) {
                // yes, remove it
                if (previous == null)  // at top?
                {
                    data = finger.next();
                } else {
                    previous.setNext(finger.next());
                }
                count--;
                // return value
                return finger.value();
            }
            // return nonvalue
            return null;
        }
```

Again, because the `SinglyLinkedListIterator` accepts a `SinglyLinked-ListElement` as its parameter, the implementation of the `OrderedList`'s iterator method is particularly simple:

```
public Iterator iterator()
// post: returns an iterator over ordered list
{
    return new SinglyLinkedListIterator(data);
}
```

The remaining size-related procedures follow those found in the implementation of `SinglyLinkedLists`.

10.2.6 Example: The Modified Parking Lot

Renter—
ambiguous
noun:
(1) one who
rents from
others,
(2) one who
rents to others.

In Section 8.2 we implemented a system for maintaining rental contracts for a small parking lot. With our knowledge of ordered structures, we now return to that example to incorporate a new feature—an alphabetical listing of contracts.

As customers rent spaces from the parking office, contracts are added to a generic list of associations between renter names and lot assignments. We now change that structure to reflect a better means of keeping track of this information—an ordered list of comparable associations. This structure is declared as an `OrderedStructure` but is assigned an instance of an `OrderedList`:

```
OrderedStructure rented = new OrderedList(); // rented spaces
```

When a renter fills out a contract, the name of the renter and the parking space information are bound together into a single `ComparableAssociation`:

```
String renter = r.readString();
// link renter with space description
rented.add(new ComparableAssociation(renter,location));
System.out.println("Space "+location.number+" rented.");
```

ParkingLot2

Notice that the renter's name is placed into a `String`. Since `Strings` support the `compareTo` method, they implement the `Comparable` interface. The default ordering is used because the call to the constructor did not provide a specific ordering.

At this point, the `rented` structure has all contracts sorted by name. To print these contracts out, we accept a new command, `contracts`:

```
if (command.equals("contracts"))
{   // print out contracts in alphabetical order
    Iterator ci = rented.iterator();
    while (ci.hasNext())
    {   // extract contract from iterator
        ComparableAssociation contract =
            (ComparableAssociation)ci.next();
        // extract person from contract
        String person = (String)contract.getKey();
        // extract parking slot description from contract
        Space slot = (Space)contract.getValue();
        // print it out
        System.out.println(person+" is renting "+slot.number);

    }
}
```

An iterator for the `OrderedStructure` is used to retrieve each of the ComparableAssociations, from which we extract and print the renters' names in alphabetical order. Here is an example run of the program (the user's input is indented):

```
    rent small Alice
Space 0 rented.
    rent large Bob
Space 9 rented.
    rent small Carol
Space 1 rented.
    return Alice
Space 0 is now free.
    return David
No space rented to David.
    rent small David
```

```
Space 2 rented.
   rent small Eva
Space 0 rented.
   quit
6 slots remain available.
```

Note that, for each of the requests for contracts, the contracts are listed in alphabetical order. This example is particularly interesting since it demonstrates that use of an ordered structure eliminates the need to sort the contracts before they are printed each time and that the interface meshes well with software that doesn't use ordered structures. While running an orderly parking lot can be a tricky business, it is considerably simplified if you understand the subtleties of ordered structures.

Exercise 10.2 *Implement an alternative* `Comparator` *that compares two parking spaces, based on slot numbers. Demonstrate that a single line will change the order of the records in the* `ParkingLot2` *program.*

10.3   Conclusions

Computers spend a considerable amount of time maintaining ordered data structures. In Java we described an ordering of data values using the comparison operator, `compareTo`, or a `Comparator`. Objects that fail to have an operator such as `compareTo` cannot be totally ordered in a predetermined manner. Still, a `Comparator` might be constructed to suggest an ordering between otherwise incomparable values. Java enforces the development of an ordering using the `Comparable` interface—an interface that simply requires the implementation of the `compareTo` method.

Once data values may be compared and put in order, it is natural to design a data structure that keeps its values in order. Disk directories, dictionaries, filing cabinets, and zip-code ordered mailing lists are all obvious examples of abstract structures whose utility depends directly on their ability to efficiently maintain a consistently ordered state. Here we extend various unordered structures in a way that allows them to maintain the natural ordering of the underlying data.

Self Check Problems

Solutions to these problems begin on page 434.

10.1   What is the primary feature of an `OrderedStructure`?

10.2   How does the user communicate the order in which elements are to be stored in an `OrderedStructure`?

10.3   What is the difference between a `compareTo` method and a comparator with a `compare` method?

10.4   Are we likely to find two objects that are equal (using their `equals` method) to be close together in an `OrderedStructure`?

10.5   Is an `OrderedVector` a `Vector`?

10.6   Is it reasonable to have an `OrderedStack`, a class that implements both the `Stack` and `OrderedStructure` interfaces?

10.7   People queue up to enter a movie theater. They are stored in an `OrderedStructure`. How would you go about comparing two people?

10.8   Sally and Harry implement two different `compareTo` methods for a class they are working on together. Sally's `compareTo` method returns −1, 0, or +1, depending on the relationship between two objects. Harry's `compareTo` method returns −6, 0, or +3. Which method is suitable?

10.9   Sally and Harry are working on an implementation of `Coin`. Sally declares the sole parameter to her `compareTo` method as type `Object`. Harry knows the `compareTo` method will always be called on objects of type `Coin` and declares the parameter to be of that type. Which method is suitable for storing `Coin` objects in a `OrderedVector`?

Problems

Solutions to the odd-numbered problems begin on page 461.

10.1   Describe the contents of an `OrderedVector` after each of the following values has been added: 1, 9, 0, −1, and 3.

10.2   Describe the contents of an `OrderedList` after each of the following values has been added: 1, 9, 0, −1, and 3.

10.3   Suppose duplicate values are added to an `OrderedVector`. Where is the oldest value found (with respect to the newest)?

10.4   Suppose duplicate values are added to an `OrderedList`. Where is the oldest value found (with respect to the newest)?

10.5   Show that the expected insertion time of an element into an `Ordered-List` is $O(n)$ in the worst case.

10.6   Show that the expected insertion time of an element into an `Ordered-Vector` is $O(n)$.

10.7   Under what conditions would you use an `OrderedVector` over an `OrderedList`?

10.8   At what point does the Java environment complain about your passing a non-`Comparable` value to an `OrderedVector`?

10.9   Write the `compareTo` method for the `String` class.

10.10   Write the `compareTo` method for a class that is to be ordered by a field, `key`, which is a `double`. Be careful: The result of `compareTo` must be an `int`.

10.11   Write the `compareTo` method for a class describing a person whose name is stored as two `Strings`: `first` and `last`. A person is "less than" another if they appear before the other in a list alphabetized by last name and then first name (as is typical).

10.12 Previous editions of the `structures` package opted for the use of a `lessThan` method instead of a `compareTo` method. The `lessThan` method would return `true` exactly when one value was `lessThan` another. Are these approaches the same, or is one more versatile?

10.13 Suppose we consider the use of an `OrderedStructure get` method that takes an integer i. This method returns the ith element of the `OrderedStructure`. What are the best- and worst-case running times for this method on `Ordered-Vector` and `OrderedList`?

10.14 Your department is interested in keeping track of information about majors. Design a data structure that will maintain useful information for your department. The roster of majors, of course, should be ordered by last name (and then by first, if there are multiple students with the same last name).

10.4 Laboratory: Computing the "Best Of"

Objective. To efficiently select the largest k values of n.

Discussion. One method to select the largest k values in a sequence of n is to sort the n values and to look only at the first k. (In Chapter 12, we will learn of another technique: insert each of the n values into a max-heap and extract the first k values.) Such techniques have two important drawbacks:

- The data structure that keeps track of the values must be able to hold $n \gg k$ values. This may not be possible if, for example, there are more data than may be held easily in memory.

- The process requires $O(n \log n)$ time. It should be possible to accomplish this in $O(n)$ time.

One way to reduce these overheads is to keep track of, at all times, the best k values found. As the n values are passed through the structure, they are only remembered if they are potentially one of the largest k values.

Procedure. In this lab we will implement a `BestOf OrderedStructure`. The constructor for your `BestOf` structure should take a value k, which is an upper bound on the number of values that will be remembered. The default constructor should remember the top 10.

An `add` method takes an `Object` and adds the element (if reasonable) in the correct location. The `get(i)` method should return the ith largest value encountered so far. The `size` method should return the number of values currently stored in the structure. This value should be between 0 and k, inclusive. The `iterator` method should return an `Iterator` over all the values. The `clear` method should remove all values from the structure.

Here are the steps that are necessary to construct and test this data structure:

1. Consider the underlying structure carefully. Because the main considerations of this structure are size and speed, it would be most efficient to implement this using a fixed-size array. We will assume that here.

2. Implement the `add` method. This method should take the value and, like a pass of insertion sort, it should find the correct location for the new value. If the array is full and the value is no greater than any of the values, nothing changes. Otherwise, the value is inserted in the correct location, possibly dropping a smaller value.

3. Implement the `get(i)`, `size`, and `clear` methods.

4. Implement the `iterator` method. A special `AbstractIterator` need not be constructed; instead, values can be added to a linear structure and the result of *that* structure's `iterator` method is returned.

To test your structure, you can generate a sequence of integers between 0 and $n - 1$. By the end, only values $n - k \ldots n - 1$ should be remembered.

Thought Questions. Consider the following questions as you complete the lab:

1. What is the (big-O) complexity of one call to the add method? What is the complexity of making n calls to add?

2. What are the advantages and disadvantages of keeping the array sorted at all times? Would it be more efficient to, say, only keep the smallest value in the first slot of the array?

3. Suppose that $f(n)$ is defined to be $n/2$ if n is even, and $3n + 1$ if n is odd. It is known that for small values of n (less than 10^{40}) the sequence of values generated by repeated application of f starting at n eventually reaches 1. Consider all the sequences generated from $n < 10,000$. What are the maximum values encountered?

4. The BestOf structure can be made more general by providing a third constructor that takes k and a Comparator. The comparisons in the BestOf class can now be recast as calls to the compare method of a Comparator. When a Comparator is not provided, an instance of the structure package's NaturalComparator is used, instead. Such an implementation allows the BestOf class to order non-Comparable values, and Comparable values in alternative orders.

Notes:

Chapter 11

Binary Trees

Concepts:
▷ Binary trees
▷ Tree traversals
▷ Recursion

I think that I shall never see
A poem lovely as a binary tree.
—Bill Amend as Jason Fox

RECURSION IS A BEAUTIFUL APPROACH TO STRUCTURING. We commonly think of recursion as a form of structuring the *control* of programs, but self-reference can be used just as effectively in the structuring of program *data*. In this chapter, we investigate the use of recursion in describing branching structures called *trees*.

Most of the structures we have already investigated are *linear*—their natural presentation is in a line. Trees branch. The result is that where there is an inherent ordering in linear structures, we find choices in the way we order the elements of a tree. These choices are an indication of the reduced "friction" of the structure and, as a result, trees provide us with the fastest ways to solve many problems.

Before we investigate the implementation of trees, we must develop a concise terminology.

11.1 Terminology

A tree is a collection of elements, called *nodes*, and relations between them, called *edges*. Usually, data are stored within the nodes of a tree. Two trees are *disjoint* if no node or edge is found common to both. A *trivial tree* has no nodes and thus no data. An isolated node is also a tree.

From these primitives we may recursively construct more complex trees. Let r be a new node and let $T_1, T_2, \ldots, T_n$ be a (possibly empty) set—a *forest*—of distinct trees. A new tree is constructed by making r the root of the tree, and establishing an edge between r and the root of each tree, T_i, in the forest. We draw trees with the root above and the trees below. Figure 11.1g is an aid to understanding this construction.

The *parent* of a node is the adjacent node appearing above it (see Figure 11.2). The *root* of a tree is the unique node with no parent. The *ancestors*

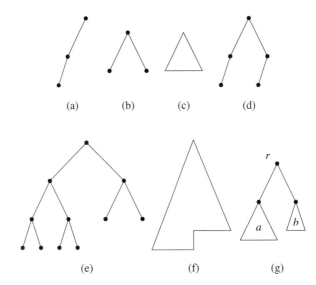

Figure 11.1 Examples of trees. Trees (a) and (b) are three-node trees. Trees are sometimes symbolized abstractly, as in (c). Tree (b) is *full*, but (d) is not. Tree (e) is not full but is *complete*. Complete trees are symbolized as in (f). Abstract tree (g) has root r and subtrees (a) and (b).

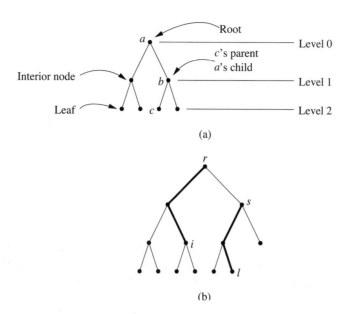

(a)

(b)

Figure 11.2 Anatomy of trees. (a) A full (and complete) tree. (b) A complete tree that is not full. Here, the unique path from node i to root r is bold: i has depth 2. Also, indicated in bold is a longest path from s to a leaf l: s has height 2 and depth 1.

of a node n are the roots of trees containing n: n, n's parent, n's parent's parent, and so on. The root is the ancestor shared by every node in the tree. A *child* of a node n is any node that has n as its parent. The *descendants* of a node n are those nodes that have n as an ancestor. A *leaf* is a node with no children. Note that n is its own ancestor and descendant. A node m is the *proper ancestor* (*proper descendant*) of a node n if m is an ancestor (descendant) of n, but not vice versa. In a tree T, the descendants of n form the *subtree* of T rooted at n. Any node of a tree T that is not a leaf is an *interior node*. Roots can be interior nodes. Nodes m and n are *siblings* if they share a parent.

A *path* is the unique shortest sequence of edges from a node n to an ancestor. The *length* of a path is the number of edges it mentions. The *height of a node* n in a tree is the length of any longest path between a leaf and n. The *height of a tree* is the height of its root. This is the maximum height of any node in the tree. The *depth* (or *level*) of a node n in its tree T is the length of the path from n to T's root. The sum of a node's depth and height is no greater than the height of the tree. The *degree of a node* n is the number of its children. The *degree of a tree* (or its *arity*) is the maximum degree of any of its nodes. A *binary tree* is a tree with arity less than or equal to 2. A 1-ary binary tree is termed *degenerate*. A node n in a binary tree is *full* if it has degree 2. In an *oriented tree* we will call one child the *left child* and the other the *right child*.

A *full binary tree* of height h has leaves only on level h, and each of its internal nodes is full. The addition of a node to a full binary tree causes its height to increase. A *complete binary tree* of height h is a full binary tree with 0 or more of the rightmost leaves of level h removed.

11.2   Example: Pedigree Charts

With the growth of the Internet, many people have been able to make contact with long-lost ancestors, not through some new technology that allows contact with spirits, but through genealogical databases. One of the reasons that genealogy has been so successful on computers is that computers can organize treelike data more effectively than people.

One such organizational approach is a pedigree chart. This is little more than a binary tree of the relatives of an individual. The root is an individual, perhaps yourself, and the two subtrees are the pedigrees of your mother and father.[1] They, of course, have two sets of parents, with pedigrees that are rooted at your grandparents.

To demonstrate how we might make use of a `BinaryTree` class, we might imagine the following code that develops the pedigree for someone named George Bush:[2]

Pedigree

```
// ancestors of George H. W. Bush
// indentation is provided to aid in understanding relations
    BinaryTree JSBush = new BinaryTree("Rev. James");
    BinaryTree HEFay = new BinaryTree("Harriet");
  BinaryTree SPBush = new BinaryTree("Samuel",JSBush,HEFay);

    BinaryTree RESheldon = new BinaryTree("Robert");
     BinaryTree MEButler = new BinaryTree("Mary");
    BinaryTree FSheldon = new BinaryTree("Flora",RESheldon,MEButler);

  BinaryTree PSBush = new BinaryTree("Prescott",SPBush,FSheldon);

    BinaryTree DDWalker = new BinaryTree("David");
    BinaryTree MABeaky = new BinaryTree("Martha");
  BinaryTree GHWalker = new BinaryTree("George",DDWalker,MABeaky);

    BinaryTree JHWear = new BinaryTree("James II");
    BinaryTree NEHolliday = new BinaryTree("Nancy");
  BinaryTree LWear = new BinaryTree("Lucretia",JHWear,NEHolliday);

  BinaryTree DWalker = new BinaryTree("Dorothy",GHWalker,LWear);

BinaryTree GHWBush = new BinaryTree("George",PSBush,DWalker);
```

---

[1] At the time of this writing, modern technology has not advanced to the point of allowing nodes of degree other than 2.

[2] This is the Texan born in Massachusetts; the other Texan was born in Connecticut.

For each person we develop a node that either has no links (the parents were not included in the database) or has references to other pedigrees stored as `BinaryTrees`. Arbitrarily, we choose to maintain the father's pedigree on the left side and the mother's pedigree along the right. We can then answer simple questions about ancestry by examining the structure of the tree. For example, who are the direct female relatives of the President?

```
// Question: What are George H. W. Bush's ancestors' names,
//   following the mother's side?
BinaryTree person = GHWBush;
while (person.right() != BinaryTree.EMPTY)
{
    person = person.right();     // right branch is mother
    System.out.println(person.value()); // value is name
}
```

The results are

```
Dorothy
Lucretia
Nancy
```

Exercise 11.1 *These are, of course, only some of the female relatives of President Bush. Write a program that prints* all *the female names found in a* `BinaryTree` *representing a pedigree chart.*

One feature that would be useful, would be the ability to add branches to a tree after the tree was constructed. For example, we might determine that James Wear had parents named William and Sarah. The database might be updated as follows:

```
// add individual directly
JHWear.setLeft(new BinaryTree("William"));
// or keep a reference to the pedigree before the update:
BinaryTree SAYancey = new BinaryTree("Sarah");
JHWear.setRight(SAYancey);
```

A little thought suggests a number of other features that might be useful in supporting the pedigree-as-**BinaryTree** structure.

11.3   Example: Expression Trees

Most programming languages involve mathematical expressions that are composed of binary operations applied to values. An example from Java is the simple expression R = 1 + (L - 1) * 2. This expression involves four operators (=, +, -, and *), and 5 values (R, 1, L, 1, and 2). Languages often represent expressions using binary trees. Each value in the expression appears as a leaf, while the operators are internal nodes that represent the reduction of two values to one (for example, L - 1 is reduced to a single value for use on the left side of the multiplication sign). The *expression tree* associated with our expression is shown in Figure 11.3a. We might imagine that the following code constructs the tree and prints −1:

```
BinaryTree v1a,v1b,v2,vL,vR,t;

// set up values 1 and 2, and declare variables
v1a = new BinaryTree(new value(1));
v1b = new BinaryTree(new value(1));
v2 = new BinaryTree(new value(2));
vL = new BinaryTree(new variable("L",0));// L=0
vR = new BinaryTree(new variable("R",0));// R=0

// set up expression
t = new BinaryTree(new operator('-'),vL,v1a);
t = new BinaryTree(new operator('*'),t,v2);
t = new BinaryTree(new operator('+'),v1b,t);
t = new BinaryTree(new operator('='),vR,t);

// evaluate and print expression
System.out.println(eval(t));
```

Calc

Once an expression is represented as an expression tree, it may be evaluated by *traversing* the tree in an agreed-upon manner. Standard rules of mathematical precedence suggest that the parenthesized expression (L-1) should be evaluated first. (The L represents a value previously stored in memory.) Once the subtraction is accomplished, the result is multiplied by 2. The product is then added to 1. The result of the addition is assigned to R. The assignment operator is treated in a manner similar to other common operators; it just has lower *precedence* (it is evaluated later) than standard mathematical operators. Thus an implementation of binary trees would be aided by a traversal mechanism that allows us to manipulate values as they are encountered.

11.4   Implementation

We now consider the implementation of binary trees. As with `List` implementations, we will construct a self-referential `BinaryTree` class. The recursive design motivates implementation of many of the `BinaryTree` operations as recursive methods. However, because the base case of recursion often involves an empty tree we will make use of a dedicated node that represents the empty tree. This simple implementation will be the basis of a large number of more advanced structures we see throughout the remainder of the text.

11.4.1   The BinaryTree Implementation

Our first step toward the development of a binary tree implementation is to represent an entire subtree as a reference to its root node. The node will maintain a reference to user data and related nodes (the node's parent and its two

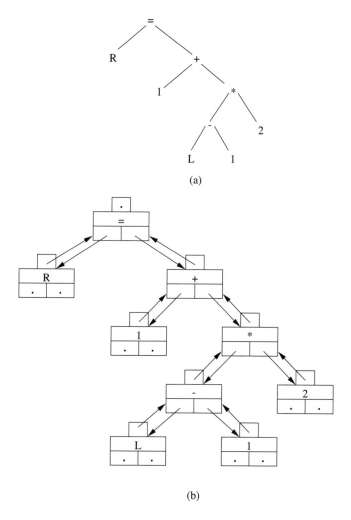

Figure 11.3 Expression trees. (a) An abstract expression tree representing `R=1+(L-1)*2`. (b) A possible connectivity of an implementation using references.

children) and directly provides methods to maintain a subtree rooted at that node. All empty trees will be represented by a single `BinaryTree` instance called `BinaryTree.EMPTY`. This approach is not unlike the "dummy nodes" provided in our study of linked lists. The `EMPTY` node allows programs to call methods on trees that are empty. If the empty tree were represented by a `null` pointer, it would be impossible to apply methods to the structure. Here is the interface (again we have omitted right-handed versions of handed operations):

BinaryTree

```
public class BinaryTree
{
    protected Object val; // value associated with node
    protected BinaryTree parent; // parent of node
    protected BinaryTree left, right; // children of node
    public static final BinaryTree EMPTY = new BinaryTree();

    private BinaryTree()
    // post: private constructor that generates the EMPTY node

    public BinaryTree(Object value)
    // post: returns a tree referencing value with two null subtrees

    public BinaryTree(Object value, BinaryTree left, BinaryTree right)
    // post: returns a tree referencing value and subtree

    public BinaryTree left()
    // post: returns reference to left subtree, or null

    public BinaryTree parent()
    // post: returns reference to parent node, or null

    public void setLeft(BinaryTree newLeft)
    // post: sets left subtree to newLeft
    //       re-parents newLeft if not null

    protected void setParent(BinaryTree newParent)
    // post: re-parents this node to parent reference, or null

    public Iterator iterator()
    // post: returns an in-order iterator of the elements

    public boolean isLeftChild()
    // post: returns true if this is a left child of parent

    public Object value()
    // post: returns value associated with this node

    public void setValue(Object value)
    // post: sets the value associated with this node
}
```

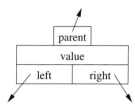

Figure 11.4 The structure of a `BinaryTree`. The parent reference opposes a left or right child reference in parent node.

Figure 11.3b depicts the use of `BinaryTree`s in the representation of an entire tree. We visualize the structure of a `BinaryTree` as in Figure 11.4. To construct such a node, we require three pieces of information: a reference to the data that the user wishes to associate with this node, and left and right references to binary tree nodes that are roots of subtrees of this node. The parent reference is determined implicitly from opposing references. The various methods associated with constructing a `BinaryTree` are as follows:

```
protected Object val; // value associated with node
protected BinaryTree parent; // parent of node
protected BinaryTree left, right; // children of node
public static final BinaryTree EMPTY = new BinaryTree();

private BinaryTree()
// post: private constructor that generates the EMPTY node
{
    val = null;
    parent = null; left = right = this;
}

public BinaryTree(Object value)
// post: returns a tree referencing value with two null subtrees
{
    val = value;
    parent = null;
    left = right = EMPTY;
}

public BinaryTree(Object value, BinaryTree left, BinaryTree right)
// post: returns a tree referencing value and subtree
{
    this(value);
    setLeft(left);
    setRight(right);
}
```

The first constructor is called exactly once—when the `BinaryTree` class is initialized. The result of this constructor is the unique node `EMPTY` that will represent the fringe of empty trees found along the edge of the binary tree. In the three-parameter variant of the constructor we make two calls to "setting" routines. These routines allow one to set the references of the left and right subtrees, but also ensure that the children of this node reference this node as their parent. This is the direct cost of implementing forward and backward references along every link. The return, though, is the considerable simplification of other code within the classes that make use of `BinaryTree` methods.

Principle 19 *Don't let opposing references show through the interface.*

When maintenance of opposing references is left to the user, there is an opportunity for references to become inconsistent. Furthermore, one might imagine implementations with fewer references (it is common, for example, to avoid the parent reference); the details of the implementation should be hidden from the user, in case the implementation needs to be changed.

Here is the code for `setLeft` (`setRight` is similar):

```
public void setLeft(BinaryTree newLeft)
// post: sets left subtree to newLeft
//       re-parents newLeft if not null
{
    if (isEmpty()) return;
    if (left.parent() == this) left.setParent(null);
    left = newLeft;
    left.setParent(this);
}
```

If the setting of the left child causes a subtree to be disconnected from this node, and that subtree considers this node to be its parent (it should), we disconnect the node by setting its parent to `null`. We then set the left child reference to the value passed in. Any dereferenced node is explicitly told to set its `parent` reference to `null`. We also take care to set the opposite parent reference by calling the `setParent` method of the root of the associated nontrivial tree. Because we want to maintain consistency between the downward child references and the upward parent references, we declare `setParent` to be `protected` to make it impossible for the user to refer to directly:

```
protected void setParent(BinaryTree newParent)
// post: re-parents this node to parent reference, or null
{
    parent = newParent;
}
```

It is, of course, useful to be able to access the various references once they have been set. We accomplish this through the accessor functions such as `left`:

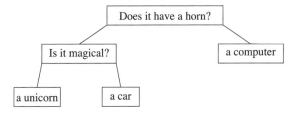

Figure 11.5 The state of the database in the midst of playing `InfiniteQuestions`.

```
public BinaryTree left()
// post: returns reference to left subtree, or null
{
    return left;
}
```

Once the node has been constructed, its value can be inspected and modified using the value-based functions that parallel those we have seen with other types:

```
public Object value()
// post: returns value associated with this node
{
    return val;
}

public void setValue(Object value)
// post: sets the value associated with this node
{
    val = value;
}
```

Once the `BinaryTree` class is implemented, we may use it as the basis for our implementation of some fairly complex programs and structures.

11.5 Example: An Expert System

Anyone who has been on a long trip with children has played the game Twenty Questions. It's not clear why this game has this name, because the questioning often continues until the entire knowledge space of the child is exhausted. We can develop a very similar program, here, called `InfiniteQuestions`. The central component of the program is a database, stored as a `BinaryTree`. At each leaf is an object that is a possible guess. The interior nodes are questions that help distinguish between the guesses.

Figure 11.5 demonstrates one possible state of the database. To simulate a questioner, one asks the questions encountered on a path from the root to some leaf. If the response to the question is positive, the questioning continues along the left branch of the tree; if the response is negative, the questioner considers the right.

Exercise 11.2 *What questions would the computer ask if you were thinking of a truck?*

Of course, we can build a very simple database with a single value—perhaps a computer. The game might be set up to play against a human as follows:

Infinite-
Questions

```
public static void main(String args[])
{
    ReadStream human = new ReadStream();
    // construct a simple database -- knows only about a computer
    BinaryTree database = new BinaryTree("a computer");

    System.out.println("Do you want to play a game?");
    while (human.readLine().equals("yes"))
    {
        System.out.println("Think of something...I'll guess it");
        play(human,database);
        System.out.println("Do you want to play again?");
    }
    System.out.println("Have a good day!");
}
```

When the game is played, we are likely to lose. If we lose, we can still benefit by incorporating information about the losing situation. If we guessed a computer and the item was a car, we could incorporate the car and a question "Does it have wheels?" to distinguish the two objects. As it turns out, the program is not that difficult.

```
public static void play(ReadStream human, BinaryTree database)
// pre: database is non-null
// post: the game is finished, and if we lost, we expanded the database
{
    if (!database.left().isEmpty())
    { // further choices; must ask a question to distinguish them
        System.out.println(database.value());
        if (human.readLine().equals("yes"))
        {
            play(human,database.left());
        } else {
            play(human,database.right());
        }
    } else { // must be a statement node
        System.out.println("Is it "+database.value()+"?");
        if (human.readLine().equals("yes"))
        {
            System.out.println("I guessed it!");
```

```
        } else {
            System.out.println("Darn.   What were you thinking of?");
            // learn!
            BinaryTree newObject = new BinaryTree(human.readLine());
            BinaryTree oldObject = new BinaryTree(database.value());
            database.setLeft(newObject);
            database.setRight(oldObject);
            System.out.println("What question would distinguish "+
                                newObject.value()+" from "+
                                oldObject.value()+"?");
            database.setValue(human.readLine());
        }
    }
}
```

The program can distinguish questions from guesses by checking to see there is a left child. This situation would suggest this node was a question since the two children need to be distinguished.

The program is very careful to expand the database by adding new leaves at the node that represents a losing guess. If we aren't careful, we can easily corrupt the database by growing a tree with the wrong topology.

Here is the output of a run of the game that demonstrates the ability of the database to incorporate new information—that is to *learn*:

```
Do you want to play a game?
yes
Think of something...I'll guess it
Is it a computer?
no
Darn.   What were you thinking of?
a car
What question would distinguish a car from a computer?
Does it have a horn?
Do you want to play again?
yes
Think of something...I'll guess it
Does it have a horn?
yes
Is it a car?
no
Darn.   What were you thinking of?
a unicorn
What question would distinguish a unicorn from a car?
Is it magical?
Do you want to play again?
yes
Think of something...I'll guess it
Does it have a horn?
yes
Is it magical?
```

```
no
Is it a car?
yes
I guessed it!
Do you want to play again?
no
Have a good day!
```

Exercise 11.3 *Make a case for or against this program as a (simple) model for human learning through experience.*

We now discuss the implementation of a general-purpose `Iterator` for the `BinaryTree` class. Not surprisingly a structure with branching (and therefore a choice in traversal order) makes traversal implementation more difficult. Next, we consider the construction of several `Iterators` for binary trees.

11.6   Traversals of Binary Trees

We have seen, of course, there is a great industry in selling calculators that allow users to enter expressions in what appear to be arbitrary ways. For example, some calculators allow users to specify expressions in *infix* form, where keys associated with operators are pressed between operands. Other brands of calculators advocate a *postfix*[3] form, where the operator is pressed only after the operands have been entered. Reconsidering our representation of expressions as trees, we observe that there must be a similar variety in the ways we traverse a `BinaryTree` structure. We consider those here.

When designing iterators for linear structures there are usually few useful choices: start at one end and visit each element until you get to the other end. Many of the linear structures we have seen provide an `elements` method that constructs an iterator for traversing the structure. For binary trees, there is no obvious order for traversing the structure. Here are four rather obvious but distinct mechanisms:

Preorder traversal. Each node is visited before any of its children are visited. Typically, we visit a node, and then each of the nodes in its left subtree, followed by each of the nodes in the right subtree. A preorder traversal of the expression tree in the margin visits the nodes in the order: $=$, R, $+$, 1, $*$, $-$, L, 1, and 2.

In-order traversal. Each node is visited after all the nodes of its left subtree have been visited and before any of the nodes of the right subtree. The in-order traversal is usually only useful with binary trees, but similar traversal mechanisms can be constructed for trees of arbitrary arity. An in-order

---

[3] Reverse Polish Notation (RPN) was developed by Jan Lukasiewicz, a philosopher and mathematician of the early twentieth century, and was made popular by Hewlett-Packard in their calculator wars with Texas Instruments in the early 1970s.

traversal of the expression tree visits the nodes in the order: R, $=$, 1, $+$, L, $-$, 1, $*$, and 2. Notice that, while this representation is similar to the expression that actually generated the binary tree, the traversal has removed the parentheses.

Postorder traversal. Each node is visited after its children are visited. We visit all the nodes of the left subtree, followed by all the nodes of the right subtree, followed by the node itself. A postorder traversal of the expression tree visits the nodes in the order: R, 1, L, 1, $-$, 2, $*$, $+$, and $=$. This is precisely the order that the keys would have to be pressed on a "reverse Polish" calculator to compute the correct result.

Level-order traversal. All nodes of level i are visited before the nodes of level $i+1$. The nodes of the expression tree are visited in the order: $=$, R, $+$, 1, $*$, $-$, 2, L, and 1. (This particular ordering of the nodes is motivation for another implementation of binary trees we shall consider later and in Problem 11.12.)

As these are the most common and useful techniques for traversing a binary tree we will investigate their respective implementations. Traversing `BinaryTree`s involves constructing an iterator that traverses the entire set of subtrees. For this reason, and because the traversal of subtrees proves to be just as easy, we discuss implementations of iterators for `BinaryTree`s.

Most implementations of iterators maintain a linear structure that keeps track of the state of the iterator. In some cases, this auxiliary structure is not strictly necessary (see Problem 11.22) but may reduce the complexity of the implementation and improve its performance.

11.6.1 Preorder Traversal

For a preorder traversal, we wish to traverse each node of the tree before any of its proper descendants (recall the node is a descendant of itself). To accomplish this, we keep a stack of nodes whose right subtrees have not been investigated. In particular, the current node is the topmost element of the stack, and elements stored deeper within the stack are more distant ancestors.

We develop a new implementation of an `Iterator` that is not declared `public`. Since it will be a member of the `structure` package, it *is* available for use by the classes of the `structure` package, including `BinaryTree`. The `BinaryTree` class will construct and return a reference to the preorder iterator when the `preorderElements` method is called:

BinaryTree

```
public AbstractIterator preorderIterator()
// post: the elements of the binary tree rooted at node are
//       traversed in preorder
{
    return new BTPreorderIterator(this);
}
```

Note that the constructor for the iterator accepts a single parameter—the root of the subtree to be traversed. Because the iterator only gives access to values stored within nodes, this is not a breach of the privacy of our binary tree implementation. The actual implementation of the BTPreorderIterator is short:

BTPreorder-
Iterator

```java
class BTPreorderIterator extends AbstractIterator
{
    protected BinaryTree root; // root of tree to be traversed
    protected Stack todo; // stack of unvisited nodes whose

    public BTPreorderIterator(BinaryTree root)
    // post: constructs an iterator to traverse in preorder
    {
        todo = new StackList();
        this.root = root;
        reset();
    }

    public void reset()
    // post: resets the iterator to retraverse
    {
        todo.clear(); // stack is empty; push on root
        if (root != null) todo.push(root);
    }

    public boolean hasNext()
    // post: returns true iff iterator is not finished
    {
        return !todo.isEmpty();
    }

    public Object get()
    // pre: hasNext()
    // post: returns reference to current value
    {
        return ((BinaryTree)todo.getFirst()).value();
    }

    public Object next()
    // pre: hasNext();
    // post: returns current value, increments iterator
    {
        BinaryTree old = (BinaryTree)todo.pop();
        Object result = old.value();

        if (!old.right().isEmpty()) todo.push(old.right());
        if (!old.left().isEmpty()) todo.push(old.left());
        return result;
    }
}
```

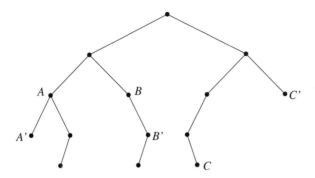

Figure 11.6   Three cases of determining the next current node for preorder traversals. Node A has a left child A' as the next node; node B has no left, but a right child B'; and node C is a leaf and finds its closest, "right cousin," C'.

As we can see, `todo` is the private stack used to keep track of references to unvisited nodes whose nontrivial ancestors have been visited. Another way to think about it is that it is the frontier of nodes encountered on paths from the root that have not yet been visited. To construct the iterator we initialize the stack. We also keep a reference to the root node; this will help reset the iterator to the correct node (when the root of the traversal is not the root of the tree, this information is vital). We then reset the iterator to the beginning of the traversal.

Resetting the iterator involves clearing off the stack and then pushing the root on the stack to make it the current node. The `hasMoreElements` method needs only to check to see if there *is* a top node of the stack, and `value` returns the reference stored within the topmost `BinaryTree` of the `todo` stack.

The only tricky method is `nextElement`. Recall that this method returns the value of the current element and then increments the iterator, causing the iterator to reference the next node in the traversal. Since the current node has just been visited, we push on any children of the node—first any right child, then any left. If the node has a left child (see node A of Figure 11.6), that node (A') is the next node to be visited. If the current node (see node B) has only a right child (B'), it will be visited next. If the current node has no children (see node C), the effect is to visit the closest unvisited right cousin or sibling (C').

It is clear that over the life of the iterator each of the n values of the tree is pushed onto and popped off the stack exactly once; thus the total cost of traversing the tree is $O(n)$. A similar observation is possible for each of the remaining iteration techniques.

11.6.2 In-order Traversal

The most common traversal of trees is in order. For this reason, the `BTInorder-Iterator` is the value returned when the `elements` method is called on a `BinaryTree`. Again, the iterator maintains a stack of references to nodes. Here, the stack contains unvisited ancestors of the current (unvisited) node.

Thus, the implementation of this traversal is similar to the code for other iterators, except for the way the stack is `reset` and for the mechanism provided in the `nextElement` method:

BTInorder-
Iterator

```
protected BinaryTree root; // root of subtree to be traversed
protected Stack todo; // stack of unvisited ancestors of current

public void reset()
// post: resets the iterator to retraverse
{
    todo.clear();
    // stack is empty.  Push on nodes from root to
    // leftmost descendant
    BinaryTree current = root;
    while (current != BinaryTree.EMPTY) {
        todo.push(current);
        current = current.left();
    }
}

public Object next()
// pre: hasNext()
// post: returns current value, increments iterator
{
    BinaryTree old = (BinaryTree)todo.pop();
    Object result = old.value();
    // we know this node has no unconsidered left children;
    // if this node has a right child,
    //    we push the right child and its leftmost descendants:
    // else
    //    top element of stack is next node to be visited
    if (!old.right().isEmpty()) {
        BinaryTree current = old.right();
        do {
            todo.push(current);
            current = current.left();
        } while (!current.isEmpty());
    }
    return result;
}
```

Since the first element considered in an in-order traversal is the leftmost descendant of the root, resetting the iterator involves pushing each of the nodes from the root down to the leftmost descendant on the auxiliary stack.

When the current node is popped from the stack, the next element of the traversal must be found. We consider two scenarios:

1. If the current node has a right subtree, the nodes of that tree have not been visited. At this stage we should push the right child, and all the nodes down to and including its leftmost descendant, on the stack.

2. If the node has no right child, the subtree rooted at the current node has been fully investigated, and the next node to be considered is the closest unvisited ancestor of the former current node—the node just exposed on the top of the stack.

As we shall see later, it is common to order the nodes of a binary tree so that left-hand descendants of a node are smaller than the node, which is, in turn, smaller than any of the rightmost descendants. In such a situation, the in-order traversal plays a natural role in presenting the data of the tree in order. For this reason, the `elements` method returns the iterator constructed by the `inorderElements` method.

11.6.3   Postorder Traversal

Traversing a tree in postorder also maintains a stack of uninvestigated nodes. Each of the elements on the stack is a node whose descendants are currently being visited. Since the first element to be visited is the leftmost descendant of the root, the `reset` method must (as with the in-order iterator) push on each of the nodes from the root to the leftmost descendant. (Note that the leftmost descendant need not be a leaf—it does not have a left child, but it may have a right.)

BTPostorder-
Iterator

```
protected BinaryTree root; // root of traversed subtree
protected Stack todo;   // stack of nodes whose descendants
                        // are currently being visited

public void reset()
// post: resets the iterator to retraverse
{
    todo.clear();
    // stack is empty; push on nodes from root to
    // leftmost descendant
    BinaryTree current = root;
    while (!current.isEmpty()) {
        todo.push(current);
        if (!current.left().isEmpty())
            current = current.left();
        else
            current = current.right();
    }
}
```

```
public Object next()
// pre: hasNext();
// post: returns current value, increments iterator
{
    BinaryTree current = (BinaryTree)todo.pop();
    Object result = current.value();
    if (!todo.isEmpty())
    {
        BinaryTree parent = (BinaryTree)todo.getFirst();
        if (current == parent.left()) {
            current = parent.right();
            while (!current.isEmpty())
            {
                todo.push(current);
                if (!current.left().isEmpty())
                    current = current.left();
                else current = current.right();
            }
        }
    }
    return result;
}
```

Here an interior node on the stack is potentially exposed twice before becoming current. The first time it may be left on the stack because the element recently popped off was the left child. The right child should now be pushed on. Later the exposed node becomes current because the popped element was its right child.

It is interesting to observe that the stack contains the ancestors of the current node. This stack describes, essentially, the path to the root of the tree. As a result, we could represent the state of the stack by a single reference to the current node.

11.6.4 Level-order Traversal

This is the family values traversal.

A level-order traversal visits the root, followed by the nodes of level 1, from left to right, followed by the nodes of level 2, and so on. This can be easily accomplished by maintaining a queue of the next few nodes to be visited. More precisely, the queue contains the current node, followed by a list of all siblings and cousins to the right of the current node, followed by a list of "nieces and nephews" to the left of the current node. After we visit a node, we enqueue the children of the node. With a little work it is easy to see that these are either nieces and nephews or right cousins of the next node to be visited.

BTLevelorder-
Iterator

```
class BTLevelorderIterator extends AbstractIterator
{
    protected BinaryTree root; // root of traversed subtree
    protected Queue todo;  // queue of unvisited relatives
```

```
        public BTLevelorderIterator(BinaryTree root)
        // post: constructs an iterator to traverse in level order
        {
            todo = new QueueList();
            this.root = root;
            reset();
        }

        public void reset()
        // post: resets the iterator to root node
        {
            todo.clear();
            // empty queue, add root
            if (!root.isEmpty()) todo.enqueue(root);
        }

        public boolean hasNext()
        // post: returns true iff iterator is not finished
        {
            return !todo.isEmpty();
        }

        public Object get()
        // pre: hasNext()
        // post: returns reference to current value
        {
            return ((BinaryTree)todo.getFirst()).value();
        }

        public Object next()
        // pre: hasNext();
        // post: returns current value, increments iterator
        {
            BinaryTree current = (BinaryTree)todo.dequeue();
            Object result = current.value();
            if (!current.left().isEmpty())
                todo.enqueue(current.left());
            if (!current.right().isEmpty())
                todo.enqueue(current.right());
            return result;
        }
    }
```

To **reset** the iterator, we need only empty the queue and add the root. When the queue is empty, the traversal is finished. When the next element is needed, we need only enqueue references to children (left to right). Notice that, unlike the other iterators, this method of traversing the tree is meaningful regardless of the degree of the tree.

11.6.5   Recursion in Iterators

Trees are recursively defined structures, so it would seem reasonable to consider recursive implementations of iterators. The difficulty is that iterators must maintain their state across many calls to `nextElement`. Any recursive approach to traversal would encounter nodes while deep in recursion, and the state of the stack must be preserved.

One way around the difficulties of suspending the recursion is to initially perform the entire traversal, generating a list of values encountered. Since the entire traversal happens all at once, the list can be constructed using recursion. As the iterator pushes forward, the elements of the list are consumed.

Using this idea, we rewrite the in-order traversal:

Recursive-
Iterators

```
protected BinaryTree root; // root of traversed subtree
protected Queue todo;  // queue of unvisited elements

public BTInorderIteratorR(BinaryTree root)
// post: constructs an iterator to traverse in in-order
{
    todo = new QueueList();
    this.root = root;
    reset();
}

public void reset()
// post: resets the iterator to retraverse
{
    todo.clear();
    enqueueInorder(root);
}

protected void enqueueInorder(BinaryTree current)
// pre: current is non-null
// post: enqueue all values found in tree rooted at current
//       in in-order
{
    if (current.isEmpty()) return;
    enqueueInorder(current.left());
    todo.enqueue(current);
    enqueueInorder(current.right());
}
public Object next()
// pre: hasNext();
// post: returns current value, increments iterator
{
    BinaryTree current = (BinaryTree)todo.dequeue();
    return current.value();
}
```

The core of this implementation is the protected method `enqueueInorder`. It simply traverses the tree rooted at its parameter and enqueues every node encountered. Since it recursively enqueues all its left descendants, then itself, and then its right descendants, it is an in-order traversal. Since the queue is a FIFO, the order is preserved and the elements may be consumed at the user's leisure.

For completeness and demonstration of symmetry, here are the pre- and postorder counterparts:

```
protected void enqueuePreorder(BinaryTree current)
// pre: current is non-null
// post: enqueue all values found in tree rooted at current
//       in preorder
{
    if (current.isEmpty()) return;
    todo.enqueue(current);
    enqueuePreorder(current.left());
    enqueuePreorder(current.right());
}

protected void enqueuePostorder(BinaryTree current)
// pre: current is non-null
// post: enqueue all values found in tree rooted at current
//       in postorder
{
    if (current.isEmpty()) return;
    enqueuePostorder(current.left());
    enqueuePostorder(current.right());
    todo.enqueue(current);
}
```

It is reassuring to see the brevity of these implementations. Unfortunately, while the recursive implementations are no less efficient, they come at the obvious cost of a potentially long delay whenever the iterator is reset. Still, for many applications this may be satisfactory.

11.7   Property-Based Methods

At this point, we consider the implementation of a number of property-based methods. Properties such as the height and fullness of a tree are important to guiding updates of a tree structure. Because the binary tree is a recursively defined data type, the proofs of tree characteristics (and the methods that verify them) often have a recursive feel. To emphasize the point, in this section we allow theorems about trees and methods that verify them to intermingle. Again, the methods described here are written for use on `BinaryTrees`, but they are easily adapted for use with more complex structures.

Our first method makes use of the fact that the root is a common ancestor of every node of the tree. Because of this fact, given a `BinaryTree`, we can identify the node as the root, or return the root of the tree containing the node's parent.

BinaryTree

```
public BinaryTree root()
// post: returns the root of the tree node n
{
    if (parent() == null) return this;
    else return parent().root();
}
```

A proof that this method functions correctly could make use of induction, based on the depth of the node involved.

If we count the number of times the `root` routine is recursively called, we compute the number of edges from the node to the root—the depth of the node. Not surprisingly, the code is very similar:

```
public int depth()
// post: returns the depth of a node in the tree
{
    if (parent() == null) return 0;
    return 1 + parent.depth();
}
```

The time it takes is proportional to the depth of the node. For full trees, we will see that this is approximately $O(\log n)$. Notice that in the `EMPTY` case we return a height of -1. This is consistent with our recursive definition, even if it does seem a little unusual. We could avoid the strange case by avoiding it in the precondition. Then, of course, we would only have put off the work to the calling routine. Often, making tough decisions about base cases can play an important role in making your interface useful. Generally, a method is more robust, and therefore more usable, if you handle as many cases as possible.

Principle 20 *Write methods to be as general as possible.*

Having computed the depth of a node, it follows that we should be able to determine the height of a tree rooted at a particular `BinaryTree`. We know that the height is simply the length of a longest path from the root to a leaf, but we can adapt a self-referential definition: the height of a tree is one more than the height of the tallest subtree. This translates directly into a clean implementation of the height function:

```
public int height()
// post: returns the height of a node in its tree
{
    if (isEmpty()) return -1;
    return 1 + Math.max(left.height(),right.height());
}
```

This method takes $O(n)$ time to execute on a subtree with n nodes (see Problem 11.9).

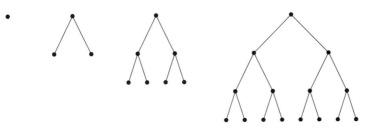

Figure 11.7   Several full (and complete) binary trees.

At this point, we consider the problem of identifying a tree that is full (see Figure 11.7). Our approach uses recursion:

```
public boolean isFull()
// post: returns true iff the tree rooted at node is full
{
    if (isEmpty()) return true;
    if (left().height() != right().height()) return false;
    return left().isFull() && right().isFull();
}
```

Again, the method is compact. Unfortunately, detecting this property appears to be significantly more expensive than computing the height. Note, for example, that in the process of computing this function on a full tree, the *height of every node* must be computed from scratch. The result is that the running time of the algorithm on full trees is $O(n \log n)$. Can it be improved upon?

To find the answer, we first prove a series of theorems about the structure of trees, with hope that we can develop an inexpensive way to test for a full tree. Our first result determines the number of nodes that are found in full trees:

Observation 11.1 *A full binary tree of height $h \geq 0$ has $2^{h+1} - 1$ nodes.*

Proof: We prove this by induction on the height of the tree. Suppose the tree has height 0. Then it has exactly one node, which is also a leaf. Since $2^1 - 1 = 1$, the observation holds, trivially.

Our inductive hypothesis is that full trees of height $k < h$ have $2^{k+1} - 1$ nodes. Since $h > 0$, we can decompose the tree into two full subtrees of height $h - 1$, under a common root. Each of the full subtrees has $2^{(h-1)+1} - 1 = 2^h - 1$ nodes, so there are $2(2^h - 1) + 1 = 2^{h+1} - 1$ nodes. This is the result we sought to prove, so by induction on tree height we see the observation must hold for all full binary trees. ◇

This observation suggests that if we can compute the height and size of a tree, we have a hope of detecting a full tree. First, we compute the size of the tree using a recursive algorithm:

```
public int size()
// post: returns the size of the subtree
{
    if (isEmpty()) return 0;
    return left().size() + right().size() + 1;
}
```

This algorithm is similar to the height algorithm: each call to size counts one more node, so the complexity of the routine is $O(n)$. Now we have an alternative implementation of isFull that compares the height of the tree to the number of nodes:

```
public boolean isFull()
// post: returns true iff the tree rooted at n is full
{
    int h = height();
    int s = size();
    return s == (1<<(h+1))-1;
}
```

Notice the return statement makes use of shifting 1 to the left $h + 1$ binary places. This efficiently computes 2^{h+1}. The result is that, given a full tree, the function returns true in $O(n)$ steps. Thus, it *is* possible to improve on our previous implementation.

There is one significant disadvantage, though. If you are given a tree with height greater than 100, the result of the return statement cannot be accurately computed: 2^{100} is a large enough number to overflow Java integers. Even rea-
Redwoods and sonably sized trees can have height greater than 100. The first implementation
sequoias come is accurate, even if it is slow. Problem 11.21 considers an efficient and accurate
to mind. solution.

We now prove some useful facts about binary trees that help us evaluate performance of methods that manipulate them. First, we consider a pretty result: if a tree has lots of leaves, it must branch in lots of places.

Observation 11.2 *The number of full nodes in a binary tree is one less than the number of leaves.*

Proof: Left to the reader.◇

With this result, we can now demonstrate that just over half the nodes of a full tree are leaves.

Observation 11.3 *A full binary tree of height $h \geq 0$ has 2^h leaves.*

Proof: In a full binary tree, all nodes are either full interior nodes or leaves. The number of nodes is the sum of full nodes F and the number of leaves L. Since, by Observation 11.2, $F = L - 1$, we know that the count of nodes is $F + L = 2L - 1 = 2^{h+1} - 1$. This leads us to conclude that $L = 2^h$ and that $F = 2^h - 1$. ◇ This result demonstrates that for many simple tree methods (like

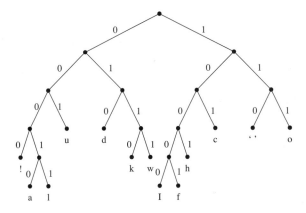

Figure 11.8   The woodchuck Huffman tree. Leaves are labeled with the characters they represent. Paths from root to leaves provide Huffman bit strings.

size) half of the time is spent processing leaves. Because complete trees can be viewed as full trees with some rightmost leaves removed, similar results hold for complete trees as well.

11.8   Example: Huffman Compression

Information within machines is stored as a series of `bits`, or 1's and 0's. Because the distribution of the patterns of 1's and 0's is not always uniform, it is possible to compress the bit patterns that are used and reduce the amount of storage that is necessary. For example, consider the following 32-character phrase:

    If a woodchuck could chuck wood!

If each letter in the string is represented by 8 bits (as they often are), the entire string takes 256 bits of storage. Clearly this catchy phrase does not use the full range of characters, and so perhaps 8 bits are not needed. In fact, there are 13 distinct characters so 4 bits would be sufficient (4 bits can represent any of 16 values). This would halve the amount of storage required, to 128 bits.

Huffman

   If each character were represented by a unique *variable-length* string of bits, further improvements are possible. *Huffman encoding* of characters allows us to reduce the size of this string to only 111 bits by assigning frequently occurring letters (like "o") short representations and infrequent letters (like "a") relatively long representations.

   Huffman encodings can be represented by binary trees whose leaves are the characters to be represented. In Figure 11.8 left edges are labeled 0, while right edges are labeled 1. Since there is a unique path from the root to each leaf, there is a unique sequence of 1's and 0's encountered as well. We will use the string

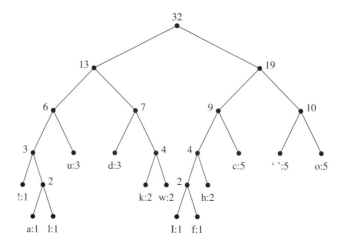

Figure 11.9 The Huffman tree of Figure 11.8, but with nodes labeled by total frequencies of descendant characters.

of bits encountered along the path to a character as its representation in the compressed output. Note also that no string is a prefix for any other (otherwise one character would be an ancestor of another in the tree). This means that, given the Huffman tree, decoding a string of bits involves simply traversing the tree and writing out the leaves encountered.

The construction of a Huffman tree is an iterative process. Initially, each character is placed in a Huffman tree of its own. The weight of the tree is the frequency of its associated character. We then iteratively merge the two most lightweight Huffman trees into a single new Huffman tree whose weight is the sum of weights of the subtrees. This continues until one tree remains. One possible tree for our example is shown in Figure 11.9.

Our approach is to use `BinaryTrees` to maintain the structure. This allows the use of recursion and easy merging of trees. Leaves of the tree carry descriptions of characters and their frequencies:

Huffman

```
class leaf
{
    int frequency; // frequency of char
    char ch;       // the character

    public leaf(char c)
    // post: construct character entry with frequency 1

    public boolean equals(Object other)
    // post: return true if leaves represent same character
}
```

Intermediate nodes carry no data at all. Their relation to their ancestors determines their portion of the encoding. The entire tree is managed by a wrapper class, huffmanTree:

```
class huffmanTree implements Comparable
{
    BinaryTree root; // root of tree
    int totalWeight;    // weight of tree

    public huffmanTree(leaf e)
    // post: construct a leaf with associated character

    public huffmanTree(huffmanTree left, huffmanTree right)
    // pre: left and right non-null
    // post: merge two trees together and merge their weights

    public int compareTo(Object other)
    // pre: other is non-null
    // post: return integer reflecting relation between values

    public boolean equals(Object that)
    // post: return true if this and that are same tree instance

    public void print()
    // post: print out strings associated with characters in tree

    protected void print(BinaryTree r, String representation)
    // post: print out strings associated with chars in tree r,
    //          prefixed by representation
}
```

This class is a Comparable because it implements the compareTo method. That method allows the trees to be ordered by their total weight during the merging process. The utility method print generates our output recursively, building up a different encoding along every path.

We now consider the construction of the tree:

```
public static void main(String args[])
{
    ReadStream r = new ReadStream();
    List freq = new SinglyLinkedList();

    // read data from input
    while (!r.eof())
    {
        char c = r.readChar();
        // look up character in frequency list
        leaf query = new leaf(c);
        leaf item = (leaf)freq.remove(query);
        if (item == null)
```

```
        {   // not found, add new leaf
            freq.addFirst(query);
        } else { // found, increment leaf
            item.frequency++;
            freq.addFirst(item);
        }
    }

    // insert each character into a Huffman tree
    Iterator li = freq.iterator();
    OrderedList trees = new OrderedList();
    while (li.hasNext())
    {
        trees.add(new huffmanTree((leaf)li.next()));
    }

    // merge trees in pairs until one remains
    Iterator ti = trees.iterator();
    while (trees.size() > 1)
    {
        // construct a new iterator
        ti = trees.iterator();
        // grab two smallest values
        huffmanTree smallest = (huffmanTree)ti.next();
        huffmanTree small = (huffmanTree)ti.next();
        // remove them
        trees.remove(smallest);
        trees.remove(small);
        // add bigger tree containing both
        trees.add(new huffmanTree(smallest,small));
    }
    // print only tree in list
    ti  = trees.iterator();
    Assert.condition(ti.hasNext(),"Huffman tree exists.");
    huffmanTree encoding = (huffmanTree)ti.next();
    encoding.print();
}
```

There are three phases in this method: the reading of the data, the construction of the character-holding leaves of the tree, and the merging of trees into a single encoding. Several things should be noted:

1. We store characters in a list. Since this list is likely to be small, keeping it ordered requires more code and is not likely to improve performance.

2. The huffmanTrees are kept in an OrderedList. Every time we remove values we must construct a fresh iterator and remove the two smallest trees. When they are merged and reinserted, the wrappers for the two smaller trees can be garbage-collected. (Even better structures for managing these details in Chapter 12.)

3. The resulting tree is then printed out. In an application, the information
   in this tree would have to be included with the compressed text to guide
   the decompression.

When the program is run on the input

```
If a woodchuck could chuck wood!
```

it generates the output:

```
Encoding of ! is 0000 (frequency was 1)
Encoding of a is 00010 (frequency was 1)
Encoding of l is 00011 (frequency was 1)
Encoding of u is 001 (frequency was 3)
Encoding of d is 010 (frequency was 3)
Encoding of k is 0110 (frequency was 2)
Encoding of w is 0111 (frequency was 2)
Encoding of I is 10000 (frequency was 1)
Encoding of f is 10001 (frequency was 1)
Encoding of h is 1001 (frequency was 2)
Encoding of c is 101 (frequency was 5)
Encoding of   is 110 (frequency was 5)
Encoding of o is 111 (frequency was 5)
```

Again, the total number of bits that would be used to represent our compressed phrase is only 111, giving us a compression rate of 56 percent. In these
days of moving bits about, the construction of efficient compression techniques
is an important industry—one industry that depends on the efficient implementation of data structures.

11.9   Example Implementation: Ahnentafel

Having given, in Section 11.2, time to the Republican genealogists, we might
now investigate the heritage of a Democrat, William Jefferson Clinton. In Figure 11.10 we see the recent family tree presented as a list. This arrangement is
called an *ahnentafel*, or ancestor table. The table is generated by performing a
level-order traversal of the pedigree tree, and placing the resulting entries in a
table whose index starts at 1.

This layout has some interesting features. First, if we have an individual
with index i, the parents of the individual are found in table entries $2i$ and
$2i + 1$. Given the index i of a parent, we can find the child (there is only one
child for every parent in a pedigree), by dividing the index by 2 and throwing
away the remainder.

We can use this as the basis of an implementation of short binary trees. Of
course, if the tree becomes tall, there is potentially a great amount of data in the
tree. Also, if a tree is not full, there will be empty locations in the table. These
must be carefully managed to keep from interpreting these entries as valid data.

1	William Jefferson Clinton
2	William Jefferson Blythe III
3	Virginia Dell Cassidy
4	William Jefferson Blythe II
5	Lou Birchie Ayers
6	Eldridge Cassidy
7	Edith Grisham
8	Henry Patton Foote Blythe
9	Frances Ellen Hines
10	Simpson Green Ayers
11	Hattie Hayes
12	James M. Cassidy
13	Sarah Louisa Russell
14	Lemma Newell Grisham
15	Edna Earl Adams

Figure 11.10   The genealogy of President Clinton, presented as a linear table. Each individual is assigned an index i. The parents of the individual can be found at locations $2i$ and $2i + 1$. Performing an integer divide by 2 generates the index of a child. Note the table starts at index 1.

While the math is fairly simple, our `Lists` are stored with the first element at location 0. The implementor must either choose to keep location 0 blank or to modify the indexing methods to make use of zero-origin indices.

One possible approach to storing tree information like this is to store entrees in key-value pairs in the list structure, with the key being the index. In this way, the tree can be stored compactly and, if the associations are kept in an ordered structure, they can be referenced with only a logarithmic slowdown.

Exercise 11.4 *Describe what would be necessary to allow support for trees with degrees up to eight (called* octtrees*). At what cost do we achieve this increased functionality?*

In Chapter 12 we will make use of an especially interesting binary tree called a *heap*. We will see the ahnentafel approach to storing heaps in a vector shortly.

11.10   Conclusions

The tree is a nonlinear structure. Because of branching in the tree, we will find it is especially useful in situations where decisions can guide the process of adding and removing nodes.

Our approach to implementing the binary tree—a tree with degree 2 or less—is to visualize it as a self-referential structure. This is somewhat at odds with an object-oriented approach. It is, for example, difficult to represent empty self-referential structures in a manner that allows us to invoke methods. To relieve the tension between these two approaches, we represent the empty tree with a unique class instance called `BinaryTree.EMPTY`.

The power of recursion on branching structures is that significant work can be accomplished with very little code. Sometimes, as in our implementation of the `isFull` method, we find ourselves subtly pushed away from an efficient solution because of overzealous use of recursion. Usually we can eliminate such inefficiencies, but we must always verify that our methods act reasonably.

Self Check Problems

Solutions to these problems begin on page 434.

11.1   Can a tree have no root? Can a tree have no leaves?

11.2   Can a binary tree have more leaves than interior nodes? Can it have more interior nodes than leaves?

11.3   In a binary tree, which node (or nodes) have greatest height?

11.4   Is it possible to have two different paths between a root and a leaf?

11.5   Why are arithmetic expressions naturally stored in binary trees?

11.6   Many spindly trees look like lists. Is a `BinaryTree` a `List`?

11.7   Suppose we wanted to make a `List` from a `BinaryTree`. How might we provide indices to the elements of the tree?

11.8   Could the queue in the level-order traversal of a tree be replaced with a stack?

11.9   Recursion is used to compute many properties of trees. What portion of the tree is usually associated with the base case?

11.10   In code that recursively traverses binary trees, how many recursive calls are usually found within the code?

11.11   What is the average degree of a node in an n-node binary tree?

Problems

Solutions to the odd-numbered problems begin on page 463.

11.1   In the following binary tree containing character data, describe the characters encountered in pre-, post- and in-order traversals.

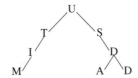

11.2   In the following tree what are the ancestors of the leaf D? What are the descendants of the node S? The root of the tree is the common ancestor of what nodes?

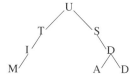

11.3   Draw an expression tree for each of the following expressions.

a. 1

b. $1 + 5 * 3 - 4/2$

c. $1 + 5 * (3 - 4)/2$

d. $(1 + 5) * (3 - 4/2)$

e. $(1 + (5 * (3 - (4/2))))$

Circle the nodes that are ancestors of the node containing the value 1.

11.4   What topological characteristics distinguish a tree from a list?

11.5   Demonstrate how the expression tree associated with the expression $R = 1 + (L - 1) * 2$ can be simplified using first the distributive property and then reduction of constant expressions to constants. Use pictures to forward your argument.

11.6   For each of the methods of `BinaryTree`, indicate which method can be implemented in terms of other `public` methods of that class or give a reasoned argument why it is not possible. Explain why it is useful to cast methods in terms of other `public` methods and not base them directly on a particular implementation.

11.7   The `BinaryTree` class is a *recursive data structure*, unlike the `List` class. Describe how the `List` class would be different if it were implemented as a recursive data structure.

11.8   The `parent` reference in a `BinaryTree` is declared `protected` and is accessed through the accessor methods `parent` and `setParent`. Why is this any different than declaring `parent` to be `public`.

11.9   Prove that efficient computation of the height of a `BinaryTree` must take time proportional to the number of nodes in the tree.

11.10   Write an `equals` method for the `BinaryTree` class. This function should return `true` if and only if the trees are similarly shaped and refer to equal values (every `Object`, including the `Objects` of the tree, has an `equals` method).

11.11   Write a static method, `copy`, that, given a binary tree, returns a copy of the tree. Because not every object implements the `copy` method, you should *not* copy objects to which the tree refers. This is referred to as a *shallow copy*.

11.12 Design a nonrecursive implementation of a binary tree that maintains node data in a `Vector`, `data`. In this implementation, element 0 of `data` references the root (if it exists). Every non-`null` element i of `data` finds its left and right children at locations $2i+1$ and $2(i+1)$, respectively. (The inverse of these index relations suggests the parent of a nonroot node at i is found at location $\lfloor(i-1)/2\rfloor$.) Any element of data that is not used to represent a node should maintain a `null` reference.

11.13 Design an *interface* for general trees—trees with unbounded degree. Make this interface as consistent as possible with `BinaryTrees` when the degree of a tree is no greater than 2.

11.14 Implement the general tree structure of Problem 11.13 using `Binary-TreeNodes`. In this implementation, we interpret the left child of a `BinaryTree-Node` to be the leftmost child, and the right child of the `BinaryTree` to be the leftmost right sibling of the node.

11.15 Write a preorder iterator for the general tree implementation of Problem 11.14.

11.16 Implement the general tree structure of Problem 11.13 using a tree node of your own design. In this implementation, each node maintains (some sort of) collection of subtrees.

11.17 Write an in-order iterator for the general tree implementation of Problem 11.16.

11.18 Determine the complexity of each of the methods implemented in Problem 11.14.

11.19 Write a method, `isComplete`, that returns `true` if and only if the subtree rooted at a `BinaryTree` on which it acts is complete.

11.20 A tree is said to be an *AVL tree* or *height balanced* if, for every node n, the heights of the subtrees of n differ by no more than 1. Write a static `BinaryTree` method that determines if a tree rooted at the referenced node is height balanced.

11.21 The `BinaryTree` method `isFull` takes $O(n \log n)$ time to execute on full trees, which, as we've seen, is not optimal. Careful thought shows that calls to `height` (an $O(n)$ operation) are made more often than is strictly necessary. Write a recursive method `info` that computes two values—the height of the tree and whether or not the tree is full. (This might be accomplished by having the sign of the height be negative if it is not full. Make sure you do not call this method on empty trees.) If `info` makes no call to `height` or `isFull`, its performance is $O(n)$. Verify this on a computer by counting procedure calls. This process is called *strengthening*, an optimization technique that often improves performance of recursive algorithms.

11.22 Demonstrate how, in an in-order traversal, the associated stack can be removed and replaced with a single reference. (Hint: We only need to know the top of the stack, and the elements below the stack top are determined *by* the stack top.)

11.23 Which other traversals can be rewritten by replacing their `Linear` structure with a single reference? How does this change impact the complexity of each of the iterations?

11.24 Suppose the nodes of a binary tree are unique and that you are given the order of elements as they are encountered in a preorder traversal and the order of the elements as they are encountered in a postorder traversal. Under what conditions can you accurately reconstruct the structure of the tree from these two traversal orders?

11.25 Suppose you are to store a k-ary tree where each internal node has k children and (obviously) each leaf has none. If $k = 2$, we see that Observation 11.2 suggests that there is one more leaf than internal node. Prove that a similar situation holds for k-ary trees with only full nodes and leaves: if there are n full nodes, there are $(k - 1)n + 1$ leaves. (Hint: Use induction.)

11.26 Assume that the observation of Problem 11.25 is true and that you are given a k-ary tree with only full nodes and leaves constructed with references between nodes. In a k-ary tree with n nodes, how many references are `null`? Considerable space might be saved if the k references to the children of an internal node were stored in a k-element array, instead of k fields. In leaves, the array needn't be allocated. In an 8-ary tree with only full nodes and leaves (an "octtree") with one million internal nodes, how many bytes of space can be saved using this array technique (assume all references consume 4 bytes).

11.11 Laboratory: Playing Gardner's Hex-a-Pawn

Objective. To use trees to develop a game-playing strategy.

Discussion. In this lab we will write a simulator for the game, Hex-a-Pawn. This game was developed in the early sixties by Martin Gardner. Three white and three black pawns are placed on a 3 × 3 chessboard. On alternate moves they may be either moved forward one square, or they may capture an opponent on the diagonal. The game ends when a pawn is promoted to the opposite rank, or if a player loses all his pieces, or if no legal move is possible.

In his article in the March 1962 *Scientific American*, Gardner discussed a method for teaching a computer to play this simple game using a relatively small number of training matches. The process involved keeping track of the different states of the board and the potential for success (a win) from each board state. When a move led directly to a loss, the computer forgot the move, thereby causing it to avoid that particular loss in the future. This *pruning* of moves could, of course, cause an intermediate state to lead indirectly to a loss, in which case the computer would be forced to prune out an intermediate move.

Gardner's original "computer" was constructed from matchboxes that contained colored beads. Each bead corresponded to a potential move, and the pruning involved disposing of the last bead played. In a modern system, we can use nodes of a tree stored in a computer to maintain the necessary information about each board state. The degree of each node is determined by the number of possible moves.

Procedure. During the course of this project you are to

1. Construct a tree of Hex-a-Pawn board positions. Each node of the tree is called a `GameTree`. The structure of the class is of your own design, but it is likely to be similar to the `BinaryTree` implementation.

2. Construct three classes of `Players` that play the game of Hex-a-Pawn. These three classes may interact in pairs to play a series of games.

Available for your use are three Javafiles:

HexBoard This class describes the state of a board. The default board is the 3×3 starting position. You can ask a board to print itself out (`toString`) or to return the `HexMoves` (`moves`) that are possible from this position. You can also ask a `HexBoard` if the current position is a win for a particular color— `HexBoard.WHITE` or `HexBoard.BLACK`. A static utility method, `opponent`, takes a color and returns the opposite color. The `main` method of this class demonstrates how `HexBoards` are manipulated.

HexBoard

HexMove This class describes a valid move. The components of the `Vector` returned from the `HexBoard.moves` contains objects of type `HexMove`. Given a `HexBoard` and a `HexMove` one can construct the resulting `HexBoard` using a `HexBoard` constructor.

HexMove

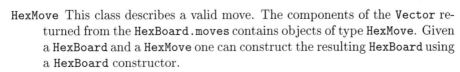

Player

Player When one is interested in constructing players that play Hex-a-Pawn, the `Player` interface describes the form of the `play` method that must be provided. The `play` method takes a `GameTree` node and an opposing `Player`. It checks for a loss, plays the game according to the `GameTree`, and then turns control over to the opposing player.

Read these class files carefully. You should not expect to modify them.

There are many approaches to experimenting with Hex-a-Pawn. One series of experiments might be the following:

1. Compile `HexBoard.java` and run it as a program. Play a few games against the computer. You may wish to modify the size of the board. Very little is known about the games larger than 3 × 3.

2. Implement a `GameTree` class. This class should have a constructor that, given a `HexBoard` and a color (a `char`, `HexBoard.WHITE` or `HexBoard.BLACK`), generates the tree of all boards reachable from the specified board position during normal game play. Alternate levels of the tree represent boards that are considered by alternate players. Leaves are winning positions for the player at hand. The references to other `GameTree` nodes are suggested by the individual moves returned from the `moves` method. A complete game tree for 3 × 3 boards has 370 nodes.

3. Implement the first of three players. It should be called `HumanPlayer`. If it hasn't already lost (i.e., if the opponent hasn't won), this player prints the board, presents the moves, and allows a human (through a `ReadStream`) to select a move. The play is then handed off to the opponent.

4. The second player, `RandPlayer`, should play randomly. Make sure you check for a loss before attempting a move.

5. The third player, called `CompPlayer`, should attempt to have the `CompPlayer` object modify the game tree to remove losing moves.

Clearly, `Player`s may be made to play against each other in any combination.

Thought Questions. Consider the following questions as you complete the lab:

1. How many board positions are there for the 3 × 4 board? Can you determine how many moves there are for a 3 × 5 board?

2. If you implement the learning machine, pit two machines against each other. Gardner called the computer to move first H.I.M., and the machine to move second H.E.R. Will H.I.M. or H.E.R. ultimately win more frequently? Explain your reasoning in a short write-up. What happens for larger boards?

3. In Gardner's original description of the game, each matchbox represented a board state *and its reflection*. What modifications to `HexBoard` and `HexMove` would be necessary to support this collapsing of the game tree?

Chapter 12
Priority Queues

Concepts:
▷ Priority queues
▷ Heaps
▷ Skew heaps
▷ Sorting with heaps
▷ Simulation

"Exactly!" said Mr. Wonka.
"I decided to invite five children
to the factory, and the one I liked best
at the end of the day
would be the winner!"
—Roald Dahl

SOMETIMES A RESTRICTED INTERFACE IS A FEATURE. The *priority queue*, like an ordered structure, appears to keep its data in order. Unlike an ordered structure, however, the priority queue allows the user only to access its smallest element. The priority queue is also similar to the `Linear` structure: values are added to the structure, and they later may be inspected or removed. Unlike their `Linear` counterpart, however, once a value is added to the priority queue it may only be removed if it is the minimum value.[1] It is precisely this restricted interface to the priority queue that allows many of its implementations to run quickly.

Priority queues are used to schedule processes in an operating system, to schedule future events in a simulation, and to generally rank choices that are generated out of order.

Think triage.

12.1 The Interface

Because we will see many contrasting implementations of the priority queue structure, we describe it as abstractly as possible in Java—with an interface:

```
public interface PriorityQueue
{
    public Comparable getFirst();
    // pre: !isEmpty()
    // post: returns the minimum value in priority queue
```

`PriorityQueue`

---

[1] We will consider priority queues whose elements are ranked in ascending order. It is, of course, possible to maintain these queues in descending order with only a few modifications.

```
public Comparable remove();
// pre: !isEmpty()
// post: returns and removes minimum value from queue

public void add(Comparable value);
// pre: value is non-null comparable
// post: value is added to priority queue

public boolean isEmpty();
// post: returns true iff no elements are in queue

public int size();
// post: returns number of elements within queue

public void clear();
// post: removes all elements from queue
}
```

Because they must be kept in order, the elements of a `PriorityQueue` are `Comparable`. In this interface the smallest values are found near the front of the queue and will be removed soonest.[2] The `add` operation is used to insert a new value into the queue. At any time a reference to the minimum value can be obtained with the `getFirst` method and is removed with `remove`. The remaining methods are similar to those we have seen before.

Notice that the `PriorityQueue` does not extend any of the interfaces we have seen previously. First, as a matter of convenience, `PriorityQueue` methods consume `Comparable` parameters and return `Comparable` values. Most structures we have encountered manipulate `Objects`. Though similar, the `PriorityQueue` is not a `Queue`. There is, for example, no `dequeue` method. Though this might be remedied, it is clear that the `PriorityQueue` need not act like a first-in, first-out structure. At any time, the value about to be removed is the current minimum value. This value might have been the first value inserted, or it might have just recently "cut in line" before larger values. Still, the priority queue is just as general as the stack and queue since, with a little work, one can associate with inserted values a priority that forces any `Linear` behavior in a `PriorityQueue`. Finally, since the `PriorityQueue` has no `elements` method, it may not be traversed and, therefore, cannot be a `Collection`.

Exercise 12.1 *An alternative definition of a* `PriorityQueue` *might not take and return* `Comparable` *values. Instead, the constructor for a* `PriorityQueue` *could be made to take a* `Comparator`. *Recall that the* compare *method of the* `Comparator` *class needn't take a* `Comparable` *value. Consider this alternative definition. Will the code be simpler? When would we expect errors to be detected?*

---

[2] If explicit priorities are to be associated with values, the user may insert a `ComparableAssociation` whose key value is a `Comparable` such as an `Integer`. In this case, the associated value—the data element—need not be `Comparable`.

The simplicity of the abstract priority queue makes its implementation relatively straightforward. In this chapter we will consider three implementations: one based on use of an `OrderedStructure` and two based on a novel structure called a *heap*. First, we consider an example that emphasizes the simplicity of our interface.

12.2   Example: Improving the Huffman Code

In the Huffman example from Section 11.8 we kept track of a pool of trees. At each iteration of the tree-merging phase of the algorithm, the two lightest-weight trees were removed from the pool and merged. There, we used an `OrderedStructure` to maintain the collection of trees:

Huffman

```
OrderedList trees = new OrderedList();
    ...
// merge trees in pairs until one remains
Iterator ti = trees.iterator();
while (trees.size() > 1)
{
    // construct a new iterator
    ti = trees.iterator();
    // grab two smallest values
    huffmanTree smallest = (huffmanTree)ti.next();
    huffmanTree small = (huffmanTree)ti.next();
    // remove them
    trees.remove(smallest);
    trees.remove(small);
    // add bigger tree containing both
    trees.add(new huffmanTree(smallest,small));
}
// print only tree in list
ti  = trees.iterator();
Assert.condition(ti.hasNext(),"Huffman tree exists.");
huffmanTree encoding = (huffmanTree)ti.next();
```

To remove the two smallest objects from the `OrderedStructure`, we must construct an `Iterator` and indirectly remove the first two elements we encounter. This code can be greatly simplified by storing the trees in a `PriorityQueue`. We then remove the two minimum values:

Huffman2

```
PriorityQueue trees = new PriorityVector();
    ...
// merge trees in pairs until one remains
while (trees.size() > 1)
{
    // grab two smallest values
    huffmanTree smallest = (huffmanTree)trees.remove();
    huffmanTree small = (huffmanTree)trees.remove();
```

```
    // add bigger tree containing both
    trees.add(new huffmanTree(smallest,small));
}
huffmanTree encoding = (huffmanTree)trees.remove();
```

After the merging is complete, access to the final result is also improved.

A number of interesting algorithms must have access to the minimum of a collection of values, and yet do not require the collection to be sorted. The extra energy required by an `OrderedVector` to keep all the values in order may, in fact, be excessive for some purposes.

12.3 A Vector-Based Implementation

Perhaps the simplest implementation of a `PriorityQueue` is to keep all the values in ascending order in a `Vector`. Of course, the constructor is responsible for initialization:

Priority-
Vector

```
protected Vector data;

public PriorityVector()
// post: constructs a new priority queue
{
    data = new Vector();
}
```

From the standpoint of adding values to the structure, the priority queue is very similar to the implementation of the `OrderedVector` structure. In fact, the implementations of the `add` method and the "helper" method `indexOf` are similar to those described in Section 10.2.2. Still, values of a priority queue are removed in a manner that differs from that seen in the `OrderedVector`. They are not removed by value. Instead, `getFirst` and the parameterless `remove` operate on the `Vector` element that is smallest (leftmost). The implementation of these routines is straightforward:

```
public Comparable getFirst()
// pre: !isEmpty()
// post: returns the minimum value in the priority queue
{
    return (Comparable)data.get(0);
}

public Comparable remove()
// pre: !isEmpty()
// post: removes and returns minimum value in priority queue
{
    Comparable result = (Comparable)data.get(0);
    data.remove(0);
    return result;
}
```

The **getFirst** operation takes constant time. The **remove** operation caches and removes the first value of the **Vector** with a linear-time complexity. This cannot be easily avoided since the cost is inherent in the way we use the **Vector** (though see Problem 12.8).

It is interesting to see the evolution of the various types encountered in the discussion of the **PriorityVector**. Although the **Vector** took an entire chapter to investigate, the abstract notion of a vector seems to be a relatively natural structure here. Abstraction has allowed us to avoid considering the minute details of the implementation. For example, we assume that **Vectors** automatically extend themselves. The abstract notion of an **OrderedVector**, on the other hand, appears to be insufficient to directly support the specification of the **PriorityVector**. The reason is that the **OrderedVector** does not support **Vector** operations like the index-based **get(i)** and **remove(i)**. These could, of course, be added to the **OrderedVector** interface, but an appeal for symmetry might then suggest implementation of the method **add(i)**. This would be a poor decision since it would then allow the user to insert elements out of order.

Principle 21 *Avoid unnaturally extending a natural interface.*

Designers of data structures spend considerable time weighing these design trade-offs. While it is tempting to make the most versatile structures support a wide variety of extensions, it surrenders the interface distinctions between structures that often allow for novel, efficient, and safe implementations.

Exercise 12.2 *Although the* **OrderedVector** *class does not directly support the* **PriorityQueue** *interface, it nonetheless can be used in a protected manner. Implement the* **PriorityVector** *using a* **protected OrderedVector**? *What are the advantages and disadvantages?*

In Section 12.4 we discuss a rich class of structures that allow us to maintain a loose ordering among elements. It turns out that even a loose ordering is sufficient to implement priority queues.

12.4 A Heap Implementation

In actuality, it is not necessary to develop a complete ranking of the elements of the priority queue in order to support the necessary operations. It is only necessary to be able to quickly identify the *minimum* value and to maintain a relatively loose ordering of the remaining values. This realization is the motivation for a structure called a *heap*.

Definition 12.1 *A heap is a binary tree whose root references the minimum value and whose subtrees are, themselves, heaps.*

An alternate definition is also sometimes useful.

Definition 12.2 *A heap is a binary tree whose values are in ascending order on every path from root to leaf.*

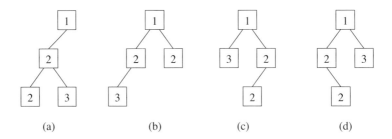

Figure 12.1 Four heaps containing the same values. Note that there is no ordering among siblings. Only heap (b) is complete.

We will draw our heaps in the manner shown in Figure 12.1, with the minimum value on the top and the possibly larger values below. Notice that each of the four heaps contains the same values but has a different structure. Clearly, there is a great deal of freedom in the way that the heap can be oriented—for example, exchanging subtrees does not violate the heap property (heaps (c) and (d) are mirror images of each other). While not every tree with these four values is a heap, many are (see Problems 12.17 and 12.18). This flexibility reduces the *friction* associated with constructing and maintaining a valid heap and, therefore, a valid priority queue. When friction is reduced, we have the potential for increasing the speed of some operations.

Principle 22 *Seek structures with reduced friction.*

This is completely obvious. We will say that a heap is a *complete heap* if the binary tree holding the values of the heap is complete. Any set of n values may be stored in a complete heap. (To see this we need only sort the values into ascending order and place them in level order in a complete binary tree. Since the values were inserted in ascending order, every child is at least as great as its parent.) The abstract notion of a complete heap forms the basis for the first of two heap implementations of a priority queue.

12.4.1 Vector-Based Heaps

As we saw in Section 11.9 when we considered the implementation of Ahnentafel structures, any complete binary tree (and therefore any complete heap) may be stored compactly in a vector. The method involves traversing the tree in level order and mapping the values to successive slots of the vector. When we are finished with this construction, we observe the following (see Figure 12.2):

1. The root of the tree is stored in location 0. If non-`null`, this location references the minimum value of the heap.

2. The left child of a value stored in location i is found at location $2i + 1$.

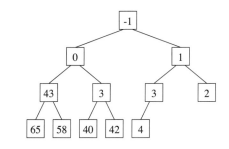

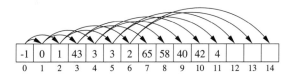

Figure 12.2 An abstract heap (top) and its vector representation. Arrows from parent to child are not physically part of the vector, but are indices computed by the heap's **left** and **right** methods.

3. The right child of a value stored in location i may be found at the location following the left child, location $2(i + 1) = (2i + 1) + 1$.

4. The parent of a value found in location i can be found at location $\lfloor \frac{i-1}{2} \rfloor$. Since division of integers in Java-like languages throws away the remainder for positive numbers, this expression is written `(i-1)/2`.

These relations may, of course, be encoded as functions. In Figure 12.2 we see the mapping of a heap to a vector, with tree relations indicated by arrows in the vector. Notice that while the vector is not maintained in ascending order, any path from the root to a leaf encounters values in ascending order. If the vector is larger than necessary, slots not associated with tree nodes can maintain a `null` reference. With this mapping in mind, we consider the constructor and `static` methods:

```
protected Vector data;   // the data, kept in heap order

public VectorHeap()
// post: constructs a new priority queue
{
    data = new Vector();
}

public VectorHeap(Vector v)
// post: constructs a new priority queue from an unordered vector
```

VectorHeap

```
{
    int i;
    data = new Vector(v.size()); // we know ultimate size
    for (i = 0; i < v.size(); i++)
    {   // add elements to heap
        add((Comparable)v.get(i));
    }
}

protected static int parent(int i)
// pre: 0 <= i < size
// post: returns parent of node at location i
{
    return (i-1)/2;
}

protected static int left(int i)
// pre: 0 <= i < size
// post: returns index of left child of node at location i
{
    return 2*i+1;
}

protected static int right(int i)
// pre: 0 <= i < size
// post: returns index of right child of node at location i
{
    return 2*(i+1);
}
```

The functions parent, left, and right are declared static to indicate that
they do not actually have to be called on any instance of a heap. Instead, their
values are functions of their parameters only.

Principle 23 *Declare object-independent functions* static.

Now consider the addition of a value to a complete heap. We know that
the heap is currently complete. Ideally, after the addition of the value the
heap will remain complete but will contain one extra value. This realization
forces us to commit to inserting a value in a way that ultimately produces a
correctly structured heap. Since the first free element of the Vector will hold a
value, we optimistically insert the new value in that location (see Figure 12.3).
If, considering the path from the leaf to the root, the value is in the wrong
location, then it must be "percolated upward" to the correct entry. We begin
by comparing and, if necessary, exchanging the new value and its parent. If the
values along the path are still incorrectly ordered, it must be because of the new
value, and we continue to percolate the value upward until either the new value
is the root or it is greater than or equal to its current parent. The only values
possibly exchanged in this operation are those appearing along the unique path

from the insertion point. Since locations that change only become smaller, the integrity of other paths in the tree is maintained.

The code associated with percolating a value upward is contained in the function `percolateUp`. This function takes an index of a value that is possibly out of place and pushes the value upward toward the root until it reaches the correct location. While the routine takes an index as a parameter, the parameter passed is usually the index of the rightmost leaf of the bottom level.

```
protected void percolateUp(int leaf)
// pre: 0 <= leaf < size
// post: moves node at index leaf up to appropriate position
{
    int parent = parent(leaf);
    Comparable value = (Comparable)(data.get(leaf));
    while (leaf > 0 &&
        (value.compareTo((Comparable)(data.get(parent))) < 0))
    {
        data.set(leaf,data.get(parent));
        leaf = parent;
        parent = parent(leaf);
    }
    data.set(leaf,value);
}
```

Adding a value to the priority queue is then only a matter of appending it to the end of the vector (the location of the newly added leaf) and percolating the value upward until it finds the correct location.

```
public void add(Comparable value)
// pre: value is non-null comparable
// post: value is added to priority queue
{
    data.add(value);
    percolateUp(data.size()-1);
}
```

Let us consider how long it takes to accomplish the addition of a value to the heap. Remember that the tree that we are working with is an n-node complete binary tree, so its height is $\lfloor \log_2 n \rfloor$. Each step of the `percolateUp` routine takes constant time and pushes the new value up one level. Of course, it may be positioned correctly the first time, but the worst-case behavior of inserting the new value into the tree consumes $O(\log n)$ time. This performance is considerably better than the linear behavior of the `PriorityVector` implementation described in Section 12.3. What is the best time? It is constant when the value added is large compared to the values found on the path from the new leaf to the root.

Next, we consider the removal of the minimum value (see Figures 12.4 and 12.5). It is located at the root of the heap, in the first slot of the vector. The removal of this value leaves an empty location at the top of the heap. Ultimately,

What is the expected time? Be careful!

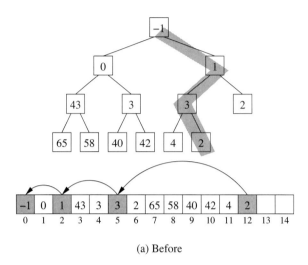

(a) Before

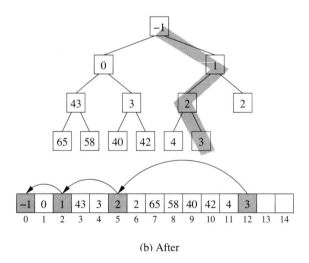

(b) After

Figure 12.3   The addition of a value (2) to a vector-based heap. (a) The value is inserted into a free location known to be part of the result structure. (b) The value is percolated up to the correct location on the unique path to the root.

when the operation is complete, the freed location will be the rightmost leaf of the bottom level, the last element of the underlying vector. Again, our approach is first to construct a tree that is the correct shape, but potentially not a heap, and then perform transformations on the tree that both maintain its shape and bring the structure closer to being a heap. Thus, when the minimum value is removed, the rightmost leaf on the bottom level is removed and re-placed at the root of the tree (Figure 12.4a and b). At this point, the tree is the correct shape, but it may not be a heap because the root of the tree is potentially too large. Since the subtrees remain heaps, we need to ensure the root of the tree is the minimum value contained in the tree. We first find the minimum child and compare this value with the root (Figure 12.5a). If the root value is no greater, the minimum value is at the root and the entire structure is a heap. If the root is larger, then it is exchanged with the true minimum—the smallest child—pushing the large value downward. At this point, the root of the tree has the correct value. All but one of the subtrees are unchanged, and the shape of the tree remains correct. All that has happened is that a large value has been pushed down to where it may violate the heap property in a subtree. We then perform any further exchanges recursively, with the value sinking into smaller subtrees (Figure 12.5b), possibly becoming a leaf. Since any single value is a heap, the recursion must stop by the time the newly inserted value becomes a leaf.

We're "heaping in shape."

Here is the code associated with the pushing down of the root:

```
protected void pushDownRoot(int root)
// pre: 0 <= root < size
// post: moves node at index root down
//    to appropriate position in subtree
{
    int heapSize = data.size();
    Comparable value = (Comparable)data.get(root);
    while (root < heapSize) {
        int childpos = left(root);
        if (childpos < heapSize)
        {
            if ((right(root) < heapSize) &&
              (((Comparable)(data.get(childpos+1))).compareTo
              ((Comparable)(data.get(childpos))) < 0))
            {
                childpos++;
            }
            // Assert: childpos indexes smaller of two children
            if (((Comparable)(data.get(childpos))).compareTo
                (value) < 0)
            {
                data.set(root,data.get(childpos));
                root = childpos; // keep moving down
            } else { // found right location
                data.set(root,value);
```

```
                        return;
                    }
            } else { // at a leaf! insert and halt
                data.set(root,value);
                return;
            }
        }
    }
```

The `remove` method simply involves returning the smallest value of the heap, but only after the rightmost element of the vector has been pushed downward.

```
public Comparable remove()
// pre: !isEmpty()
// post: returns and removes minimum value from queue
{
    Comparable minVal = getFirst();
    data.set(0,data.get(data.size()-1));
    data.setSize(data.size()-1);
    if (data.size() > 1) pushDownRoot(0);
    return minVal;
}
```

Each level of recursion pushes a large value down into a smaller heap on a path from the root to a leaf. Therefore, the performance of `remove` is $O(\log n)$, an improvement over the behavior of the `PriorityVector` implementation.

Since we have implemented all the required methods of the `PriorityQueue`, the `VectorHeap` implements the `PriorityQueue` and may be used wherever a priority queue is required.

The advantages of the `VectorHeap` mechanism are that, because of the unique mapping of complete trees to the `Vector`, it is unnecessary to explicitly store the connections between elements. Even though we are able to get improved performance over the `PriorityVector`, we do not have to pay a space penalty. The complexity arises, instead, in the code necessary to support the insertion and removal of values.

12.4.2   Example: Heapsort

Any priority queue, of course, can be used as the underlying data structure for a sorting mechanism. When the values of a heap are stored in a `Vector`, an empty location is potentially made available when they are removed. This location could be used to store a removed value. As the heap shrinks, the values are stored in the newly vacated elements of the `Vector`. As the heap becomes empty, the `Vector` is completely filled with values in descending order.

Unfortunately, we cannot make assumptions about the structure of the values initially found in the `Vector`; we are, after all, sorting them. Since this approach depends on the values being placed in a heap, we must consider one more operation: a constructor that "heapifies" the data found in a `Vector` passed to it:

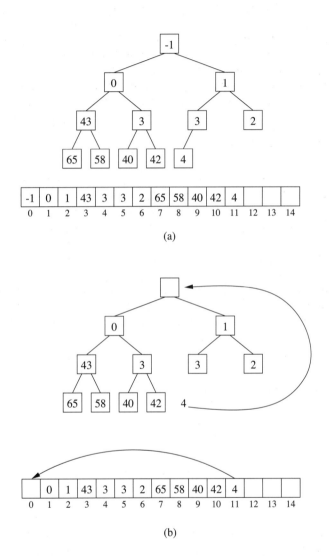

(a)

(b)

Figure 12.4 Removing a value from the heap shown in (a) involves moving the rightmost value of the vector to the top of the heap as in (b). Note that this value is likely to violate the heap property but that the subtrees will remain heaps.

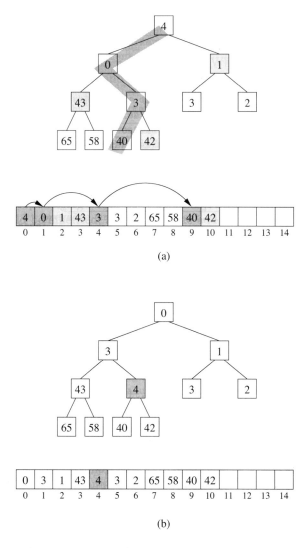

Figure 12.5 Removing a value (continued). In (a) the newly inserted value at the root is pushed down along a shaded path following the smallest children (lightly shaded nodes are also considered in determining the path). In (b) the root value finds, over several iterations, the correct location along the path. Smaller values shift upward to make room for the new value.

```java
public VectorHeap(Vector v)
// post: constructs a new priority queue from an unordered vector
{
    int i;
    data = new Vector(v.size()); // we know ultimate size
    for (i = 0; i < v.size(); i++)
    {   // add elements to heap
        add((Comparable)v.get(i));
    }
}
```

The process of constructing a heap from an unordered **Vector** obviously takes the time of n **add** operations, each of which is $O(n)$. The worst-case cost of "heapifying" is, therefore, $O(n \log n)$. (This can be improved—see Problem 12.10.)

Now, the remaining part of the heapsort—removing the minimum values and placing them in the newly freed locations—requires n **remove** operations. This phase also has worst-case complexity $O(n \log n)$. We have, therefore, another sorting algorithm with $O(n \log n)$ behavior and little space overhead.

The feature of a heap that makes the sort so efficient is its short height. The values are always stored in as full a tree as possible and, as a result, we may place a logarithmic upper bound on the time it takes to insert and remove values. In Section 12.4.3 we investigate the use of unrestricted heaps to implement priority queues. These structures have *amortized* cost that is equivalent to heaps built atop vectors.

12.4.3   Skew Heaps

The performance of **Vector**-based heaps is directly dependent on the fact that these heaps are complete. Since complete heaps are a minority of all heaps, it is reasonable to ask if efficient priority queues might be constructed from unrestricted heaps. The answer is yes, if we relax the way we measure performance.

We consider, here, the implementation of heaps using dynamically structured binary trees. A direct cost of this decision is the increase in space. Whereas a **Vector** stores a single reference, the binary tree node keeps an additional three references. These three references allow us to implement noncomplete heaps, called *skew heaps*, in a space-efficient manner (see Problem 12.21). Here are the protected data and the constructor for this structure:

```java
protected BinaryTree root;
protected int count;

public SkewHeap()
// post: creates an empty priority queue
{
    root = BinaryTree.EMPTY;
    count = 0;
}
```

SkewHeap

Notice that we keep track of the size of the heap locally, rather than asking the `BinaryTree` for its size. This is simply a matter of efficiency, but it requires us to maintain the value within the `add` and `remove` procedures. Once we commit to implementing heaps in this manner, we need to consider the implementation of each of the major operators.

The implementation of `getFirst` simply references the value stored at the root. Its implementation is relatively straightforward:

```
public Comparable getFirst()
// pre: !isEmpty()
// post: returns the minimum value in priority queue
{
    return (Comparable)(root.value());
}
```

As with all good things, this will eventually seem necessary.

Before we consider the implementation of the `add` and `remove` methods, we consider a (seemingly unnecessary) operation, `merge`. This method takes two heaps and merges them together. This is a *destructive* operation: the elements of the participating heaps are consumed in the construction of the result. Our approach will be to make `merge` a recursive method that considers several cases. First, if either of the two heaps participating in the merge is empty, then the result of the merge is the other heap. Otherwise, both heaps contain at least a value—assume that the minimum root is found in the left heap (if not, we can swap them). We know, then, that the result of the merge will be a reference to the root node of the left heap. To see how the right heap is merged into the left we consider two cases:

1. If the left heap has no left child, make the right heap the left child of the left heap (see Figure 12.6b).

2. Otherwise, exchange the left and right children of the left heap. Then merge (the newly made) left subheap of the left heap with the right heap (see Figure 12.6d).

Notice that if the left heap has one subheap, the right heap becomes the left subheap and the merging is finished. Here is the code for the `merge` method:

```
protected static BinaryTree merge(BinaryTree left,
                                  BinaryTree right)
{
    if (left.isEmpty()) return right;
    if (right.isEmpty()) return left;
    Comparable leftVal = (Comparable)(left.value());
    Comparable rightVal = (Comparable)(right.value());
    BinaryTree result;
    if (rightVal.compareTo(leftVal) < 0)
    {
        result = merge(right,left);
    } else {
```

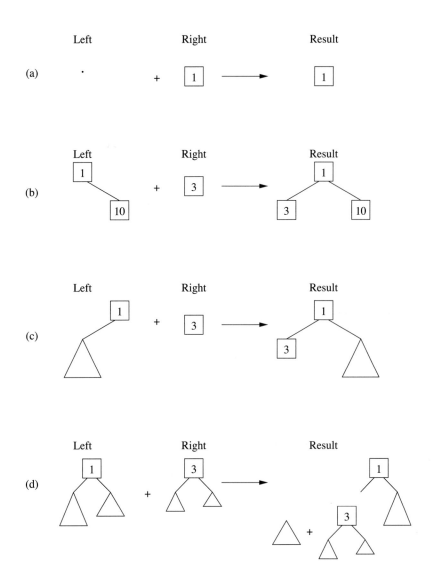

Figure 12.6 Different cases of the **merge** method for **SkewHeaps**. In (a) one of the heaps is empty. In (b) and (c) the right heap becomes the left child of the left heap. In (d) the right heap is merged into what was the right subheap.

```
        result = left;
        // assertion left side is smaller than right
        // left is new root
        if (result.left().isEmpty())
        {
            result.setLeft(right);
        } else {
            BinaryTree temp = result.right();
            result.setRight(result.left());
            result.setLeft(merge(temp,right));
        }
    }
    return result;
}
```

Once the merge method has been defined, we find that the process of adding a value or removing the minimum is relatively straightforward. To add a value, we construct a new BinaryTree containing the single value that is to be added. This is, in essence, a one-element heap. We then merge this heap with the existing heap, and the result is a new heap with the value added:

```
public void add(Comparable value)
// pre: value is non-null comparable
// post: value is added to priority queue
{
    BinaryTree smallTree = new BinaryTree(value);
    root = merge(smallTree,root);
    count++;
}
```

To remove the minimum value from the heap we must extract and return the value at the root. To construct the smaller resulting heap we detach both subtrees from the root and merge them together. The result is a heap with all the values of the left and right subtrees, but not the root. This is precisely the result we require. Here is the code:

```
public Comparable remove()
// pre: !isEmpty()
// post: returns and removes minimum value from queue
{
    Comparable result = (Comparable)(root.value());
    root = merge(root.left(),root.right());
    count--;
    return result;
}
```

The remaining priority queue methods for skew heaps are implemented in a relatively straightforward manner.

Because a skew heap has unconstrained topology (see Problem 12.16), it is possible to construct examples of skew heaps with degenerate behavior. For

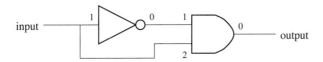

Figure 12.7   A circuit for detecting a rising logic level.

example, adding a new maximum value can take $O(n)$ time. For this reason we cannot put very impressive bounds on the performance of any individual operation. The skew heap, however, is an example of a self-organizing structure: inefficient operations spend some of their excess time making later operations run more quickly. If we are careful, time "charged against" early operations can be *amortized* or redistributed to later operations, which we hope will run very efficiently. This type of analysis can be used, for example, to demonstrate that $m > n$ skew heap operations applied to a heap of size n take no more than $O(m \log n)$ time. On average, then, each operation takes $O(\log n)$ time. For applications where it is expected that a significant number of requests of a heap will be made, this performance is appealing.

12.5   Example: Circuit Simulation

Consider the electronic digital circuit depicted in Figure 12.7. The two devices shown are *logic gates*. The wires between the gates propagate electrical signals. Typically a zero voltage is called *false* or *low*, while a potential of 3 volts or more is *true* or *high*.

The triangular gate, on the left, is an *inverter*. On its output (pin 0) it "inverts" the logic level found on the input (pin 1): false becomes true and true becomes false. The gate on the right is an *and-gate*. It generates a true on pin 0 exactly when both of its inputs (pins 1 and 2) are true.

The action of these gates is the result of a physical process, so the effect of the inputs on the output is delayed by a period of time called a *gate delay*. Gate delays depend on the complexity of the gate, the manufacturing process, and environmental factors. For our purposes, we'll assume the gate delay of the inverter is 0.2 nanosecond (ns) and the delay of the and-gate is 0.8 ns.

The question is, what output is generated when we toggle the input from low to high and back to low several times? To determine the answer we can build the circuit, or simulate it in software. For reasons that will become clear in a moment, simulation will be more useful.

The setup for our simulation will consist of a number of small classes. First, there are a number of components, including an `Inverter`; an `And`; an input, or `Source`; and a voltage sensor, or `Probe`. When constructed, gates are provided gate delay values, and Sources and Probes are given names. Each of these components has one or more pins to which wires can be connected. (As with real circuits, the outputs should connect only to inputs of other components!) Finally, the voltage level of a particular pin can be set to a particular level. As an example of the interface, we list the public methods for the And gate:

Circuit

```
class And extends Component
{
    public And(double delay)
    // pre: delay >= 0.0ns
    // post: constructs and gate with indicated gate delay

    public void set(double time, int pinNum, int level)
    // pre: pinNum = 1 or 2, level = 0/3
    // post: updates inputs and generates events on
    //       devices connected to output
}
```

Notice that there is a time associated with the set method. This helps us document when different events happen in the component. These events are simulated by a comparable Event class. This class describes a change in logic level on an input pin for some component. As the simulation progresses, Events are created and scheduled for simulation in the future. The ordering of Events is based on an event time. Here are the details:

```
class Event implements Comparable
{
    protected double time;      // time of event
    protected int level;        // voltage level
    protected Connection c;     // gate/pin

    public Event(Connection c, double t, int l)
    // pre: c is a valid pin on a gate
    // post: constructs event for time t to set pin to level l
    {
        this.c = c;
        time = t;
        level = l;
    }

    public void go()
    // post: informs target component of updated logic on pin
    {
        c.component().set(time,c.pin(),level);
    }

    public int compareTo(Object other)
    // pre: other is non-null
    // post: returns integer representing relation between values
```

```
        {
            Event that = (Event)other;
            if (this.time < that.time) return -1;
            else if (this.time == that.time) return 0;
            else return 1;
        }
    }
```

The `Connection` mentioned here is simply a component's input pin.

Finally, to orchestrate the simulation, we use a priority queue to correctly simulate the order of events. The following method simulates a circuit by removing events from the priority queue and setting the logic level on the appropriate pins of the components. The method returns the time of the last event to help monitor the progress of the simulation.

```
public class Circuit
{
    static PriorityQueue eventQueue; // main event queue

    public static double simulate()
    // post: run simulation until event queue is empty;
    //       returns final clock time
    {
        double low = 0.0;        // voltage of low logic
        double high = 3.0;       // voltage of high logic
        double clock = 0.0;
        while (!eventQueue.isEmpty())
        {   // remove next event
            Event e = (Event)eventQueue.remove();
            // keep track of time
            clock = e.time;
            // simulate the event
            e.go();
        }
        System.out.println("-- circuit stable after "+clock+" ns --");
        return clock;
    }
}
```

As events are processed, the logic level on a component's pins are updated. If the inputs to a component change, new `Events` are scheduled one gate delay later for each component connected to the output pin. For `Sources` and `Probes`, we write a message to the output indicating the change in logic level. Clearly, when there are no more events in the priority queue, the simulated circuit is stable. If the user is interested, he or she can change the logic level of a `Source` and resume the simulation by running the `simulate` method again.

We are now equipped to simulate the circuit of Figure 12.7. The first portion of the following code sets up the circuit, while the second half simulates the effect of toggling the input several times:

```
public static void main(String[] args)
{
    int low = 0;     // voltage of low logic
    int high = 3;    // voltage of high logic
    eventQueue = new SkewHeap();
    double time;

    // set up circuit
    Inverter not = new Inverter(0.2);
    And and = new And(0.8);
    Probe output = new Probe("output");
    Source input = new Source("input",not.pin(1));

    input.connectTo(and.pin(2));
    not.connectTo(and.pin(1));
    and.connectTo(output.pin(1));

    // simulate circuit
    time = simulate();
    input.set(time+1.0,0,high); // first: set input high
    time = simulate();
    input.set(time+1.0,0,low);  // later: set input low
    time = simulate();
    input.set(time+1.0,0,high); // later: set input high
    time = simulate();
    input.set(time+1.0,0,low);  // later: set input low
    simulate();
}
```

When run, the following output is generated:

```
1.0 ns: output now 0 volts
-- circuit stable after 1.0 ns --
2.0 ns: input set to 3 volts
2.8 ns: output now 3 volts
3.0 ns: output now 0 volts
-- circuit stable after 3.0 ns --
4.0 ns: input set to 0 volts
-- circuit stable after 5.0 ns --
6.0 ns: input set to 3 volts
6.8 ns: output now 3 volts
7.0 ns: output now 0 volts
-- circuit stable after 7.0 ns --
8.0 ns: input set to 0 volts
-- circuit stable after 9.0 ns --
```

When the input is moved from low to high, a short spike is generated on the output. Moving the input to low again has no impact. The spike is generated by the *rising edge* of a signal, and its width is determined by the gate delay of the inverter. Because the spike is so short, it would have been difficult to detect it using real hardware.[3] Devices similar to this edge detector are important tools for detecting changing states in the circuits they monitor.

12.6 Conclusions

We have seen three implementations of priority queues: one based on a `Vector` that keeps its entries in order and two others based on heap implementations. The `Vector` implementation demonstrates how any ordered structure may be adapted to support the operations of a priority queue.

Heaps form successful implementations of priority queues because they relax the conditions on "keeping data in priority order." Instead of maintaining data in sorted order, heaps maintain a competition between values that becomes progressively more intense as the values reach the front of the queue. The cost of inserting and removing values from a heap can be made to be as low as $O(\log n)$.

If the constraint of keeping values in a `Vector` is too much (it may be impossible, for example, to allocate a single large chunk of memory), or if one wants to avoid the uneven cost of extending a `Vector`, a dynamic mechanism is useful. The `SkewHeap` is such a mechanism, keeping data in general heap form. Over a number of operations the skew heap performs as well as the traditional `Vector`-based implementation.

Self Check Problems

Solutions to these problems begin on page 435.

12.1   Is a `PriorityQueue` a `Queue`?

12.2   Is a `PriorityQueue` a `Linear` structure?

12.3   How do you interpret the weight of a Huffman tree? How do you interpret the depth of a node in the tree?

12.4   What is a min-heap?

12.5   `Vector`-based heaps have $O(\log n)$ behavior for insertion and removal of values. What structural feature of the underlying tree guarantees this?

12.6   Why is a `PriorityQueue` useful for managing simulations base on events?

---

[3] This is a very short period of time. During the time the output is high, light travels just over 2 inches!

Problems

Solutions to the odd-numbered problems begin on page 467.

12.1 Draw the state of a `HeapVector` after each of the values 3, 4, 7, 0, 2, 8, and 6 are added, in that order.

12.2 Consider the heap | 0 | 2 | 1 | 3 | 7 | 4 | 6 | 8 |

    a. What does this heap look like when drawn as a tree?

    b. What does this heap look like (in array form) when a value is removed?

12.3 Below is a `SkewHeap`. What does it look like after a value is removed?

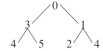

12.4 How might you use priorities to simulate a LIFO structure with a priority queue?

12.5 Is a `VectorHeap` a `Queue`? Is it an `OrderedStructure`?

12.6 How might you use priorities to simulate a FIFO structure with a priority queue?

12.7 Suppose a user built an object whose `compareTo` and `equals` methods were inconsistent. For example, values that were `equals` might also return a negative value for `compareTo`. What happens when these values are added to a `PriorityVector`? What happens when these values are added to a `SkewHeap`?

12.8 We have seen that the cost of removing a value from the `Priority-Vector` takes linear time. If elements were stored in descending order, this could be reduced to constant time. Compare the ascending and descending implementations, discussing the circumstances that suggest the use of one implementation over the other.

12.9 What methods would have to be added to the `OrderedVector` class to make it possible to implement a `PriorityVector` using only a private `Ordered-Vector`?

12.10 Reconsider the "heapifying" constructor discussed in Section 12.4.2. Instead of adding n values to an initially empty heap (at a cost of $O(n \log n)$), suppose we do the following: Consider each interior node of the heap in order of decreasing array index. Think of this interior node as the root of a potential subheap. We know that its subtrees are valid heaps. Now, just push this node down into its (near-)heap. Show that the cost of performing this heapify operation is linear in the size of the `Vector`.

12.11 Design a more efficient version of `HeapVector` that keeps its values in order only when necessary: When values are added, they are appended to the end of the existing heap and a `nonHeap` flag is set to `true`. When values are removed, the `nonHeap` flag is checked and the `Vector` is heapified if necessary. What are the worst-case and best-case running times of the **add** and **remove** operations? (You may assume that you have access to the heapify of Problem 12.10.)

12.12 Consider the unordered data:

4	2	7	3	1	0	5	6

What does this **Vector** look like after it has been heapified?

12.13 Consider the in-place **Vector**-based heapsort.

a. A min-heap is particularly suited to sorting data in place into which order: ascending or descending?

b. What is the worst-case time complexity of this sort?

c. What is the best-case time complexity of this sort?

12.14 Suppose we are given access to a min-heap, but not the code that supports it. What changes to the *comparable data* might we make to force the min-heap to work like a max-heap?

12.15 Suppose we are to find the kth largest element of a heap of n values. Describe how we might accomplish this efficiently. What is the worst-case running time of your method? Notice that if the problem had said "set of n values," we would require a heapify operation like that found in Problem 12.10.

12.16 Demonstrate that any binary tree that has the heap property can be generated by inserting values into a skew heap in an appropriate order. (This realization is important to understanding why an amortized accounting scheme is necessary.)

12.17 Suppose you are given n distinct values to store in a full heap—a heap that is maintained in a full binary tree. Since there is no ordering between children in a heap, the left and right subheaps can be exchanged. How many equivalent heaps can be produced by only swapping children of a node?

12.18 Given n distinct values to be stored in a heap, how many heaps can store the values? (Difficult.)

12.19 What proportion of the binary trees holding n distinct values are heaps?

12.20 Suppose that n randomly selected (and uniformly distributed) numbers are inserted into a complete heap. Now, select another number and insert it into the heap. How many levels is the new number expected to rise?

12.21 The mapping strategy that takes a complete binary tree to a **vector** can actually be used to store general trees, albeit in a space-inefficient manner. The strategy is to allocate enough space to hold the lowest, rightmost leaf, and to maintain null references in nodes that are not currently being used. What is the worst-case **Vector** length needed to store an n-element binary tree?

12.22 Write an **equals** method for a **PriorityVector**. It returns **true** if each pair of corresponding elements removed from the structures would be equal. What is the complexity of the **equals** method? (Hint: You may not need to remove values.)

12.23 Write an `equals` method for a `HeapVector`. It returns `true` if each pair of corresponding elements removed from the structures would be equal. What is the complexity of the `equals` method? (Hint: You may need to remove values.)

12.24 Write an `equals` method for a `SkewHeap`. It returns `true` if each pair of corresponding elements removed from the structures would be equal. What is the complexity of the `equals` method? (Hint: You may need to remove values.)

12.25 Show that the implementation of the `PriorityVector` can be improved by not actually keeping the values in order. Instead, only maintain the minimum value at the left. Demonstrate the implementation of the `add` and `remove` methods.

12.26 Suppose you are a manufacturer of premium-quality videocassette recorders. Your XJ-6 recorder allows the "user" to "program" 4096 different future events to be recorded. Of course, as the time arrives for each event, your machine is responsible for turning on and recording a program.

  a. What information is necessary to correctly record an event?

  b. Design the data structure(s) needed to support the XJ-6.

12.7 Laboratory: Simulating Business

Objective. To determine if it is better to have single or multiple service lines.

Discussion. When we are waiting in a fast food line, or we are queued up at a bank, there are usually two different methods of managing customers:

1. Have a single line for people waiting for service. Every customer waits in a single line. When a teller becomes free, the customer at the head of the queue moves to the teller. If there are multiple tellers free, one is picked randomly.

2. Have multiple lines—one for each teller. When customers come in the door they attempt to pick the line that has the shortest wait. This usually involves standing in the line with the fewest customers. If there are multiple choices, the appropriate line is selected randomly.

It is not clear which of these two methods of queuing customers is most efficient. In the single-queue technique, tellers appear to be constantly busy and no customer is served before any customer that arrives later. In the multiple-queue technique, however, customers can take the responsibility of evaluating the queues themselves.

Note, by the way, that some industries (airlines, for example) have a mixture of both of these situations. First class customers enter in one line, while coach customers enter in another.

Procedure. In this lab, you are to construct a simulation of these two service mechanisms. For each simulation you should generate a sequence of customers that arrive at random intervals. These customers demand a small range of services, determined by a randomly selected service time. The simulation is driven by an event queue, whose elements are ranked by the event time. The type of event might be a customer arrival, a teller freeing up, etc.

For the single line simulation, have the customers all line up in a single queue. When a customer is needed, a single customer (if any) is removed from the customer queue, and the teller is scheduled to be free at a time that is determined by the service time. You must figure out how to deal with tellers that are idle—how do they wait until a customer arrives?

For the multiple line simulation, the customers line up at their arrival time, in one of the shortest teller queues. When a teller is free, it selects the next customer from its dedicated queue (if any). A single event queue is used to drive the simulation.

To compare the possibilities of these two simulations, it is useful to run the same random customers through both types of queues. Think carefully about how this might be accomplished.

Thought Questions. Consider the following questions as you complete the lab:

1. Run several simulations of both types of queues. Which queue strategy seems to process all the customers fastest?

2. Is their a difference between the average wait time for customers between the two techniques?

3. Suppose you simulated the ability to jump between lines in a multiple line simulation. When a line has two or more customers than another line, customers move from the end one line to another until the lines are fairly even. You see this behavior frequently at grocery stores. Does this change the type of underlying structure you use to keep customers in line?

4. Suppose lines were dedicated to serving customers of varying lengths of service times. Would this improve the average wait time for a customer?

Notes:

Chapter 13

Search Trees

He looked to the right of him.
No caps.
He looked to the left of him.
No caps.
...
Then he looked up into the tree.
And what do you think he saw?
—Esphyr Slobodkina

STRUCTURES ARE OFTEN THE SUBJECT OF A SEARCH. We have seen, for example, that binary search is a natural and efficient algorithm for finding values within ordered, randomly accessible structures. Recall that at each point the algorithm compares the value sought with the value in the middle of the structure. If they are not equal, the algorithm performs a similar, possibly recursive search on one side or the other. The pivotal feature of the algorithm, of course, was that the underlying structure was in order. The result was that a value could be efficiently *found* in approximately logarithmic time. Unfortunately, the modifying operations—add and remove—had complexities that were determined by the linear nature of the vector.

Heaps have shown us that by relaxing our notions of order we can improve on the linear complexities of adding and removing values. These logarithmic operations, however, do not preserve the order of elements in any obviously useful manner. Still, if we were somehow able to totally order the elements of a binary tree, then an algorithm like binary search might naturally be imposed on this branching structure.

13.1 Binary Search Trees

The *binary search tree* is a binary tree whose elements are kept in order. This is easily stated as a recursive definition.

Definition 13.1 *A binary tree is a* binary search tree *if it is trivial, or if every node is simultaneously greater than or equal to each value in its left subtree, and less than or equal to each value in its right subtree.*

To see that this is a significant restriction on the structure of a binary tree, one need only note that if a maximum of n distinct values is found at the root,

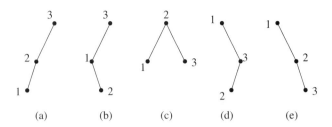

Figure 13.1   Binary search trees with three nodes.

all other values must be found in the left subtree. Figure 13.1 demonstrates the many trees that can contain even three distinct values. Thus, if one is not too picky about the value one wants to have at the root of the tree, there are still a significant number of trees from which to choose. This is important if we want to have our modifying operations run quickly: ideally we should be as nonrestrictive about the outcome as possible, in order to reduce the friction of the operation.

One important thing to watch for is that even though our definition allows duplicate values of the root node to fall on either side, our code will prefer to have them on the left. This preference is arbitrary. If we assume that values equal to the root will be found in the left subtree, but in actuality some are located in the right, then we might expect inconsistent behavior from methods that search for these values. In fact, this is not the case.

To guide access to the elements of a binary search tree, we will consider it an implementation of an `OrderedStructure`, supporting the following methods:

Binary–
SearchTree

```
public class BinarySearchTree
    extends AbstractStructure implements OrderedStructure
{
    public BinarySearchTree()
    // post: constructs an empty binary search tree
```

Unlike the `BinaryTree`, the `BinarySearchTree` provides only one `iterator` method. This method provides for an in-order traversal of the tree, which, with some thought, allows access to each of the elements in order.

Maybe even with no thought!

13.2   Example: Tree Sort

Because the `BinarySearchTree` is an `OrderedStructure` it provides the natural basis for sorting. The algorithm of Section 10.2.3 will work equally well here, provided the allocation of the `OrderedStructure` is modified to construct a `BinarySearchTree`. The binary search structure, however, potentially provides significant improvements in performance. If the tree can be kept reasonably short, the cost of inserting each element is $O(\log n)$. Since n elements are ultimately added to the structure, the total cost is $O(n \log n)$.[1] As we have seen in Chapter 11, all the elements of the underlying binary tree can be visited in linear time. The resulting algorithm has a potential for $O(n \log n)$ time complexity, which rivals the performance of sorting techniques using heaps. The advantage of binary search trees is that the elements need not be removed to determine their order. To attain this performance, though, we must keep the tree as short as possible. This will require considerable attention.

13.3 Example: Associative Structures

Associative structures play an important role in making algorithms efficient. In these data structures, *values* are associated with *keys*. Typically (though not necessarily), the keys are unique and aid in the retrieval of more complete information—the value. In a `Vector`, for example, we use integers as indices to find values. In an `AssociativeVector` we can use any type of *object*. The *SymbolTable* associated with the `PostScript` lab (Section 9.5) is, essentially, an associative structure.

Associative structures are an important feature of many symbol-based systems. Here, for example, is a first approach to the construction of a general-purpose symbol table, with potentially logarithmic performance:

SymTab

```java
import structure.*;
import java.util.Iterator;
public class SymTab
{
    protected BinarySearchTree table;
    public SymTab()
    // post: constructs empty symbol table
    {
        table = new BinarySearchTree();
    }

    public boolean contains(Comparable symbol)
    // pre: symbol is non-null string
    // post: returns true iff string in table
    {
        ComparableAssociation a =
            new ComparableAssociation(symbol,null);
        return table.contains(a);
    }

    public void add(Comparable symbol, Object value)
    // pre: symbol non-null
    // post: adds/replaces symbol-value pair in table
```

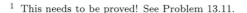

[1] This needs to be proved! See Problem 13.11.

```
        {
            ComparableAssociation a =
                new ComparableAssociation(symbol,value);
            if (table.contains(a)) table.remove(a);
            table.add(a);
        }

        public Object get(Comparable symbol)
        // pre: symbol non null
        // post: returns token associated with symbol
        {
            ComparableAssociation a =
                new ComparableAssociation(symbol,null);
            if (table.contains(a)) {
                a = (ComparableAssociation)table.get(a);
                return a.getValue();
            } else {
                return null;
            }
        }

        public Object remove(Comparable symbol)
        // pre: symbol non null
        // post: removes value associated with symbol and returns it
        //       if error returns null
        {
            ComparableAssociation a =
                new ComparableAssociation(symbol,null);
            if (table.contains(a)) {
                a = (ComparableAssociation)table.remove(a);
                return a.getValue();
            } else {
                return null;
            }
        }
    }
```

Based on such a table, we might have a program that reads in a number of alias-name pairs terminated by the word END. After that point, the program prints out the fully translated aliases:

```
    public static void main(String args[])
    {
        SymTab table = new SymTab();
        ReadStream r = new ReadStream();
        String alias, name;
        // read in the alias-name database
        do
        {
            alias = r.readString();
```

```
            if (!alias.equals("END"))
            {
                name = r.readString();
                table.add(alias,name);
            }
        } while (!alias.equals("END"));
        // enter the alias translation stage
        do
        {
            name = r.readString();
            while (table.contains(name))
            {
                // translate alias
                name = (String)table.get(name);
            }
            System.out.println(name);
            r.skipWhite();
        } while (!r.eof());
    }
```

Given the input:

```
three 3
one unity
unity 1
pi three
END

one
two
three
pi
```

the program generates the following output:

```
1
two
3
3
```

We will consider general associative structures in Chapter 14, when we discuss `Dictionaries`. We now consider the details of actually supporting the `BinarySearchTree` structure.

13.4   Implementation

In considering the implementation of a `BinarySearchTree`, it is important to remember that we are implementing an `OrderedStructure`. The methods of the `OrderedStructure` accept and return values that are to be compared with one another. By default, we assume that the data are `Comparable` and that the natural order suggested by the `NaturalComparator` is sufficient. If alternative orders are necessary, or an ordering is to be enforced on elements that do not directly implement a `compareTo` method, alternative `Comparator`s may be used. Essentially the only methods that we depend upon are the compatibility of the `Comparator` and the elements of the tree.

We begin by noticing that a `BinarySearchTree` is little more than a binary tree with an imposed order. We maintain a reference to a `BinaryTree` and explicitly keep track of its size. The constructor need only initialize these two fields and suggest an ordering of the elements to implement a state consistent with an empty binary search tree:

BinarySearch-
Tree

```
protected BinaryTree root;
protected int count;
protected Comparator ordering;


public BinarySearchTree()
// post: constructs an empty binary search tree
{
    this(new NaturalComparator());
}

public BinarySearchTree(Comparator alternateOrder)
// post: constructs an empty binary search tree
{
    root = BinaryTree.EMPTY;
    count = 0;
    ordering = alternateOrder;
}
```

As with most implementations of `OrderedStructure`s, we develop a method to find the correct location to insert the value and then use that method as the basis for implementing the public methods—add, `contains`, and `remove`. Our approach to the method `locate` is to have it return a reference to the location that identifies the correct point of insertion for the new value. This method, of course, makes heavy use of the `ordering`. Here is the Java code for the method:

```
protected BinaryTree locate(BinaryTree root, Object value)
// pre: root and value are non-null
// post: returned: 1 - existing tree node with the desired value, or
//                 2 - the node to which value should be added
{
    Object rootValue = root.value();
    BinaryTree child;

    // found at root: done
    if (rootValue.equals(value)) return root;
    // look left if less-than, right if greater-than
    if (ordering.compare(rootValue,value) < 0)
```

```
    {
        child = root.right();
    } else {
        child = root.left();
    }
    // no child there: not in tree, return this node,
    // else keep searching
    if (child.isEmpty()) {
        return root;
    } else {
        return locate(child, value);
    }
}
```

The approach of the `locate` method parallels binary search. Comparisons are made with the `root`, which serves as a median value. If the value does not match, then the search is refocused on either the left side of the tree (among smaller values) or the right side of the tree (among larger values). In either case, if the search is about to step off the tree, the current node is returned: if the value were added, it would be a child of the current node.

Once the `locate` method is written, the `contains` method must check to see if the node returned by `locate` actually equals the desired value:[2]

```
public boolean contains(Object value)
// post: returns true iff val is a value found within the tree
{
    if (root.isEmpty()) return false;

    BinaryTree possibleLocation = locate(root,value);
    return value.equals(possibleLocation.value());
}
```

It now becomes a fairly straightforward task to add a value. We simply locate the value in the tree using the `locate` function. If the value was not found, `locate` returned a node off of which a leaf with the desired value may be added. If, however, `locate` has found an equivalent value, we must insert the new value as the right child of the predecessor of the node returned by `locate`.[3]

```
public void add(Object value)
// post: adds a value to binary search tree
{
    BinaryTree newNode = new BinaryTree(value);
```

---

[2] We reemphasize at this point the importance of making sure that the `equals` method for an object is consistent with the ordering suggested by the `compare` method of the particular `Comparator`.

[3] With a little thought, it is clear to see that this is a correct location. If there are two copies of a value in a tree, the second value added is a descendant and predecessor (in an in-order traversal) of the located value. It is also easy to see that a predecessor has no right child, and that if one is added, *it* becomes the predecessor.

```
// add value to binary search tree
// if there's no root, create value at root
if (root.isEmpty())
{
    root = newNode;
} else {
    BinaryTree insertLocation = locate(root,value);
    Object nodeValue = insertLocation.value();
    // The location returned is the successor or predecessor
    // of the to-be-inserted value
    if (ordering.compare(nodeValue,value) < 0) {
        insertLocation.setRight(newNode);
    } else {
        if (!insertLocation.left().isEmpty()) {
            // if value is in tree, we insert just before
            predecessor(insertLocation).setRight(newNode);
        } else {
            insertLocation.setLeft(newNode);
        }
    }
}
count++;
}
```

Our add code makes use of the protected "helper" function, predecessor, which returns a pointer to the node that immediately precedes the indicated root:

```
protected BinaryTree predecessor(BinaryTree root)
{
    Assert.pre(!root.isEmpty(), "No predecessor to middle value.");
    Assert.pre(!root.left().isEmpty(), "Root has left child.");
    BinaryTree result = root.left();
    while (!result.right().isEmpty()) {
        result = result.right();
    }
    return result;
}
```

A similar routine can be written for successor, and would be used if we preferred to store duplicate values in the right subtree.

We now approach the problem of removing a value from a binary search tree. Observe that if it is found, it might be an internal node. The worst case occurs when the root of a tree is involved, so let us consider that problem.

There are several cases. First (Figure 13.2a), if the root of a tree has no left child, the right subtree can be used as the resulting tree. Likewise (Figure 13.2b), if there is no right child, we simply return the left. A third case (Figure 13.2c) occurs when the left subtree has no right child. Then, the right subtree—a tree with values no smaller than the left root—is made the right subtree of the left.

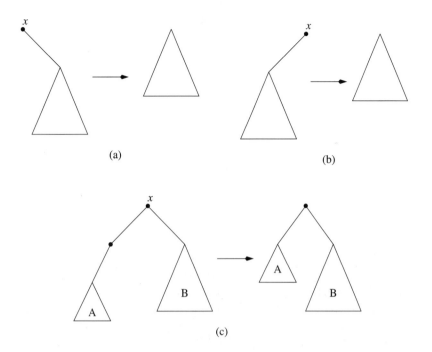

Figure 13.2   The three simple cases of removing a root value from a tree.

The left root is returned as the result. The opposite circumstance could also be true.

We are, then, left to consider trees with a left subtree that, in turn, contains a right subtree (Figure 13.3). Our approach to solving this case is to seek out the predecessor of the root and make it the new root. Note that even though the predecessor does not have a right subtree, it may have a left. This subtree can take the place of the predecessor as the right subtree of a nonroot node. (Note that this is the result that we would expect if we had recursively performed our node-removing process on the subtree rooted at the predecessor.)

Finally, here is the Java code that removes the top `BinaryTree` of a tree and returns the root of the resulting tree:

```
protected BinaryTree removeTop(BinaryTree topNode)
{
    // remove topmost BinaryTree from a binary search tree
    BinaryTree left  = topNode.left();
    BinaryTree right = topNode.right();
    // disconnect top node
    topNode.setLeft(BinaryTree.EMPTY);
    topNode.setRight(BinaryTree.EMPTY);
    // Case a, no left BinaryTree
```

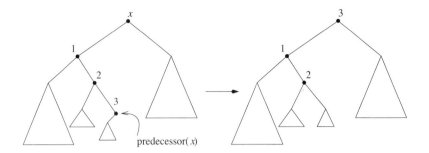

Figure 13.3   Removing the root of a tree with a rightmost left descendant.

```
//   easy: right subtree is new tree
if (left.isEmpty()) { return right; }
// Case b, no right BinaryTree
//   easy: left subtree is new tree
if (right.isEmpty()) { return left; }
// Case c, left node has no right subtree
//   easy: make right subtree of left
BinaryTree predecessor = left.right();
if (predecessor.isEmpty())
{
    left.setRight(right);
    return left;
}
// General case, slide down left tree
//   harder: successor of root becomes new root
//           parent always points to parent of predecessor
BinaryTree parent = left;
while (!predecessor.right().isEmpty())
{
    parent = predecessor;
    predecessor = predecessor.right();
}
// Assert: predecessor is predecessor of root
parent.setRight(predecessor.left());
predecessor.setLeft(left);
predecessor.setRight(right);
return predecessor;
}
```

With the combined efforts of the removeTop and locate methods, we can now
simply locate a value in the search tree and, if found, remove it from the tree.
We must be careful to update the appropriate references to rehook the modified
subtree back into the overall structure.

Notice that inserting and removing elements in this manner ensures that the in-order traversal of the underlying tree delivers the values stored in the nodes in a manner that respects the necessary ordering. We use this, then, as our preferred iteration method.

```
public Iterator iterator()
// post: returns iterator to traverse BST
{
    return root.inorderIterator();
}
```

The remaining methods (`size`, etc.) are implemented in a now-familiar manner.

Exercise 13.1 *One possible approach to keeping duplicate values in a binary search tree is to keep a list of the values in a single node. In such an implementation, each element of the list must appear externally as a separate node. Modify the* `BinarySearchTree` *implementation to make use of these lists of duplicate values.*

Each of the time-consuming operations of a `BinarySearchTree` has a worst-case time complexity that is proportional to the height of the tree. It is easy to see that checking for or adding a leaf, or removing a root, involves some of the most time-consuming operations. Thus, for logarithmic behavior, we must be sure that the tree remains as short as possible.

Unfortunately, we have no such assurance. In particular, one may observe what happens when values are inserted in descending order: the tree is heavily skewed to the left. If the same values are inserted in ascending order, the tree can be skewed to the right. If these values are distinct, the tree becomes, essentially, a singly linked list. Because of this behavior, we are usually better off if we shuffle the values beforehand. This causes the tree to become, on average, shorter and more balanced, and causes the expected insertion time to become $O(\log n)$.

Considering that the tree is responsible for maintaining an order among data values, it seems unreasonable to spend time shuffling values before ordering them. In Section 13.5 we find out that the process of adding and removing a node can be modified to maintain the tree in a relatively balanced state, with only a little overhead.

13.5   Splay Trees

Because the process of adding a new value to a binary search tree is *deterministic*—it produces the same result tree each time—and because inspection of the tree does not modify its structure, one is stuck with the performance of any degenerate tree constructed. What might work better would be to allow the tree to reconfigure itself when operations appear to be inefficient.

The *splay tree* quickly overcomes poor performance by rearranging the tree's nodes on the fly using a simple operation called a *splay*. Instead of performing

Splay: to spread outward.

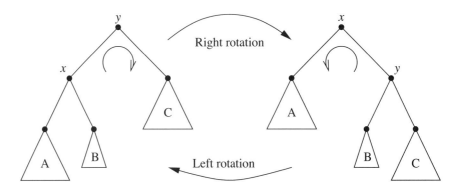

Figure 13.4   The relation between rotated subtrees.

careful analysis and optimally modifying the structure whenever a node is added or removed, the splay tree simply moves the referenced node to the top of the tree. The operation has the interesting characteristic that the average depth of the ancestors of the node to be splayed is approximately halved. As with skew heaps, the performance of a splay tree's operators, when amortized over many operations, is logarithmic.

The basis for the splay operation is a pair of operations called *rotations* (see Figure 13.4). Each of these rotations replaces the root of a subtree with one of its children. A right rotation takes a left child, x, of a node y and reverses their relationship. This induces certain obvious changes in connectivity of subtrees, but in all other ways, the tree remains the same. In particular, there is no structural effect on the tree above the original location of node y. A left rotation is precisely the opposite of a right rotation; these operations are inverses of each other.

The code for rotating a binary tree about a node is a method of the `Binary-Tree` class. We show, here, `rotateRight`; a similar method performs a left rotation.

Finally, a right handed method!

BinaryTree-
Node

```
protected void rotateRight()
// pre: this node has a left subtree
// post: rotates local portion of tree so left child is root
{
    BinaryTree parent = parent();
    BinaryTree newRoot = left();
    boolean wasChild = parent != null;
    boolean wasLeftChild = isLeftChild();

    // hook in new root (sets newRoot's parent, as well)
    setLeft(newRoot.right());
```

```
        // puts pivot below it (sets this's parent, as well)
        newRoot.setRight(this);

        if (wasChild) {
            if (wasLeftChild) parent.setLeft(newRoot);
            else              parent.setRight(newRoot);
        }
    }
```

For each rotation accomplished, the nonroot node moves upward by one level. Making use of this fact, we can now develop an operation to splay a tree at a particular node. It works as follows:

- If x is the root, we are done.

- If x is a left (or right) child of the root, rotate the tree to the right (or left) about the root. x becomes the root and we are done.

- If x is the left child of its parent p, which is, in turn, the left child of its grandparent g, rotate right about g, followed by a right rotation about p (Figure 13.5a). A symmetric pair of rotations is possible if x is a left child of a left child. After double rotation, continue splay of tree at x with this new tree.

- If x is the right child of p, which is the left child of g, we rotate left about p, then right about g (Figure 13.5b). The method is similar if x is the left child of a right child. Again, continue the splay at x in the new tree.

After the splay has been completed, the node x is located at the root of the tree. If node x were to be immediately accessed again (a strong possibility), the tree is clearly optimized to handle this situation. It is *not* the case that the tree becomes more balanced (see Figure 13.5a). Clearly, if the tree is splayed at an extremal value, the tree is likely to be extremely unbalanced. An interesting feature, however, is that the depth of the nodes on the original path from x to the root of the tree is, on average, halved. Since the average depth of these nodes is halved, they clearly occupy locations closer to the top of the tree where they may be more efficiently accessed.

To guarantee that the splay has an effect on all operations, we simply perform each of the binary search tree operations as before, but we splay the tree at the node accessed or modified during the operation. In the case of `remove`, we splay the tree at the parent of the value removed.

13.6 Splay Tree Implementation

Because the splay tree supports the binary search tree interface, we extend the `BinarySearchTree` data structure. Methods written for the `SplayTree` hide or *override* existing code inherited from the `BinarySearchTree`.

SplayTree

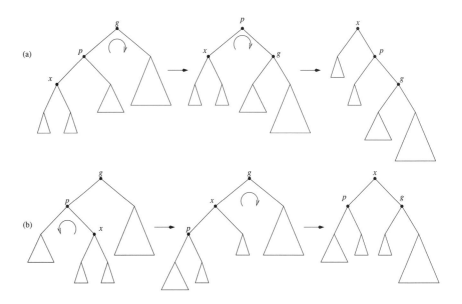

Figure 13.5   Two of the rotation pairs used in the splaying operation. The other cases are mirror images of those shown here.

```
public class SplayTree extends BinarySearchTree
    implements OrderedStructure
{
    public SplayTree()
    // post: construct a new splay tree

    public SplayTree(Comparator alternateOrder)
    // post: construct a new splay tree

    public void add(Object val)
    // post: adds a value to the binary search tree

    public boolean contains(Object val)
    // post: returns true iff val is a value found within the tree

    public Object get(Object val)
    // post: returns object found in tree, or null

    public Object remove(Object val)
    // post: removes one instance of val, if found

    protected void splay(BinaryTree splayedNode)
```

```
        public Iterator iterator()
        // post: returns iterator that traverses tree nodes in order
    }
```

As an example of how the splay operation is incorporated into the existing binary tree code, we look at the `contains` method. Here, the root is reset to the value of the node to be splayed, and the splay operation is performed on the tree. The postcondition of the splay operation guarantees that the splayed node will become the root of the tree, so the entire operation leaves the tree in the correct state.

```
    public boolean contains(Object val)
    // post: returns true iff val is a value found within the tree
    {
        if (root.isEmpty()) return false;

        BinaryTree possibleLocation = locate(root,val);
        if (val.equals(possibleLocation.value())) {
            splay(root = possibleLocation);
            return true;
        } else {
            return false;
        }
    }
```

One difficulty with the splay operation is that it potentially modifies the structure of the tree. For example, the `contains` method—a method normally considered nondestructive—potentially changes the underlying topology of the tree. This makes it difficult to construct iterators that traverse the `SplayTree` since the user may use the value found from the iterator in a read-only operation that inadvertently modifies the structure of the splay tree. This *can* have disastrous effects on the state of the iterator. A way around this difficulty is to have the iterator keep only that state information that is necessary to help reconstruct—with help from the structure of the tree—the complete state of our traditional nonsplay iterator. In the case of the `SplayTreeIterator`, we keep track of two references: a reference to an "example" node of the tree and a reference to the current node inspected by the iterator. The example node helps recompute the root whenever the iterator is reset. To determine what nodes would have been stored in the stack in the traditional iterator—the stack of unvisited ancestors of the current node—we consider each node on the (unique) path from the root to the current node. Any node whose left child is also on the path is an element of our "virtual stack." In addition, the top of the stack maintains the current node (see Figure 13.6).

It can also wreck your day.

The constructor sets the appropriate underlying references and resets the iterator into its initial state. Because the `SplayTree` is dynamically restructuring, the root value passed to the constructor may not always be the root of the tree. Still, one can easily find the root of the current tree, given a node: follow parent pointers until one is `null`. Since the first value visited in an inorder

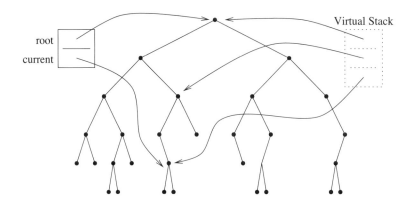

Figure 13.6 A splay tree iterator, the tree it references, and the contents of the virtual stack driving the iterator.

traversal is the leftmost descendant, the reset method travels down the leftmost branch (logically pushing values on the stack) until it finds a node with no left child.

SplayTree-
Iterator

```
protected BinaryTree tree; // node of splay tree, root computed
protected BinaryTree current; // current node
// In this iterator, the "stack" normally used is implied by
// looking back up the path from the current node.  Those nodes
// for which the path goes left are on the stack

public SplayTreeIterator(BinaryTree root)
// pre: root is the root of the tree to be traversed
// post: constructs a new iterator to traverse splay tree
{
    tree = root;
    reset();
}

public void reset()
// post: resets iterator to smallest node in tree
{
    current = tree;
    if (!current.isEmpty()) {
        current = current.root();
        while (!current.left().isEmpty()) current = current.left();
    }
}
```

The current node points to, by definition, an unvisited node that is, logically, on the top of the outstanding node stack. Therefore, the `hasNext` and `get` methods may access the current value immediately.

```
public boolean hasNext()
// post: returns true if there are unvisited nodes
{
    return !current.isEmpty();
}

public Object get()
// pre: hasNext()
// post: returns current value
{
    return current.value();
}
```

All that remains is to move the iterator from one state to the next. The **next** method first checks to see if the current (just visited) element has a right child. If so, **current** is set to the leftmost descendant of the right child, effectively popping off the current node and pushing on all the nodes physically linking the current node and its successor. When no right descendant exists, the subtree rooted at the current node has been completely visited. The next node to be visited is the node under the top element of the virtual stack—the closest ancestor whose left child is also an ancestor of the current node. Here is how we accomplish this in Java:

```
public Object next()
// pre: hasNext()
// post: returns current element and increments iterator
{
    Object result = current.value();
    if (!current.right().isEmpty()) {
        current = current.right();
        while (!current.left().isEmpty())
        {
            current = current.left();
        }
    } else {
        // we're finished with current's subtree.  We now pop off
        // nodes until we come to the parent of a leftchild ancestor
        // of current
        boolean lefty;
        do
        {
            lefty = current.isLeftChild();
            current = current.parent();
        } while (current != null && !lefty);
        if (current == null) current = BinaryTree.EMPTY;
    }
    return result;
}
```

The iterator is now able to maintain its position through splay operations.

Again, the behavior of the splay tree is logarithmic when amortized over a number of operations. Any particular operation may take more time to execute, but the time is usefully spent rearranging nodes in a way that tends to make the tree shorter.

From a practical standpoint, the overhead of splaying the tree on every operation may be hard to justify if the operations performed on the tree are relatively random. On the other hand, if the access patterns tend to generate degenerate binary search trees, the splay tree can improve performance.

13.7 An Alternative:Red-Black Trees

A potential issue with both traditional binary search trees and splay trees is the fact that they potentially have bad performance if values are inserted or accessed in a particular order. Splay trees, of course, work hard to make sure that repeated accesses (which seem likely) will be efficient. Still, there is no absolute performance guarantee.

One could, of course, make sure that the values in a tree are stored in as perfectly balanced a manner as possible. In general, however, such techniques are both difficult to implement and costly in terms of per-operation execution time.

Exercise 13.2 *Describe a strategy for keeping a binary search tree as short as possible. One example might be to unload all of the values and to reinsert them in a particular order. How long does your approach take to* **add** *a value?*

Because we consider the performance of structures using big-O notation, we implicitly suggest we might be happy with performance that is within a constant of optimal. For example, we might be happy if we could keep a tree balanced within a factor of 2. One approach is to develop a structure called a *red-black tree*.

For accounting purposes only, the nodes of a red-black tree are imagined to be colored red or black. Along with these colors are several simple rules that are constantly enforced:

1. Every red node has two black children.

2. Every leaf has two black (**EMPTY** is considered black) children.

3. Every path from a node to a descendent leaf contains the same number of black nodes.

The result of constructing trees with these rules is that the height of the tree measured along two different paths cannot differ by more than a factor of 2: two red nodes may not appear contiguously, and every path must have the same number of black nodes. This would imply that the height of the tree is $O(\log_2 n)$.

Exercise 13.3 *Prove that the height of the tree with n nodes is no worse than* $O(\log_2 n)$.

Of course, the purpose of data abstraction is to be able to maintain the consistency of the structure—in this case, the red-black tree rules—as the structure is probed and modified. The methods `add` and `remove` are careful to maintain the red-black structure through at most $O(\log n)$ rotations and re-colorings of nodes. For example, if a node that is colored black is removed from the tree, it is necessary to perform rotations that either convert a red node on the path to the root to black, or reduce the *black height* (the number of black nodes from root to leaf) of the entire tree. Similar problems can occur when we attempt to add a new node that must be colored black.

The code for red-black trees can be found online as `RedBlackTree`. While the code is too tedious to present here, it is quite elegant and leads to binary search trees with very good performance characteristics.

The implementation of the `RedBlackTree` structure in the **structure** package demonstrates another approach to packaging a binary search tree that *is* important to discuss. Like the `BinaryTree` structure, the `RedBlackTree` is defined as a recursive structure represented by a single node. The `RedBlackTree` also contains a dummy-node representation of the `EMPTY` tree. This is useful in reducing the complexity of the tests within the code, and it supports the notion that leaves have children with color, but most importantly, it allows the user to call `static` methods that are defined even for red-black trees with no nodes. This approach—coding inherently recursive structures as recursive classes—leads to *side-effect free* code. Each method has an effect on the tree at hand but does not modify any global structures. This means that the user must be very careful to record any side effects that might occur. In particular, it is important that methods that cause modifications to the structure return the "new" value of the tree. If, for example, the root of the tree was the object of a `remove`, that reference is no longer useful in maintaining contact with the tree.

To compare the approaches of the `BinarySearchTree` wrapper and the recursive `RedBlackTree`, we present here the implementation of the `SymTab` structure we investigated at the beginning of the chapter, but cast in terms of `RedBlackTree`s. Comparison of the approaches is instructive (important differences are highlighted with uppercase comments).

```
import structure.*;
import java.util.Iterator;
public class RBSymTab
{
    protected RedBlackTree table; // comparable associations

    public RBSymTab()
    // post: constructs empty symbol table
    {
        table = RedBlackTree.EMPTY; // NO NEW PERFORMED
```

RBSymTab

```
    }

    public boolean contains(Comparable symbol)
    // pre: symbol is non-null string
    // post: returns true iff string in table
    {
        return table.contains(new ComparableAssociation(symbol,null));
    }

    public void add(Comparable symbol, Object value)
    // pre: symbol non-null
    // post: adds/replaces symbol-value pair in table
    {
        ComparableAssociation a = new ComparableAssociation(symbol,value);
        if (table.contains(a)) table = table.remove(a);
        table = table.add(a);
    }

    public Object get(Comparable symbol)
    // pre: symbol non-null
    // post: returns token associated with symbol
    {
        ComparableAssociation a = new ComparableAssociation(symbol,null);
        if (table.contains(a)) {
            a = (ComparableAssociation)table.get(a);
            return a.getValue();
        } else {
            return null;
        }
    }

    public Object remove(Comparable symbol)
    // pre: symbol non-null
    // post: removes value associated with symbol and returns it
    //       if error returns null
    {
        ComparableAssociation a = new ComparableAssociation(symbol,null);
        if (table.contains(a)) {
            a = (ComparableAssociation)table.get(a);
            table = table.remove(a);
            return a.getValue();
        } else {
            return null;
        }
    }
}
```

The entire definition of RedBlackTrees is available in the structure package, when $O(\log n)$ performance is desired. For more details about the structure, please see the documentation within the code.

13.8 Conclusions

A binary search tree is the product of imposing an order on the nodes of a binary tree. Each node encountered in the search for a value represents a point where a decision can be accurately made to go left or right. If the tree is short and fairly balanced, these decisions have the effect of eliminating a large portion of the remaining candidate values.

The binary search tree is, however, a product of the history of the insertion of values. Since every new value is placed at a leaf, the internal nodes are left untouched and make the structure of the tree fairly static. The result is that poor distributions of data can cause degenerate tree structures that adversely impact the performance of the various search tree methods.

To combat the problem of unbalanced trees, various rotation-based optimizations are possible. In splay trees, rotations are used to force a recently accessed value and its ancestors closer to the root of the tree. The effect is often to shorten degenerate trees, resulting in an amortized logarithmic behavior. A remarkable feature of this implementation is that there is no space penalty: no accounting information needs to be maintained in the nodes.

Self Check Problems

Solutions to these problems begin on page 435.

13.1 What motivates the use of *binary* search trees?

13.2 Suppose values have only been added into a `BinarySearchTree`. Where is the first node added to the tree? Where is the last node added to the tree?

13.3 What is an associative structure?

13.4 Which node becomes the root after a tree is rotated left?

13.5 Is the right rotation the reverse of the left rotation?

13.6 If two values are equal (using `equals`) are they found near each other in a `BinarySearchTree`?

13.7 Why is it so difficult to construct an `Iterator` for a `SplayTree`?

13.8 What is the primary advantage of a red-black tree over a splay tree?

Problems

Solutions to the odd-numbered problems begin on page 468.

13.1 What distinguishes a binary search tree from a binary tree?

13.2 Draw all three-node integer-valued trees whose nodes are visited in the order 1-2-3 in an in-order traversal. Which trees are binary search trees?

13.3 Draw all three-node integer-valued trees whose nodes are visited in the order 1-2-3 in a preorder traversal. Which trees are binary search trees?

13.4   Draw all three-node integer-valued trees whose nodes are visited in the order 1-2-3 in a postorder traversal. Which trees are binary search trees?

13.5   Redraw the following binary search tree after the root has been removed.

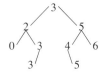

13.6   Redraw the tree shown in Problem 13.5 after the leaf labeled 3 is removed.

13.7   Redraw the tree shown in Problem 13.5 after it is splayed at the leaf labeled 3.

13.8   The `locate` methods from `OrderedVector`s and `BinarySearchTree`s are very similar. They have, for example, similar best-case behaviors. Explain why their behaviors differ in the worst case.

13.9   Prove that, if values are distinct, any binary search tree can be constructed by appropriately ordering insertion operations.

13.10   In splay trees rotations are performed, possibly reversing the parent-child relationship between two equal values. It is now possible to have a root node with a right child that is equal. Explain why this will not cause problems with each of the current methods `locate`, `add`, and `remove`.

13.11   Describe the topology of a binary search tree after the values 1 through n have been inserted in order. How long does the search tree take to construct?

13.12   Describe the topology of a splay tree after the values 1 through n have been inserted in order. How long does the splay tree take to construct?

13.13   Because the `remove` method of binary search trees prefers to replace a node with its predecessor, one expects that a large number of `remove`s will cause the tree to lean toward the right. Describe a scheme to avoid this problem.

13.14   Suppose n distinct values are stored in a binary tree. It is noted that the tree is a min-heap *and* a binary search tree. What does the tree look like?

13.15   As we have seen, the splay tree requires the construction of an iterator that stores a single reference to the tree, rather than an unlimited number of references to ancestors. How does this reduction in space utilization impact the running time of the iterator?

13.16   Write an `equals` method for binary search trees. It should return `true` if both trees contain equal values.

13.17   Having answered Problem 13.16, is it possible to accurately use the same method for splay trees?

13.18   Write a `copy` method for binary search trees. The result of the `copy` should be equal to the original. Carefully argue the utility of your approach.

13.19   Prove that the expected time to perform the `next` method of the splay tree iterator is constant time.

13.9   Laboratory: Improving the BinarySearchTree

Objective. To understand it is possible to improve an implementation.

Discussion. As we have seen in the implementation of the `BinarySearchTree` class, the insertion of values is relative to the root of the tree. One of the situations that must be handled carefully is the case where more than one node can have the same key. If equal keys are allowed in the binary search tree, then we must be careful to have them inserted on one side of the root. This behavior increases the complexity of the code, and when there are many duplicate keys, it is possible that the tree's depth can be increased considerably.

Procedure. An alternative approach is to have all the nodes with similar keys stored in the same location. When the tree is constructed in this manner, then there is no need to worry about keeping similar keys together—they're *always together*.

In this lab, we will implement a `BinaryMultiTree`—a `BinarySearchTree`-like structure that stores a multiset (a set of values with potential duplicates). We are not so concerned with the set features, but we are demanding that different values are kept in sorted order in the structure. In particular, the traversal of the `BinaryMultiTree` should return the values in order.

In this implementation, a `BinaryTree` is used to keep track of a `List` of values that are equal when compared with the `compare` method of the `ordering` `Comparator`. From the perspective of the structure, there is no distinguishing the members of the list. Externally, the interface to the `BinaryMultiTree` is exactly the same as the `BinarySearchTree`, but the various methods work with values stored in `Lists`, as opposed to working with the values directly. For example, when we look at a value stored in a node, we find a `List`. A `getFirst` of this `List` class picks out an example that is suitable, for example, for comparison purposes.

Here are some things to think about during your implementation:

1. The `size` method does not return the number of nodes; it returns the number of values stored in all the nodes. The bookkeeping is much the same as it was before, but `size` is an upper bound on the actual size of the search tree.

2. The `add` method compares values to the heads of lists found at each node along the way. A new node is created if the value is not found in the tree; the value is inserted in a newly created `List` in the `BinaryTreeNode`. When an equal key is found, the search for a location stops, and the value is added to the `List`. A carefully considered `locate` method will help considerably here.

3. The `contains` method is quite simple: it returns `true` if the `getFirst` of any of the `Lists` produces a similar value.

4. The `get` method returns one of the matching values, if found. It should probably be the same value that would be returned if a `remove` were executed in the same situation.

5. The `iterator` method returns an `Iterator` that traverses all the values of the `BinarySearchTree`. When a list of equal values is encountered, they are all considered before a larger value is returned.

When you are finished, test your code by storing a large list of names of people, ordered only by last name (you will note that this is a common technique used by stores that keep accounts: "Smith?" "Yes!" "Are you Paul or John?"). You should be able to roughly sort the names by inserting them into a `BinaryMultiTree` and then iterating across its elements.

Thought Questions. Consider the following questions as you complete the lab:

1. Recall: What is the problem with having equal keys stored on either side of an equal-valued root?

2. Does it matter what type of `List` is used? What kinds of operations are to be efficient in this `List`?

3. What is the essential difference between implementing the tree as described and, say, just directly storing linked lists of equivalent nodes in the `BinarySearchTree`?

4. An improved version of this structure might use a `Comparator` for primary and secondary keys. The primary comparison is used to identify the correct location for the value in the `BinaryMultiTree`, and the secondary key could be used to order the keys that appear equal using the primary key. Those values that are equal using the primary key are kept within an `OrderedStructure` that keeps track of its elements using the secondary key `Comparator`.

Notes:

Chapter 14

Maps

*X is very useful
if your name is
Nixie Knox.
It also
comes in handy
spelling ax
and extra fox.*
—Theodor Seuss Geisel

WE HAVE SEEN THAT AN ASSOCIATION ESTABLISHES A LINK between a *key* and a *value*. An *associative array* or *map* is a structure that allows a disjoint set of keys to become associated with an arbitrary set of values. The convenience of an associative array is that the values used to index the elements need not be comparable and their range need not be known ahead of time. Furthermore, there is no upper bound on the size of the structure. It is able to maintain an arbitrary number of different pieces of information simultaneously. The analogy with a mathematical map or function stems from the notion that every key has at most associated value. Maps are sometimes called *dictionaries* because of the uniqueness of the association of words and definitions in a household dictionary. Needless to say, a map structure would nicely support the storage of dictionary definitions.

14.1   Example Revisited: The Symbol Table

In Chapter 13 we stored the words and their translations (name-alias pairs) in a structure called a `SymTab`. This structure forms a good basis for a more general-purpose approach. Here, we suggest a slightly modified program to accomplish exactly the same task. The names of the methods, however, have been changed to suggest slight improvements in the *semantics* of structure:

```
public static void main(String args[])
{
    Map table = new MapList();
    ReadStream r = new ReadStream();
    String alias, name;
```

SymMap

```
                  // read in the alias-name database
                  do
                  {
                      alias = r.readString();
                      if (!alias.equals("END"))
                      {
                          name = r.readString();
                          table.put(alias,name); // was called add, but may modify
                      }
                  } while (!alias.equals("END"));
                  // enter the alias translation stage
                  System.out.println("Table contains aliases: "+
                                      table.keySet());
                  // enter the alias translation stage
                  do
                  {
                      name = r.readString();
                      while (table.containsKey(name)) // was contains; more explicit
                      {
                          name = (String)table.get(name); // translate alias
                      }
                      System.out.println(name);
                      r.skipWhite();
                  } while (!r.eof());
              }
```

The differences between this implementation and that of Section 13.3 involve improvements in clarity. The method add was changed to put. The difference is that put suggests that the key-value pair is replaced if it is already in the Map. We also check for a value in the domain of the Map with containsKey. There might be a similar need to check the range; that would be accomplished with containsValue. Finally, we make use of a method, keySet, that returns a Set of values that are possible keys. This suggests aliases that might be typed in during the translation phase. Other methods might return a collection of values.

Thus we see that the notion of a Map formalizes a structure we have found useful in the past. We now consider a more complete description of the interface.

14.2   The Interface

In Java, a Map can be found within the java.util package. Each Map structure must have the following interface:

Map

```
public interface Map
{
    public abstract int size();
    // post: returns the number of entries in the map
```

```
        public abstract boolean isEmpty();
        // post: returns true iff this map does not contain any entries

        public abstract boolean containsKey(Object k);
        // pre: k is non-null
        // post: returns true iff k is in the domain of the map

        public abstract boolean containsValue(Object v);
        // pre: v is non-null
        // post: returns true iff v is the target of at least one map entry;
        // that is, v is in the range of the map

        public abstract Object get(Object k);
        // pre: k is a key, possibly in the map
        // post: returns the value mapped to from k, or null

        public abstract Object put(Object k, Object v);
        // pre: k and v are non-null
        // post: inserts a mapping from k to v in the map

        public abstract Object remove(Object k);
        // pre: k is non-null
        // post: removes any mapping from k to a value, from the mapping

        public abstract void putAll(Map other);
        // pre: other is non-null
        // post: all the mappings of other are installed in this map,
        // overriding any conflicting maps

        public abstract void clear();
        // post: removes all map entries associated with this map

        public abstract Set keySet();
        // post: returns a set of all keys associated with this map

        public abstract Structure values();
        // post: returns a structure that contains the range of the map

        public abstract Set entrySet();
        // post: returns a set of (key-value) pairs, generated from this map

        public abstract boolean equals(Object other);
        // pre: other is non-null
        // post: returns true iff maps this and other are entry-wise equal

        public abstract int hashCode();
        // post: returns a hash code associated with this structure
    }
```

The put method places a new key-value pair within the Map. If the key was already used to index a value, that association is replaced with a new association between the key and value. In any case, the put method returns the value replaced or null. The get method allows the user to retrieve, using a key, the value from the Map. If the key is not used to index an element of the Map, a null value is returned. Because this null value is not distinguished from a stored value that is null, it is common to predicate the call to get with a call to the containsKey method. This method returns true if a key matching the parameter can be found within the Map. Sometimes, like human associative memory, it is useful to check to see if a *value* is found in the array. This can be accomplished with the containsValue method.

Aside from the fact that the keys of the values stored within the Map should be distinct, there are no other constraints on their type. In particular, the keys of a Map need only be accurately compared using the equals method. For this reason, it is important that a reasonable key equality test be provided.

There are no iterators provided with maps. Instead, we have a Map return a Set of keys (a keySet as previously seen), a Set of key-value pairs (entrySet), or any Structure of values (values). (The latter must not be a Set because values may be duplicated.) Each of these, in turn, can generate an Iterator with the iterator method. Because keys might not implement the Comparable class, there is no obvious ordering of the entries in a Map. This means that the keys generated from the keySet and the values encountered during an iteration over the values structure may appear in different orders. To guarantee the correct association, use the Iterator associated with the entrySet method.

14.3   Simple Implementation: MapList

One approach to this problem, of course, is to store the values in a List. Each mapping from a key to a value is kept in an Association which, in turn, is stored in a List. The result is what we call a MapList; we saw this in Section 14.2, though we referred to it as a generic Map structure. The approach is fairly straightforward. Here is the protected data declaration and constructors:

MapList

```
protected List data;
public MapList()
// post: constructs an empty map, based on a list
{
    data = new SinglyLinkedList();
}

public MapList(Map source)
// post: constructs a map with values found in source
{
    this();
    putAll(source);
}
```

It is conventional for complex structures to have a *copy constructor* that generates a new structure using the entries found in another `Map`. Notice that we don't make any assumptions about the particular *implementation* of the `Map` we copy from; it may be a completely different implementation.

Most of the other methods are fairly straightforward. For example, the `put` method is accomplished by finding a (possible) previous `Association` and replacing it with a fresh construction. The previous value (if any) is returned.

```
public Object put(Object k, Object v)
// pre: k and v are non-null
// post: inserts a mapping from k to v in the map
{
    Association temp = new Association(k,v);
    Association result = (Association)data.remove(temp);
    data.add(temp);
    if (result == null) return null;
    else return result.getValue();
}
```

The `Set` constructions make use of the `Set` implementations we have discussed in passing in our discussion of Lists:

```
public Set keySet()
// post: returns a set of all keys associated with this map
{
    Set result = new SetList();
    Iterator i = data.iterator();
    while (i.hasNext())
    {
        Association a = (Association)i.next();
        result.add(a.getKey());
    }
    return result;
}


public Set entrySet()
// post: returns a set of (key-value) pairs, generated from this map
{
    Set result = new SetList();
    Iterator i = data.iterator();
    while (i.hasNext())
    {
        Association a = (Association)i.next();
        result.add(a);
    }
    return result;
}
```

(We will discuss the implementation of various `Iterators` in Section 14.4; they are filtering iterators that modify `Associations` returned from subordinate iterators.) Notice that the uniqueness of keys in a `Map` suggests they form a `Set`,

yet this is checked by the Set implementation in any case. The values found
in a Map are, of course, not necessarily unique, so they are stored in a general
Structure. Any would do; we make use of a List for its simplicity:

```
public Structure values()
// post: returns a structure that contains the range of the map
{
    Structure result = new SinglyLinkedList();
    Iterator i = new ValueIterator(data.iterator());
    while (i.hasNext())
    {
        result.add(i.next());
    }
    return result;
}
```

Exercise 14.1 *What would be the cost of performing a* containsKey *check on
a* MapList*? How about a call to* containsValue*?*

Without giving much away, it is fairly clear the answers to the above exercise
are not constant time. It would seem quite difficult to get a $O(1)$ performance
from operators like contains and remove. We discuss the possibilities in the
next section.

14.4   Constant Time Maps: Hash Tables

Clearly a collection of associations is a useful approach to filling the needs of
the map. The costs associated with the various structures vary considerably.
For Vectors, the cost of looking up data has, on average, $O(n)$ time complexity.
Because of limits associated with being linear, all the $O(n)$ structures have
similar performance. When data can be ordered, sorting the elements of the
Linear structure improves the performance in the case of Vectors: this makes
sense because Vectors are random access structures whose intermediate values
can be accessed given an index.

When we considered binary search trees—a structure that also stores Comparable values—we determined the values could be found in logarithmic time.
At each stage, the search space can be reduced by a factor of 2. The difference
between logarithmic and linear algorithms is very dramatic. For example, a
balanced BinarySearchTree or an ordered Vector might find one number in a
million in 20 or fewer compares. In an unordered Vector the expected number
of compares increases to 500,000.

Is it possible to improve on this behavior? With hash tables, the answer
is, amazingly, *yes*. With appropriate care, the hash table can provide access
to an arbitrary element in roughly constant time. By "roughly," we mean that
as long as sufficient space is provided, each potential key can be reserved an
undisturbed location with probability approaching 1.

How is this possible? The technique is, actually, rather straightforward. Here is an example of how hashing occurs in real life:

I was just going to say that.

> We head to a local appliance store to pick up a new freezer. When we arrive, the clerk asks us for *the last two digits* of our home telephone number! Only then does the clerk ask for our last name. Armed with that information, the clerk walks directly to a bin in a warehouse of hundreds of appliances and comes back with the freezer in tow.

The technique used by the appliance store was *hashing*. The "bin" or *bucket* that contains the object is identified by the last two digits of the phone number of the future owner. If two or more items were located in the bin, the name could be used to further distinguish the order.

An alternative approach to the "addressing" of the bins might be to identify each bin with the first letter of the name of the customer. This, however, has a serious flaw, in that it is likely that there will be far more names that begin with S than with, say, K. Even when the entire name is used, the names of customers are unlikely to be evenly distributed. These techniques for addressing bins are less likely to uniquely identify the desired parcel.

That would be a large number of bins!

The success of the phone number technique stems from generating an identifier associated with each customer that is both random and evenly distributed.[1]

14.4.1 Open Addressing

We now implement a hash table, modeled after the `Hashtable` of Java's `java.-util` package. All elements in the table are stored in a fixed-length array whose length is, ideally, prime. Initialization ensures that each slot within the array is set to `null`. Eventually, slots will contain references to associations between keys and values. We use an array for speed, but a `Vector` would be a logical alternative.

Hashtable

```
protected static Association reserved =
           new Association("reserved",null);
protected Association data[];
protected int count;
protected int capacity;
protected final double loadFactor = 0.6;

public Hashtable(int initialCapacity)
// pre: initialCapacity > 0
// post: constructs a new Hashtable
//       holding initialCapacity elements
{
```

---

[1] Using the last two digits of the telephone number makes for an evenly distributed set of values. It is *not* the case that the first two digits of the exchange would be useful, as that is not always random. In our town, where the exchange begins with 45, no listed phones have extensions beginning with 45.

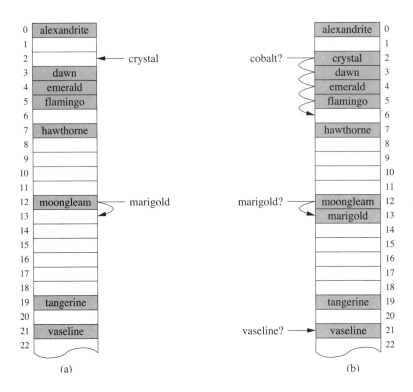

Figure 14.1   Hashing color names of antique glass. (a) Values are hashed into the first available slot, possibly after rehashing. (b) The lookup process uses a similar approach to possibly find values.

```
        data = new Association[initialCapacity];
        capacity = initialCapacity;
        count = 0;
    }

    public Hashtable()
    // post: constructs a new Hashtable
    {
        this(997);
    }
```

The key and value management methods depend on a function, `locate`, that finds a good location for a value in the structure. First, we use an index-producing function that "hashes" a value to a slot or bucket (see Figure 14.1). In Java, every `Object` has a function, called `hashCode`, that returns an integer to be used for precisely this purpose. For the moment, we'll assume the hash code is the alphabet code ($a = 0$, $b = 1$, etc.) of the first letter of the word. The

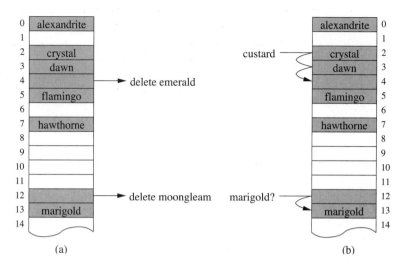

Figure 14.2 (a) Deletion of a value leaves a shaded reserved cell as a place holder. (b) A reserved cell is considered empty during insertion and full during lookup.

hash code for a particular key (2 for the word "crystal") is used as an index to the first slot to be considered for storing or locating the value in the table. If the slot is empty, the value can be stored there. If the slot is full, it is possible that another value already occupies that space (consider the insertion of "marigold" in Figure 14.1). When the keys of the two objects do not match, we have a *collision*. A *perfect hash function* guarantees that (given prior knowledge of the set of potential keys) no collisions will occur. When collisions do occur, they can be circumvented in several ways. With *open addressing*, a collision is resolved by generating a new hash value, or *rehashing*, and reattempting the operation at a new location.

Slots in the hash table logically have two states—empty (`null`) or full (a reference to an object)—but there is also a third possibility. When values are removed, we replace the value with a *reserved* value that indicates that the location potentially impacts the lookup process for other cells during insertions. That association is represented by the empty shaded cell in Figure 14.2a. Each time we come across the reserved value in the search for a particular value in the array (see Figure 14.2b), we continue the search as though there had been a collision. We keep the first reserved location in mind as a possible location for an insertion, if necessary. In the figure, this slot is used by the inserted value "custard."

When large numbers of different-valued keys hash or rehash to the same locations, the effect is called *clustering* (see Figure 14.3). *Primary clustering* is when several keys hash to the same initial location and rehash to slots with potential collisions with the same set of keys. *Secondary clustering* occurs when

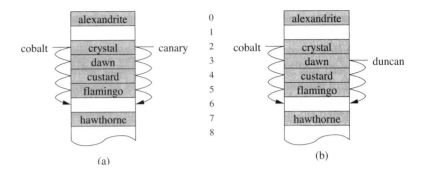

Figure 14.3   (a) *Primary clustering* occurs when two values that hash to the same slot continue to compete during rehashing. (b) Rehashing causes keys that initially hash to different slots to compete.

keys that initially hash to different locations eventually rehash to the same sequence of slots.

In this simple implementation we use *linear probing* (demonstrated in Figures 14.1 to 14.3). Any rehashing of values occurs a constant distance from the last hash location. The linear-probing approach causes us to wrap around the array and find the next available slot. It does not solve either primary or secondary clustering, but it is easy to implement and quick to compute. To avoid secondary clustering we use a related technique, called *double hashing*, that uses a second hash function to determine the magnitude of the constant offset (see Figure 14.4). This is not easily accomplished on arbitrary keys since we are provided only one `hashCode` function. In addition, multiples and factors of the hash table size (including 0) must also be avoided to keep the `locate` function from going into an infinite loop. Still, when implemented correctly, the performance of double hashing can provide significant improvements over linear-probing.

We now discuss our implementation of hash tables. First, we consider the `locate` function. Its performance is important to the efficiency of each of the public methods.

```
protected int locate(Object key)
{
    // compute an initial hash code
    int hash = Math.abs(key.hashCode() % capacity);
    // keep track of first unused slot, in case we need it
    int firstReserved = -1;
    while (data[hash] != null)
    {
        if (data[hash] == reserved) {
            // remember reserved slot if we fail to locate value
```

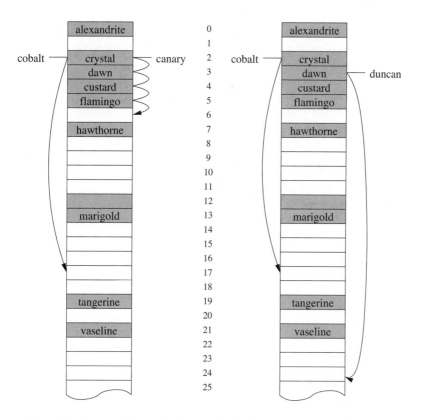

Figure 14.4 The keys of Figure 14.3 are rehashed by an offset determined by the alphabet code ($a = 1$, $b = 2$, etc.) of the *second* letter. No clustering occurs, but strings must have two letters!

```
            if (firstReserved == -1) firstReserved = hash;
        } else  {
            // value located? return the index in table
            if (key.equals(data[hash].getKey())) return hash;
        }
        // linear probing; other methods would change this line:
        hash = (1+hash)%capacity;
    }
    // return first empty slot we encountered
    if (firstReserved == -1) return hash;
    else return firstReserved;
}
```

To measure the difficulty of finding an empty slot by hashing, we use the *load factor*, α, computed as the ratio of the number of values stored within the table to the number of slots used. For open addressing, the load factor cannot exceed 1. As we shall see, to maintain good performance we should keep the load factor small as possible. Our maximum allowable load factor is a constant `loadFactor`. Exceeding this value causes the array to be reallocated and copied over (using the method `extend`).

When a value is added, we simply locate the appropriate slot and insert a new association. If the ideal slot already has a value (it must have an equal key), we return the replaced association. If we replace the reference to an empty cell with the `reserved` association, we return `null` instead.

```
public Object put(Object key, Object value)
// pre: key is non-null object
// post: key-value pair is added to hash table
{
    if (loadFactor*capacity <= (1+count)) {
        extend();
    }
    int hash = locate(key);
    Association a = data[hash];
    if (a == null || a == reserved)
    {   // logically empty slot; just add association
        data[hash] = new Association(key,value);
        count++;
        return null;
    } else {
        // full slot; add new and return old value
        Object oldValue = a.getValue();
        a.setValue(value);
        return oldValue;
    }
}
```

The `get` function works similarly—we simply return the value from within the key-located association or `null`, if no association could be found.

```
public Object get(Object key)
// pre: key is non-null Object
// post: returns value associated with key, or null
{
    int hash = locate(key);
    Association a = data[hash];
    if (a == null || a == reserved) return null;
    return data[hash].getValue();
}
```

The `containsKey` method is similar. To verify that a value is within the table we build `contains` from the `elements` iterator:

```
public boolean containsValue(Object value)
// pre: value is non-null Object
```

```
// post: returns true iff hash table contains value
{
    Iterator i = iterator();
    while (i.hasNext())
    {
        Object nextValue = i.next();
        // the value we seek?
        if (nextValue != null &&
            nextValue.equals(value)) return true; // yes!
    }
    // no value found
    return false;
}

public boolean containsKey(Object key)
// pre: key is a non-null Object
// post: returns true if key appears in hash table
{
    int hash = locate(key);
    return data[hash] != null && data[hash] != reserved;
}
```

The containsValue method is difficult to implement efficiently. This is one of the trade-offs of having a structure that is fast by most other measures.

To remove a value from the Hashtable, we locate the correct slot for the value and remove the association. In its place, we leave a reserved mark to maintain consistency in locate.

```
public Object remove(Object key)
// pre: key is non-null object
// post: removes key-value pair associated with key
{
    int hash = locate(key);
    Association a = data[hash];
    if (a == null || a == reserved) {
        return null;
    }
    count--;
    Object oldValue = a.getValue();
    data[hash] = reserved; // in case anyone depends on us
    return oldValue;
}
```

Hash tables are not made to be frequently traversed. Our approach is to construct sets of keys, values, and Associations that can be, themselves, traversed. Still, to support the Set construction, we build a single iterator (a HashtableIterator) that traverses the Hashtable and returns the Associations. Once constructed, the association-based iterator can be used to generate the key- and value-based iterators.

The protected iterator is similar to the `Vector` iterator. A current index points to the cell of the current non-`null` (and nonreserved) association. When the iterator is incremented, the underlying array is searched from the current point forward to find the next non-`null` entry. The iterator must eventually inspect every element of the structure, even if very few of the elements are currently used.[2]

Given an iterator that returns `Associations`, we can construct two different public filtering iterators, a `ValueIterator` and a `KeyIterator`. Each of these maintains a protected internal "slave" iterator and returns, as the iterator is incremented, values or keys associated with the respective elements. This design is much like the design of the `UniqueFilter` of Section 7.5. The following code, for example, implements the `ValueIterator`:

ValueIterator

```
class ValueIterator extends AbstractIterator
{
    protected Iterator slave;

    public ValueIterator(Iterator slave)
    // pre: slave is an iterator returning Association elements
    // post: creates a new iterator returning associated values
    {
        this.slave = slave;
    }

    public boolean hasNext()
    // post: returns true if current element is valid
    {
        return slave.hasNext();
    }

    public Object next()
    // pre: hasNext()
    // post: returns current value and increments iterator
    {
        Association pair = (Association)((AbstractIterator)slave).next();
        return pair.getValue();
    }
}
```

Once these iterators are defined, the `Set` and `Structure` returning methods are relatively easy to express. For example, to return a `Structure` that contains the values of the table, we simply construct a new `ValueIterator` that uses the `HashtableIterator` as a source for `Associations`:

Hashtable

```
public Structure values()
```

---

[2] The performance of this method could be improved by linking the contained associations together. This would, however, incur an overhead on the add and remove methods that may not be desirable.

```
// post: returns a Structure that contains the (possibly repeating)
// values of the range of this map.
{
    List result = new SinglyLinkedList();
    Iterator i = new ValueIterator(new HashtableIterator(data));
    while (i.hasNext())
    {
        result.add(i.next());
    }
    return result;
}
```

It might be useful to have direct access to iterators that return keys and values. If that choice is made, the `keys` method is similar but constructs a `KeyIterator` instead. While the `ValueIterator` and `KeyIterator` are protected, they may be accessed publicly when their identity has been removed by the `elements` and `keys` methods, respectively.

This is a form of identity laundering.

14.4.2 External Chaining

Open addressing is a satisfactory method for handling hashing of data, if one can be assured that the hash table will not get too full. When open addressing is used on nearly full tables, it becomes increasingly difficult to find an empty slot to store a new value.

One approach to avoiding the complexities of open addressing—reserved associations and table extension—is to handle collisions in a fundamentally different manner. *External chaining* solves the collision problem by inserting all elements that hash to the same bucket into a single collection of values. Typically, this collection is a singly linked list. The success of the hash table depends heavily on the fact that the average length of the linked lists (the *load factor* of the table) is small and the inserted objects are uniformly distributed. When the objects are uniformly distributed, the *deviation* in list size is kept small and no list is much longer than any other.

The process of locating the correct slot in an externally chained table involves simply computing the initial `hashCode` for the key and "modding" by the table size. Once the appropriate bucket is located, we verify that the collection is constructed and the value in the collection is updated. Because our `List` classes do not allow the retrieval of internal elements, we may have to remove and reinsert the appropriate association.

```
public Object put(Object key, Object value)
// pre: key is non-null object
// post: key-value pair is added to hash table
{
    List l = locate(key);
    Association newa = new Association(key,value);
    Association olda = (Association)l.remove(newa);
    l.addFirst(newa);
```

Chained-
HashTable

```
      if (olda != null)
      {
          return olda.getValue();
      }
      else
      {
          count++;
          return null;
      }
  }
```

Most of the other methods are implemented in a similar manner: they locate the appropriate bucket to get a `List`, they search for the association within the `List` to get the association, and then they manipulate the key or value of the appropriate association.

One method, `contains`, essentially requires the iteration over two dimensions of the hash table. One loop searches for non-`null` buckets in the hash table—buckets that contain associations in collections—and an internal loop that explicitly iterates across the `List` (the `containsKey` method can directly use the `contains` method provided with the collection). This is part of the price we must pay for being able to store arbitrarily large numbers of keys in each bucket of the hash table.

```
public boolean containsValue(Object value)
// pre: value is non-null Object
// post: returns true iff hash table contains value
{
    Iterator elements = iterator();

    while (elements.hasNext())
    {
        if (value.equals(elements.next())) return true;
    }
    return false;
}
```

At times the implementations appear unnecessarily burdened by the interfaces of the underlying data structure. For example, once we have found an appropriate `Association` to manipulate, it is difficult to modify the key. This is reasonable, though, since the value of the key is what helped us locate the bucket containing the association. If the key could be modified, we could insert a key that was inconsistent with its bucket's location.

Another subtle issue is the selection of the collection class associated with the bucket. Since linked lists have poor linear behavior for most operations, it might seem reasonable to use more efficient collection classes—for example, tree-based structures—for storing data with common hash codes. The graph of Figure 14.5 demonstrates the performance of various ordered structures when asked to construct collections of various sizes. It is clear that while `SplayTrees`

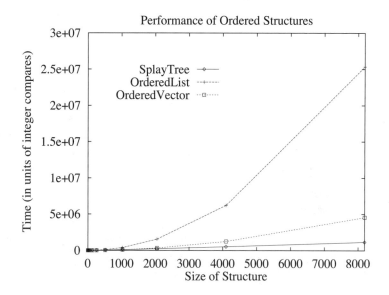

Figure 14.5 The time required to construct large ordered structures from random values.

provide better ultimate performance, the simple linear structures are more efficient when the structure size is in the range of expected use in chained hash tables (see Figure 14.6). When the average collection size gets much larger than this, it is better to increase the size of the hash table and re-insert each of the elements (this is accomplished with the `Hashtable` method, `extend`).

14.4.3 Generation of Hash Codes

Because any object might eventually be stored within a hash table, and because data abstraction hides the details of implementation, it is important for implementors to provide a `hashCode` method for their classes whenever possible.

Principle 24 *Provide a method for hashing the objects you implement.*

When a `hashCode` method *is* provided, it is vital that the method return the same `hashCode` for any pair of objects that are identified as the same under the `equals` method. If this is not the case, then values indexed by equivalent keys can be stored in distinct locations within the hash table. This can be confusing for the user and often incorrect.

Principle 25 *Equivalent objects should return equal hash codes.*

The generation of successful hash codes can be tricky. Consider, for example, the generation of hash codes for `String`s. Recall that the purpose of the hash

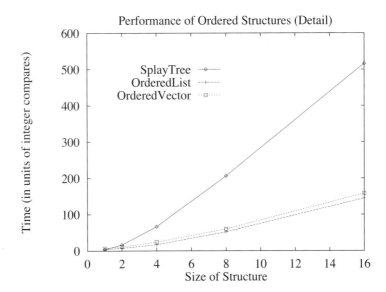

Figure 14.6   The time required to construct small ordered structures from random values.

code generation function is to distribute `String` values uniformly across the hash table.

Most of the approaches for hashing strings involve manipulations of the characters that make up the string. Fortunately, when a character is cast as an integer, the internal representation (often the ASCII encoding) is returned, usually an integer between 0 and 255. Our first approach, then, might be to use the first character of the string. This has rather obvious disadvantages: the first letters of strings are not uniformly distributed, and there isn't any way of generating hash codes greater than 255.

Our next approach would be to sum all the letters of the string. This is a simple method that generates large-magnitude hash codes if the strings are long. The main disadvantage of this technique is that if letters are transposed, then the strings generate the same hash values. For example, the string `"dab"` has $100 + 97 + 98 = 295$ as its sum of ASCII values, as does the string `"bad"`. The string `"bad"` and `"bbc"` are also equivalent under this hashing scheme. Figure 14.7 is a histogram of the number of words that hash, using this method, to each slot of a 997 element hash table. The periodic peaks demonstrate the fact that some slots of the table are heavily preferred over others. The performance of looking up and modifying values in the hash table will vary considerably, depending on the slot that is targeted by the hash function. Clearly, it would be useful to continue our search for a good mechanism.

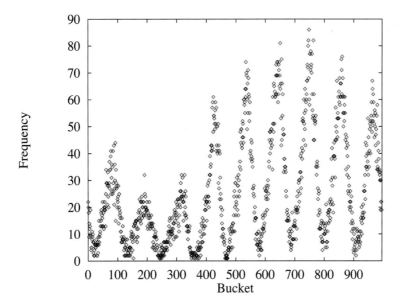

Figure 14.7 Numbers of words from the UNIX spelling dictionary hashing to each of the 997 buckets of a default hash table, if sum of characters is used to generate hash code.

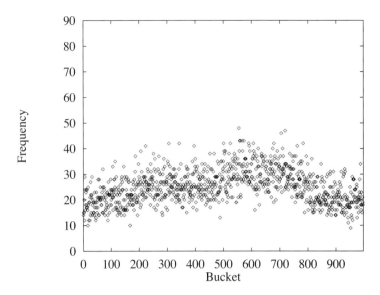

Figure 14.8   Frequency of dictionary words hashing to each of 997 buckets if characters are weighted by powers of 2 to generate hash code.

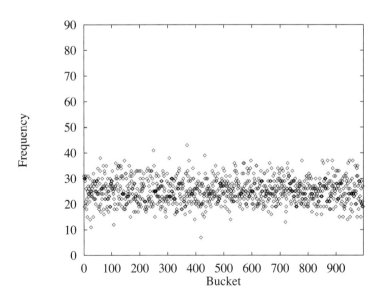

Figure 14.9   Frequency of words from dictionary hashing to each of 997 buckets if hash code is generated by weighting characters by powers of 256.

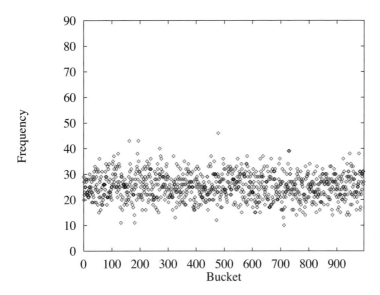

Figure 14.10 Frequency of words from dictionary hashing to each of 997 buckets, using the Java `String` hash code generation.

Another approach might be to weight each character of the string by its position. To ensure that even very short strings have the potential to generate large hash values, we can provide exponential weights: the hash code for an l character string, s, is

$$\sum_{i=0}^{l-1} s[i]c^i$$

where c is usually a small integer value. When c is 2, each character is weighted by a power of 2, and we get a distribution similar to that of Figure 14.8. While this is closer to being uniform, it is clear that even with exponential behavior, the value of $c = 2$ is too small: not many words hash to table elements with large indices. When $c = 256$, the hash code represents the first few characters of the string exactly (see Figure 14.9). Java currently hashes with $c = 31$.

The hashing mechanism used by Java `String`s in an early version of Java's development environment (see Figure 14.10) used a combination of weightings that provided a wide range of values for short strings and was efficient to compute for longer strings. Unfortunately, the constant-time algorithm was not suitable for distinguishing between long and nearly identical strings often found, say, in URLs.

Many of the data structures we have investigated are classes that contain multiple objects of unspecified type. When hashing entire container classes, it can be useful to compose the codes of the contained elements.

Method	Successful	Unsuccessful
Linear probes	$\frac{1}{2}\left(1 + \frac{1}{(1-\alpha)}\right)$	$\frac{1}{2}\left(1 + \frac{1}{(1-\alpha)^2}\right)$
Double hashing	$\frac{1}{\alpha}\log\frac{1}{(1-\alpha)}$	$\frac{1}{1-\alpha}$
External chaining	$1 + \frac{1}{2}\alpha$	$\alpha + e^\alpha$

Figure 14.11 Performance of hashing methods, as a function of α, the load factor. Formulas are for the number of association compares needed to locate the correct value or to demonstrate that the value cannot be found.

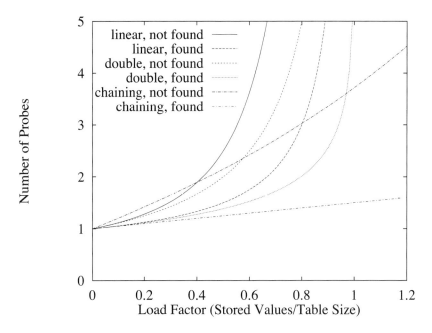

Figure 14.12 The shape of the performance curves for various hashing techniques. Our hash table implementation uses linear probing.

14.4.4 Hash Codes for Collection Classes

Each of the techniques used to generate hash codes from a composition of characters of `Strings` can be used to compose hash codes of objects in collection classes. The features of primary importance for the construction of hash codes are:

1. Whenever two structures are equal, using the `isEqual` methods, the `hashCode` method should return the same value.

2. For container structures—structures whose only purpose is to hold values—the state of the structure itself should be transparent; the state of the structure should not be included in the `hashCode`.

The first item was discussed before, but it is the most common error leading to difficulties with the use of `Hashtables`. When the `hashCodes` do not match for objects that are logically equal, the objects have a high probability of entering into different locations of the table. Accesses that should interact do not.

The second consideration is understood if we consider self-modifying structures like `SplayTrees` or `Hashtables` whose external state may be modeled by several distinct internal states. The construction of the hash code should consider those bits of information that enter into identifying equal structures. In the case of the `SplayTree`, for example, we might use the sum of the hash codes of the values that appear within the tree.

In general, the following first attempt at a `hashCode` method, taken from the `AbstractStructure` type, is reasonable:

```
public int hashCode()
// post: generate a hashcode for the structure: sum of
// all the hash codes of elements
{
    Iterator i = iterator();
    int result = 0;
    while (i.hasNext())
    {
        Object o = i.next();
        if (o != null) result += o.hashCode();
    }
    return result;
}
```

Abstract-
Structure

As we can see here, we must constantly be on the watch for values that may potentially be `null` references. For some structures, of course, such an approach may lead to intolerable amounts of time computing `hashCodes` for large structures.

One last point concerns the `hashCodes` associated with recursively defined structures. If the recursive structure is visible externally, that is, the structure could be referenced at several points, it may be suitable to define the `hashCode` to be the value contained within a single node of the structure. This certainly fulfills the primary obligation of a hashing function, but it also serves to separate the structure from the hash code. In our case, we choose to make a recursive definition, similar to the following definition found in `BinaryTree`:

BinaryTree

```
public int hashCode()
// post: return sum of hashcodes of the contained values
{
    if (isEmpty()) return 0;
    int result = left().hashCode() + right().hashCode();
    if (value() != null) result += value().hashCode();
    return result;
}
```

14.4.5 Performance Analysis

For open addressing, the load factor α obviously cannot exceed 1. As the load factor approaches 1, the performance of the table decreases dramatically. By counting the number of *probes* or association compares needed to find a value (a successful search) or to determine that the value is not among the elements of the map (an unsuccessful search), we can observe the relative performance of the various hashing techniques (see Figures 14.11 and 14.12). Notice that the number of probes necessary to find an appropriate key is a function of the load factor, and not directly of the number of keys found in the table.

When a hash table exceeds the threshold load factor, the entire table is forced to expand, and each of the keys is rehashed. Looking at the graph in Figure 14.12, we select our threshold load factor to be 60 percent, the point at which the performance of linear probing begins to degrade. When we expand the hash table, we make sure to at least double its size. For the same reasons that doubling is good when a `Vector` is extended, doubling the size of the hash table improves the performance of the hash table without significant overhead.

14.5   Ordered Maps and Tables

In fact, better hash functions probably avoid order!

A significant disadvantage of the `Map` interface is the fact that the values stored within the structure are not kept in any particular order. Often we wish to efficiently maintain an ordering among key-value pairs. The obvious solution is to construct a new `OrderedMap` that builds on the interface of the `Map`, but where methods may be allowed to assume parameters that are `Comparable`:

OrderedMap

```
public interface OrderedMap extends Map
{
}
```

When we do this, the methods of the `Map` are inherited. As a result, the types of the key-based methods manipulate `Object`s and not `Comparable`s. Because we desire to maintain order among comparable keys, we have a general precondition associated with the use of the data structure—that keys provided and returned are treated as `Comparable` objects.

Even with comparable keys, it is not easy to construct a `Hashtable` whose `keys` iterator returns the keys in order. The hash codes provided for `Comparable` objects are not required (and unlikely) to be ordered in a way consistent with the `compareTo` function. We therefore consider other `OrderedStructure`s to maintain the order among `ComparableAssociations`.

We will call our implementation of the `OrderedMap` a `Table`. As a basis for the implementation, we depend on the `SplayTree` class. `OrderedLists` and `OrderedVectors` could also provide suitable implementations for small applications. The `Table` maintains a single protected data item—the `SplayTree`. The constructor is responsible for allocating the `SplayTree`, leaving it initialized in its empty state:

```
protected OrderedStructure data;

public Table()
// post: constructs a new table
{
    data = new SplayTree();
}

public Table(Table other)
{
    data = new SplayTree();
    Iterator i = other.entrySet().iterator();
    while (i.hasNext())
    {
        java.util.Map.Entry o = (java.util.Map.Entry)i.next();
        put(o.getKey(),o.getValue());
    }
}
```

Table

When a key-value pair is to be put into the `Table`, a `ComparableAssociation` is constructed with the key-value pair, and it is used to look up any previous association using the same key. If the association is present, it is removed. In either case, the new association is inserted into the tree. While it seems indirect to remove the pair from the table to update it, it maintains the integrity of the `ComparableAssociation` and therefore the `SplayTree`. In addition, even though two `keys` may be logically equal, it is possible that they may be distinguishable. We insert the actual key-value pair demanded by the user, rather than perform a partial modification. Theoretically, removing and inserting a value into the `SplayTree` costs the same as finding and manipulating the value in place. Next, we see the method for `put` (`get` is similar):

```
public Object put(Object key, Object value)
// pre: key is non-null object
// post: key-value pair is added to table
{
    ComparableAssociation ca =
        new ComparableAssociation((Comparable)key,value);
    // fetch old key-value pair
    ComparableAssociation old =
        (ComparableAssociation)data.remove(ca);
    // insert new key-value pair
    data.add(ca);
    // return old value
    if (old == null) return null;
    else return old.getValue();
}
```

While most of the other methods follow directly from considering Hash-
tables and SplayTrees, the contains method—the method that returns true
exactly when a particular value is indexed by a key in the table—potentially requires a full traversal of the SplayTree. To accomplish this, we use an Iterator
returned by the SplayTree's elements methods. We then consider each association in turn, returning as soon as an appropriate value is found:

```
public boolean containsValue(Object value)
// pre: value is non-null object
// post: returns true iff value in table
{
    Iterator i = iterator();
    while (i.hasNext())
    {
        Object nextValue = i.next();
        if (nextValue != null &&
            nextValue.equals(value)) return true;
    }
    return false;
}
```

Next, our Table must provide an Iterator to be used in the construction
of the keySet and entrySet. The approach is similar to the Hashtable—
we construct a private Association-returning Iterator and then return its
KeyIterator or ValueIterator. Because every value returned from the Splay-
Tree's iterator is useful,[3] we need not implement a special-purpose iterator for
Tables; instead, we use the SplayTree's iterator directly. Since Comparable-
Associations extend Associations, the KeyIterator generates an Iterator
that returns the comparable keys as Objects to be cast later.

---

[3] Compare this with, perhaps, a Vector iterator that might be used to traverse a Vector-based
Hashtable.

```
public Set keySet()
{
    Set result = new SetList();
    Iterator i = new KeyIterator(data.iterator());
    while (i.hasNext())
    {
        result.add(i.next());
    }
    return result;
}

public Set entrySet()
{
    Set result = new SetList();
    Iterator i = data.iterator();
    while (i.hasNext())
    {
        result.add(i.next());
    }
    return result;
}
```

Previous hard work greatly simplifies this implementation! Since no hashing occurs, it is not necessary for any of the `keys` of a `Table` to implement the `hashCode` method. They must, though, implement the `compareTo` method since they are `Comparable`. Thus, each of the methods runs in amortized logarithmic time, instead of the near-constant time we get from hashing.

Exercise 14.2 *Modify the* `Table` *structure to make use of* `RedBlackTree`*s, instead of* `SplayTree`*s.*

Exercise 14.3 *It is common to allow ordered structures, like* `OrderedMap`*, to use a* `Comparator` *to provide an alternative ordering. Describe how this approach might be implemented.*

14.6   Example: Document Indexing

Indexing is an important task, especially for search engines that automatically index keywords from documents retrieved from the Web. Here we present the skeleton of a document indexing scheme that makes use of a `Map` to keep track of the vocabulary.

Given a document, we would like to generate a list of words, each followed by a list of lines on which the words appear. For example, when provided Gandhi's seven social sins:

```
politics without principle
pleasure without conscience
  wealth without work
```

```
knowledge without character
 business without morality
  science without humanity
             and
   worship without sacrifice
```

(It is interesting to note that `programming without comments` is not among these!) The indexing program should generate the following output:

```
and: 7
business: 5
character: 4
conscience: 2
humanity: 6
knowledge: 4
morality: 5
pleasure: 2
politics: 1
principle: 1
sacrifice: 8
science: 6
wealth: 3
without: 1 2 3 4 5 6 8
work: 3
worship: 8
```

In this program we make use of Java's `StreamTokenizer` class. This class takes a stream of data and converts it into a stream of tokens, some of which are identified as words. The process for constructing this stream is a bit difficult, so we highlight it here.

Index

```java
public static void main(String args[])
{
    try {
        InputStreamReader isr = new InputStreamReader(System.in);
        java.io.Reader r = new BufferedReader(isr);
        StreamTokenizer s = new StreamTokenizer(r);
            ...
    } catch (java.io.IOException e) {
        Assert.fail("Got an I/O exception.");
    }
}
```

Each of the objects constructed here provides an additional layer of filtering on the base stream, `System.in`. The body of the main method is encompassed by the `try` statement in this code. The `try` statement catches errors generated by the `StreamTokenizer` and rewraps the exception as an assertion failure.

We begin by associating with each word of the input an initially empty list of line numbers. It seems reasonable, then, to use the vocabulary word as a key and the list of lines as the value. Our `Map` provides an ideal mechanism to maintain the data. The core of the program consists of reading word tokens from the stream and entering them into the `Map`:

```
// allocate the symbol table (uses comparable keys)
Map t = new Table();
int token;
// we'll not consider period as part of identifier
s.ordinaryChar('.');
// read in all the tokens from file
for (token = s.nextToken();
     token != StreamTokenizer.TT_EOF;
     token = s.nextToken())
{
    // only tokens we care about are whole words
    if (token == StreamTokenizer.TT_WORD)
    {
        // get wrapper for integer
        Integer line = new Integer(s.lineno());
        // each set of lines is maintained in a List
        List l;

        // look up symbol
        if (t.containsKey(s.sval))
        {   // symbol is there, get line # list
            l = (List)t.get(s.sval);
            l.addLast(line);
        } else {
            // not found, create new list
            l = new DoublyLinkedList();
            l.addLast(line);
            t.put(s.sval,l);
        }
    }
}
```

Here, we use a `Table` as our `Map` because it is important that the entries be sorted alphabetically. As the tokens are read from the input stream, they are looked up in the `Map`. Since the `Map` accepts comparable keys, it is important to use a (comparable) `String` to allow the words to index the structure. If the key is within the `Map`, the value associated with the key (a list) is updated by appending the current line number (provided by the stream's `lineno` method) to the end of the list. If the word is not found, a new list is allocated with the current line appended, and the fresh word–list pair is inserted into the table.

The next section of the program is responsible for generating the output:

```
// printing table involves tandem key-value iterators
Iterator ti = t.keySet().iterator();
Iterator ki = t.values().iterator();
```

```
while (ti.hasNext())
{
    // print symbol
    System.out.print(ti.next()+": ");
    // print out (and consume) each line number
    List l = (List)ki.next();
    while (!l.isEmpty())
    {
        System.out.print(l.removeFirst()+" ");
    }
    System.out.println();
    // increment iterators
}
```

Here, two iterators—one for keys and one for values—are constructed for the Map and are incremented in parallel. As each word is encountered, it is printed out along with the list of line numbers, generated by traversing the list with an iterator.

Because we used a Table as the underlying structure, the words are kept and printed in sorted order. If we had elected to use a Hashtable instead, the output would appear shuffled. The order is neither alphabetical nor the order in which the words are encountered. It is the result of the particular hash function we chose to locate the data.

14.7   Conclusions

In this chapter we have investigated two structures that allow us to access values using a key or index from an arbitrary domain. When the keys can be uniformly distributed across a wide range of values, hashing is an excellent technique for providing constant-time access to values within the structure. The cost is extra time necessary to hash the value, as well as the extra space needed to keep the load factor small enough to provide the expected performance.

When the keys are comparable, and order is to be preserved, we must depend on logarithmic behavior from ordered structures we have seen before. In our implementation of Tables, the SplayTree was used, although any other OrderedStructure could be used instead.

Because of the nonintuitive nature of hashing and hash tables, one of the more difficult tasks for the programmer is to generate useful, effective hash code values. Hash functions should be designed specifically for each new class. They should be fast and deterministic and have wide ranges of values. While all Objects inherit a hashCode function, it is important to update the hashCode method whenever the equals method is changed; failure to do so leads to subtle problems with these useful structures.

Self Check Problems

Solutions to these problems begin on page 436.

14.1 What access feature distingishes `Map` structures from other structrues we have seen?

14.2 What is the load factor of a hash table?

14.3 In a hash table is it possible to have a load factor of 2?

14.4 Is a constant-time performance guaranteed for hash tables?

14.5 What is a hash collision?

14.6 What are the qualities we seek in a hash function?

14.7 Under what condition is a `MapList` preferable to a `Hashtable`?

14.8 Many of our more complex data structures have provided the under-pinnings for efficient sorts. Is that the case for the `Hashtable`? Does the `Table` facilitate sorting?

Problems

Solutions to the odd-numbered problems begin on page 469.

14.1 Is it possible for a hash table to have two entries with equal keys?

14.2 Is it possible for a hash table to have two entries with equal values?

14.3 Suppose you have a hash table with seven entries (indexed 0 through 6). This table uses open addressing with the hash function that maps each letter to its alphabet code ($a = A = 0$, etc.) modulo 7. Rehashing is accomplished using linear-probing with a jump of 1. Describe the state of the table after each of the letters D, a, d, H, a, and h are added to the table.

14.4 Suppose you have a hash table with eight entries (indexed 0 through 7). The hash mechanism is the same as for Problem 14.3 (alphabet code modulo 7), but with a linear probe jump of 2. Describe what happens when one attempts to add each of the letters A, g, g, a, and g, in that order. How might you improve the hashing mechanism?

14.5 When using linear probing with a rehashing jump size of greater than 1, why is it necessary to have the hash table size and jump size be relatively prime?

14.6 Design a `hashCode` method for a class that represents a telephone number.

14.7 Design a `hashCode` method for a class that represents a real number.

14.8 Suppose two identifiers—`Strings` composed of letters—were considered equal even if their cases were different. For example, `AGEdwards` would be equal to `AgedWards`. How would you construct a hash function for strings that was "case insensitive"?

14.9   When 23 randomly selected people are brought together, chances are greater than 50 percent that two have the same birthday. What does this tell us about uniformly distributed hash codes for keys in a hash table?

14.10   Write a `hashCode` method for an `Association`.

14.11   Write a `hashCode` method for a `Vector`. It should only depend on hash codes of the `Vector`'s elements.

14.12   Write a `hashCode` method for a `BinaryTree`. Use recursion.

14.13   Write a `hashCode` method for a `Hashtable`. (For some reason, you'll be hashing hash tables into other hash tables!) Must the hashing mechanism look at the value of *every* element?

14.14   The Java hash function for `String`s computes a hash code based on a fixed maximum number of characters of the string. Given that `String`s have no meaningful upper bound in length, describe how an effective, constant-time hashing algorithm can be constructed. (Hint: If you were to pick, say, eight characters to represent a string of length l, which would you choose?)

14.15   Since URLs differ mostly toward their end (at high indices), write code that efficiently computes a hash code based on characters $l - x_i$ where $x_i = 2^i$ and $i = 0, 1, 2, \ldots$ How fast does this algorithm run? Is it better able to distinguish different URLs?

14.16   A hash table with *ordered linear probing* maintains an order among keys considered during the rehashing process. When the keys are encountered, say, in increasing order, the performance of a failed lookup approaches that of a successful search. Describe how a key might be inserted into the ordered sequence of values that compete for the same initial table entry.

14.17   Isn't the hash table resulting from Problem 14.16 just an ordered `Vector`? (Hint: No.) Why?

14.18   If we were to improve the iterators for `Map`s, we might add an iterator that returned key-value pairs. Is this an improvement in the interface?

14.19   Design a hash function for representing the state of a checkerboard.

14.20   Design a hash function for representing the state of a tic-tac-toe board. (It would—for strategy reasons—be useful to have mirror images of a board be considered equal.)

14.21   One means of potentially reducing the complexity of computing the hash code for `String`s is to compute it once—when the `String` is constructed. Future calls to `hashCode` would return the precomputed value. Since the value of a `String` never changes, this has potential promise. How would you evaluate the success of such a method?

14.22   Explain how a `Map` might be useful in designing a spelling checker. (Would it be useful to have the words `bible` and `babble` stored near each other?)

14.8 Laboratory: The Soundex Name Lookup System

Objective. To use a `Map` structure to keep track of similar sounding names.

Discussion. The United States National Archives is responsible for keeping track of the census records that, according to the Constitution, must be gathered every 10 years. After a significant amount of time has passed (70 or more years), the census records are made public. Such records are of considerable historical interest and a great many researchers spend time looking for lost ancestors among these records.

To help researchers find individuals, the censuses are often indexed using a phonetic system called *Soundex*. This system takes a name and produces a short string called the Soundex key. The rules for producing the Soundex key of a name are precisely:

1. The entire name is translated into a series of digit characters:

Digit	Letter of name
'1'	b, p, f, v
'2'	c, s, k, g, j, q, x, z
'3'	d, t
'4'	l
'5'	m, n
'6'	r
'7'	*all other letters*

   For example, `O'Niell` would be translated into the string 757744.

2. All double digits are reduced to single digits. Thus, 757744 would become 7574.

3. The first digit is replaced with the first letter of the original name, in uppercase. Thus, 7574 would become 0574.

4. All 7's are removed. Thus, 0574 becomes 054.

5. The string is truncated to four characters. If the resulting string is shorter than four characters, it is packed with enough '0' characters to bring the length to four. The result for `O'Niell` would be 0540. Notice that, for the most part, the nonzero characters represent the significant sounded letters of the beginning of the name.

Other names translate to Soundex keys as follows:

Bailey	becomes	B400
Ballie	becomes	B400
Knuth	becomes	K530
Scharstein	becomes	S623
Lee	becomes	L000

Procedure. You are to write a system that takes a list of names (the UNIX spelling dictionary is a good place to find names) and generates an ordered map whose entries are indexed by the Soundex key. The values are the actual names that generated the key. The input to the program is a series of names, and the output is the Soundex key associated with the name, along with all the names that have that same Soundex key, in alphabetical order.

Pick a data structure that provides performance: the response to the query should be nearly instantaneous, even with a map of several thousand names.

Thought Questions. Consider the following questions as you complete the lab:

1. What is the Soundex system attempting to do when it encodes many letters into one digit? For example, why are 'd' and 't' both encoded as '3'?

2. Why does the Soundex system ignore any more than the first four sounds in a name?

Notes:

Chapter 15

Graphs

...314159...
—π (digits 176452–176457)

RELATIONS ARE OFTEN AS USEFUL AS DATA. The process of building and accessing a data structure can be thought of as a means of effectively focusing the computation. Linear structures record the history of their accesses, ordered structures perform incremental sorting, and binary trees encode decisions about the partitioning of collections of data.

The most general mechanism for encoding relations between data is the *graph*. Simple structures, like arrays, provide implicit connections, such as adjacency, between stored values. Graphs are more demanding to construct but, as a result, they can encode more detailed information. Indeed, the versatility of graphs allows them to represent many of the most difficult theoretical problems of computer science.

This chapter investigates two traditional implementations of graphs, as well as several standard algorithms for analyzing their structure. We first agree on some basic terminology.

15.1 Terminology

A *graph* G consists of a collection of *vertices* $v \in V_G$ and relations or *edges* $(u, v) \in E_G$ between them (see Figure 15.1). An edge is *incident to* (or *mentions*) each of its two component vertices. A graph is *undirected* if each of its edges is considered a set of two unordered vertices, and *directed* if the mentioned vertices are ordered (e.g., referred to as the *source* and *destination*). A graph S is a *subgraph* of G if and only if $V_S \subseteq V_G$ and $E_S \subseteq E_G$. Simple examples of graphs include the *list* and the *tree*.

In an undirected graph, the number of edges (u, v) incident to a vertex u is its *degree*. In a directed graph, the outgoing edges determine its *out-degree* (or just *degree*) and incoming edges its *in-degree*. A *source* is a vertex with no incoming edges, while a *sink* is a vertex with no outgoing edges.

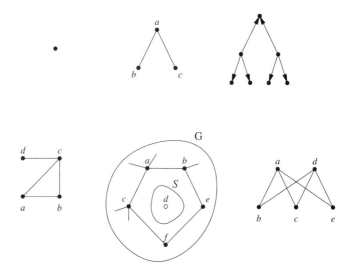

Figure 15.1   Some graphs. Each node a is adjacent to node b, but never to d. Graph G has two components, one of which is S. The directed tree-shaped graph is a directed, acyclic graph. Only the top left graph is complete.

Two edges (u, v) and (v, w) are said to be *adjacent*. A *path* is a sequence of n distinct, adjacent edges $(v_0, v_1), (v_1, v_2), \ldots, (v_{n-1}, v_n)$. In a *simple path* the vertices are distinct, except for, perhaps, the *end points* v_0 and v_n. When $v_0 = v_n$, the simple path is a *cycle*.

Two vertices u and v are *connected* (written $u \rightsquigarrow v$) if and only if a simple path of the graph mentions u and v as its end points. A subgraph S is a *Components* *connected component* (or, often, just a *component*) if and only if S is a largest *are always* subgraph of G such that for every pair of vertices $u, v \in V_S$ either $u \rightsquigarrow v$ or *connected.* $v \rightsquigarrow u$. A connected component of a directed graph G is *strongly connected* if $u \rightsquigarrow v$ and $v \rightsquigarrow u$ for all pairs of vertices $u, v \in V_S$.

A graph containing no cycles is *acyclic*. A directed, acyclic graph (*DAG*) plays an important role in solving many problems. A *complete graph* G contains an edge (u, v) for all vertices $u, v \in V_G$.

15.2   The Graph Interface

Graph

Vertices of a graph are usually labeled with application-specific information. As a result, our implementations of a graph structure depend on the user specifying unique labels for vertices. In addition, edges may be labeled, but not necessarily uniquely. It is common, for example, to specify weights or lengths for edges. All the graph implementations allow addition and removal of vertices and edges:

```
public interface Graph extends Structure
{
    public void add(Object label);
    // pre: label is a non-null label for vertex
    // post: a vertex with label is added to graph
    //        if vertex with label is already in graph, no action

    public void addEdge(Object vtx1, Object vtx2, Object label);
    // pre: vtx1 and vtx2 are labels of existing vertices
    // post: an edge (possibly directed) is inserted between
    //        vtx1 and vtx2.

    public Object remove(Object label);
    // pre: label is non-null vertex label
    // post: vertex with "equals" label is removed, if found

    public Object removeEdge(Object vLabel1, Object vLabel2);
    // pre: vLabel1 and vLabel2 are labels of existing vertices
    // post: edge is removed, its label is returned

    public Object get(Object label);
    // post: returns actual label of indicated vertex

    public Edge getEdge(Object label1, Object label2);
    // post: returns actual edge between vertices

    public boolean contains(Object label);
    // post: returns true iff vertex with "equals" label exists

    public boolean containsEdge(Object vLabel1, Object vLabel2);
    // post: returns true iff edge with "equals" label exists

    public boolean visit(Object label);
    // post: sets visited flag on vertex, returns previous value

    public boolean visitEdge(Edge e);
    // pre: sets visited flag on edge; returns previous value

    public boolean isVisited(Object label);
    // post: returns visited flag on labeled vertex

    public boolean isVisitedEdge(Edge e);
    // post: returns visited flag on edge between vertices

    public void reset();
    // post: resets visited flags to false

    public int size();
    // post: returns the number of vertices in graph
```

```
        public int degree(Object label);
        // pre: label labels an existing vertex
        // post: returns the number of vertices adjacent to vertex

        public int edgeCount();
        // post: returns the number of edges in graph

        public Iterator iterator();
        // post: returns iterator across all vertices of graph

        public Iterator neighbors(Object label);
        // pre: label is label of vertex in graph
        // post: returns iterator over vertices adj. to vertex
        //       each edge beginning at label visited exactly once

        public Iterator edges();
        // post: returns iterator across edges of graph
        //       iterator returns edges; each edge visited once

        public void clear();
        // post: removes all vertices from graph

        public boolean isEmpty();
        // post: returns true if graph contains no vertices

        public boolean isDirected();
        // post: returns true if edges of graph are directed
    }
```

Because edges can be fully identified by their constituent vertices, edge operations sometimes require pairs of vertex labels. Since it is useful to implement both directed and undirected graphs, we can determine the type of a specific graph using the isDirected method. In undirected graphs, the addition of an edge effectively adds a directed edge in both directions. Many algorithms keep track of their progress by visiting vertices and edges. This is so common that it seems useful to provide direct support for adding (visit), checking (isVisited), and removing (reset) marks on vertices and edges.

Two iterators—generated by iterator and edges—traverse the vertices and edges of a graph, respectively. A special iterator—generated by neighbors—traverses the vertices adjacent to a given vertex. From this information, outbound edges can be determined.

Before we discuss particular implementations of graphs, we consider the abstraction of vertices and edges. From the user's point of view a vertex is a label. Abstractly, an edge is an association of two vertices and an edge label. In addition, we must keep track of objects that have been visited. These features of vertices and edges are independent of the implementation of graphs; thus we commit to an interface for these objects early. Let's consider the Vertex class.

```
class Vertex
{
    public Vertex(Object label)
    // post: constructs unvisited vertex with label

    public Object label()
    // post: returns user label associated w/vertex

    public boolean visit()
    // post: returns, then marks vertex as being visited

    public boolean isVisited()
    // post: returns true iff vertex has been visited

    public void reset()
    // post: marks vertex unvisited

    public boolean equals(Object o)
    // post: returns true iff vertex labels are equal
}
```

Vertex

This class is similar to an Association: the label portion of the Vertex cannot be modified, but the visited flag can be freely set and reset. Two Vertex objects are considered equal if their labels are equal. It is a bare-bones interface. It should also be noted that the Vertex is a nonpublic class. Since a Vertex is not visible through the Graph interface, there is no reason for the user to have access to the Vertex class.

Because the Edge class is visible "through" the Graph interface (you might ask why—see Problem 15.8), the Edge class is declared public:

```
public class Edge
{
    public Edge(Object vtx1, Object vtx2, Object label,
                boolean directed)
    // post: edge associates vtx1 and vtx2; labeled with label
    //       directed if "directed" set true

    public Object here()
    // post: returns first node in edge

    public Object there()
    // post: returns second node in edge

    public void setLabel(Object label)
    // post: sets label of this edge to label

    public Object label()
    // post: returns label associated with this edge

    public boolean visit()
```

Edge

```
                   // post: visits edge, returns whether previously visited

                   public boolean isVisited()
                   // post: returns true iff edge has been visited

                   public boolean isDirected()
                   // post: returns true iff edge is directed

                   public void reset()
                   // post: resets edge's visited flag to initial state

                   public boolean equals(Object o)
                   // post: returns true iff edges connect same vertices
              }
```

As with the `Vertex` class, the `Edge` can be constructed, visited, and reset. Unlike its `Vertex` counterparts, an `Edge`'s label may be changed. The methods `here` and `there` provide access to labels of the vertices mentioned by the edge. These method names are sufficiently ambiguous to be easily used with undirected edges and convey a slight impression of direction for directed edges. Naming of these methods is important because they are used by those who wish to get vertex information while traversing a (potentially directed) graph.

15.3   Implementations

As "traditional" as this science gets, anyway!

Now that we have a good feeling for the graph interface, we consider traditional implementations. Nearly every implementation of a graph has characteristics of one of these two approaches. Our approach to specifying these implementations, however, will be dramatically impacted by the availability of object-oriented features. We first discuss the concept of a partially specified *abstract class* in Java.

15.3.1   Abstract Classes Reemphasized

Normally, when a class is declared, code for each of the methods must be provided. Then, when an instance of the class is constructed, each of the methods can be applied to the resulting object. As is common with our design approach, however, it is useful to partially implement a class and later finish the implementation by *extending* the class in a particular direction. The partial base class is *abstract*; it cannot be constructed because some of the methods are not completely defined. The extension to the class *inherits* the methods that have been defined and specifies any incomplete code to make the class *concrete*.

Again, we use abstract classes in our design of various graph implementations. Each implementation will be declared abstract, with the `abstract` keyword:

GraphMatrix   `abstract public class GraphMatrix extends AbstractStructure implements Graph`

Our approach will be to provide all the code that can be written without considering whether the graph is undirected or directed. When we must write code that is dependent on the "directedness" of the graph, we delay it by writing just an abstract header for the particular method. For example, we will need to add edges to our graph, but the implementation depends on whether or not the graph is directed. Looking ahead, here is what the declaration for addEdge looks like in the abstract class GraphMatrix:

```
abstract public void addEdge(Object v1, Object v2, Object label);
// pre: vtx1 and vtx2 are labels of existing vertices
// post: an edge (possibly directed) is inserted between
//       vtx1 and vtx2.
```

That's it! It is simply a *promise* that code will eventually be written.

Once the abstract class is described as fully as possible, we extend it, committing the graph to being undirected or directed. The directed version of the Graph implementation, called GraphMatrixDirected, specifies the addEdge method as follows:

```
public class GraphMatrixDirected extends GraphMatrix
{
    public void addEdge(Object vLabel1, Object vLabel2, Object label)
    // pre: vLabel1 and vLabel2 are labels of existing vertices
    // post: an edge is inserted between vLabel1 and vLabel2;
    //       if edge is new, it is labeled with label (can be null)
    {
        GraphMatrixVertex vtx1,vtx2;
    }
}
```

GraphMatrix-
Directed

Because we declare the class GraphMatrixDirected to be an extension of the GraphMatrix class, all the code written for the GraphMatrix class is inherited; it is as though it had been written for the GraphMatrixDirected class. By providing the missing pieces of code (tailored for directed graphs), the extension class becomes concrete. We can actually construct instances of the GraphMatrixDirected class.

A related concept, *subtyping*, allows us to use any extension of a class wherever the extended class could be used. We call the class that was extended the *base type* or *superclass*, and the extension the *subtype* or *subclass*. Use of subtyping allows us to write code like

```
GraphMatrix g = new GraphMatrixDirected();

g.add("Alice");
g.add("Bob");
g.addEdge("Alice","Bob","helps"); // "Alice helps Bob!"
```

Because GraphMatrixDirected is an extension of GraphMatrix, it *is* a Graph-Matrix. Even though we cannot construct a GraphMatrix, we can correctly

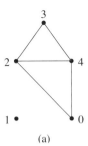
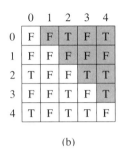

(a)   (b)

Figure 15.2 (a) An undirected graph and (b) its adjacency matrix representation. Each nontrivial edge is represented twice across the diagonal—once in the gray and once in the white—making the matrix symmetric.

manipulate concrete subtypes using the methods described in the abstract class. In particular, a call to the method `addEdge` calls the method of `GraphMatrix-Directed`.

We now return to our normally scheduled implementations!

15.3.2 Adjacency Matrices

An $n \times n$ matrix of booleans is sufficient to represent an arbitrary graph of relations among n vertices. We simply store `true` in the boolean at matrix location $[u][v]$ to represent the fact that there is an edge between u and v (see Figure 15.2), and `false` otherwise. Since entries $[u][v]$ and $[v][u]$ are independent, the representation is sufficient to describe directed graphs as well. Our convention is that the first index (the row) specifies the source and the second index (the column) indicates the destination. To represent undirected graphs, we simply duplicate the entry $[u][v]$ at entry $[v][u]$. This is called an *adjacency matrix* representation of a graph. The abstract graphs of Figures 15.2a and 15.3a are represented, respectively, by the matrices of Figures 15.2b and 15.3b.

Beware: Edges on the diagonal appear exactly once.

One difficult feature of our implementation is the arbitrary labeling of vertices and edges. To facilitate this, we maintain a `Dictionary` that translates a vertex label to a `Vertex` object. To help each vertex keep track of its associated index we extend the `Vertex` class to include methods that manipulate an `index` field. Each index is a small integer that identifies the dedicated row and column that maintain adjacency information about each vertex. To help allocate the indices, we keep a free list (see Section 8.2) of available indices.

One feature of our implementation has the potential to catch the unwary programmer by surprise. Because we keep a `Map` of vertex labels, it is important that the vertex label class implement the `hashCode` function in such a way as to guarantee that if two labels are equal (using the `equals` method), they have the same `hashCode`.

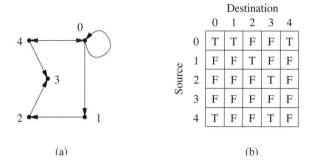

		Destination				
		0	1	2	3	4
Source	0	T	T	F	F	T
	1	F	F	T	F	F
	2	F	F	F	T	F
	3	F	F	F	F	F
	4	T	F	F	T	F

(a) (b)

Figure 15.3 (a) A directed graph and (b) its adjacency matrix representation. Each edge appears exactly once in the matrix.

We can now consider the protected data and constructors for the `GraphMatrix` class:

```
protected int size;        // allocation size for graph
protected Edge data[][];   // matrix - array of arrays
protected Map dict;   // translates labels->vertices
protected List freeList;   // available indices in matrix
protected boolean directed; // graph is directed


protected GraphMatrix(int size, boolean dir)
{
    this.size = size; // set maximum size
    directed = dir;   // fix direction of edges
    // the following constructs a size x size matrix
    data = new Edge[size][size];
    // label to index translation table
    dict = new Hashtable(size);
    // put all indices in the free list
    freeList = new SinglyLinkedList();
    for (int row = size-1; row >= 0; row--)
        freeList.add(new Integer(row));
}
```

GraphMatrix

To construct the graph, the user specifies an upper bound on the number of vertices. We allocate `size` arrays of length `size`—a two-dimensional array. By default, the array elements are `null`, so initially there are no edges. We then put each of the indices into the list of available vertex indices.

This constructor is declared protected. It takes a second parameter, `directed`, that identifies whether or not the graph constructed is to act like a directed graph. When we extend the graph to implement either directed or undirected graphs, we write a public constructor to call the abstract protected class's constructor with an appropriate boolean value:

GraphMatrix-
Directed

```
public GraphMatrixDirected(int size)
// pre: size > 0
// post: constructs an empty graph that may be expanded to
//       at most size vertices.  Graph is directed if dir true
//       and undirected otherwise
{
    super(size,true);
}
```

As we discussed before, this technique allows the implementor to selectively inherit the code that is common between directed and undirected graphs. Since we hide the implementation, we are free to reimplement either type of graph without telling our users, perhaps allowing us to optimize our code.

Returning to the `GraphMatrix` class, the `add` method adds a labeled vertex. If the vertex already exists, the operation does nothing. If it is new to the graph, an index is allocated from the free list, a new `Vertex` object is constructed, and the label-vertex association is recorded in the `Map`. The newly added vertex mentions no edges, initially.

GraphMatrix

```
public void add(Object label)
// pre: label is a non-null label for vertex
// post: a vertex with label is added to graph;
//        if vertex with label is already in graph, no action
{
    // if there already, do nothing
    if (dict.containsKey(label)) return;

    Assert.pre(!freeList.isEmpty(), "Matrix not full");
    // allocate a free row and column
    int row = ((Integer) freeList.removeFirst()).intValue();
    // add vertex to dictionary
    dict.put(label, new GraphMatrixVertex(label, row));
}
```

Removing a vertex reverses the `add` process. We must, however, be sure to set each element of the vertex's matrix row and column to `null`, removing any mentioned edges (we may wish to add a new, isolated vertex with this index in the future). When we remove the vertex from the `Map`, we "recycle" its index by adding it to the list of free indices. As with all of our `remove` methods, we return the previous value of the label. (Even though the labels match using `equals`, they may not be precisely the same; once returned the user can extract any unknown information from the previous label before the value is collected as garbage.)

```
public Object remove(Object label)
// pre: label is non-null vertex label
// post: vertex with "equals" label is removed, if found
{
    // find and extract vertex
```

```
        GraphMatrixVertex vert;
        vert = (GraphMatrixVertex)dict.remove(label);
        if (vert == null) return null;
        // remove vertex from matrix
        int index = vert.index();
        // clear row and column entries
        for (int row=0; row<size; row++) {
            data[row][index] = null;
            data[index][row] = null;
        }
        // add node index to free list
        freeList.add(new Integer(index));
        return vert.label();
    }
```

Within the graph we store references to Edge objects. Each Edge records all of the information necessary to position it within the graph, including whether it is directed or not. This allows the equals method to work on undirected edges, even if the vertices were provided in the opposite order (see Problem 15.12). To add an edge to the graph, we require two vertex labels and an edge label. The vertex labels uniquely identify the vertices within the graph, and the edge label is used to form the value inserted within the matrix at the appropriate row and column. To add the edge, we construct a new Edge with the appropriate information. This object is written to appropriate matrix entries: undirected graphs update one or two locations; directed graphs update just one. Here is the addEdge method for undirected graphs:

```
    public void addEdge(Object vLabel1, Object vLabel2, Object label)
    // pre: vLabel1 and vLabel2 are labels of existing vertices, v1 & v2
    // post: an edge (undirected) is inserted between v1 and v2;
    //       if edge is new, it is labeled with label (can be null)
    {
        GraphMatrixVertex vtx1,vtx2;
        // get vertices
        vtx1 = (GraphMatrixVertex) dict.get(vLabel1);
        vtx2 = (GraphMatrixVertex) dict.get(vLabel2);
        // update matrix with new edge
        Edge e = new Edge(vtx1.label(), vtx2.label(), label, false);
        data[vtx1.index()][vtx2.index()] = e;
        data[vtx2.index()][vtx1.index()] = e;
    }
```

GraphMatrix-
Undirected

Here is a similar method for directed graphs:

```
    public void addEdge(Object vLabel1, Object vLabel2, Object label)
    // pre: vLabel1 and vLabel2 are labels of existing vertices
    // post: an edge is inserted between vLabel1 and vLabel2;
    //       if edge is new, it is labeled with label (can be null)
    {
```

GraphMatrix-
Directed

```
                    GraphMatrixVertex vtx1,vtx2;
                    // get vertices
                    vtx1 = (GraphMatrixVertex) dict.get(vLabel1);
                    vtx2 = (GraphMatrixVertex) dict.get(vLabel2);
                    // update matrix with new edge
                    Edge e = new Edge(vtx1.label(), vtx2.label(), label, true);
                    data[vtx1.index()][vtx2.index()] = e;
                }
```

The differences are quite minor, but the two different subtypes allow us to write specialized code without performing explicit run-time tests.[1]

The `removeEdge` method removes and returns the label associated with the `Edge` found between two vertices. Here is the undirected version (the directed version is similar):

GraphMatrix-
Undirected

```
public Object removeEdge(Object vLabel1, Object vLabel2)
// pre: vLabel1 and vLabel2 are labels of existing vertices
// post: edge is removed, its label is returned
{
    // get indices
    int row = ((GraphMatrixVertex)dict.get(vLabel1)).index();
    int col = ((GraphMatrixVertex)dict.get(vLabel2)).index();
    // cache old value
    Edge e = data[row][col];
    // update matrix
    data[row][col] = null;
    data[col][row] = null;
    if (e == null) return null;
    else return e.label();
}
```

The `get`, `getEdge`, `contains`, and `containsEdge` methods return information about the graph in an obvious way. Modifying the objects returned by these methods can be dangerous: they have the potential of invalidating the state of the underlying graph implementation.

Each of the `visit`-type methods passes on requests to the underlying object. For example, the `visit` method simply refers the request to the associated `Vertex`:

GraphMatrix

```
public boolean visit(Object label)
// post: sets visited flag on vertex, returns previous value
{
    Vertex vert = (Vertex) dict.get(label);
    return vert.visit();
}
```

---

[1] This is somewhat misleading, as the obvious run-time tests are replaced by less obvious decreases in performance due to subtyping. Still, the logical complexity of the code can be dramatically reduced using these techniques.

The process of resetting the visitation marks on a graph traverses each of the vertices and edges, resetting them along the way.

We now consider the implementation of each of the three iterators. The first, generated by `iterator`, traverses the vertices. The values returned by the `Iterator` are vertex labels. This `Iterator` is easily constructed by returning the value of the `Map`'s `keys` function! *But I reiterate myself.*

```
public Iterator iterator()
// post: returns traversal across all vertices of graph
{
    return dict.keySet().iterator();
}
```

The `neighbors` iterator, which traverses the edges adjacent to a single vertex, considers only the outgoing edges. We simply look up the index associated with the vertex label and scan across the row, building up a list of vertex labels that are adjacent using each of the edges. By putting these values in a list, we can return a `ListIterator` that will give us iterative access to each of the adjacent vertex labels. With this information we may retrieve the respective edges with `getEdge` if necessary.

```
public Iterator neighbors(Object label)
// pre: label is label of vertex in graph
// post: returns traversal over vertices adj. to vertex
//       each edge beginning at label visited exactly once
{
    GraphMatrixVertex vert;
    vert = (GraphMatrixVertex) dict.get(label);
    List list = new SinglyLinkedList();
    for (int row=size-1; row>=0; row--)
    {
        Edge e = data[vert.index()][row];
        if (e != null) {
            if (e.here().equals(vert.label()))
                list.add(e.there());
            else list.add(e.here());
        }
    }
    return list.iterator();
}
```

All that remains is to construct an iterator over the edges of the graph. Again, we construct a list of the edges and return the result of the `iterator` method invoked on the list. For directed edges, we include every edge; for undirected edges we include only the edges found in, say, the lower half of the array (including the diagonal). Here is the version for the undirected graph:

```
public Iterator edges()
// post: returns traversal across all edges of graph (returns Edges)
```

GraphMatrix-
Undirected

```
{
    List list = new SinglyLinkedList();
    for (int row=size-1; row>=0; row--)
        for (int col=size-1; col >= row; col--) {
            Edge e = data[row][col];
            if (e != null) list.add(e);
        }
    return list.iterator();
}
```

The great advantage of the adjacency matrix representation is its simplicity. The access to a particular edge in a graph of size n can be accomplished in constant time. Other operations, like **remove**, appear to be more complex, taking $O(n)$ time. The disadvantage is that the implementation may vastly overestimate the storage required for edges. While we have room for storing $O(n^2)$ directed edges, some graphs may only need to make use of $O(n)$ edges. Graphs with superlinear numbers of edges are called *dense;* all other graphs are *sparse.* When graphs are sparse, most of the elements of the adjacency matrix are not used, leading to a significant waste of space. Our next implementation is particularly suited for representing sparse graphs.

15.3.3 Adjacency Lists

Recalling the many positive features of a linked list over a fixed-size array, we now consider the use of an *adjacency list.* As with the adjacency matrix representation, we maintain a **Map** for identifying the relationship between a vertex label and the associated **Vertex** object. Within the vertex, however, we store a collection (usually a linked list) of edges that mention this vertex. Figures 15.4 and 15.5 demonstrate the adjacency list representations of undirected and directed graphs. The great advantage of using a collection is that it stores only edges that appear as part of the graph.

As with the adjacency matrix implementation, we construct a privately used extension to the **Vertex** class. In this extension we reference a collection of edges that are incident to this vertex. In directed graphs, we collect edges that mention the associated vertex as the source. In undirected graphs any edge incident to the vertex is collected. Because the edges are stored within the vertices, most of the actual implementation of graphs appears within the implementation of the extended vertex class. We see most of the implementation here:

GraphListVertex

```
class GraphListVertex extends Vertex
{
    protected Structure adjacencies; // adjacent edges
    public GraphListVertex(Object key)
    // post: constructs a new vertex, not incident to any edge
    {
        super(key); // init Vertex fields
        adjacencies = new SinglyLinkedList(); // new list
    }
```

```
    public void addEdge(Edge e)
    // pre: e is an edge that mentions this vertex
    // post: adds edge to this vertex's adjacency list
    {
        if (!containsEdge(e)) adjacencies.add(e);
    }

    public boolean containsEdge(Edge e)
    // post: returns true if e appears on adjacency list
    {
        return adjacencies.contains(e);
    }

    public Edge removeEdge(Edge e)
    // post: removes and returns adjacent edge "equal" to e
    {
        return (Edge)adjacencies.remove(e);
    }

    public Edge getEdge(Edge e)
    // post: returns the edge that "equals" e, or null
    {
        Iterator edges = adjacencies.iterator();
        while (edges.hasNext())
        {
            Edge adjE = (Edge)edges.next();
            if (e.equals(adjE)) return adjE;
        }
        return null;
    }

    public int degree()
    // post: returns the degree of this node
    {
        return adjacencies.size();
    }

    public Iterator adjacentVertices()
    // post: returns iterator over adj. vertices
    {
        return new GraphListAIterator(adjacentEdges(), label());
    }

    public Iterator adjacentEdges()
    // post: returns iterator over adj. edges
    {
        return adjacencies.iterator();
    }
}
```

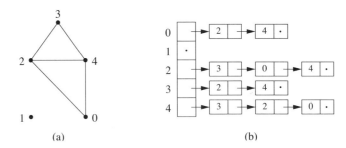

Figure 15.4   (a) An undirected graph and (b) its adjacency list representation. Each edge is represented twice in the structure. (Compare with Figure 15.2.)

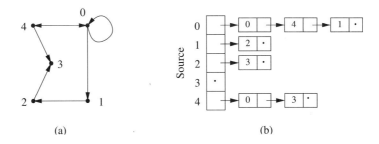

Figure 15.5   (a) A directed graph and (b) its adjacency list representation. Each edge appears once in the source list. (Compare with Figure 15.3.)

The constructor initializes its **Vertex** fields, and then constructs an empty adjacency list. Elements of this list will be **Edge** objects. Most of the other methods have obvious behavior.

The only difficult method is **getEdge**. This method returns an edge from the adjacency list that logically equals (i.e., is determined to be equal through a call to **Edge**'s **equals** method) the edge provided. In an undirected graph the order of the vertex labels may not correspond to the order found in edges in the edge list. As a result, **getEdge** returns a *canonical edge* that represents the edge specified as the parameter. This ensures that there are not multiple instances of edges that keep track of shared information.

We are now ready to implement most of the methods required by the **Graph** interface. First, we consider the protected **GraphList** constructor:

```
protected Map dict; // label to vertex dictionary
protected boolean directed; // is graph directed?

protected GraphList(boolean dir)
```

```
{
    dict = new Hashtable();
    directed = dir;
}
```

Our approach to extending the abstract `GraphList` type to support directed and undirected graphs is similar to that described in the adjacency matrix implementation. With the list-based implementation, though, we need not provide an upper bound on the number of vertices that will appear in the graph. This is because the underlying structures automatically extend themselves, if necessary.

The process of adding and removing a vertex involves simple manipulations of the `Map`. Here, for example, is the code for adding a new vertex to the graph:

```
public void add(Object label)
// pre: label is a non-null label for vertex
// post: a vertex with label is added to graph;
//       if vertex with label is already in graph, no action
{
    if (dict.containsKey(label)) return; // vertex exists
    GraphListVertex v = new GraphListVertex(label);
    dict.put(label,v);
}
```

To add an edge to the graph we insert a reference to the `Edge` object in the appropriate adjacency lists. For a directed graph, we insert the edge in the list associated with the source vertex. For an undirected graph, a reference to the edge must be inserted into both lists. It is important, of course, that a *reference* to a single edge be inserted in both lists so that changes to the edge are maintained consistently. Here, we show the undirected version:

```
public void addEdge(Object vLabel1, Object vLabel2, Object label)
// pre: vLabel1 and vLabel2 are labels of existing vertices, v1 & v2
// post: an edge (undirected) is inserted between v1 and v2;
//       if edge is new, it is labeled with label (can be null)
{
    GraphListVertex v1 = (GraphListVertex) dict.get(vLabel1);
    GraphListVertex v2 = (GraphListVertex) dict.get(vLabel2);
    Edge e = new Edge(v1.label(), v2.label(), label, false);
    v1.addEdge(e);
    v2.addEdge(e);
}
```

GraphList-
Undirected

Removing an edge simply reverses this process:

```
public Object removeEdge(Object vLabel1, Object vLabel2)
// pre: vLabel1 and vLabel2 are labels of existing vertices
// post: edge is removed, its label is returned
{
    GraphListVertex v1 = (GraphListVertex) dict.get(vLabel1);
```

```
        GraphListVertex v2 = (GraphListVertex) dict.get(vLabel2);
        Edge e = new Edge(v1.label(), v2.label(), null, false);
        v2.removeEdge(e);
        e = v1.removeEdge(e);
        if (e == null) return null;
        else return e.label();
    }
```

Notice that to remove an edge a "pattern" edge must be constructed to identify (through `equals`) the target of the remove.

Now that we can remove edges, we can remove a vertex. Since the removal of a vertex should remove incident edges, it is important that each of the adjacency lists be checked. Our approach is to iterate across each of the vertices and remove any edge that mentions that vertex. This requires some care. Here is the directed version:

GraphList-
Directed

```
public Object remove(Object label)
// pre: label is non-null vertex label
// post: vertex with "equals" label is removed, if found
{
    GraphListVertex v = (GraphListVertex)dict.get(label);

    Iterator vi = iterator();
    while (vi.hasNext())
    {
        Object v2 = vi.next();
        if (!label.equals(v2)) removeEdge(v2,label);
    }
    dict.remove(label);
    return v.label();
}
```

The complexity of this method counterbalances the simplicity of adding a vertex to the graph.

Many of the remaining edge and vertex methods have been greatly simplified by our having extended the `Vertex` class. Here, for example, is the `degree` method:

```
public int degree(Object label)
// pre: label labels an existing vertex
// post: returns the number of vertices adjacent to vertex
{
    Assert.condition(dict.containsKey(label), "Vertex exists.");
    return ((GraphListVertex) dict.get(label)).degree();
}
```

This code calls the `GraphListVertex degree` method. That, in turn, calls the `size` method of the underlying collection, a `SinglyLinkedList`. Most of the remaining methods are simply implemented.

At this point, it is useful to discuss the implementation of iterators for the adjacency list representation. Like the adjacency matrix implementation, the `iterator` method simply returns the result of the `keys` iterator on the underlying `Map`. Each of the values returned by the iterator is a vertex label, which is exactly what we desire.

The `neighbors` iterator should return an iterator over the neighbors of the provided vertex. Since each vertex maintains a `Collection` of edges, the `iterator` method of the collection returns `Edge` values. Our approach is similar to the approach we used in constructing the iterators for `Maps`: we construct a private, special-purpose iterator that drives the `Collection` iterator as a slave. The process of extracting the "other" vertex from each edge encountered is made complex by the fact that "this" vertex can appear as either the source or destination vertex when the graph is undirected.

The `Edge`'s iterator has similar complexities. The easiest approach is to construct a list of edges by traversing each of the edge lists found in each of the vertices. The result is an iterator over the resulting list. Here is the code for the constructor of our private `GraphListEIterator` class:

```
protected Iterator edges;

public GraphListEIterator(Map dict)
// post: constructs a new iterator across edges of
//       vertices within dictionary
{
    List l = new DoublyLinkedList();
    Iterator dictIterator = dict.values().iterator();
    while (dictIterator.hasNext())
    {
        GraphListVertex vtx =
            (GraphListVertex)dictIterator.next();
        Iterator vtxIterator = vtx.adjacentEdges();
        while (vtxIterator.hasNext())
        {
            Edge e = (Edge)vtxIterator.next();
            if (vtx.label().equals(e.here())) l.addLast(e);
        }
    }
    edges = l.iterator();
}
```

Each of the edges is traversed in the construction of the iterator, so there is considerable overhead just during initialization. Once constructed, however, the traversal is quick. An alternative implementation would distribute the cost over each step of the traversal. Construction of the iterator would be less expensive, but each step of the traversal would be slightly slower. In the end, both methods consume similar amounts of time. If, however, partial traversals of the edge lists are expected, the alternative implementation has its merits.

With two implementations of graphs in mind, we now focus on a number of examples of their use.

15.4   Examples: Common Graph Algorithms

Because the graph structure is so flexible there are many good examples of graph applications. In this section, we investigate a number of beautiful algorithms involving graphs. These algorithms provide a cursory overview of the problems that may be cast as graph problems, as well as techniques that are commonly used to solve them.

15.4.1   Reachability

Once data are stored within a graph, it is often desirable to identify vertices that are reachable from a common source (see Figure 15.6). One approach is to treat the graph as you would a maze and, using search techniques, find the reachable vertices. For example, we may use *depth-first search*: each time we visit an unvisited vertex we seek to further deepen the traversal.

The following code demonstrates how we might use recursion to search for unvisited vertices:

Reachability

```
static void reachableFrom(Graph g, Object vertexLabel)
// pre: g is a non-null graph, vertexLabel labels a vertex of g
// post: unvisited vertices reachable from vertex are visited
{
    g.visit(vertexLabel);   // visit this vertex

    // recursively visit unvisited neighbor vertices
    Iterator ni = g.neighbors(vertexLabel);
    while (ni.hasNext())
    {
        Object neighbor = ni.next(); // adjacent node label
        if (!g.isVisited(neighbor))
        {
            reachableFrom(g,neighbor); // depth-first search
        }
    }
}
```

We clear each **Vertex**'s visited flag with a call to **reset**, and then call **reachableFrom** with the graph and the source vertex for the reachability test. Before the call to **reachableFrom**, the vertex labeled with the **vertexLabel** has not been visited. After the call, every vertex reachable from the vertex has been visited. Some vertices may be left unvisited and are not reachable from the source. So, to determine whether you may reach one vertex from another, the following code can be used:

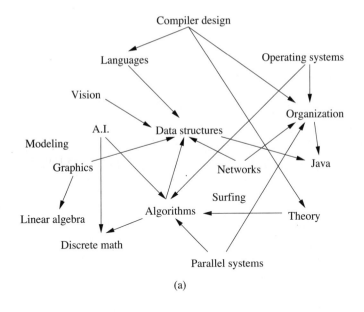

(a)

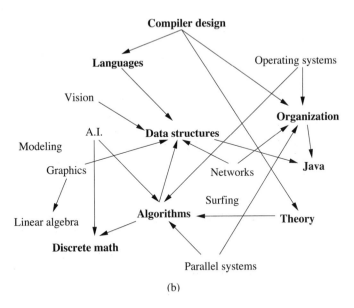

(b)

Figure 15.6   Courses you might be expected to have taken if you're in a compiler design class. (a) A typical prerequisite graph (classes point to prerequisites). Note the central nature of data structures! (b) Bold courses can be reached as requisite courses for compiler design.

```
g.reset();
reachableFrom(g,sourceLabel);
canGetThere = g.isVisited(destinationLabel);
```

In Section 9.3 we discussed the use of a `Linear` structure to maintain the state of a search of a maze. The use of a `Stack` led to a depth-first search. Here, however, no `Stack` appears! The reason is that the act of calling the procedure recursively maintains an implied stack of local variables.

How long does it take to execute the procedure? Suppose that, ultimately, we visit the reachable vertices V_r. Let E_r be the edges of the graph found among the vertices of V_r. Clearly, each vertex of V_r is visited, so there is one call to `reachableFrom` from each vertex $v \in V_r$. For each call, we ask each destination vertex if it has been visited or not. There is one such test for every edge within E_r. Thus, the total time is $O(|V_r| + |E_r|)$. Since $|E_r| \geq |V_r - 1|$ (every new vertex is visited by traversing a new edge), the algorithm is dominated by the number of edges actually investigated. Of course, if the graph is dense, this is bounded above by the square of the number of vertices.

In an undirected graph the reachable vertices form a component of the graph. To count the components of a graph (the undirected version of the graph of Figure 15.6 has three components), we iterate across the vertices of the graph, calling the `reachableFrom` procedure on any vertex that has not yet been visited. Since each unvisited vertex is not reachable from those that have been encountered before, the number of searches determines the number of components.

15.4.2 Topological Sorting

Occasionally it is useful to list the vertices of a graph in such a way as to make the edges point in one direction, for example, toward the front of the list. Such graphs have to be directed and acyclic (see Problem 15.13). A listing of vertices with this property is called a *topological sort*.

One technique for developing a topological sort involves keeping track of a counter or virtual timer. The timer is incremented every time it is read. We now visit each of the nodes using a depth-first search, labeling each node with two *time stamps*. These time stamps determine the span of time that the algorithm spends processing the descendants of a node. When a node is first encountered during the search, we record the *start time*. When the recursive depth-first search returns from processing a node, the timer is again read and the *finish time* is recorded. Figure 15.7 depicts the intervals associated with each vertex of the graph of Figure 15.6. (As arbitrary convention, we assume that a vertex iterator would encounter nodes in the diagram in "reading" order.)

One need only observe that the finish time of a node is greater than the finish time of any node it can reach. (This depth-first search may have to be started at several nodes if there are several independent components, or if the graph is not strongly connected.) The algorithm, then, simply lists the vertices in the order in which they are finished. For our course graph we generate one

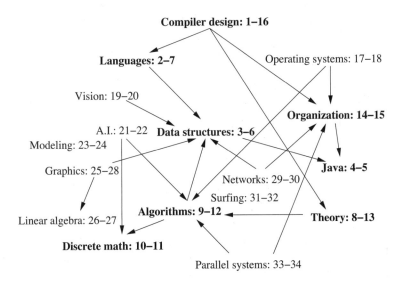

Figure 15.7 The progress of a topological sort of the course graph. The time interval following a node label indicates the time interval spent processing that node or its descendants. Dark nodes reachable from compiler design are all processed during the interval [1–16]—the interval associated with compiler design.

of many course schedules that allow students to take courses without violating course requirements:

Vertices Ordered by Finish Time					
5.	Java	15.	Organization	27.	Linear algebra
6.	Data structures	16.	Compiler design	28.	Graphics
7.	Languages	18.	Operating systems	30.	Networks
11.	Discrete math	20.	Vision	32.	Surfing
12.	Algorithms	22.	A.I.	34.	Parallel systems
13.	Theory	24.	Modeling		

Actually, the time stamps are useful only for purposes of illustration. In fact, we can simply append vertices to the end of a queue at the time that they would normally be finished. Here is a sample code:

TopoSort

```
public static List topoSort(Graph g)
// pre: g is non-null
// post: returns list of all vertices of g, topologically ordered
{
    // construct result list
    List l = new DoublyLinkedList();
    Iterator vi = g.elements();
    for (vi.reset(); vi.hasNext(); vi.next())
    {
        // perform depth-first search on unvisited vertices
        if (!g.isVisited(vi.value()))
        {
            DFS(g,vi.value(),l);
        }
    }
    // result is queue of vertex labels
    return l;
}

static protected void DFS(Graph g, Object n, List l)
// post: performs depth-first search enqueuing
//       unvisited descendants of node n into l
{
    g.visit(n); // mark node visited
    Iterator ei = g.neighbors(n); // get neighbors
    while (ei.hasNext())
    {
        Object neighbor = ei.next();
        // potentially deepen search if neighbor not visited
        if (!g.isVisited(neighbor)) {
            DFS(g,neighbor,l);
        }
    }
    l.addLast(n); // add this value once decendants added
}
```

These functions are declared as static procedures of a program that might make use of a topological sort. Alternatively, they could be written as methods of a graph, reducing the complexity of method calls.

15.4.3 Transitive Closure

Previously we discussed a reachability algorithm that determines if it is possible to reach any particular vertex from a particular source. It is also useful to compute the *transitive closure* of a graph: for *each pair* of vertices $u, v \in V$, *is v reachable from u?* These questions can be answered by $O(|V|)$ calls to the depth-first search algorithm (leading to an algorithm that is $O(|V|(|V|+|E|))$), or we can look for a more direct algorithm that has similar behavior.

One algorithm, *Warshall's algorithm*, computes reachability for each pair of vertices by modifying the graph. When the algorithm is applied to a graph, edges are added until there is an edge for every pair of connected vertices (u, v). The concept behind Warshall's algorithm is relatively simple. Two connected vertices u and v are either directly connected, or the path from u to v passes through an intermediate node w. The algorithm simply considers each node and connects all pairs of nodes u and v that can be shown to use w as an intermediate node. Here is a Java implementation:

Warshall

```java
static void warshall(Graph g)
// pre: g is non-null
// post: g contains edge (a,b) if there is a path from a to b
{
    Iterator uiter = g.iterator();
    Iterator viter = g.iterator();
    Iterator witer = g.iterator();

    while (witer.hasNext())
    {
        Object w = witer.next();
        while (uiter.hasNext())
        {
            Object u = uiter.next();
            while (viter.hasNext())
            {
                Object v = viter.next();
                // check for edge from u to v via w
                if (g.containsEdge(u, w) &&
                    g.containsEdge(w, v))
                {
                    g.addEdge(u, v, null);
                }
            }
        }
    }
}
```

This algorithm is clearly $O(|V|^3)$: each iterator visits $|V|$ vertices and (for adjacency matrices) the check for existence of an edge can be performed in constant time.

To see how the algorithm works, we number the vertices in the order they are encountered by the vertex iterator. After k iterations of the outer loop, all "reachability edges" of the subgraph containing just the first k vertices are completely determined. The next iteration extends this result to a subgraph of $k + 1$ vertices. An inductive approach to proving this algorithm correct (which we avoid) certainly has merit.

15.4.4 All Pairs Minimum Distance

A slight modification of Warshall's algorithm gives us a method for computing the minimum distance between all pairs of points. The method is due to Floyd. Again, we use three loops to compute the new edges representing reachability, but these edges are now labeled, or *weighted*, with integer distances that indicate the current minimum distance between each pair of nodes. As we consider intermediate nodes, we merge minimum distance approximations by computing and updating the distance if the sum of path lengths through an intermediate node w is less than our previous approximation. Object orientation makes this code somewhat cumbersome:

Floyd

```
static void floyd(Graph g)
// post: g contains edge (a,b) if there is a path from a to b
{
    Iterator uiter = g.iterator();
    Iterator viter = g.iterator();
    Iterator witer = g.iterator();

    while (witer.hasNext())
    {
        Object w = witer.next();
        while (uiter.hasNext())
        {
            Object u = uiter.next();
            while (viter.hasNext())
            {
                Object v = viter.next();
                if (g.containsEdge(u,w) && g.containsEdge(w,v))
                {
                    Edge leg1 = g.getEdge(u,w);
                    Edge leg2 = g.getEdge(w,v);
                    int leg1Dist =
                        ((Integer)leg1.label()).intValue();
                    int leg2Dist =
                        ((Integer)leg2.label()).intValue();
                    int newDist = leg1Dist+leg2Dist;
```

```
                    if (g.containsEdge(u,v))
                    {
                        Edge across = g.getEdge(u,v);
                        int acrossDist =
                            ((Integer)across.label()).intValue();
                        if (newDist < acrossDist)
                            across.setLabel(new Integer(newDist));
                    } else {
                        g.addEdge(u,v,new Integer(newDist));
                    }
                }
            }
        }
    }
}
```

Clearly, edge labels could contain more information than just the path length. For example, the path itself could be constructed, stored, and produced on request, if necessary. Again, the complexity of the algorithm is $O(|V|^3)$. This is satisfactory for dense graphs, especially if they're stored in adjacency matrices, but for sparse graphs the checking of all possible edges seems excessive. Indeed, other approaches can improve these bounds. We leave some of these for your next course in algorithms!

15.4.5 Greedy Algorithms

We now consider two examples of *greedy* algorithms—algorithms that compute optimal solutions to problems by acting in the optimal or "most greedy" manner at each stage in the algorithm. Because both algorithms seek to find the best choice for the next step in the solution process, both make use of a priority queue.

Minimum Spanning Tree

The solution to many network problems involves identifying a *minimum spanning tree* of a graph. A minimum spanning tree of an edge-weighted graph is a tree that connects every vertex of a component whose edges have minimum total edge weight. Such a tree might represent the most inexpensive way to connect several cities with telephone trunk lines. For this reason, we will interpret the weights as edge lengths. For the purposes of our discussion, we will assume that the graph under consideration is composed of a single component. (If the graph contains multiple components, we can compute a minimum spanning forest with multiple applications of the minimum spanning tree algorithm.)

MCST

The process of constructing a minimum spanning tree involves starting with a shortest edge and then iteratively incorporating a shortest edge that connects a new node to the tree. The process stops when $|V| - 1$ edges have been added to the tree.

```
static public void mcst(Graph g)
// pre: g is a graph
// post: edges of minimum spanning tree of a component are visited
{
    // keep edges ranked by length
    PriorityQueue q = new SkewHeap();
    Object v = null;         // current vertex
    Edge e;                  // current edge

    g.reset();               // clear visited flags

    // select a smallest edge in graph for initial tree
    ComparableEdge shortest = null;
    Iterator ei = g.edges();

    v = null;
    while (ei.hasNext())
    {
        ComparableEdge possible =
            new ComparableEdge((Edge)ei.next());
        if (shortest == null ||
            possible.compareTo(shortest) < 0)
            shortest = possible;
    }
    if (shortest == null) return; // no shortest edge
    else v = shortest.here();

    // at this point v is a vertex mentioned by shortest edge
    e = null;
    while (v != null)
    {
        // v is a (possibly new) vertex
        if (!g.isVisited(v))
        {
            // visit incoming edge and vertex v
            if (e!=null) g.visitEdge(g.getEdge(e.here(),e.there()));
            g.visit(v);

            // now add all the outgoing edges from v
            Iterator ai = g.neighbors(v);
            while (ai.hasNext()) {
                // turn it into outgoing edge
                e = g.getEdge(v,ai.next());
                // add the edge to the queue
                q.add(new ComparableEdge(e));
            }
        }
        if (!q.isEmpty())
        {
            // grab next shortest edge
```

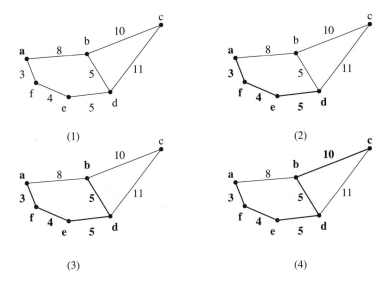

Figure 15.8   The progress of a minimum spanning tree computation. Bold vertices and edges are part of the tree. Vertex **a** is adjacent to the shortest edge. At each stage, a shortest external edge adjacent to the tree is incorporated.

```
        e = (Edge)q.remove();

        // does this edge take us somewhere new?
        v = e.there();
        if (g.isVisited(v)) v = e.here();
    } else {
        // couldn't get to new vertex (we're done)
        v = null;
    }
  }
}
```

First, we use a priority queue to rank edges based on length. As we re- move the edges from the queue, the smallest edges are considered first (see Figure 15.8). When an edge is considered that includes an unvisited vertex, we visit it, logically adding it to the minimum spanning tree. We then add any edges that are outward-bound from the newly visited node. At any time, the priority queue contains only edges that mention at least one node of the tree. If, of course, an edge is considered that mentions two previously visited nodes, the edge is unnecessary, as the nodes are already connected by a path in the tree (albeit a potentially long one). When the priority queue "runs dry," the tree is fully computed.

The result of the algorithm will be visited marks on all nodes and edges that participate in the tree. The first loop looks for a shortest edge.[2] We use the source vertex to "prime" the greedy algorithm.

The main loop of the algorithm will run as long as a vertex is potentially added to the tree. If the vertex has already been visited, the next shortest edge is greedily considered. If the vertex has not been visited, then the edge that mentions it is visited and added to the tree (the initial vertex has no incoming edge). Its outbound edges are then added to the list of those to be considered. Eventually, all vertices and edges are processed once, leading to a running time of $O(|V| + |E|)$.

Notice that, indirectly, the initial vertex guarantees that a shortest edge is added to the tree first.

Single-Source Shortest Paths

The minimum spanning tree algorithm is related to a fast, single-source, shortest-path algorithm attributed to Dijkstra. In this algorithm, we desire the minimum-length paths from a single source to all other nodes. We expect the algorithm, of course, to run considerably faster than the all-pairs version. This algorithm also runs in time proportional to $O(|V| + |E|)$ due to the fact that it uses much the same control as the minimum spanning tree. Here is the code:

Dijkstra

```
public static Map dijkstra(Graph g, Object start)
// pre: g is a graph; start is source vertex
// post: returns a dictionary of vertex-based results
//       value is association (total-distance,prior-edge)
{
    // keep a priority queue of distances from source
    PriorityQueue q = new SkewHeap();
    Map result = new Table(); // results, sorted by vertex
    Object v = start;        // last vertex added
    // result is a (total-distance,previous-edge) pair
    ComparableAssociation possible =
        new ComparableAssociation(new Integer(0),null);
    // as long as we add a new vertex...
    while (v != null)
    {
        if (!result.containsKey(v))
        {
            // visit node v - record incoming edge
            result.put(v,possible);
            // vDist is shortest distance to v
            int vDist = ((Integer)possible.getKey()).intValue();

            // compute and consider distance to each neighbor
```

---

[2] We use ComparableEdges here, an extension to an edge that assumes that the labels implement Comparable.

```
                    Iterator ai = g.neighbors(v);
                    while (ai.hasNext())
                    {
                        // get edge to neighbor
                        Edge e = g.getEdge(v,ai.next());
                        // construct (distance,edge) pair for possible result
                        possible = new ComparableAssociation(
                          new Integer(vDist+((Integer)e.label()).intValue()),
                          e);
                        q.add(possible);      // add to priority queue
                    }
                }
                // now, get closest (possibly unvisited) vertex
                if (!q.isEmpty())
                {
                    possible = (ComparableAssociation)q.remove();
                    // get destination vertex (take care w/undirected graphs)
                    v = ((Edge)possible.getValue()).there();
                    if (result.containsKey(v))
                        v = ((Edge)possible.getValue()).here();
                } else {
                    // no new vertex (algorithm stops)
                    v = null;
                }
            }
        }
        return result;
    }
```

Unlike the minimum cost spanning tree algorithm, we return a `Table` of results. Each entry in the `Table` has a vertex label as a key. The value is an association between the total distance from the source to the vertex, and (in the nontrivial case) a reference to the last edge that supports the minimum-length path.

We initially record trivial results for the source vertex (setting its distance to zero) and place every outgoing edge in the priority queue (see Figure 15.9). Unlike the minimum spanning tree algorithm, we rank the edges based on *total* distance from the source. These edges describe how to extend, in a nearest-first, greedy manner, the paths that pass from the source through visited nodes. If, of course, an edge is dequeued that takes us to a vertex with previously recorded results, it may be ignored: some other path from the source to the vertex is shorter. If the vertex has not been visited, it is placed in the `Table` with the distance from the source (as associated with the removed edge). New outbound edges are then enqueued.

The tricky part is to rank the edges by the distance of the destination vertex from the source. We can think of the algorithm as considering edges that fall within a neighborhood of increasing radius from the source vertex. When the boundary of the neighborhood includes a new vertex, its minimum distance from the source has been determined.

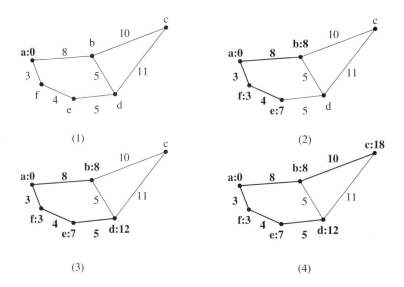

Figure 15.9   The progress of a single-source, shortest-path computation from source **a**. As nodes are incorporated, a minimum distance is associated with the vertex. Compare with Figure 15.8.

Since every vertex is considered once and each edge possibly twice, the worst-case performance is $O(|V|+|E|)$, an improvement over the $O(|V|^3)$ performance for sparse graphs.

15.5   Conclusions

In this chapter we have investigated two traditional implementations of graphs. The adjacency matrix stores information about each edge in a square matrix while the adjacency list implementation keeps track of edges that leave each vertex. The matrix implementation is ideal for dense graphs, where the number of actual edges is high, while the list implementation is best for representing sparse graphs.

Our approach to implementing graph structures is to use partial implementations, called abstract classes, and extend them until they are concrete, or complete. Other methods are commonly used, but this has the merit that common code can be shared among similar classes. Indeed, this inheritance is one of the features commonly found in object-oriented languages.

This last section is, in effect, a stepping stone to an investigation of algorithms. There are many approaches to answering graph-related questions, and because of the dramatic differences in complexities in different implementations, the solutions are often affected by the underlying graph structure.

Finally, we note that many of the seemingly simple graph-related problems cannot be efficiently solved with *any* reasonable representation of graphs. Those problems are, themselves, a suitable topic for many future courses of study.

Self Check Problems

Solutions to these problems begin on page 436.

15.1   What is the difference between a graph and a tree?

15.2   What is the difference between an undirected graph and a directed graph?

15.3   Under what conditions would you use an adjacency matrix over an adjacency list implementation of a graph?

15.4   What do we know if the adjacency matrix is symmetric?

15.5   What is the time potentially required to add an edge to a graph represented as an adjacency list? What if the graph is represented using an adjacency matrix?

15.6   What is a spanning tree of a graph?

15.7   What is a minimum spanning tree of a weighted graph?

15.8   What is the transitive closure of a graph?

15.9   What is the topological ordering of vertices of a graph?

15.10   Under what conditions is a topological sort of the vertices of a graph possible?

Problems

Solutions to the odd-numbered problems begin on page 471.

15.1   Draw the adjacency matrix and list representations of the following (undirected and complete) graph:

15.2   Draw the adjacency matrix and list representations of the following (directed) graph:

15.3   Draw the adjacency matrix and list representations of a complete tree with seven nodes and undirected edges.

15.4   What are the transitive closures of each of the following graphs?

(a)   (b)

15.5   Suppose that we use an $n \times n$ boolean matrix to represent the edges of a directed graph. Assume, as well, that the diagonal elements are all **true**. How should we interpret the nth power of this adjacency matrix?

15.6   What topological characteristics distinguish a general graph from a general tree?

15.7   Consider the following (simplified) map of the world:

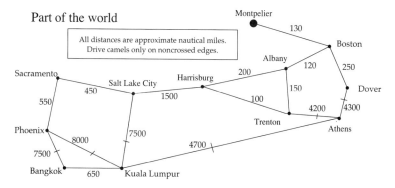

a. Compute the shortest air distance to each of the cities from scenic Montpelier, Vermont. Redraw the map with distances to cities and include only the air routes that support the most direct travel to Vermont.

b. Suppose you're interested in setting up a network among the capitals. Redraw the map to depict the minimum spanning network.

c. Suppose you're interested in setting up a Camel Express system. Redraw the map to depict the minimum spanning road systems that don't cross bodies of water (indicated by crossed edges).

15.8   Explain why it is necessary that the **Edge** class "show through" the **Graph** interface. (Hint: Consider implementations of the **Iterator** constructed by the **edges** method.)

15.9   Compare and contrast the performance of the adjacency list and adjacency matrix implementations of graphs.

15.10 For both implementations of graphs, write a method, `isSink`, that returns `true` if and only if the vertex indicated is a sink. (A sink has out-degree 0.)

15.11 For both implementations of graphs, write a method, `isSource`, that returns `true` if and only if the vertex indicated is a source. (A source has in-degree 0.)

15.12 In an undirected graph, it is possible for a single edge to be represented by `Edge` objects whose vertices appear in opposite orders. Describe how a general `equals` method for `Edge`s might be written.

15.13 Explain why graphs with topologically sortable vertices must be (1) directed and (2) acyclic.

15.14 Suppose we have a cycle-free graph that describes the dependencies between Java modules. How would you compute the order of compilations that had to occur?

Topological sorting solves this, given no cycles.

15.15 It is a fairly common practice to traverse the vertices and edges of a graph. Consider a new implementation of graphs that keeps a `Map` of vertices as well as an unordered `List` of edges. This makes traversal of edges simple. What is the complexity of each of the other `Graph` operations?

15.16 Extend the all-pairs minimum distance algorithm to keep track of the shortest *path* between the nodes.

15.17 Explain why it is sometimes more efficient to compute the distance from a single source to all other nodes, even though a particular query may be answered with a partial solution.

15.18 Under what conditions can a graph component have nonunique minimum spanning trees?

15.19 Prove that a minimum spanning tree of a graph component must include a shortest edge.

15.20 It is possible, in Dijkstra's algorithm, that an edge removed from the priority queue is not useful: it takes us to a previously visited node. Some of these extraneous edges can be avoided by not placing an edge in the priority queue if the destination has already been visited. Is it still possible to encounter an edge to a previously visited node?

15.6 Laboratory: Converting Between Units

Objective. To perform the transitive closure of a graph.

Discussion. An interesting utility available on UNIX systems is the `units` program. With this program you can convert between one unit and another. For example, if you were converting between feet and yards, you might have the following interaction with the `units` program:

```
You have: yard
You want: inch
Multiply by 36.0
```

The program performs its calculations based on a database of values which has entries that appear as follows:

```
1 yard 3 foot
1 foot 12 inch
1 yard 39.37 inch
```

Notice that there is no direct conversion between yards and inches.

In this lab you are to write a program that computes the relations between units. When the program starts, it reads in a database of values that describe the ratios between units. Each unit becomes a node of a graph, and the conversions are directed edges between related units. Note that the edges of the graph must be directed because the factor that converts inches to yards is the reciprocal of the factor that converts yards to inches.

In order to deduce conversions between distantly related units, it will be necessary for you to construct the closure of the graph. The labels associated with adjacent edges are multiplied together to label the direct edge.

Once your program reads the unit conversion database, the program should prompt for the source units and the destination units. It should then print out the conversion factor used to multiply the source units by to get the destination units. If the units do not appear to be related, you should print out a message that indicates that fact. Prompting continues until the user enters a blank line for the source units.

Thought Questions. Consider the following questions as you complete the lab:

1. There are two approaches to this problem: (1) construct the closure of the graph, or (2) perform a search from the source unit node to the destination unit node. What are the trade-offs to the two approaches?

2. What does it mean if the graph is composed of several disconnected components?

Notes:

Appendix A

Answers

Concepts:
▷ Self check problem solutions
▷ Solutions to selected problems

*From north, south, east, and west
every man who had a shade of
red in his hair had tramped into the city
to answer the advertisement.*
—Sir Arthur Conan Doyle

This section contains answers to many problems presented to the reader in the text. In the first section, we provide answers to self check problems. In the second section, we provide answers to odd-numbered problems found in the text.

A.1   Solutions to Self Check Problems

Chapter 0

Problems begin on page 3.

0.1   Answers to all self check problems are found, here, in Appendix A.

0.2   Large programs take time to write and involve complex structures. Large programs *may* take a long time to run, however many programs are large because they more effectively manipulate the data and, in the end, they *may* run faster than an equivalent short program.

0.3   The author of this text made it briefer than most texts to make it possible for students to spend less time reading and more time practicing writing programs.

0.4   No. They are, essentially, rules of thumb. Because programmers spend considerable time attacking new problems, principles are useful for *guiding* the design process, but not *determining* the design.

Chapter 1

Problems begin on page 26.

1.1   Abstraction, in computer science, is the process of removing or hiding unnecessary details of a definition.

1.2   Procedural abstraction removes unnecessary details of an implementation by hiding them within the bodies of procedures or methods.

1.3   Data abstraction removes the unnecessary details of an implementation by hiding them within the protected portion of a data structure.

1.4   In Java, a message is sent to an object by calling a method.

1.5   A class provides the details of an implementation of a data structure. An object is a particular instance (or, sometimes, an *instantiation*) of a class. Objects take up memory; classes are simply models for objects. A class need not be instantiated. `java.lang.Math` is an example of a instance-free class.

1.6   A method is identified by its name and the types of each of its parameters. The return type, in Java, is not part of its signature.

1.7   An interface describes those aspects of a data structure or class that are publicly visible; it forms a contract between the implementor and the user of a class. The implementation describes the particular details necessary to make a workable object. Those portions of the implementation that are not part of the interface are usually hidden from the user.

1.8   An accessor provides read-only access to an implementation's data, directly or indirectly. It does not modify the structure. A mutator allows the user to modify the state of an object. It may also return a structure's data.

1.9   The `Object` class is the most general class in Java. Every object is of type `Object`. A general purpose class manipulates objects of the most general type possible.

1.10   An object is an instance of a class. A reference provides a means of refering to a particular object. If a reference refers to no particular object, this is indicated by a `null` value.

1.11   Programmers make use of a class when they import them into their programs. For some classes you implement you may be the only user.

Chapter 2

Problems begin on page 37.

2.1   The pre- and postconditions provide a slight increase in formality that allows the user of the data structure to identify exactly what will happen when a method is run.

2.2   If a method has no precondition it may be called at any time.

2.3   A method with no postcondition does not have any predictable result. If a method does not have a predictable result, it is not generally useful.

2.4   Because hidden code is called by other methods. These methods act, essentially, like users of your hidden code.

Chapter 3

Problems begin on page 64.

3.1   Arrays and `Vectors` are both randomly accessed, container objects. Both can have their sizes determined at run-time. Since both are objects, either may be `null`, a condition that is often to be avoided.

Arrays are a feature of Java and enjoy access using square bracket (`[]`) notation, while `Vectors` are accessed using their `get` and `set` methods. Arrays are declared to hold a specific type of object, determined by the user, and when accessed, they return objects of that type. `Vectors` always hold objects of type `Object`, the most general type possible. A value accessed from a vector is always of type `Object`; the result must be cast to suggest and verify the desired type.

The most important feature of the `Vector` class is the notion of *extensibility*. `Vectors` may be lengthened by the `add` method. Arrays must be explictly reallocated and copied. The vector data abstraction supports this automatically, and efficiently.

3.2 The `add(v)` method appends a value to the end of the `Vector`. The `add(i,v)` method inserts a value into a `Vector` so that `v` will be found at location `i`. Any values found at `i` or higher are shifted to higher slots in the process.

3.3 The `add` methods insert new values into the `Vector`, logically increasing its size. No existing values are changed. The `set(i,v)` method *replaces* the value at location `i`.

3.4 The `remove` method either removes the first occurrence of a value `v`, or a value found at a location `i`. Both decrease the logical size of the `Vector`.

3.5 The size is the number of storage locations logically available in the `Vector`. Usually, the size corresponds to the number of items stored within the `Vector`. The capacity is the number of memory references currently allocated to the `Vector`. The capacity indicates how large the vector's size can get before the underlying array must be reallocated and copied over. Ideally, the capacity provides enough room so that the size can increase without a significant risk of reallocation.

3.6 The use of a `Vector` allows us to concentrate on the manipulation of the words that remain in the list, not the allocation and reallocation of the word list, itself.

3.7 This avoids destroying data. Starting at the low end of the `Vector` causes each moved value to destroy an unmoved value.

3.8 The doubling of the size effectively delays the next reallocation of the `Vector` for a long time. Since reallocation involves moving every element of the `Vector`, reallocation is to be avoided, if possible. The doubling reduces the average number of times a single value is copied from approximately $\frac{n}{2}$ to 1.

3.9 The code allocates an array of `initialCapacity` `Objects` and assigns a reference to the array to `elementData`. The array previously referenced by `elementData` is potentially lost. Each element of the array is `null`; no element of the array refers to any particular `Object`.

3.10 Constructors, like other methods, are identified by the types of their parameters. A constructor is called when the `new` keyword is encountered. Following the `new` keyword is the type of object to be constructed, and the parameters used to select and execute the appropriate constructor. The variable `v` is constructed with the parameterless constructor and has size 0 and capacity 10. The variable `w` is constructed with the single-parameter (an `int`) constructor and has size 0 and capacity 1000. `w` will not have to be reallocated as soon as `v`, but it initially consumes more memory.

3.11 The row is bounded by the height and the column by the width. The row, in Java and most modern languages, is the first index provided. This is motivated by the notation used in mathematics.

Chapter 4

Problems begin on page 99.

4.1   The function $f(x) = x$ is $O(x)$. Let $c = 1$, and $n_0 = 1$.

4.2   The function $f(x) = 3x$ is $O(x)$. Let $c = 3$ and $n_0 = 1$.

4.3   If $x + 900$ is $O(x)$, set $c = 901$ and $n_0 = 1$.

4.4   It grows with rate $O(x)$. Set $c = 450$ and $n_0 = 1$.

4.5 $\log_2 2 = 1$, $\sqrt{2} \approx 1.414$, $x = 2$, $x! = 2$, $x^2 = 4$, $2^x = 4$, and $30x = 60$. The largest is $30x$.

$\log_2 4 = 2$, $\sqrt{4} = 2$, $x = 4$, $x^2 = 16$, $2^x = 16$, $x! = 24$, and $30x = 120$. The largest is $30x$.

$\log_2 16 = 4$, $\sqrt{16} = 4$, $x = 16$, $x^2 = 256$, $30x = 480$, $2^x = 65,536$, and $x! = 20,922,789,888,000$. The largest is $x!$.

$\log_2 64 = 6$, $\sqrt{64} = 8$, $x = 64$, $30x = 1920$, $x^2 = 4096$,

$$2^x = 18,446,744,073,709,551,616$$

and

$$x! = \begin{aligned} &126,886,932,185,884,164,103,433,389,335, \\ &161,480,802,865,516,174,545,192,198,801, \\ &894,375,214,704,230,400,000,000,000,000. \end{aligned}$$

$x!$ is the largest, by far. This ordering of these functions is maintained for all values of $x > 30$.

4.6   A base case, self-reference, and, in the self-reference, progress toward the base case.

4.7   Assume there are 400 million people in the U.S. Reading children (say ages 10 to 18) represent, say 20 percent of the population, or 80 million people. The book is read by, say, 60 million U.S. children. Suppose the book has 750 pages, read at 1 minute per page. Each child takes approximately 10 hours to read the text (they get faster near the end), yielding a hit of 600 million child-hours of extra-curricular reading. A child-year we approximate at 2000 hours. The result is about 300 thousand child-years of reading. (If parents read this book aloud to their 2 children, this might cut the time in half, but the children would likely read the text themselves, again.)

4.8   It is easy to see that that postmaster would never return more than 21 penny stamps when a single 21 cent stamp would do. Similary, the postmaster would never return 37 or more 21 cent stamps in change, since 21 letter stamps would suffice. Both $c_1(x)$ and $c_{21}(x)$ must, then be $O(1)$. The remainder of at least $x - (0.20 + 36 \times 0.21)$ dollars change must be accommodated by 37 cent stamps. The function $c_{37}(x)$ is clearly linear, $O(x)$.

Chapter 5

Problems begin on page 132.

5.1   It is useful to have a temporary object reference so that the two values can be exchanged without forgetting one of the two references.

5.2   You are using insertion sort. As you encounter the values, you insert them into the list represented on your piece of paper.

5.3   You are using selection sort. You extract minimum values one at a time until all values have been listed in increasing order.

5.4   It is valid. This is a first stage of a sort involving merging. Merge months 1 and 2. Then merge months 3 and 4. Then merge each of these two piles. Note that after the month sorting pass the checks are nearly in order.

5.5   This is a form of radix sort. It works because she expects that the mail is fairly evenly distributed. Notice that the street number has lower priority than the street name. If she walks down the even side of each street and up the odd side, how would you suggest she change this algorithm?

5.6   The `compareTo` method returns a value that is less than, equal to, or greater than 0 if this object is less than, equal to, or greater than the parameter. Essentially, the `compareTo` method determines if a `swap` is necessary in most sorting algorithms.

Chapter 7

Problems begin on page 160.

7.1   Typical code is as follows:

```
Enumeration e = x.elements();

while (e.hasMoreElements())
{
    System.out.println(e.nextElement());
}
```

7.2   Typical code is as follows:

```
Iterator i = x.iterator();

while (i.hasNext())
{
    System.out.println(i.next());
}
```

7.3   It is important, in this case, to make sure that you assign the value of the `Iterator` variable to an `Integer` variable using a cast:

```
// w is a Vector of integer values:
Iterator iter = w.iterator();

while (iter.hasNext())
{
```

```
        Integer I = (Integer)iter.next();
        int n = I.intValue();
        if ((n % 2) == 0) System.out.println(n);
    }
```

7.4   The code makes use of a `boolean` value and the `Math.sqrt` function.

```
boolean perfectSoFar = true;

// attempt to read a first value
if (g.hasNext())
{
    Integer I = (Integer)g.next();
    int i = I.intValue();
    // attempt to read second, and on, while perfect
    while (perfectSoFar && g.hasNext())
    {
        Integer J = (Integer)g.next();
        int j = J.intValue();
        // compute integer square root
        int k = (int)Math.sqrt(j+i);
        // it's working if i+j is a perfect square
        perfectSoFar = perfectSoFar && ((i+j) == (k*k));
        // save current value
        i = j;
    }
}
if (perfectSoFar) System.out.println("Perfect!");
```

Chapter 8

Problems begin on page 200.

8.1   The `List` allocates and frees memory in small units, while the `Vector` actually seeks to avoid changes in allocation. This is because the `Vector` class must copy any data in the `Vector` at the time of reallocation, while a `List` does not. The `List` type allows for the efficient insertion and deletion of values within the structure, while the `Vector` class requires linear time, on average.

8.2   The use of references allows the `List` structures to rearrange their values more easily. For example, in most `List` structures, it is fairly simple to add or remove a value at the front of the list

8.3   The structure is a `List` if (1) it implements each of the methods required by the `List` interface, and (2) it implements the `List` interface directly or indirectly.

8.4   If C extends `SinglyLinkedList`, it is a (specific kind of) `SinglyLinked-List`. Since all `SinglyLinkedLists` are extensions of `AbstractLists`, C is an `AbstractList`. Since at least one (in actuality, all) of these classes implements `List`, C is a `List` as well. C is not a `DoublyLinkedList` because C does not extend that class.

8.5   No. Both the `DoublyLinkedList` and `SinglyLinkedList` classes are direct extensions of `AbstractList`; they are both `AbstractLists`, but one is not an extension of the other.

8.6   The `tail` reference facilitates getting to the far end of the list. It makes it possible, for example, to add an element to the end of the list in constant time. If `tail` was eliminated, it would be necessary to traverse the entire list to find the far end; this operation is $O(n)$.

8.7   It is not directly useful. We might arrange to have the `tail` reference point to the last element, but keeping that reference up to date is relatively difficult. It is possible, though, and the result is, essentially, a circular list.

8.8   Because it uses less space. A `ListVector` needs room to store one reference to each element; other `List` implementations also need to store one or more references.

8.9   The abstract class only attempts to provide implementations of methods that are generic, or shared among all implementations of the `List` class.

8.10   It gets added at the tail of the list. The `remove` method will remove and return this value.

8.11   It is the second element. The first element occurs in position 0.

Chapter 9

Problems begin on page 233.

9.1   A `Stack` is an interface that extends a `Linear`. It is therefore a `Linear`. It is not a `List` because it does not directly or indirectly extend that interface. It is not an `AbstractLinear`; a `Stack` is an interface and does extend the `AbstractLinear` class. (A particular *implementation* of a `Stack` is likely to extend an `AbstractStack`, which extends an `AbstractLinear`.) Stacks and Queues are both `Linear` objects, but otherwise unrelated.

9.2   The `Stack` is an interface that does not extend `List`; they are unrelated. A `StackList` is an implementation of the `Stack` interface that uses a `List` in its implementation. It is not, however, a `List` itself. (You can see this because the `StackList` class does not have some `List` methods: for example, `get(i)`.) The `StackList` is an implementation of a `Stack`.

9.3   `Queue` is more general than `QueueList`. It makes it impossible for us to depend on features of a `QueueList` implementation. If we wish to change our actual types from `QueueList` to `QueueVector`, the change is relatively simple and painless.

9.4   No. The `Queue` is an interface and, for practical purposes cannot be constructed. If you want to construct a value for a `Queue` variable, you must pick an implementation and construct an instance of that type.

9.5   Your car is in a queue. The first car in is the first car to leave.

9.6   It is a stack. The last page you visited is the first page you recall.

9.7   The first solution you find is the shortest possible.

9.8   The stack-based mechanism is more similar to human maze-solving strategy. The breadth-first approach involves keeping track of and reconsidering an increasing number of options. If you are walking, the stack-based approach is simpler.

9.9   The reason is that it is possible for the `Queue` to "wrap around" the array.

Chapter 10

Problems begin on page 260.

10.1   The values within an `OrderedStructure` are maintained in some agreed-upon order.

10.2   The user specifies a `compareTo` method for each class potentially stored in an ordered structure. This method is at least useful for determining the relative ordering of two objects of that class.

10.3   The `compareTo` method is a feature of a class, and is used to order the instances of the class. The `compareTo` method is typically fixed, and cannot be changed to suit the particular need. A `Comparator`, on the other hand, is an object itself, with a `compare` method that compares two objects. Each `Comparator` instance may choose to order the objects in a different manner. Thus, the `Comparator` approach provides greater flexibility, while the `compareTo` approach leaves the ordering of objects up to the designer of the original class.

10.4   Yes. It is best if the ordering mechanism keeps `equals` objects near each other. Otherwise, inconsistencies can result.

10.5   No. A `Vector` allows the insertion of values in the center of the structure. An `OrderedVector` must disallow this, in order to maintain the internal order of the structure.

10.6   No. The values in a `Stack` are ordered by their entry time, not necessarily the object's value.

10.7   The people are ordered according to their arrival time.

10.8   They're both equally suitable. As long as the value returned is negative, 0, or positive, that is all that is needed to determine the order of two values. Harry, though, might do well to see why Sally's method seems more symmetric.

10.9   Sally's method will work, and Harry's will not. The `OrderedVector` does not know ahead of time what type will be stored within the structure. It must call, then, the `compareTo` method that takes a general `Object`. Harry will not have written this method, and the program will complain when the `OrderedVector` attempts to compare two of Harry's `Coins`.

Chapter 11

Problems begin on page 297.

11.1   Yes, in both cases, but only if the tree is empty.

11.2   Yes, but barely. There is always just one fewer full nodes than leaves. A spindly tree—a tree with no nodes of degree 2—can have as many interior nodes as it wants, but it always has exactly one leaf.

11.3   The root has the greatest height, if there is a root.

11.4 No. If there were two paths, then some node would have two parents. Nodes have at most one parent.

11.5 Because the operations in arithmetic expressions usually involve at most two operands. Each operand is represented by an independent subtree of an operator node.

11.6 A `BinaryTree` is not a `List` because, among other things, it has no notion of indexing.

11.7 Any of the traversals encounter each element at some point. The index associated with an element in a `BinaryTree` might be the relative position of the node in the traversal of the `BinaryTree`.

11.8 Not easily. The queue makes sure that the nodes on a level are all visited around the same time. Use of a stack would make it possible to visit nodes at a deeper level before all the nodes at a relatively shallow level had been encountered.

11.9 Usually the base case is found near the leaves. The recursion starts at the root, and follows the branches outward. It stops when it gets to the leaves.

11.10 Usually 2. Each call investigates one subtree.

11.11 It is $\frac{n-1}{n}$, very close to 1 for large n. The sum of the degrees is the number of edges in the tree. Since every edge attaches one node directly or indirectly to the root, there are $n-1$ edges. The average, then, is as indicated.

Chapter 12

Problems begin on page 325.

12.1 No. A `PriorityQueue` cannot guarantee that the first value entering the structure is the first out.

12.2 No. A `PriorityQueue` must accept `Comparable` values. A `Linear` structure has no such constraint.

12.3 The weight corresponds to the total number of occurrences of the letters found within the tree. The depth of a node is the number of bits associated with the encoding of the information at the node.

12.4 A min-heap is a tree of values whose minimum is found at the root, and whose subtrees are either empty or min-heaps themselves.

12.5 Because the tree is complete, we can be sure that it has minimum $(O(\log n))$ height.

12.6 Events have associated times. The time of the event determines when it should be simulated. The timing of events is neither LIFO nor FIFO, so a time-as-priority scheme is useful.

Chapter 13

Problems begin on page 351.

13.1 The `compareTo` operator identifies one of two orderings for unequal values. Thus at each stage it is natural to have degree 2.

13.2 The first node is at the root, the last node is at a leaf.

13.3 Any structure where a value is selected by providing a key.

13.4 The right child. Everything to the left of the right child in the original tree moves to the left side of the final tree.

13.5 It is. Look at Figure 13.4.

13.6 Not necessarily. One may be at the root of a large tree, and the other, having just been added, may be found at a leaf quite far away.

13.7 The `SplayTree` potentially changes topology whenever it is referenced. The `Iterator` must be capable of maintaining its state while the tree is splayed.

13.8 The red-black tree is always very close to balanced. It has height that is always $O(\log_2 n)$. The splay tree has no such guarantee.

Chapter 14

Problems begin on page 385.

14.1 The `Map` structure is associative. It allows the user to specify separate keys and values. Previous structures have depended heavily on `compareTo` methods to order values.

14.2 It is the percentage of the table entries that contain key-value pairs.

14.3 Yes. If the hash table uses external chaining, the number of entries in the table can be smaller than the number of key-value pairs.

14.4 It is not guaranteed. In practice, if the load factor is kept low, the number of comparisons can be expected to be very low.

14.5 A collision occurs when two different keys attempt to hash to the same location. This can occur when the two keys directly map to the same bucket, or as the result of rehashing due to previous collisions for one or both of the keys.

14.6 It should be fast, reproducible, and it should spread keys as uniformly as possible across the hash table. This is usually accomplished by attempting to filter out any nonuniform features of the key distribution.

14.7 When space is tight, the extra space required by a `Hashtable`'s low load factor makes a `MapList` somewhat preferable. Since a `MapList` is slower than a `Hashtable` in the expected case, and since a `MapList` has the overhead of links between elements, this preference is relatively infrequent.

14.8 The `Hashtable` does not help with sorting, precisely because the hashing mechanism is unlikely to be correlated with any useful ordering of the keys. On the other hand, the `Table` structure does provide, essentially, a sorting mechanism based on binary search trees. Key-value pairs are placed in the table, and they are encountered in sorted order when iterating across the keys.

Chapter 15

Problems begin on page 421.

15.1 A tree does not have cycles; a graph can. All trees are graphs, but not all graphs are trees.

15.2 An undirected graph has oriented edges–edges that establish a potentially one-way relation between vertices. The edges of an undirected graph establish a symmetric relationship.

15.3 You use an adjacency matrix when more edges appear in the graph than not. If the percentage of potential edges is low, an adjacency list is more efficient.

15.4 The graph is undirected. Each edge is essentially represented by two directed edges.

15.5 For the adjacency list, it takes $O(|V|)$ potentially, since you must check to see if the edge is possibly in the graph already. In the adjacency matrix implementation, it is constant time because the edge is represented by one or two spots in a matrix.

15.6 A tree of edges that includes every vertex. Spanning trees are not possible for disconnected graphs; in that case, a spanning forest is required.

15.7 Of all of the spanning trees of a graph, a minimum spanning tree is one whose total edge weight is least.

15.8 The transitive closure of a graph includes edge (u, v) if and only if one can reach vertex v from vertex u.

15.9 It is an ordering of vertices such that the (directed) edges of the graph all point in one direction.

15.10 If the graph is directed and acyclic.

A.2   Solutions to Odd-Numbered Problems

Chapter 0

Problems begin on page 3.

0.1 Right here, in the back of the book.

0.3 There are many resources available at `http://www.cs.williams.edu/JavaStructures`.

0.5 There are many resources available from `http://www.javasoft.com`.

0.7 There are a number of great texts associated with Java.

0.9 These pages are mirrored at `http://www.mhhe.com/javastructures`.

Chapter 1

Problems begin on page 26.

1.1 `int, double, char, boolean`.

1.3 (a) `java.lang.Double` extends `java.lang.Number`, (b) `java.lang.Integer` extends `java.lang.Number`, (c) `java.lang.Number` extends `java.lang.Object`, (d) `java.util.Stack` extends `java.util.Vector`, (e) `java.util.Hashtable` extends `java.util.Dictionary`.

1.5 The program

```
import structure.Association;
public class ModAssoc
{
    public static void main(String args[])
    {
        Association a = new Association("key","value");
```

```
                    a.theKey = null; // illegal access; generates compile error
         }
    }
```

generates the compile-time error

```
    ModAssoc.java:9: theKey has protected access in structure.Association
                    a.theKey = null; // illegal access; generates compile error
                    ^
    1 error
```

It is a compile-time error, because field access is determined by the compiler.
1.7   The following code approximates π using the technique stated. This version of gcd is particularly fast.

```
    import java.util.Random;
    public class Pi
    {
        static int gcd(int a, int b)
        // post: iteratively compute the gcd of two values
        {
            while (a*b!=0) // a and b not zero
            {   // reduce larger by smaller
                if (a < b) b %= a;
                else       a %= b;
            }
            return a+b; // a or b is zero; return other
        }

        public static void main(String args[])
        {
            int least = 0;
            int trials = 1000000;
            Random g = new Random();
            // perform the trials
            for (int i = 0; i < trials; i++)
            {
                // pick a random fraction, and test for a gcd of 1;
                // the fraction is in lowest terms
                if (gcd(Math.abs(g.nextInt())%10000,
                        Math.abs(g.nextInt())%10000) == 1) least++;
            }
            System.out.println("pi is approximately:");
            System.out.println("# "+Math.sqrt(6.0*trials/least));
        }
    }
```

1.9   The code for StopWatch is precisely the code of the structure package Clock object:

```
    package structure;
```

```
public class Clock
{
    // we use a native-code library for structures
    protected boolean running;  // is the clock on?
    protected long strt;        // starting millisecond count
    protected long accum;       // total milliseconds

    public Clock()
    // post: returns a stopped clock
    {
        running = false;
        strt = 0;
        accum = 0;
    }

    public void start()
    // post: clock is stopped
    // pre: starts clock, begins measuring possibly accumulated time
    {
        running = true;
        strt = System.currentTimeMillis();
    }

    public void stop()
    // pre: clock is running
    // post: stops clock, and accumulates time
    {
        running = false;
        accum += (System.currentTimeMillis()-strt);
    }

    public double read()
    // pre: clock is stopped
    // post: returns the accumulated time on the clock
    {
        return (double)accum/(double)1000.0;
    }

    public void reset()
    // post: stops running clock and clears the accumulated time
    {
        running = false;
        accum = 0;
    }

    public String toString()
    // post: returns a string representation of the clock
    {
        return "<Clock: "+read()+" seconds>";
    }
```

```
    }

1.11

    246.76047636306453 Hz

1.13

    import structure.Assert;
    public class Radio {
        protected boolean isOn;              // is the radio on
        protected boolean isFM;              // is the radio tuned to FM
        protected double tunedTo;            // current radio freq
        protected double tunedToAM;          // current AM radio freq
        protected double tunedToFM;          // current FM radio freq
        protected double FMFreq[];           // presets for FM
        protected double AMFreq[];           // presets for AM
        protected double AMPreset = 1030.0;  // factory setting for AM
        protected double FMPreset = 88.5;    // factory setting for FM

        public Radio()
        // post: constructs a radio, initially tuned to FM.
        // FM presets are 88.5, and AM presets are 1030.
        {
            FMFreq = new double[12];
            AMFreq = new double[12];
            for (int i = 0; i < 12; i++)
            {
                FMFreq[i] = FMPreset;
                AMFreq[i] = AMPreset;
            }
            on();
            AM();
            press(1);
            FM();
            press(1);
            off();
        }

        public boolean isOn()
        // post: returns true iff the radio is on
        {
            return isOn;
        }

        public boolean isFM()
        // post: returns true iff the radio is set to FM
        {
            return isFM;
        }
```

```
protected boolean validAM(double f)
// post: returns true iff f is a valid AM frequency
{
    return (530 <= f && f <= 1610) && (0.0 == f % 10.0);
}

protected boolean validFM(double f)
// post: returns true iff f is a valid FM frequency
{
    return (87.9 <= f) && (f <= 107.9) && ((((int)(f*10+0.5))-879)%2) == 0;
}

public void set(int button, double frequency)
// pre: radio is on and
//   button is between 1 and 12, and
//   frequency is a multiple of 10 if set to AM, or .2 if set to FM
// post: sets the indicated preset if the frequency is valid
{
    if (!isOn()) return;
    Assert.pre(button >= 1 && button <= 12, "Button value between 1 and 12.");
    if (isFM() && validFM(frequency)) FMFreq[button-1] = frequency;
    if ((!isFM()) && validAM(frequency)) AMFreq[button-1] = frequency;
}

public void press(int button)
// pre: button is between 1 and 12
// post: tunes radio to preset indicated by button
{
    if (isFM()) tune(FMFreq[button-1]);
    else tune(AMFreq[button-1]);
}

public void tune(double freq)
// pre: radio is on and frequency is valid for current AM/FM setting
// post: tunes the indicated radio frequency
{
    if (!isOn()) return;
    if (isFM() && validFM(freq)) tunedTo = tunedToFM = freq;
    else if ((!isFM()) && validAM(freq)) tunedTo = tunedToAM = freq;
}

public double frequency()
// post: returns the frequency that the radio is tuned to.
{
    return tunedTo;
}

public void AM()
// post: sets frequency range to AM; tunes radio to last AM freq
{
```

```
        isFM = false;
        tunedTo = tunedToAM;
    }

    public void FM()
    // post: sets frequency range to FM; tunes radio to last FM freq
    {
        isFM = true;
        tunedTo = tunedToFM;
    }

    public void on()
    // post: turns radio on
    {
        isOn = true;
    }

    public void off()
    // post: turns radio off
    {
        isOn = false;
    }

    public String toString()
    // post: generates a string representing the radio.
    {
        String result = "<Radio: ";
        if (isOn()) result += "turned on, ";
        else result += "turned off, ";
        if (isFM()) {
            result += "tuned to FM frequency "+tunedTo+"\n";
            result += "current AM frequency is "+tunedToAM+"\n";
        } else {
            result += "tuned to AM frequency "+tunedTo+"\n";
            result += "current FM frequency is "+tunedToFM+"\n";;
        }
        int i;
        result += "FM presets: ";
        for (i = 1; i <= 12; i++)
        {
            result += " "+FMFreq[i-1];
        }
        result += "\n";
        result += "AM presets: ";
        for (i = 1; i <= 12; i++)
        {
            result += " "+AMFreq[i-1];
        }
        result += "\n";
        result += ">";
```

```
            return result;
        }
    }
```

Chapter 2

Problems begin on page 37.

2.1   Precondition: none. Postcondition: returns the length of the string.

2.3   Precondition: the string provided as the parameter is non-null. Post-condition: returns a new string consisting of chars of this string followed by characters of parameter string.

2.5   This is a good exercise with most programs.

2.7   Precondition: the value must have magnitude no greater than 1. The postcondition can be gleaned from the Sun API web pages: "Returns the arc sine of an angle, in the range of $-\pi/2$ through $\pi/2$. Special cases:

- If the argument is NaN or its absolute value is greater than 1, then the result is NaN.

- If the argument is positive zero, then the result is positive zero; if the argument is negative zero, then the result is negative zero."

Programmers should remember that the angle cannot generally be retrieved from the inverse trigonometric functions unless both the numerator and denominator are remembered.

Chapter 3

Problems begin on page 65.

3.1   The size is the actual number of elements in use; the capacity is the number of cells allocated in the underlying array.

3.3   The trimToSize method allows the programmer to reduce the memory used by a Vector to the absolute minimum. In cases where doubling is used, or where there is shrinkage in the size of the Vector, there may be considerable savings. It is possible to trim the size of a Vector by copying it to a new Vector that is constructed using a capacity that is the exact size needed. The old Vector is reclaimed. In fact, this is often how the process is accomplished internally.

3.5   Here is the code, from the structure package implementation.

```
public int indexOf(Object elem, int index)
// post: returns index of element equal to object, or -1; starts at index
{
    int i;
    for (i = index; i < elementCount; i++)
    {
        if (elem.equals(elementData[i])) return i;
    }
```

```
            return -1;
    }
```

Clearly, the function returns −1 when the value cannot be found. Returning 0 would be incorrect, since 0 is a possible index for the Vector. On average, it takes $\frac{n}{2}$ to find the value.

3.7 This approach will not work. Removing values from the front and inserting them at the rear of the Vector keeps the elements in the original order. A better approach is to iteratively remove the first element from the Vector, and add it to a new result Vector at the zero location.

3.9 Using the default settings of Sun's Java 1.1.2 compiler under Solaris(TM), an array of approximately 1 million strings can be allocated. Can you write a program to determine the upper bound?

3.11 Here is the modified rewrite method:

```
public static Vector rewrite(Vector s)
// pre: s is a string of letters and strings
// post: returns a string rewritten by productions
{
    Vector result = new Vector();
    for (int pos = 0; pos < s.size(); pos++)
    {
        // rewrite according to two different rules
        if (s.get(pos) instanceof Vector)
        {
            result.add(rewrite((Vector)s.get(pos)));
        } else if (S == s.get(pos)) {
            result.add(T);
        } else if (T == s.get(pos)) {
            result.add(U);
        } else if (U == s.get(pos)) {
            result.add(V);
        } else if (V == s.get(pos)) {
            result.add(W);
        } else if (W == s.get(pos)) {
            Vector temp = new Vector();
            temp.add(S);
            result.add(temp);
            result.add(U);
        }
    }
    return result;
}
```

3.13 These methods must both assume, as preconditions, that the values stored within the Matrix are of type Double. The add method must require that the matrices are the same shape. The multiply method must verify that the number of columns of the left Matrix is the same as the number of rows of the right Matrix. Each of these conditions should be checked by formal assertions.

3.15 This is a partial implementation of an alternative `Matrix` class:

```
import structure.Vector;
import structure.Assert;

public class Matrix {
    protected int width;        // width of the matrix
    protected int height;       // height of the matrix
    protected Vector data;

    public Matrix(int rows, int cols)
    {
        data = new Vector(rows*cols);
        width = cols;
        height = rows;
    }
    public Object get(int row, int col)
    // pre: 0 <= row < height(), 0 <= col < width()
    // post: returns object at (row, col)
    {
        Assert.pre(0 <= row && row < height, "Row in bounds.");
        Assert.pre(0 <= col && col < width, "Col in bounds.");
        return data.get(row*width+col);
    }

    public void set(int row, int col, Object value)
    // pre: 0 <= row < height(), 0 <= col < width()
    // post: changes location (row,col) to value
    {
        Assert.pre(0 <= row && row < height, "Row in bounds.");
        Assert.pre(0 <= col && col < width, "Col in bounds.");
        data.set(row*width+col,value);
    }

    public String toString()
    {
        int i, j;
        String result = "<Matrix:\n";
        for (i = 0; i < height; i++)
        {
            for (j = 0; j < width; j++)
            {
                result += "\t"+get(i,j);
            }
            result += "\n";
        }
        return result + ">";
    }

    public static void main(String[] args)
```

```
    {
        int w = 3;
        int h = 10;
        Matrix m = new Matrix(h,w);
        int i, j;
        for (i = 0; i < h; i++)
        {
            for (j = 0; j < w; j++)
            {
                m.set(i,j,new Double(((double)i+1)/((double)j+1)));
            }
        }
        System.out.println(m);
    }
}
```

The advantages of this implementation are increased speed (only one Vector
lookup is necessary), and size (only one Vector is necessary; any overhead to
a Vector occurs once). Most matrix-like structures are implemented in this
manner in C-like languages. The disadvantage is that Matrix structures must
be rectangular: every row must be the same length. This can be avoided by
changing the computation of the index in the alternate implementation, but
that requires recompilation of the code.

3.17

```
    import structure.Assert;
    import structure.Vector;
    public class SymmetricMatrix
    {
        protected int size;   // size of matrix
        protected Vector rows;         // vector of row vectors

        public SymmetricMatrix()
        // post: constructs empty matrix
        {
            this(0);
        }

        public SymmetricMatrix(int h)
        // pre: h >= 0
        // post: constructs an h row by w column matrix
        {
            size = h;  // initialize size
            // allocate a vector of rows
            rows = new Vector(size);
            for (int r = 0; r < size; r++)
            {   // each row is allocated and filled with nulls
                Vector theRow = new Vector(r+1);
                rows.add(theRow);
                for (int c = 0; c < r+1; c++)
```

```
            {
                theRow.add(null);
            }
        }
    }

    public Object get(int row, int col)
    // pre: 0 <= row < size(), 0 <= col < size()
    // post: returns object at (row, col)
    {
        Assert.pre(0 <= row && row < size, "Row in bounds.");
        Assert.pre(0 <= col && col < size, "Col in bounds.");
        if (row < col) return get(col,row);
        else {
            Vector theRow = (Vector)rows.get(row);
            return theRow.get(col);
        }
    }

    public void set(int row, int col, Object value)
    // pre: 0 <= row < size(), 0 <= col < size
    // post: changes location (row,col) to value
    {
        Assert.pre(0 <= row && row < size, "Row in bounds.");
        Assert.pre(0 <= col && col < size, "Col in bounds.");
        if (row < col) set(col,row,value);
        else
        {
            Vector theRow = (Vector)rows.get(row);
            theRow.set(col,value);
        }
    }

    public int size()
    // post: returns number of rows in matrix
    {
        return size;
    }

    public String toString()
    // post: returns string description of matrix
    {
        StringBuffer s = new StringBuffer();
        s.append("<SymmetricMatrix:\n");
        for (int r = 0; r < size(); r++)
        {
            for (int c = 0; c < size(); c++)
            {
                s.append("  "+get(r,c));
            }
```

```
            s.append("\n");
        }
        s.append(">");
        return s.toString();
    }
}
```

Chapter 4

Problems begin on page 100.

4.1   Accessing a value in an array is $O(1)$ time. The same is true with the `get` method. The difference is absorbed in the constant associated with big-O notation.

4.3   The running time is $O(\log n)$. The function loops approximately $\log_2 n$ times.

4.5   This "standard" approach to matrix multiplication is $O(n^3)$.

4.7   The lower bound on adding a value to the end of the `Vector` is constant time as well: $\Omega(1)$. The doubling of the size of the array may affect the upper bound, but not the lower bound.

4.9   The complexity is $O(n)$: we must construct a new string with space that has `a.size()+1` characters, and we must copy them all over. Notice that, from a theoretical standpoint, it is no more complex than adding a character to the end of a zero-terminated mutable string. The time is still determined, in that case, by a search for the end of the string: $O(n)$ time.

4.11   The function grows as a linear function, $O(n)$. The linear term n outstrips the logarithmic term $\log n$. Select $c = 2$ and $n_0 = 1$. (Proof omitted.)

4.13   The rate is $O(1)$. Select $c = 1.5$ and $n_0 = 1$. (Proof omitted.)

4.15 $O(\tan n)$. If no "traditional" bound can be found, we can make use of the fact that every function f is $O(f)$.

4.17   Here is a recursive implementation:

```
public static void syr(int s0)
{
    System.out.print(s0+" ");
    if (s0 == 1) System.out.println();
    else if ((s0 % 2) == 0) syr(s0/2);
    else syr(s0*3+1);
}
```

4.19   This answer is discussed in detail in *Java Elements* by Bailey and Bailey:

```
public static void drawLine(int x0, int y0, int x1, int y1)
// pre: drawing window d is non-null
// post: a line is drawn on d from (x0,y0) to (x1,y1)
{
    int mx = (x0+x1)/2;                    // midpoint
    int my = (y0+y1)/2;
    int dx = Math.abs(x1-x0);              // span in x and y direction
    int dy = Math.abs(y1-y0);
```

```
        if (dx <= 1 && dy <= 1)  // very close end points
        {
            d.draw(new Pt(x1,y1));        // draw destination
        } else if (dx > 1 || dy > 1)
        {
            drawLine(x0,y0,mx,my);        // draw first half
            drawLine(mx,my,x1,y1);        //    and second half
        }
    }
```

4.21   The complexity of this function is $O(n)$ where n is the smaller of the two values.

```
    public static int mult(int a, int b)
    {
        if (a < 0) return -mult(-a,b);
        if (a == 0) return 0;
        if (a == 1) return b;
        if (a < b) return mult(a-1,b)+b;
        else return mult(b,a);
    }
```

4.23   Let us prove this by induction. First, note that if $n = 0$, then

$$5^n - 4n - 1 = 1 + 0 - 1 = 0$$

Since 16 divides 0 evenly, the observation holds for $n = 0$. Now, assume that the observation holds for all values less than n, and specifically in the case of $n - 1$. We have, then, that

$$5^{n-1} - 4(n - 1) - 1$$

is divisible by 16. Multiplying by 5 we get

$$5^n - 20(n - 1) - 5$$

which is also divisible by 16. That is not quite the desired expression. At this point we add $16(n - 1)$, a multiple of 16:

$$
\begin{aligned}
& 5^n - 20(n - 1) + 16(n - 1) - 5 \\
= \ & 5^n - 4(n - 1) - 5 \\
= \ & 5^n - 4n + 4 - 5 \\
= \ & 5^n - 4n - 1
\end{aligned}
$$

Clearly, this expression is divisible by 16, so the observation holds for n. By induction on n, we see the result holds for all $n \geq 0$.

4.25   It is clear to see that n^d can be rewritten as $n^{c+(d-c)} = n^c \cdot n^{d-c}$. Since $d \geq c$, then $d - c \geq 0$ and, for $n \geq 1$, $n^{d-c} \geq 1$. We have, therefore, that $n^d \geq n^c$ for all $n \geq 1$. This is sufficient to demonstrate that n^c is $O(n^d)$ for any $d \geq c$.

4.27   Clearly, the sum of the first n odd integers is

$$2\left(\sum_{i=0}^{n} i\right) - n = n(n+1) - n = n^2$$

4.29   Since $\log n$ is monotonic and increasing, the $\log n$ bounds $\log i$ above for $i \leq n$. The result is, then, trivial.

4.31   This is a good problem to perform in a later lab. Keeping a log of errors is instructive and points to weaknesses in our understanding of the systems we use.

4.33   The best strategy is to decrease the size of the Vector by a factor of 2 when the number of elements within the Vector falls below $\frac{1}{3}$. An interesting experiment would be to simulate the expansion and contraction of Vectors over time with random inserts and deletes. What are the characteristics of the various expansion and reduction policies?

Chapter 5

Problems begin on page 133.

5.1   The two values a and b can be exchanged with the following code:

```
a=b-a;
b=b-a;
a=a+b;
```

5.3   Bubble sort, as presented in the text, performs comparisons in a data-independent manner. Its behavior, then, is always $O(n^2)$.

5.5   All cases take $O(n^2)$ time. Selection sort does not improve the ordering of the data by selecting a value. It is often worse than the modified bubble sort.

5.7   The author ran the following test sorts on arrays of randomly selected integers. Winner for each test is indicated in italics.

	Insertion Sort		Quicksort	
n	Compares	Time (ms)	Compares	Time (ms)
2	1	0.0	1	0.0
4	4	0.0	2	0.0
8	17	0.0	6	0.0
16	51	*0.0*	42	0.0010
32	213	0.0	125	0.0
64	1,008	*0.0010*	217	0.0010
128	3,923	*0.0020*	595	0.0040
256	17,465	*0.0010*	1,234	0.0020
512	64,279	0.0040	3,492	*0.0020*
1,024	255,250	0.016	6,494	*0.0010*
2,048	1,064,222	0.067	18,523	*0.0020*
4,096	4,245,882	0.265	31,930	*0.0050*
8,192	16,816,801	1.092	76,093	*0.012*
16,384	66,961,345	4.424	179,017	*0.027*

5.9   It is relatively simple to construct a counterexample array. Here is one:

| 19 | 28 | 29 | 46 | 55 |

An immediate pass through the 10's digits does not change the array. If this is followed by a pass on the units bits, you get

| 55 | 46 | 28 | 19 | 29 |

which is clearly not sorted. If this was, however, the first pass, a second pass then generates

| 19 | 28 | 29 | 46 | 55 |

which is sorted.

5.11   In late 2001 the author informally measured the speed of an assignment using the Java 2 HotSpot(TM) virtual machine under Mac OS/X running on a Macintosh Powerbook G3 at approximately 2 nanoseconds. The speed of other operations measured in units of a basic assignment were approximately:

Integer assignment	1
Add to integer	1
Multiply by integer	1
Integer array entry assignment	3
Iteration of empty loop	9
Vector entry assignment	70

5.13   As presented, insertion and mergesort are stable. Selection and quicksort are not stable. Selection sort can easily be made stable. For quicksort to be made stable, the partition function needs to be reconsidered.

5.15   The following modifications are made to the standard `quickSort` program:

```
protected static Random gen;
public static void quickSort(int data[], int n)
// post: the values in data[0..n-1] are in ascending order
{
    gen = new Random();
    quickSortRecursive(data,0,n-1);
}


private static int partition(int data[], int left, int right)
// pre: left <= right
// post: data[left] placed in the correct (returned) location
{
    if (left < right) {
        int x = left+(Math.abs(gen.nextInt()) % (right-left+1));
        swap(data,left,x);
    }
    while (true)
        ...
}
```

It is important to construct a new random number generator at most once per sort or it will lose its random behavior. Here, we have used an instance variable, but it could be passed along to the `partition` method.

5.17 This solution was derived from the iterative version. Since the iteration has a loop that runs the index toward 0, the recursive call happens *before* the work loop:

```
public static void insertionSort(int data[], int n)
// pre: 0 <= n <= data.length
// post: values in data[0..n-1] are in ascending order
{
    if (n > 1)
    {
        // sort the first n-1 values
        insertionSort(data,n-1);
        // take the last unsorted value
        int temp = data[n-1];
        int index; // a general index
        // ...and insert it among the sorted:
        for (index = n-1; 0 < index && temp < data[index-1]; index--)
        {
            data[index] = data[index-1];
        }
        // reinsert value
        data[index] = temp;
    }
}
```

5.19 The worst-case running time cannot be determined since given any particular upper bound, there is a nonzero probability that a run of shuffle sort will exceed that bound. The revised assumption allows a worst-case running time to be determined. Here is the questionable code to perform this sort:

```
public static void shuffleSort(int data[], Random gen)
// pre: gen is initialized, data contain only valid values
// post: data are sorted
{
    int n = data.length;
    while (true)
    {
        // check to see if data is in order
        boolean inOrder = true;
        for (int i = 1; i < n && inOrder; i++)
        {
            inOrder = inOrder && data[i-1] <= data[i];
        }
        // if it is sorted, return!
        if (inOrder) return;
        // nope: shuffle the values again
        shuffle(data,gen);
    }
```

```
        }
```

Notice we check to see if the data are in order *before* shuffling. This is advanta-geous.

Chapter 7

Problems begin on page 161.

7.1   `AbstractIterator` is an implementation of the `Iterator` class, it must implement the methods of the `Iterator`.

7.3   The main difference is that a prime number iterator returns `Integer` values, rather than `ints`.

```java
import structure.*;
import java.util.Iterator;

public class PrimeIterator extends AbstractIterator
{
    protected Vector primes;
    protected int current;

    public PrimeIterator()
    // post: construct a generator that delivers primes starting at 2
    {
        reset();
    }

    public void reset()
    // post: reset the generator to return primes starting at 2
    {
        primes = new Vector();
        primes.add(new Integer(2));
        current = 0;
    }

    public boolean hasNext()
    // post: returns true - an indication that there are always more primes
    {
        return true;
    }

    public Object get()
    {
        return primes.get(current);
    }

    public Object next()
    // post: geneate the next prime
    {
        Integer N = (Integer)get();
```

```
                current++;
                if (current >= primes.size())
                {
                    int n = N.intValue();
                    int i, f;
                    Integer F;
                    do
                    {
                        if (n == 2) n = 3;
                        else n = n + 2;
                        for (i = 0; i < primes.size(); i++)
                        {
                            F = (Integer)primes.get(i);
                            f = F.intValue();
                            if ((n%f) == 0) break;
                        }
                    } while (i < primes.size());
                    primes.add(new Integer(n));
                }
                return N;
            }
        }
```

7.5   This solution uses `OrderedLists`, which appear in Chapter 10. Another approach is to store values in a `Vector` using insertion sort, or to store all the values in a `Vector`, and perform quicksort.

```
import structure.*;
import java.util.Iterator;

public class OrderedIterator extends AbstractIterator
{
    protected OrderedList data;
    protected AbstractIterator li;
    protected Iterator iter;

    public OrderedIterator(Iterator subIterator)
    // pre: subIterator valid and generates a finite number of elements
    // post: returns elements returned by subIterator, in reverse order
    {
        data = new OrderedList();
        iter = subIterator;
        while (subIterator.hasNext())
        {
            data.add(subIterator.next());
        }
        li = (AbstractIterator)data.iterator();
    }

    public void reset()
    // post: resets the iterator to next return the last element of the
```

```
    // sub-iterator
    {
        li.reset();
    }

    public boolean hasNext()
    // post: returns true if there are more values to be returned from iterator.
    {
        return li.hasNext();
    }

    public Object next()
    // post: returns the previous element of the sub-iterator; advances iter
    {
        return li.next();
    }

    public Object get()
    // post: returns next element of iterator, does not advance
    {
        return li.get();
    }
}
```

7.7   This involves constructing two classes and an interface. The `Predicate`
interface has the following form:

```
public interface Predicate
{
    public boolean select(Object item);
    // pre: item is a valid object
    // post: returns true or false, depending on the predicate tested
}
```

A particular `Predicate` returns `true` if and only if the `String` object handed
to it is 10 characters or longer.

```
public class LongString implements Predicate
{
    public boolean select(Object o)
    // pre: o is a String
    // post: returns true if string is longer than 10 characters
    {
        String s = (String)o;
        return s.length() > 10;
    }
}
```

We now have the specification of a `PredicateIterator`:

```
import structure.*;
import java.util.Iterator;
```

```
public class PredicateIterator extends AbstractIterator
{
    protected Iterator iter;
    protected Predicate p;
    protected Object current;
    public PredicateIterator(Predicate p, Iterator subIterator)
    {
        iter = subIterator;
        this.p = p;
        reset();
    }

    public void reset()
    {
        current = null;
        while (iter.hasNext())
        {
            Object temp = iter.next();
            if (p.select(temp)) {
                current = temp;
                break;
            }
        }
    }

    public boolean hasNext()
    {
        return (current != null);
    }

    public Object get()
    {
        return current;
    }

    public Object next()
    {
        Object result = current;
        current = null;
        while (iter.hasNext())
        {
            Object temp = iter.next();
            if (p.select(temp)) {
                current = temp;
                break;
            }
        }
        return result;
    }
```

```
        }
```

Chapter 8

Problems begin on page 200.

8.1   The methods `size`, `isEmpty`, `clear`, `addFirst`, `addLast`; `remove()` and `remove(Object)`; all `add` methods; `contains`, `indexOf`, and `lastIndexOf` methods; and all methods otherwise inherited from the `Structure` object.

8.3   It is a suitable structure:

1. It is a naturally dynamic structure: there is no bound on the number of elements that may be saved in a `List`.

2. Each element of the `List` can be accessed randomly by specifying its location with respect to the head of the list—its index.

3. Although the access time is likely to be proportional to the index provided, it is unlikely that users would notice the slowdown associated with the access.

8.5

```java
public void reverse()
// post: this list is in reverse order.
// post: the list is reversed, destructively
{
    SinglyLinkedListElement previous = null;
    SinglyLinkedListElement finger = head;

    while (finger != null)
    {
        SinglyLinkedListElement next = finger.next();
        finger.setNext(previous);
        previous = finger;
        finger = next;
    }
    head = previous;
}

public int size()
// post: returns the number of elements in the list
{
    return size(head);
}

protected int size(SinglyLinkedListElement e)
// pre: e is an element of the list, or null
// post: returns the number of elements in the sublist headed by e
{
    if (e == null) return 0;
```

```
        else return 1 + size(e.next());
    }

    public boolean contains(Object o)
    // pre: o is a valid object
    // post: returns true if a value in this list is "equals" to o
    {
        return contains(o,head);
    }

    protected boolean contains(Object o,SinglyLinkedListElement e)
    // pre: o is a valid object, e is the head of a sublist of this
    // post: returns true if a value in this sublist is equals to o
    {
        if (e == null) return false;
        if (e.value().equals(o)) return true;
        return contains(o,e.next());
    }
```

8.7 This is a hard problem. It is made easier if we imagine the list to be linear, and then work out the boundary conditions.

```
    public void reverse()
    // post: this list is in reverse order.
    {
        if (tail == null) return;
        SinglyLinkedListElement previous = tail;
        SinglyLinkedListElement finger = tail.next();
        tail.setNext(null); // now, it's a singly linked list
        tail = finger;

        while (finger != null)
        {
            SinglyLinkedListElement next = finger.next();
            finger.setNext(previous);
            previous = finger;
            finger = next;
        }
    }
```

8.9 Here's the add method from the CircularList implementation:

```
    public void add(int i, Object o)
    // pre: 0 <= i <= size()
    // post: adds ith entry of list to value o
    {
        Assert.pre((0 <= i) && (i <= size()),"Index in range.");
        if (i == 0) addFirst(o);
        else if (i == size()) addLast(o);
        else {
            SinglyLinkedListElement previous = tail;
```

```
                    SinglyLinkedListElement next = tail.next();
                    while (i > 0)
                    {
                        previous = next;
                        next = next.next();
                        i--;
                    }
                    SinglyLinkedListElement current =
                        new SinglyLinkedListElement(o,next);
                    count++;
                    previous.setNext(current);
                }
            }
```

8.11 Because we have backed up the reference, it is farther away from the references that need to be manipulated. In general, the construction of the head and tail references will take longer and operations will execute more slowly. Clearly, though, the method `removeLast` has the potential for great improvement; it becomes an $O(1)$ operation, instead of $O(n)$.

8.13 Theoretically, we expect the following outcome:

1. For `addFirst`, all linked list implementations perform better than `Vector`. Singly linked lists are only slightly better than circular and doubly linked lists.

2. For `remove(Object)` a `Vector` takes $O(n)$ time to find and $O(n)$ time to remove the value. The removal is constant time for linked implementations.

3. For `removeLast`, `Vector`, doubly and circularly linked list classes are all potentially much faster than singly linked lists.

8.15

```
public int size()
// post: returns the number of elements in the list
{
    return size(head);
}


protected int size(SinglyLinkedListElement e)
// pre: e is an element of the list, or null
// post: returns the number of elements in the sublist headed by e
{
    if (e == null) return 0;
    else return 1 + size(e.next());
}
```

8.17 If we add new words to the end of the list, the final vocabulary list is in an order that is well correlated to decreasing frequency. If words are used infrequently, they will likely appear later in the input and thus in the list. Frequently used words are likely to be encountered quickly. This is a help: we want high-frequency words to appear near the front of the vocabulary list to terminate the search quickly.

Chapter 9

Problems begin on page 233.

9.1   The stack contains values $n - m$ from 1 (at the bottom) to $n - m$ (on the top).

9.3   One additional stack is necessary.

```
public static void copy(Stack s, Stack t)
// pre: s and t are valid stacks; t is empty
// post: the elements of s are copied to t, in order
{
    Stack temp = new StackList();
    while (!s.isEmpty()) temp.push(s.pop());
    // Assertion: the elements of the stack are reversed, in temp
    while (!temp.isEmpty())
    {
        Object item = temp.pop();
        s.push(item); t.push(item);
    }
}
```

9.5   Determine the size of the queue, say, n. Perform n dequeue operations, enqueuing the result both at the end of the original as well as the copy:

```
public static void copy(Queue q, Queue r)
// pre: q and r are valid queues; r is empty
// post: the elements of q are copied to r, in order
{
    int n = q.size();
    for (int i = 0; i < n; i++)
    {
        Object item = q.dequeue();
        q.enqueue(item); r.enqueue(item);
    }
}
```

9.7   The following recursive program should do the trick. Note that the elements of the queue are stored on the stack that manages recursion!

```
public static void reverse(Queue q)
// pre: q is a valid queue
// post: the elements of q are reversed
{
    if (!q.isEmpty())
    {
        Object o = q.dequeue();
```

```
        reverse(q);
        q.enqueue(o);
    }
}
```

9.9   At any time, the elements of the stack are in decreasing order from the top to the bottom. Any values that are missing from top to bottom must have been pushed and popped off already. Thus, at any point in the sequence if you pop off two values l and ultimately k ($k < l$), then all values between k and l must already have been popped off before l.

Thus, for $n = 4$, there are several impossible sequences: those that mention $3, 1, 2$ in order, or $4, 1, 2$, or $4, 1, 3$, or $4, 2, 3$.

9.11   It is only possible to remove elements from a queue in the order they are inserted. Thus, it is only possible to remove the elements in the order $1, 2, 3, \ldots, n$.

9.13   Suppose that we have two stacks, `head` and `tail`. The bottom of `head` contains the head of the `queue`, while the bottom of `tail` contains the tail of the queue. Enqueuing takes time proportional to the size of `tail`, while dequeuing takes time proportional to `head`.

9.15   This is a queue structure, where the elements contain lists of food items.

Chapter 10

Problems begin on page 261.

10.1

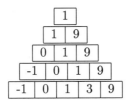

10.3   The older value is found in a location with a lower index.

10.5   To insert a value into an `OrderedList` we must execute the following procedure:

```
public void add(Object value)
// pre: value is non-null
// post: value is added to the list, leaving it in order
{
    SinglyLinkedListElement previous = null; // element to adjust
    SinglyLinkedListElement finger = data;   // target element
    Comparable cValue = (Comparable)value;   // inserted value
    // search for the correct location
    while ((finger != null) &&
            ordering.compare(finger.value(),cValue) < 0)
    {
        previous = finger;
```

```
            finger = finger.next();
        }
        // spot is found, insert
        if (previous == null) // check for insert at top
        {
            data = new SinglyLinkedListElement(cValue,data);
        } else {
            previous.setNext(
                new SinglyLinkedListElement(cValue,previous.next()));
        }
        count++;
    }
```

The initialization statements do not take any time. The `while` loop executes once for each smaller value. In the worst case, the value inserted is larger than all values within the list; the loop must be executed n times. Actual insertion involves the construction of a new `SinglyLinkedListElement`—constant time. The overal time is, then, $O(n)$.

10.7   An `OrderedVector` is faster at finding the correct location for a value, but an `OrderedList` is faster at performing the insertion. Both, then, have $O(n)$ insertion time. The main distinction between the two is in `get`-type accesses. The `OrderedVector` can make use of the binary search approach, while the `OrderedList` cannot. When you expect many accesses, the `OrderedVector` is a better structure.

10.9   Here is a straightforward implementation:

```
public int compareTo(Object other)
// pre: other is a valid String
// post: returns value <, ==, or > to 0 if this <, ==, or > that
{
    String that = (String)other;
    int thisLen = this.length();
    int thatLen = that.length();
    char thisc, thatc;
    int i;
    // as long as one string has a character
    for (i = 0; i < thisLen || i < thatLen; i++)
    {
        thisc = (i < thisLen) ? this.charAt(i) : 0; // char or 0
        thatc = (i < thatLen) ? that.charAt(i) : 0; // char or 0
        if (thisc != thatc)
        {
            return (int)(thisc - thatc);
        }
    }
    // strings are the same
    return 0;
}
```

The proprietary code for the method is also available from Sun at `www.sun.com`.

10.11 This performs a comparison between objects of type `Person`, containing first and last names stored as `String` types:

```
public int compareTo(Object other)
// pre: this and other are people with first and last names
// post: returns relationship between people based on last name, or
// first name if last names are the same.
{
    Person that = (Person)other;
    // compare last names
    int lastCompare = this.last.compareTo(that.last);
    if (lastCompare != 0) return lastCompare;
    // compare first names if necessary
    return this.first.compareTo(that.first);
}
```

10.13 For the `OrderedVector`, the get method consistently involves a binary search method that demands $O(\log n)$ time; best-, expected-, and worst-case behaviors are logarithmic.

For the `OrderedList` the get method is linear: searching for larger values takes a proportionately longer time. The best case is constant time; the average and worst case are $O(n)$.

Chapter 11

Problems begin on page 297.

11.1　In a preorder traversal: U, T, I, M, S, D, A, D.
In a postorder traversal: M, I, T, A, D, D, S, U.
In an in-order traversal: M, I, T, U, S, A, D, D.

11.3

```
a. (1)  b.      (-)       c.  (+)          d.      (*)      e. (+)
            (+)      /        (1)     /          (+)   -       (1)   *
         (1)   *   4 2               *    2    (1) 5 3 /          5   -
              5 3                  5    -           4 2             3  /
                                 3    4                              4 2
```

11.5　We see that

$$R = 1 + (L - 1) * 2$$
$$R = 1 + 2L - 2$$
$$R = 2L - 1$$

In terms of expression trees this becomes:

```
       =                    =                    =
    R    +               R    +               R    -
      1    *    =>         1    -    =>         *    -
```

```
       - 2                    *      *       L 2    2 1
       L 1                    L 2    1 2
```

11.7 The `List` classes, if defined recursively, would, probably, have more recursively defined functions. For example, many of the index-based methods (e.g., `get(i)` and `set(i,v)`, would be defined recursively: they would work on the current element if $i = 0$, and otherwise recursively act on the next element.

11.9 Here is an outline of the proof: If the time is less than linear in the number of nodes, then some node is not considered during the computation. Suppose that, in the computation of the height of a tree, node x does not need to be considered. We can, then, construct a tree of similar structure, except that a very tall subtree—a tree tall enough to change the height of the overall tree—can be hung from a descendant of x. Since x is not considered in the height computation of the original tree, the height of the revised tree will not be computed correctly, because the height-determining subtree hangs from below x.

11.11 This is very similar to the implementation of the `clone` method.

```java
public BinaryTree copy()
// post: contructs a structural copy of this binary tree
{
    if (isEmpty()) return this;      // don't copy the empty tree
    return new BinaryTree(value(),left().copy(),right().copy());
}
```

11.13 Our implementation is the same as that of Problem 11.14. Another approach keeps track of a `Vector` of children.

11.15

```java
import structure.*;
public class TreeIterator extends AbstractIterator
{
    protected Tree root;
    protected Stack todo;
    public TreeIterator(Tree root)
    {
        todo = new StackList();
        this.root = root;
        reset();
    }

    public void reset()
    // post: resets the iterator to retraverse
    {
        todo.clear();
        // stack is empty.  Push on the current node.
        if (root != null) todo.push(root);
    }

    public boolean hasNext()
```

```
// post: returns true iff iterator is not finished
{
    return !todo.isEmpty();
}

public Object get()
// pre: hasNext()
// post: returns reference to current value
{
    return ((Tree)todo.getFirst()).value();
}

public Object next()
// pre: hasNext();
// post: returns current value, increments iterator
{
    Tree old = (Tree)todo.pop();
    Object result = old.value();
    Stack s = new StackList();
    Tree child = old.oldest();
    while (!child.isEmpty())
    {
        s.push(child);
        child = child.siblings();
    }
    while (!s.isEmpty())
    {
        todo.push(s.pop());
    }
    return result;
}
}
}
```

11.17 Left to the reader.

11.19 This version is part of the `BinaryTree` implementation.

```
public boolean isComplete()
// post: returns true iff the tree rooted at node is complete
{
    int leftHeight, rightHeight;
    boolean leftIsFull, rightIsFull;
    boolean leftIsComplete, rightIsComplete;
    if (isEmpty()) return true;
    leftHeight = left().height();
    rightHeight = right().height();
    leftIsFull = left().isFull();
    rightIsFull = right().isFull();
    leftIsComplete = left().isComplete();
    rightIsComplete = right().isComplete();

    // case 1: left is full, right is complete, heights same
```

```
        if (leftIsFull && rightIsComplete &&
            (leftHeight == rightHeight)) return true;
        // case 2: left is complete, right is full, heights differ
        if (leftIsComplete && rightIsFull &&
            (leftHeight == (rightHeight + 1))) return true;
        return false;
    }
```

11.21 Here we implement the method as described. Note the important changes to isFull and height.

```
    protected int info()
    // pre: this tree is not empty
    // post: height of tree if it is full, or negative of that value
    //       if the tree is not full
    {
        if (left().isEmpty() && right().isEmpty()) return 0;
        int leftInfo = left.info();
        int rightInfo = right.info();
        int result = 1+Math.max(Math.abs(leftInfo),Math.abs(rightInfo));
        if (leftInfo<0 || rightInfo < 0 || leftInfo != rightInfo)
            result = -result;
        return result;
    }


    public int height()
    // post: returns the height of a node in its tree
    {
        if (isEmpty()) return -1;
        return Math.abs(info());
    }


    public boolean isFull()
    // post: returns true iff the tree rooted at node is full
    {
        if (isEmpty()) return true;
        return info() >= 0;
    }
```

11.23 The simplicity of the in-order iterator fix is that, given a node that you are currently processing, finding the next node is fairly simple. In the in-order case, for example, finding the next node to consider is no worse than the height of the tree.

Preorder traversals simply need to move left if there is a left child, or move right if there is a right child, or move up until we leave a left subtree and there is a right subtree: we then go to the right. Complexity is no worse than height of the tree between iterations.

In the case of postorder, we must always move upward. If we arise from a left subtree, head back down the right. If we arise from a right subtree, stop at the parent. Complexities are similar.

For level-order traversal, we must increase the complexity considerably because of the difficulty of moving between sibling nodes. To move right, we go up until we arise from a left subtree and head down a *similar number* of levels to the leftmost child (if any). If there is no such sibling, we must head to the root and down to the leftmost descendant at the next level down. This code is quite complex, but can be accomplished. A queue is a better solution!

11.25 If there are $n = 0$ full nodes, there is one node, a leaf, so the observation holds. Now, suppose the condition holds for all values less than n. The root of the tree has degree k. The k subtrees each have subtrees with $n_0, n_1, \ldots, n_{k-1}$ full nodes. By the inductive hypothesis, these subtrees have $(k-1)n_i + 1$ leaves. The total for all subtrees is

$$\sum_{i=0}^{k}(k-1)n_i + 1 = (k-1)(n-1) + k = (k-1)n + 1 - k + k = (k-1)n + 1$$

and the theorem holds. By mathematical induction on n, the theorem holds for all $g \geq 0$.

Chapter 12

Problems begin on page 326.

12.1

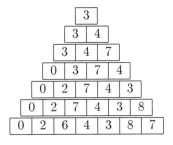

12.3

```
            1
       3         2
     4   5     4
```

12.5 A `VectorHeap` is not a `Queue` because it does not support the FIFO ordering. It is not an `OrderedStructure`.

12.7 For a `PriorityVector`, only the `compareTo` method is used to locate the correct position. Equal priorities may appear separated, but they will appear to be consistent from the point of view of `compareTo`. The same is true with `SkewHeaps`.

12.9 In fact, no additional methods are necessary.

12.11 Notice first that `heapify` of Problem 12.10 is linear even if the data are already a heap. For `add`, the best- and worst-case running times can be made constant: simply add the value to the end of the `Vector`. For the `remove` method, the best-case time is $O(\log n)$ when no heapify is necessary. In the worst case, the time is $O(n)$, if a heapify is necessary.

12.13

a. Descending. The minimum value is removed and swapped with the last element of the `Vector`.

b. The worst-case time-complexity is $O(n \log n)$, when the data are all unique.

c. The best-case time-complexity is $O(n)$, when all the data are the same. Removing a value from a heap in this case requires constant time.

12.15 First, we suppose that k is a constant determined at compile time. We can, then, keep an `OrderedVector` of k of the largest values, and a heap of the remaining values. When we add a value, we first add it into the `OrderedVector` (in constant time), and then remove the last element and insert it into a heap of the remaining values. As we remove values from the `Vector`, we can absorb values from the heap as necessary. The worst-case running time is $O(\log n)$.

12.17 Every full node has two states: swapped and unswapped. Since no full node can undo the swapping of another node, every swap has a unique effect. Since there are $\frac{n}{2}$ interior nodes that may be swapped, there are $2^{\frac{n}{2}}$ different heaps related by swapping children.

12.19 This percentage is quite small. Every node (save the root) has a parent. The chance that the child is less than the parent is 50 percent. We have, then, that 1 in 2^{n-1} trees is a heap. (This is easy to see if we just consider the degenerate trees.)

12.21 The `Vector` could be as large as $2^n - 1$ elements. Consider a rightmost degenerate tree.

12.23 Certainly this can be accomplished in $O(n \log n)$ time.

12.25 We simply add new values to the end of the `Vector`, checking to see if the new value should be swapped for the old minimum. When we are asked to remove a value, we hand over the leftmost value and heapify the rest of the `Vector`. Adding is constant time; removing is linear time.

Chapter 13

Problems begin on page 351.

13.1   The nodes of a binary search tree are kept in an order that allows them to be inspected in increasing order with an in-order traversal.

13.3

```
      1      1     1      1      1
     2      2    2   3    2      2
    3      3              3      3
```

Only the last is a binary search tree.

13.5

13.7

13.9 One need only observe that values are added as a leaf in a unique location. A level-order traversal of the binary search tree desired gives an appropriate order for insertion.

13.11 This is, effectively, the construction of a Linear structure, a degenerate rightmost search tree. Behavior is $O(n^2)$. (The best-case running time for arbitrary order is $O(n \log n)$.)

13.13 Have it first use the successor, then predecessor, then successor, and so on. Another possibility is to pick randomly, with equal probability.

13.15 At each stage of the iteration, there may be a significant search—perhaps as great as $O(n)$—for the next value. Over the entire iteration, however, the total expense is only linear.

13.17 Yes. However, one must be careful to avoid causing splays of the trees by directly accessing the tree itself. Such behavior could increase the cost of the iteration.

13.19 Provided that no splays occur during the iteration, it is fairly simple to see that each edge of the splay tree is traversed twice during the iteration. Over n next calls, this averages out to be two iterations of a loop in the next method per call.

Chapter 14

Problems begin on page 385.

14.1 No. If the keys were equal, the second key inserted would have found the first.

14.3 The state of the table changes as follows:

Index	0	1	2	3	4	5	6
Insert D				D			
Insert a	a			D			
Insert d	a			D	d		
Insert H	a	H		D	d		
Insert a	a	H	a	D	d		
Insert h	a	H	a	D	d	h	

14.5 As was the case with Problem 14.4, it is possible to have a hash table appear full when, in fact, it is only partially full.

14.7 Get the integer representation of the real number. Simply call `Double.-doubleToLongBits(d)`. The result is a suitable hash code when reduced to an `int`. The Sun implementation performs the exclusive-or of the two `int`s that make up the `longword`.

14.9 It is best to design a hash table to be several times larger than the data to be stored. If this is not done, the collisions will decrease the performance considerably.

14.11 This technique has all the disadvantages of exclusive-or, but with little knowledge of the contained data, it is suitable. The Sun implementation overflows after the first seven or eight entries.

```
public int hashCode()
// post: returns the hashcode associated with non-null values of this
// vector
{
    int result = 0;
    for (int i = 0; i < size(); i++)
    {
        Object temp = get(i);
        if (temp != null) result = result ^ temp.hashCode();
    }
    return result;
}
```

14.13 This technique works for all collections:

```
public int hashCode()
{
    int result = 0;
    Iterator it = iterator();
    while (it.hasNext())
    {
        Object temp = it.next();
        if (temp != null) result = result ^ temp.hashCode();
    }
    return result;
}
```

14.15 The value of i can get to be as large as $\log_2 l$, so the algorithm is potentially logarithmic in the length of the string.

14.17 No. It's only ordered from the perspective of rehashing. The smallest value, for example, may appear in any location to which it hashes—anywhere in the table.

14.19 One approach would be to hash together all the coordinates for each of the checker pieces. Another approach is to consider each of the rows to be a 12-bit integer, where each useful square is represented by 3 bits that encode empty, red, red-king, black, or black-king. The hash code for the entire board is then the exclusive-or of all rows, where each is shifted by three bits.

14.21 One would have to count the number of times that the `hashCode` method for the `String` class was called and compute the expected frequency per `String`. (It is likely that this value is larger than 1; compiled `Strings` are manipulated fairly frequently, for example, in the lifetime of a compiled program.) If this value is larger than 1, the hash code could be computed once, at only the cost of space. If the average length of a `String` was short—say 4 or less, the storage of the hash code might not be space efficient.

Chapter 15

Problems begin on page 421.

15.1

	a	b	c	d
a	F	T	T	T
b	T	F	T	T
c	T	T	F	T
d	T	T	T	F

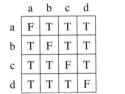

15.3

	0	1	2	3	4	5	6
0	F	T	T	F	F	F	F
1	T	F	F	T	T	F	F
2	T	F	F	F	F	T	T
3	F	T	F	F	F	F	F
4	F	T	F	F	F	F	F
5	F	F	T	F	F	F	F
6	F	F	T	F	F	F	F

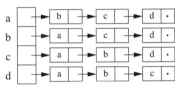

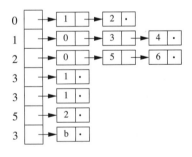

15.5 The power matrix describes which nodes are connected with paths of n or fewer edges: those with zero entries cannot be reached in n steps.

15.7

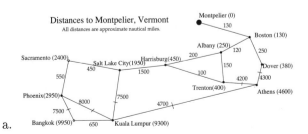

a.

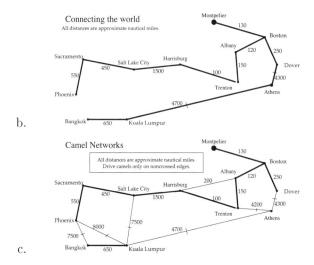

b.

c.

15.9 This is discussed fully in the text. The adjacency list is used when the graph is relatively sparse, and is likely to use less space than the adjacency matrix implementation. The adjacency matrix is used when graphs with more than $O(n)$ edges connect n nodes. It allows for fast access to specific edges—all in constant time, but at the cost of $O(n^2)$ space.

15.11 For the adjacency list, we must check each node's list to see if the potential source node is mentioned. In the adjacency matrix we check for non-null entries in the column associated with the row (don't check the diagonal entry).

15.13 An undirected edge may be considered a 2-cycle. Topological sorting depends on the transitivity of the ordering suggested by the edges. If there is a cycle, the edges do not suggest a consistent order.

15.15 Adding a vertex to the graph can be accomplished in near constant time. Adding an edge involves a $O(e)$ check for the presence of the edge already. Removing a vertex involves a $O(e)$ scan through the edges to remove those connected to the vertex. The edge iterator is ideally constructed from the list iterator. The vertex iterator is constructed from an iterator over the Map.

15.17 This can happen if multiple queries are made regarding a single source. One calculation of all solutions is less expensive than computing several partial solutions; some aspects of different solutions are shared.

15.19 Suppose it did not. This assumption leads to a contradiction.

Appendix B

Beginning with Java

Concepts:

▷ A sip of Java

I love the java jive and it loves me.
—Milton Drake and Ben Oakland

THE JAVA PROGRAMMING LANGUAGE WAS DESIGNED at Sun Microsystems as a simple, object-oriented, portable programming language for supporting Internet-based products. With large numbers of students, educators, and developers writing applications once written in languages such as C, C++, Fortran, and Pascal, the language is developing rapidly. As it gains wider acceptance, it will be increasingly important for programmers of these other languages to become familiar with the important features and paradigms introduced by Java. This Appendix serves as a quick introduction to the features of Java. Other, more in-depth treatments are available over the Internet or through your bookstore or local library.

B.1 A First Program

The main focus of a Java programmer is to write *classes*. These classes are templates for structures called *objects*. In most environments, the code supporting each class is placed in a dedicated file by the same name (class `Sort` is found in `Sort.java`). Writing a Java program involves writing a class definition. Here is a good first program to consider:

```java
import structure.*;

public class MyFirstProgram
{
    public static void main(String[] arguments)
    {
        // print a message to the standard output stream
        System.out.println("Look Mom: know Java!");
    }
}
```

At the top of the program, the `import` statement searches the programming environment for a *package* or library of classes called `structure`:

```
import structure.*;
```

and makes all of them (.*) available for use within the program. The `structure` package is the subject of this book; the applications of this text will include this `import` statement. Other packages available with Java include `java.lang`— the package of items automatically imported (this includes, for example, the definition of `System` and `String`); `java.io`—the package that provides access to special-purpose I/O facilities; and `java.util`—a package that contains utility classes, including random number generators, date objects, and simple data structures. Documentation for these packages is freely available online from `developer.java.sun.com` and in a wide variety of trade books.

The class is marked `public`:

```
public class MyFirstProgram
```

which means that it is available for access by anyone who wants to use the class—in particular anyone who wants to run the class as a program.

Classes that contain a *method* called `main` may be run as applications:

```
public static void main(String[] arguments)
```

When the application is run, the `main` method is executed. The sole parameter (here, `arguments`) is an array of `Strings` that are passed to it from the programming environment. One common mistake is to incorrectly declare the `main` method. The result is that a method `main` is declared, but the method required to run the application is not present. In such cases, the error

```
Exception in thread "main" java.lang.NoSuchMethodError: main
```

is common.

Any text on a line following a double-slash (//) is considered a comment:

```
// print a message to the standard output stream
```

and is ignored by the compiler. You can make multiple line comments by enclosing the text between `/*` and `*/`.

The computer prints a single string to the standard output:

```
System.out.println("Look Mom: know Java!");
```

The `print` method is part of the `out` stream from the `System` object. This dotted notation is used to provide names of data and methods within an object. For example, another name for the `main` procedure is `MyFirstProgram.main`.

Java is case sensitive; it is important to make sure identifiers are all in the same case. By convention, packages and methods begin with lowercase letters, while classes begin with uppercase.

Occasionally, two packages contain classes with the same name. If both classes are imported simultaneously, they are only accessible if prefixed by their respective package names. While the package system is a convenient means of compartmentalizing name spaces, programmers are encouraged to consider potential naming conflicts with common packages before designing their own classes. Still, over time with a moving target like the Java run-time environment, naming conflicts are sometimes difficult to avoid.

B.2 Declarations

The *scope* of an identifier—the name of a variable, method, or class—is the range of code that may legally access the identifier. Variables in Java may be declared in a number of different places:

- Variables must be declared within a class or method. Variables declared within a method are local to the method and may not be accessed outside the method. Variables declared within the class are instance variables whose access is determined by access keywords.

- Variables and values declared within a class are visible to any method declared as part of the class. Depending on the protection of the variable, it may be seen in subclasses, within the class's package, or globally.

- Variables and values declared within a method can be seen within code following the declaration that is delimited by the tightest enclosing braces. Ideally variables are declared at the top of a method, but they may be declared at the top of the block where they are used.

Methods may only be declared within a class. Unlike Pascal, they may *not* be nested. An understanding of the access control keywords for Java is important to understanding their scope. Section B.8 discusses this topic in considerable detail.

B.2.1 Primitive Types

Two types of data are available through Java–*primitive* types and *reference* types. Primitive types include integers, floating point numbers, booleans, and characters:

Name	Type	Range	Default Value
`boolean`	Boolean	**true** or **false**	**false**
`char`	Character data	Any character	`'\0'` (null)
`int`	Integer	$-2^{31} \ldots 2^{31} - 1$	0
`long`	Long integer	$-2^{63} \ldots 2^{63} - 1$	0
`float`	Real	$-3.4028E38 \ldots 3.4028E38$	0.0
`double`	Double precision real	$-1.7977E308 \ldots 1.7977E308$	0.0

Java variables are automatically initialized to their default values, but programmers are best advised to initialize variables before they are used.

Java supports a large variety of operators for primitive data types. Here are the most common, in decreasing order of precedence:

Operator	Meaning
++	Unary increment
--	Unary decrement
!	Logical not
* / %	Multiplication, division, remainder
+ -	Addition, subtraction
< <= => >	Numeric comparison
== !=	Primitive and reference equality test
&&	Logical and
||	Logical or
=	Assignment

Notice that assignment (=) is an operator and can be used to generate complex (and unreadable) expressions:

```
int a, b, c = 0;
a = 1 + b = 1 + c; // a = (1 + (b = (1 + c)))
```

leaves c at 0 and sets b to 1 and a to 2. Pascal programmers should note that the assignment (=) and equality (==) operators are easily confused (although the compiler is often capable of detecting such mistakes). The assignment and equality tests work on references as well, but not the objects to which they refer.

Programmers should be aware that the division operator (/) returns only the integer portion of the quotient when both operands are integers. The remainder operator (%) recovers the remainder after division. As usual, one should perform integer division and remainder on negative numbers with care.

Characters in Java are encoded using a very general mechanism called *unicode*, which is a superset of ASCII characters. Characters are surrounded by apostrophes and have the following shorthands familiar to C and C++ programmers:

Escaped character	Meaning	Escaped character	Meaning
'\b'	Backspace	'\f'	Form feed
'\r'	Carriage return	'\n'	New line
'\t'	Tab	'\''	Apostrophe
'\"'	Quotation mark	'\\'	Backslash

Primitive types may be explicitly *converted* to other types through *casting*. When information would not be lost, Java may perform the type conversion automatically. The following removes the fractional component of a `double` value:

```
double d = -3.141;
int i = (int)d;
```

Unlike C-style languages, Java does not automatically convert non-`boolean` expressions to `true` or `false` values.

B.2.2 Reference Types

Java does not have explicit pointers. Instead, more tightly controlled *references* are provided. Reference types include arrays and objects. Arrays in Java must be explicitly allocated and, as a result, may have run-time-determined bounds. The following code demonstrates several means of initializing arrays; all are identical.

```
int primes1[] = {2,3,5,7,11};
int primes2[] = new int[5];
int primes3[] = primes2;
primes[0] = 2;
primes[1] = 3;
primes[2] = 5;
primes[3] = 7;
primes[4] = 11;
```

The arrays `primes2` and `primes3` refer to the same dynamically allocated memory; `primes1` refers to another chunk of memory with similar values. An array or object may be referred to by more than one reference variable at the same time. Thus, the result of comparing `primes1==primes2` is `false` (the references refer to different memory), but `primes2==primes3` is `true`. The length of an array may be determined by inspecting its length property: `primes2.length` is 5.

Every reference either refers to no object (called a `null` reference) or an instance of an object of the appropriate type. Arrays may be `null`, in which case they refer to no memory.

References to objects perform a level of indirection. Thus

```
String s;
s = new String("Measure for measure must be answered.");
System.out.println(s.length());
```

calls the `length` method referred to by the `String s`. If s were `null`, the indirection would be impossible, leading to a `null pointer exception`. The following code, then, generates a null pointer exception:

But remember: Java has no pointers!

```
String s; // a null reference since no string allocated
System.out.println(s.length()); // illegal!
```

Java works hard to ensure that references do not point to invalid objects. In traditional languages, significant errors can be incorporated into programs by incorrectly allocating or freeing dynamic memory. Java's approach is to force the user to explicitly allocate each nonprimitive object and rely on a *garbage collector* to free allocated memory, but only after it is known to be unreferenced. This approach has some cost associated with it (the garbage collector has no hints as to where to find likely garbage), but a reference is guaranteed to never point to invalid memory.

B.3   Important Classes

Several classes are used in nearly every Java program. As with all classes, they are also fully documented online.

B.3.1   The ReadStream Class

Strangely, Java makes little effort to support input of primitive types from streams. As a result, the `structure` package provides a simple class for performing Pascal-like reading of primitive values from the keyboard. A `ReadStream` can be attached (much like a filter) to an input stream and can then be made to read primitive values. It is, perhaps, best to learn by observing an example:

ReadStream

```
ReadStream r = new ReadStream();
int i;

for (r.skipWhite(); !r.eof(); r.skipWhite())
{
    i = r.readInt();
    if (isPrime(i)) System.out.println(i);
}
r.close();
```

Here, a new `ReadStream` is created. By default, it is attached to the standard input stream, `System.in`. The method `skipWhite` scans and disposes of characters on the input, as long as they are white space (including tabs and end-of-line marks). The `eof` method returns `true` if no more data are available on the `ReadStream`. Finally, `readInt` reads in an integer from the stream. The value is stored in `i`. `ReadStream`s are capable of reading in all the primitive types, including `double`s and `boolean`s:

Method	Reads
r.readChar()	next char from stream r
r.readBoolean()	next boolean from stream r
r.readInt()	next int from stream r
r.readLong()	next long from stream r
r.readFloat()	next float from stream r
r.readDouble()	next double from stream r
r.readString()	next word, returned as String, from stream r
r.readLine()	next line, returned as String, from stream r
r.readln()	next line, returning no value, from stream r
r.skipWhite()	until next nonwhitespace from stream r
r.eof()	returns true iff no more data in stream r
r.eoln()	returns true iff no more data on line from stream r

B.3.2 The PrintStream Class

Simple output can be accomplished by writing the `PrintStream System.out`. While the interface for the standard output is not as flexible as it is in many languages, it is suitable for rudimentary communication. The methods include:

Method	Writes
`System.out.print(<primitive>)`	Primitive to standard output
`System.out.println(<primitive>)`	Primitive, followed by new line
`System.out.print(o)`	Representation of `Object o`
`System.out.println(o)`	`Object o` followed by new line

An important feature of this interface is that any subclass of `Object`—really, any class—has a `toString` method. This method is invoked by the `print` and `println` methods to generate a readable form of the `Object`.

B.3.3 Strings

Strings, in Java, are implemented as immutable objects. These objects are special in a number of ways. First, strings may be initialized to string constants, which are delimited by double quotation marks (`"`). Secondly, the addition operator (`+`) is overloaded to mean string concatenation. When strings are concatenated with other primitive types, the primitive type is converted to a string before concatenation. Thus, the following program constructs and prints one string of the first n integers:

```
String s = "";
int i;
for (i = 1; i <= 10; i++)
{
    s = s + " " + i;
}
System.out.println(s);
```

Each `String` value is allocated dynamically from the heap, and may not be modified. Thus, this program actually constructs 11 different `String`s, and we are printing only the last.

Other `String` methods include:

Method	Computes
`s.length()`	s's length
`s.charAt(i)`	the ith character (starts at 0)
`s.compareTo(t)`	integer relating s and t
`s.equals(t)`	`true` if string s has same value as t
`s.indexOf(c)`	index of c in s
`s.indexOf(t)`	index of beginning of match of t in s
`s.substring(start,end)`	substring of s between `start` and `end`

B.4   Control Constructs

Java provides many of the forms of control found in other languages, including conditional and multiple-choice statements, and various forms of looping constructs. Also included are a number of convenience operations that allow unusual forms of control.

B.4.1   Conditional Statements

Java provides several conditional statements. The `if` statement allows code to be conditionally executed, based on a `boolean` expression. Its general form is

```
if (<condition>) <statement>
```

If the boolean `<condition>` is `true`, the `<statement>` is executed. If the `<condition>` is `false`, `<statement>` is ignored. Unlike Pascal-style languages, there is no `then` keyword; instead, the parentheses around the `<condition>` are required. An alternative form is the `if-then-else` statement:

```
if (<condition>)
    <then-statement>
else
    <else-statement>
```

In this form the `<then-statement>` is executed if the `<condition>` is `true`; otherwise the `<else-statement>` is executed. Since the semicolon is part of many statements, it is often the case that the `then` part of the `if` terminates with a semicolon just before the keyword `else`. When `if` statements are nested, the `else` matches the closest `if` statement that doesn't yet contain an `else`. Thus, the following statement checks for various values of integer `i`:

```
if (i == 0)
    System.out.println("zero");
else if (i == 1)
    System.out.println("one");
else if (i == 2)
    System.out.println("two");
```

Such instances of cascading `if` statements are so common it is useful to express them as multiple-choice `switch` statements:

```
switch (<expression>)
{
    case <constant1>: <statement1>; break;
    case <constant2>: <statement2>; break;
        ...
    default: <default-statement>; break;
}
```

When the `<expression>` takes on any of the values `<constant1>`, `<constant2>`, and so forth, the respective `<statement>` is executed. The `break` statement is not strictly part of the `switch`, but if it is missing, the control falls through the various cases until a `break` is encountered. It is a good habit to introduce `break` statements regularly in the switch. The `default` case is executed if none of the `cases` match. It is a good idea to include a `default` statement in `switch` statements and perform an appropriate action. It is interesting to note that the `structure` package does not make use of the `switch` statement. The cascading `if` statements, given previously, might be recoded as

```
switch (i)
{   // note: order doesn't matter if breaks are used:
    case 1: System.out.println("one"); break;
    case 0: System.out.println("zero"); break;
    case 2: System.out.println("two"); break;
    default: // do nothing!
}
```

B.4.2 Loops

Loops are an important part of most programs. Casting your code using the appropriate loop is important to making your programs as understandable as possible. Java, like C-based languages, provides three types of looping constructs. In order of popularity, they are the `for` loop, the `while` loop, and the `do-while` loop. Unlike Fortran and Pascal, each of the loops can be used—with some modification—as a substitute for any of the others. As a result, most programmers use rules of thumb. Some prefer to always cast loops as `for` loops, while others attempt to avoid the `for` loop altogether. The best advice is to use the style of loop that seems most natural—but be prepared to defend your choice.

The most general of the three looping constructs is the `for` loop. It has the form

```
for (<initialization>; <continue-test>; <iteration>)
    <statement>
```

When the loop is encountered, the `<initialization>` is executed. At that point, the loop is started and the `<continue-test>` (a `boolean`) is evaluated. If `true`, the body of the loop (`<statement>`) is executed. If `false`, the loop is finished, and the execution continues at the statement that follows. After each execution of the loop body, the `<iteration>` statement is executed before reevaluation of the `<continue-test>`.

Here are some idiomatic `for` loops. First, to loop n times, the statement

```
for (i = 0; i < n; i++) ...
```

is used. Programmers unfamiliar with C-style languages might prefer

```
for (i = 1; i <= n; i++) ...
```

but this often detracts from the readability of the code. Besides, many operations on Strings and arrays require a range of values from 0 to n-1. Stick with the idiom, whenever possible.

The statement

```
for (i = r.readInt(); i != 0; i = r.readInt());
```

reads in integers from a stream until one is zero. Notice that the empty statement (a lone semicolon) provides the body of the loop.

To loop forever, one need only use:

```
for (;;) ...
```

Here, the empty <continue-test> is interpreted as true. The equivalent

```
for (;true;) ...
```

is less idiomatic and not frequently used but is just as effective.

Often—as in the last example—it is useful to be able to terminate or control the loop from within its body. If, for example, we wish to consume the characters in a file before the first space, we write:

```
for ( ; !r.eof(); )
{
    char c = r.readChar();
    if (c == ' ') break;
}
```

This loop terminates when the end-of-file mark is read on the ReadStream or when a space character is encountered; break statements terminate the tightest enclosing loop or switch statement.

Sometimes it is useful to jump to the next iteration of the loop from within the body. Here's an example of the use of continue:

```
for (i = 0; i < n; i++)
{
    if (i == 2) System.out.println("two is prime");
    if ((i % 0) == 0) continue;
    // only odd numbers remain
    ... test for prime ...
}
```

This loop does not look for primes among even numbers (other than 2). When an even number is encountered, it jumps to the i++ statement to begin the next iteration of the loop.

The two remaining loops are straightforward in comparison. The while loop has the form

```
while (<continue-condition>) <statement>
```

It is equivalent to the `while` loop in many languages. It could be cast as an equivalent `for` loop:

```
for (; <continue-condition>; ) <statement>
```

Another loop, the `do-while` loop, is a `while` loop with its test at the bottom:

```
do {
    <statement>
} while (<continue-condition>)
```

The `<statement>` is executed at least once, and the loop continues as long as the `<continue-condition>` is `true`. (Compare with the `repeat-until` loop of Pascal, whose condition is an *exit* condition.)

In the `structure` package, there are approximately 70 `for` loops, 135 `while` loops, and exactly one `do-while` loop.

I'm rewriting the `do-while`!

B.5 Methods

Methods are declared within classes. Unless declared otherwise, methods may only act on instances of an object. If there are no instances of an object, these methods may not be called. If, on the other hand, a method is declared `static`, it exists (and may be called) no matter the number of instances. This explains the need to bootstrap the Java application with a `static` method, `main`.

Methods are declared much as they are in C. Here, for example, is a (very inefficient) method that checks to see if n is prime:

```
static boolean isPrime(int n)
{
    int factor;
    for (factor = 2; factor < n; factor++)
    {
        if ((n % factor) == 0) return false;
    }
    return true;
}
```

Somewhere later we find:

```
if (isPrime(2)) System.out.println("Two is prime.");
```

n is passed by value—changing the value of n will not change the value of the actual parameter passed to it. Unlike Pascal and C++ there are no means of passing the parameter by reference or as a variable parameter. And, unlike C, we have no means of generating a pointer to simulate passing by reference. *All primitive values are passed by value.* Being references, all variables referring to objects pass the object by reference. The reference, of course, cannot be changed. All this makes it difficult, for example, to exchange the value of two parameters as you can easily do in most other languages.

B.6   Inheritance and Subtyping

Many object-oriented languages provide support for two useful concepts: inheritance and subtyping. Java is no exception.

B.6.1   Inheritance

Suppose, for example, we develop a class to perform the functions of a stopwatch. It might be declared as follows:

```
public class stopWatch
{
    protected double currentTime;
    protected boolean running;
    public stopWatch() {...} // code omitted for brevity
    public void start() {...} // start the watch
    public void stop() {...} // stop the watch
    public double read() {...} // read the time
}
```

This watch provides three methods once the `stopWatch` is constructed. The state of the watch is maintained in the protected `running` and `currentTime` variables. A watch with more features could be declared as

```
public class lapWatch extends stopWatch
{
    protected double memory[50];
    protected int lapNumber;
    public lapWatch() {...}
    public void startLap() {...}
    public double recallLap(int number) {...}
}
```

This class inherits the definitions in the `stopWatch` definition. It is as though all the definitions found in the `stopWatch` class were textually included in the definition of the `lapWatch`. In this way we think of the definitions added by the `lapWatch` class as extending the definition of the `stopWatch`.

Every class declared in Java is an extension of some other class. Even the `stopWatch` definition is a type extension: it extends the definition of `Object` (short for `java.lang.Object`). The `Object` class provides several interesting methods, including `toString`—which generates a `String` representation of the watch—and `hashCode`—which generates an integer that ideally represents the state of the watch (see Section 14.4.1). Since `lapWatch` extends `stopWatch`, it indirectly extends `Object`, inheriting methods like `toString`.

Type extension is useful in reducing the amount of code that must be rewritten for each class. Whenever a new class must be written, a similar type of object may be extended to inherit the hard work of previous programmers. In Java, however, the extension of types actually serves to promote a stronger relationship between types of objects—that one type of object may be substituted for another wherever it appears. This is called *subtyping*.

B.6.2   Subtyping

It is often the case that programmers do not realize the full potential of the code they write. Thus, in Pascal-like languages, it is difficult to design data structures that are capable of holding generic information. For example, it is not obvious how to write a general-purpose definition of "a list of things" because the definition of "thing" must be completely determined when the code is written. Another result is that a "list of integers" and a "list of reals" must be distinct definitions since the lists contain different types.

Java increases the utility of types by relaxing the type-checking system so that wherever a class `stopWatch` is referred to, any type extension of a `stopWatch` (including our `lapWatch`) works just as well. We say that `stopWatch` is a *supertype* or *base class* and `lapWatch` is a *subtype* or *subclass*. The rule is that

> *Wherever a supertype can be used, a subtype works just as well.*

The following code makes use of subtyping:

```
stopWatch minny = new lapWatch();
minny.start();
  ...
minny.stop();
System.out.println("Elapsed time is "+minny.read());
```

Even though `minny` refers to a `lapWatch`, we are informing the compiler that we want to use only the `stopWatch` features of `minny`. Since `minny`'s actual type (`lapWatch`) is an extension of the `stopWatch`, certainly the `stopWatch` methods are all available (though they may have `lapWatch`-like behavior if the `lapWatch` *overrides* their behavior).

In C++ the compiler and programmer are responsible for ensuring that operations work on compatible types. In Java, the object to which `minny` refers keeps track of its actual type. On occasion it is useful to verify that the type information known to the compiler is consistent with that known to the object. This is accomplished by a form of casting. We can improve the program's knowledge of `minny`'s type in the following manner:

```
( (lapWatch)minny ).startLap()
```

By placing the `lapWatch` type in parentheses, the run-time system verifies that `labWatch` is a supertype of `minny`'s actual type (it is). The object is not modified in any way. After casting, the value of the expression is of type `lapWatch` and the `startLap` method can be correctly invoked.

In Java, the way that subtypes are determined is by inheritance. Any type that extends another is automatically a subtype. Language designers are not completely convinced that subtyping and inheritance go hand in hand, but in Java they do.

B.6.3   Interfaces and Abstract Classes

The Java *interface* allows the programmer to specify a template for verifying the methods provided by a class definition. An interface is specified much like a class, but methods may not have associated bodies. We might, for example, have an interface for things that may be started and stopped:

```
public interface timer
{
    public void start();   // this can be started
    public void stop();    // and stopped
}
```

As new classes are developed, their `public` methods may support one or more interfaces. Since the `stopWatch` supports both the `start` and `stop` methods, the following definition of `stopWatch` requests that the compiler verify that the `stopWatch` supports the `timer` interface. The result is a `stopWatch` that is also a `timer`:

```
public class stopWatch implements timer
{
    protected double currentTime;
    protected boolean running;
    public stopWatch() {...}
    public void start() {...} // start the watch
    public void stop() {...} // stop the watch
    public double read() {...} // read the time
}
```

Since interfaces have no actual code associated with them, it is impossible to explicitly create objects of the interface type. It is possible, however, to use subtyping to generate references to objects that implement `timer` features:

```
timer minny = new lapWatch();
```

`minny`, in this case, is a `timer` that (via the `stopWatch` class) is really a reference to a `lapWatch`. The previous discussion of casting would apply to this example as well.

Sometimes it is useful to develop partial or *abstract* classes. These classes are partially implemented and demand extension before the class becomes *concrete*. If, for example, we had several choices for actually constructing a `stopWatch`, we might use the following definition:

```
abstract public class stopWatch
{
    protected double currentTime;
    protected boolean running;
    public stopWatch() {...}
    abstract public void start(); // start the watch
    abstract public void stop(); // stop the watch
    public double read() {...} // read the time
}
```

Here, we indicate to the compiler that the `start` and `stop` methods are part of the `stopWatch` definition, but we're not willing to commit to an actual implementation at this time (perhaps there are choices, or we just don't know how). Notice, by the way, that we have committed to the protected data and the definition of the `read` method, so this is *not* like an `interface`. Still, because there is no code associated with the `start` and `stop` methods, no instances of the class can actually be constructed. We must depend on references to subtypes—instances of extensions to this class—if we want to use a `stopWatch` in our code. We warn the compiler that we are working with an incompletely specified class by attaching the `abstract` keyword to the definition of the class and any method headers that are left unspecified.

Notice, by the way, any concrete extension of the latest `stopWatch` class must specify code for the `start` and `stop` methods. Thus, the last definition of `lapWatch` must either specify those methods completely or be declared abstract itself.

Java suffers somewhat from a desire to avoid mistakes of the past. As a result it is impossible to have a single class extend multiple superclasses at the same time. This *multiple inheritance* introduces some sticky problems into language design. Still, it *is* possible for a single class to implement multiple interfaces at the same time. The careful and conservative programmer is often rewarded with easily understood code.

B.7 Use of the Assert Command

In Java 1.4, Sun introduced the `assert` keyword. This control construct allows the programmer to write assertions directly in the code at a native level, without the need for classes like `structure.Assert`. Careful use also allows the programmer to remove all traces of the assertion easily, and for improved performance.

Programmers with access to Java 1.4 should investigate the `assert` control construct. It has the following two forms:

```
assert <condition>;

assert <condition>:<message>;
```

The first of the two forms evaluates the `<condition>` and if it is `true`, continues exectution with the next statement. If the `<condition>` is `false`, an assertion error is thrown.

The second form of the statement allows the programmer to pass information (`<message>`) about the failed statement to the program.

Because assertions are a relatively new feature to Java, they must be explicitly enabled. You should read your compiler's documentation to determine how to enable this feature. Compilers that do not have the feature enabled will report a warning or error if the `assert` keyword is encounterd.

Until the `assert` statement is supported by a large number of environments, we still recommend the use of a system like `structure.Assert`, which allows the consistent checking of assertions in all current Java programming environments.

B.8   Use of the Keyword Protected

Before I built a wall I'd ask to know
What I was walling in or walling out,
And to whom I was like to give offense.
—Robert Frost

AT EVERY TURN, this text has advocated the use of the access-control keyword `protected`. Because of the complexity of access control in the Java language, it is important that the case for the use of `protected` be adequately argued. With some reservation, we do that here.

To make the best use of data abstraction, we have argued that each data structure be considered from two vantage points: the *interface* and the *implementation*. Again, the interface describes a public contract between the implementor and the user. The private implementation informs the machine how the demands of the contract may be met.

For both parties—the user and implementor—to agree on a structure's behavior, its interface must be visible wherever it is used. The "user," of course, may be the structure itself, another structure within the same package, or some entity external to the package. We suggest the use of the word `public` to describe classes, methods, and fields that are to be visible to the user. (It is almost never necessary to make data fields public since they are only accessed through public methods.)

The implementation, on the other hand, should be hidden from the user as much as possible. Only the implementor should be able to see the internal workings of the structure. When implementations are protected in this way, then it is possible for the implementor to make changes to the implementation without affecting the user's applications—as long as contracts are met. Indeed, languages with *dynamic loading* of classes, like Java, make it possible for implementors of data structures to update applications that have already been compiled. For maintenance and reliability reasons, this is a feature.

Unfortunately, the *means* of protecting the implementation is not very clear in Java. To understand the problem we review access control briefly, and suggest further investigation by the reader.

Of the widely used languages, Java is the first to provide two levels of encapsulation: *class* and *package*. Clearly, the class provides a means of grouping together related fields and methods. It is important for an implementor to be able to see all the fields and methods within a class, but only selected elements should be visible to the user.

The package provides an (increasingly common) method for grouping related classes together. It also serves to partition the name space (we can refer to two types of `Vectors`: `structure.Vector` and `java.util.Vector`). Since access protections are sensitive to whether or not access to a field or method occurs from within the same package, the language designers clearly had a feeling that there should be a difference in visibility between inter- and intrapackage access.

There are two types of access for classes: `public` and default. Default classes are private and not visible outside the containing package. For methods (and data) there are four types of access. In increasing constraint, they are `public`, `protected`, default, and `private`:

- `public`—methods declared `public` are always visible. This is an ideal keyword for use in describing interfaces.

- `protected`—class methods declared as `protected` are visible to any class declared in the same package, as well as any extension to the class whether or not it is in the same package.

- default or friendly—class methods declared without any keyword are visible to any class declared in the same package, as well as any extension to the class *within the same package*.

- `private`—class methods are not visible outside of the class.

For our purposes it seems best to commit to one level of protection for the implementation: `protected`. What follows is an informal defense of that decision.

First, the use of `public` provides no control over the access of methods and fields. It would be possible, then, for users to access the implementation directly, undermining the control provided by the interface. For even the simplest data structures, access to the implementation undermines any effort to keep the structure in a consistent state. The following principle has been demonstrated regularly in major software systems:

Principle 26 *Make it `public` and they will use it.*

Even if you don't want them to.

The use of the `private` access control is far too restrictive. Suppose we are interested in constructing two types of lists—a `SimpleList` and an extension, a `ComplexList`. The `SimpleList` has a field, `head`, that references the first element of the list. Clearly, this field should be declared `protected`; manipulating the head of the list without going through a method is likely to put the list into an inconsistent state. Now, suppose that the `ComplexList` manipulates the list in a way that requires manipulating the head of the list in a manner not previously provided. Declaring `head` to be `private` makes it impossible for the `ComplexList` to access the field directly. We might be tempted to provide access through a method of `SimpleList`, but *we are then forced to restate our argument as it applies to methods*. If, then, we are to have an effective extension of types, the `private` keyword cannot be the preferred method of access control.

If one uses the default access control, it is only possible for a class inside the package to access the associated field. While it seems unconstrained to allow all classes within the same package to access the field (after all, we may be interested in protecting fields from a package co-resident), the protection against extension outside the package is *too* constraining. If the concern is access to implementation information outside the package, the class should be declared `final` to indicate that extension is not allowed.[1] If extension is allowed, *all extensions should have equal access*.

What remains, then, is the use of the `protected` access control. Fields and methods of a class are available to classes within the same package, *as well as extensions to the class that reside outside the package*. Use of this keyword protects fields and methods from unrelated agents outside the package. Since all extensions are provided equal access, extensions to the package are welcomed and are likely to occur.

A special warning is necessary for the "everyday programmer." Since the motivation for use of packages is subtle and their use introduces considerable bureaucratic overhead in current programming environments, the tendency is to develop one's software in the *default* or *user package*. This is particularly dangerous since, within that package, there is no distinction between access controls that are not `private`. Therefore absolute hiding of the implementation is particularly dangerous since, within that package, there is no distinction between `public`, `protected`, and default access. It follows, then, that absolute hiding of the implementation is only possible with the `private` keyword.

For most purposes, the `protected` keyword is suitable. The reader should be aware, however, that its use here is not an adoption of an ideal, but an acceptance of what's available. In short, while Java is not perfect, it is a work in progress and we may reasonably expect improvements in its access control.

Principle 27 *Fight imperfection.*

---

[1] It should be pointed out that Sun's widespread use of `final` in their own classes serves to destroy one of the features most sought in this type of language—type extension and code reuse. As it stands now, it is impossible to implement many reasonable class extensions without rewriting the base class, and even then the subtype relation is lost.

Appendix C

Collections

PERHAPS ONE OF THE MOST IMPORTANT changes to the Java environment over the past few years has been the introduction of a set of classes informally called the *collection classes*. This group of classes fills out `java.util`, bringing many commonly used data structures under one roof. For example, there is a `Stack` class. Unfortunately, there is no `Queue`.

C.1   Collection Class Features

Whenever possible, this text borrows interfaces from the `Collection` classes so that students may better understand what is in store for them when they enter full time into the wild. The notable cases of this borrowing include:

java.util.Enumeration The old iteration mechanism.

java.util.Iterator The new iteration mechanism, still not outfitted with some methods introduced in the first edition of this text.

java.util.Comparator An interface for specifying wrappers for comparison methods.

java.lang.Comparable An interface we introduced in a different form in the first edition, now brought into line with the new `Comparable` interface to avoid a forced name clash.

java.util.Map.Entry The interface describing `Association`-like classes.

The user should, as always, be aware that those features that are borrowed from the Java environment must be explicitly imported. For example, all programs that use `Iterator` classes would do well to import `java.util.Iterator`. Programmers should avoid importing all features from the `java.util` package, since there are likely to be significant clashes with Sun's class definitions.

C.2   Parallel Features

Whenever possible, the design approach outlined in this text is followed. This mirrors, in many ways, the approach of the the design of the `Collection` classes: interfaces are developed, followed by abstract base classes that implement the shared features of all implementations of the interface, followed by solid implementations that extend the abstract base classes.

The following features parallel the `Collection` classes, but with reduced functionality. For pedegogical reasons many occasionally useful features have been dropped to highlight the important features of the parallel class or interface. Included are:

structure.Structure The common interface for all `Collection`-like structures in the `structure` package.

structure.Map The interface for associative structures.

structure.List The interface for random-access, indexable, and extensible structures.

Each interface is implemented in several ways with, for example, `StackList` interpreted as a `Stack` constructed using an underlying `List` type. In many cases, these structures correspond to similar structures found in `java.util`. The programmer should be aware that moving to the use of `java.util` may introduce new methods or slight differences in the interface. For the most part, the `structure` library is a superset of those classes found in `java.util`.

C.3 Conversion

Most structures in the `structure` package extend the `AbstractStructure` class. One feature of this base class is the method `values`. The `values` method returns an object that implements `Collection`. This allows the programmer to convert `structure` package objects for use in the `Collection` system. It avoids, for the most part, the introduction of the complexities of supporting the needs of the masses, and focuses on the task at hand, learning about classic data structures.

At the time of this writing, alternative copy constructors are being incorporated into most structures to allow the conversion from `Collection` objects. This will allow the mixed use of structures.

Appendix D

Documentation

Concepts:
▷ Class hierarchy
▷ Principles

'My name is Ozymandius, King of Kings,
Look on my Works, ye Mighty, and despair!'
Nothing beside remains. Round the decay
Of the colossal Wreck, boundless and bare
The lone and level sands stretch far away.
—Percy Bysshe Shelley

D.1   Structure Package Hierarchy

The `structure` package contains a large number of interfaces and implementations of common data structures. The relationship between these is indicated below. Private structures are, of course, not available for direct use by users. Indentation indicates extension or implementation: `GraphList` is an implementation of the `Graph` and `Structure` interfaces.

Assert	§2.2
BinaryTree	§11.4
BitSet	
CharSet	
Clock	
Collection (java.util)	
StructCollection	
Comparable (java.lang)	
ComparableAssociation	§10.1.2
Comparator (java.util)	
NaturalComparator	
ReverseComparator	
DoublyLinkedListElement	§8.5
Edge	§15.2
ComparableEdge	§15.4.5
Error (java.lang)	
FailedAssertion	
FailedInvariant	
FailedPostcondition	
FailedPrecondition	
Iterator (java.util)	§7.2

D.2 Principles

1. The principled programmer understands a principle well enough to form an opinion about it. (Page 3)

2. Free the future: reuse code. (Page 17)

3. Design and abide by interfaces as though you were the user. (Page 25)

4. Declare data fields `protected`. (Page 25)

5. Test assertions in your code. (Page 35)

6. Maintaining a consistent interface makes a structure useful. (Page 51)

7. Recursive structures must make "progress" toward a "base case." (Page 83)

8. Never modify a data structure while an associated `Enumeration` is live. (Page 150)

9. When manipulating references, draw pictures. (Page 177)

10. Every public method of an object should leave the object in a consistent state. (Page 179)

11. Symmetry is good. (Page 182)

12. Test the boundaries of your structures and methods. (Page 185)

13. Question asymmetry. (Page 189)

14. Assume that values returned by iterators are read-only. (Page 199)

15. Understand the complexity of the structures you use. (Page 223)

16. Declare parameters of overriding methods with the most general types possible. (Page 244)

17. Avoid multiple casts of the same object by assigning the value to a temporary variable. (Page 246)

18. Consider your code from different points of view. (Page 257)

19. Don't let opposing references show through the interface. (Page 274)

20. Write methods to be as general as possible. (Page 288)

21. Avoid unnaturally extending a natural interface. (Page 307)

22. Seek structures with reduced friction. (Page 308)

23. Declare object-independent functions `static`. (Page 310)

24. Provide a method for hashing the objects you implement. (Page 371)

25. Equivalent objects should return equal hash codes. (Page 371)

26. Make it `public` and they will use it. (Page 489)

27. Fight imperfection. (Page 490)

Appendix E

Environments

The structure package is used in a large number of programming environments. All code and examples associated with this text are available, free of charge, from the Internet. These are the details of downloading using this software with MetroWerks Code Warrior. Most environments have similar procedures. Details for alternate environments can be found at

http://www.cs.williams.edu/JavaStructures.

E.1 Downloading Software

Available at the book web site are a number of files, including source and executable code, documentation, examples, problem solutions, etc. A particularly useful way to set up a local environment is to download the entire structure package *kit*. This is a "jar," "zip," or "tar" file. Once the file has been downloaded to your local environment, dearchive the files into a web-visible directory. The result is a mirror of the entire site.

It is important to note that the dearchiving should only decompress one level of the archive. Within the archive are zip and jar files that are Java libraries. These should not be decompressed; instead they can be downloaded from the local site for local installation. We discuss these details below.

E.2 Creating Libraries

For the purposes of this discussion, we assume you are using CodeWarrior, Learning Edition. Other environments have similar features. You are encouraged to visit the web site for more details on installation in other environments.

1. Start the CodeWarrior IDE. This is found on the program's menu on Windows machines, and in the CodeWarrior installation folder on Macintosh computers.

2. From the file menu select New.

3. Select Java Stationery from the Project panel. Type the name of the library in the Name field. You may select an alternative folder to place it in. Make sure you keep the Create Folder checkbox checked. Press OK.

4. Open the JDK1.1 group, and select Java Library stationery.

5. Once the project is created, open the Sources group and select Trivial-Class. Press Delete. This removes an unnecessary file containing an example main method.

6. Now, switch back to the operating system (Windows or the Finder) and copy all the Java sources that are part of the library, into the project folder.

7. Switch back to the IDE. Select the Sources group. From the menu, select Project>>Add Files

   - In the file types, make sure you have Source Files.
   - Select all the files (control-A on Windows, apple-A on Macintosh).
   - Press add. The desired files will be added to the Sources group.

   You may have to add other jar files to the Classes group.

8. In the project pane, select the Targets tab. Double click on the Java Library target.

   - In Target Settings, change nothing.
   - In Java Output, set Name to library name (e.g., structure.jar).
   - Select Compress and Generate Manifest.
   - Press Save and close the window.

9. Select the Files tab, and from the menu select Project>>Make.

10. Select Files>>Exit. The library can be found in the project folder.

The process is fairly complex, but it is not necessary unless you are constructing your own library.

E.3   Creating Project Stationery

The construction of project stationery for starting projects is useful in cases where libaries are involved in classroom situations. To create custom project stationery:

1. Make a new project.

2. Select the Application stationery. You may extend on other stationery, as you see fit.

3. Name the project with the desired stationery name. A typical name might be CS101 Starter.

4. Switch to the O/S, and copy the necessary jar files into the project folder. *These should be copies; do not use the originals.*

5. Once the project is created, modify the `TrivialApplication` file to import the libraries you need. For example:

```
// Author:
// Instructor:
// Lab:

import structure.*;
public class Application
{
    public static void main(String[] args)
    {
        System.out.println("Howdy world?");
    }
}
```

6. Notice that I changed the name of the class to `Application`. This makes your work feel a little less trivial. This will involve saving the new class as `Application.java`, and changing the `Applications Settings>>Java Target`:

   - `Main Class` should be `Application`
   - `Java Output` should be `Application.zip`
   - `Output type` should be `Application`

7. Delete the `TrivialApplication` file from the project, if necessary, and add the `Application` file to the project.

8. Run and test the code until it works as a good sample program.

9. Select `Project>>Remove Object Code`. OK this operation.

10. Select `Files>>Exit`.

11. Clean up the project folder so that all that remains is

    - The project file
    - The libraries
    - The `Application.java` source file

    Everything else should be removed.

12. Copy the folder to the `Stationery folder` in MetroWerks: on Windows machines this is:

    `\MetroWerks\CW Learning Edition\Stationery\Java\JDK 1.1`

13. Next time you start a new project, the stationery should be part of the `Java>>JDK 1.1` choice.

Appendix F
Further Reading

An active scientist is an active reader. There are many books available to study Java programming; most may be found in your trade-book store. The following books are written by important contributors to science, and are generally recognized as classic and important contributions to our understanding of computation and problem solving.

* Gamma, E. et al. *Design Patterns*. Addison-Wesley.
  The versatility of objects is quite difficult to appreciate without seeing many good examples of their use. This book demonstrates many common (and soon to become common) design strategies for solving problems from the most mundane to the most severely complex.

* Bentley, Jon. *Programming Pearls*. Addison-Wesley.
  Jon Bentley wrote an important monthly column for the Communications of the Association for Computing Machinery. This volume, and *More Programming Pearls* investigate program design and experimental technique. Bentley, an avid programmer, demonstrates the *art* of programming.

* Polya, G. *How to Solve It*. Princeton University Press.
  A wonderful gem of a book about developing approaches to solving problems. Polya's discussion is in the context of mathematics, but it readily transfers to the search for solutions in any discipline.

* Berlekamp et al. *Winning Ways for Your Mathematical Plays*. A.K.Peters.
  A classic work. Three volumes that analyze an impressively large number of games and puzzles. For those looking for medium-sized programming exercises, this book is a good resource.

* Knuth, Donald. *The Art of Computer Programming*. Addison-Wesley.
  A fundamental work on data structures, algorithms, and other topics of computer science. Donald Knuth has committed a substantial portion of his professional career to documenting successful approaches to implementing abstract data types and algorithms. These volumes are an important part of the library of a computer scientist.

* Brooks, Frederick. *The Mythical Man-Month*. Addison-Wesley.
  Project management may never be well understood, but the peculiar difficulties with managing some large software projects are well documented in this wonderfully written work.

Appendix G

Glossary

abstract In Java, the keyword used to describe an incomplete method—a method whose signature is provided, but whose code has been left for future implementation.

abstract data type A data structure that, in a protected manner, represents a value along with the public methods that allow the access and manipulation of the value.

abstraction The process of focusing attention on those features of an object or system that are obviously shared between the implementor and the user.

accessor A method that returns the state or a portion of the state of an abstract data type.

algorithm A detailed approach to solving a problem.

array An object that provides access to zero or more similar values that, abstractly, are stored adjacently in memory and may be accessed through indexing.

assertion A statement of something that is assumed to be true about the state of the machine.

asymptotic analysis The determination of long-range trends in a program's use of space and time.

byte code Small integers or "codes" that describe operations to be interpreted by a machine.

cast (1) For primitive types, a request by the programmer to convert one type to another. (2) For object types, an indication of a programmer assertion—to be tested at compile or run-time—that a reference is an instance of the indicated type.

class A description of an abstract data type; a template for generating new objects.

class file A file that contains the virtual byte codes (among other things) compiled from a Java program.

comments Notes or sketchy clues written by the programmer in human readable form and attached, in some manner, to a program; these annotations serve to describe the desired behavior of the program.

compiler A mechanism for translating a program from one form to another. A Java compiler translates Java source code into "byte code" for Java's "virtual machine."

complexity An arbitrary measure of how difficult it is to implement an algorithm, or to run an algorithm within specific constraints.

constructor A method (whose name is the same as the enclosing class) that is responsible for consistently initializing the state of a new object.

contract An agreement between two parties that allows both parties to work independently using common assumptions about their relationship. In Java, the interface provides a means of specifying a contract between the implementor and user of a class.

data structure An organization of memory used to represent a class of abstract data values.

design A well-considered plan for accomplishing something; always a potentially beautiful thing.

deterministic Accomplished in a reproducible, determined manner.

execute To perform the actions associated with the instructions of a program.

finger An informal device for holding one's attention.

function A method that returns a value.

hash table A data structure that uses hash codes to organize data in a manner that makes it possible to (usually) find the data value in the structure quickly.

hash function A means of mapping data values to a set of integers; the function is usually deterministic, returning equal integers for equal values.

heap A recursively defined structure that is either (1) empty, or (2) contains an extreme (e.g., minimum or maximum) value and a collection of smaller subheaps that hold the remaining values.

indexing The process of selecting one of several values stored in a structure through a computation that possibly occurs while the program is running. Without indexed types (e.g., arrays and vectors), efficiently accessed structures are difficult to implement.

interface (1) Informally, the collection of a class's accessible signatures. (2) Formally, a template that forms the basis for the accessible methods of a Java class.

interpreter A mechanism for enacting ("executing") the instructions of a program. In Java, the virtual machine *interprets* the byte code generated by the compiler.

iterator A data structure that can be used to access the values stored in a subordinate structure. Iterators usually access their values in a predictable, well-defined manner.

mutator A method that potentially modifies the state of an abstract data type; mutators take an abstract data type from one valid state to another.

null A reference that does not refer to anything.

nil Null.

object An instance of a class. In Java, all non-primitive values are objects.

pointer A general form of reference. A pointer can be directly manipulated, while a reference may only be assigned. Java uses references, which are considered safer because they are tightly controlled by the language.

polymorphism The ability to manipulate several types of data with common code. Polymorphism is an important part of code reuse.

postcondition A logical statement about the state of the object or machine that will be true if the precondition was met just before the method was executed.

precondition A logical statement about the state of the object or machine that should be true if the postcondition is to be fulfilled.

programmer Ideally, the person in control of the behavior of a program.

queue A first-in, first-out (FIFO) structure. Items enqueued earliest are dequeued first. Compare with "stack."

reference A compact means of representing a value; in most languages references are addresses of the referenced value in memory. A reference may not represent any value, in which case it is "null."

signature The form of a method: the method's name along with the types of each of its parameters. In Java, the return type is not considered part of the signature; two method references are considered to be the same if their signatures are identical.

source file A file that contains Java language instructions, usually written by a programmer; source files are identified by a `.java` suffix.

stack A last-in, first-out (LIFO) structure. Items pushed on most recently are popped off first. Compare with "queue."

state The values assumed by a data structure. For example, an `int` takes on 2^{32} different states. States of a data structure are often restricted by the ways that they are implemented.

subtype A possibly more restrictive type that may serve in the place of a supertype.

supertype A generalization of one or more subtypes. The use of supertypes allows methods to manipulate different types through common code—polymorphism.

tree A structure that is either (1) empty, or (2) a root value plus a collection of smaller subtrees.

virtual Not real; not realized.

virtual machine A program that simulates the behavior of a machine that may not exist.

Index